Beyond El Barrio

Beyond El Barrio

Everyday Life in Latina/o America

EDITED BY
Gina M. Pérez,
Frank A. Guridy, and
Adrian Burgos, Jr.

NEW YORK UNIVERSITY PRESS
New York and London

NEW YORK UNIVERSITY PRESS
New York and London
www.nyupress.org

References to Internet websites (URLs) were accurate at the time of writing.
Neither the author nor New York University Press is responsible for URLs
that may have expired or changed since the manuscript was prepared.

Library of Congress Cataloging-in-Publication Data

Beyond el barrio : everyday life in Latina/o America /
edited by Gina M. Pérez, Frank A. Guridy, and Adrian Burgos, Jr.
p. cm.
Includes bibliographical references and index.
ISBN 978-0-8147-9128-8 (cloth : alk. paper) — ISBN 978-0-8147-9129-5
(pbk.   ) — ISBN 978-0-8147-6800-6 (e-book)
1. Hispanic Americans—Social conditions. 2. Hispanic Americans—
Social life and customs. 3. Hispanic American neighborhoods.
4. Community life—United States. 5. City and town life—United States.
I. Pérez, Gina M., 1968– II. Guridy, Frank Andre. III. Burgos, Adrian, 1969–
E184.S75B49   2010
973'.0468—dc22   2010020185

New York University Press books

Manufactured in the United States of America
c 10 9 8 7 6 5 4 3 2 1
p 10 9 8 7 6 5 4 3 2 1

For Baron, Deborah, and Dolly

Contents

Acknowledgments

Beyond El Barrio is a product of more than a decade's worth of conversations among the co-editors, anthology contributors, as well as countless other colleagues and friends. The idea for the project emerged from discussions among the co-editors as we finished our dissertations in the early 2000s and were fortunate enough to receive fellowships and tenure track positions that allowed us the time, space, and financial and intellectual support to advance new scholarly interests. As a Research Associate at the Center for Puerto Rican Studies at Hunter College, City University of New York (Pérez), a scholar-in-residence at the Schomburg Center for Research and Black Culture (Guridy), and an Assistant Professor at the University of Illinois (Burgos), we benefited from critical institutional support and the generosity and guidance of colleagues, mentors, and students. We are deeply grateful to all of our colleagues at the Centro, the Schomburg, and Illinois for nurturing and guiding us during those critical years as we transitioned from graduate school to our professional careers.

We are particularly grateful to all the anthology contributors. We thank them for the intellectual excitement they brought to this project, as well as their extraordinary patience and flexibility over the years. We have been particularly fortunate to have presented our work—both as a collective and individually—in a variety of ways, and this anthology is certainly stronger as a result of the feedback generated from these presentations. We offer special thanks to Alex Vasquez and the Office of the Provost at Wheaton College, where we first presented our work in 2002. Without the extraordinary organizational skills of María Elena Cepeda, the first Beyond El Barrio symposium would never have happened. We are grateful for the financial and intellectual support she and Macalester College provided for "Beyond El Barrio: Symposium for New Directions in Latina/o Studies," that took place in April 2005. A subsequent symposium at the University of Illinois in Spring 2007 provided another important moment for many of the contributors to present their work and to receive helpful feedback. Burgos would like to thank in particular the Dean of Liberal Arts and Sciences, Sarah Mangelsdorf, for much needed institutional and financial support, as well as then-graduate student Jennifer Guiliano as co-organizer of the symposium. Pérez is grateful to Micaela di Leonardo, Jane Collins, and Brett Williams for organizing the Advanced Seminar "New Landscapes of Inequality" at the School for American Research in March 2006, where she benefited significantly from feedback on her work as well as larger conceptualizations for the anthology. We also offer our deepest thanks to John McKiernan-González and Cary Cordova for coming to the rescue when we struggled to find an appropriate image for the anthology's book cover. The image "Rhythmo del Pueblo," perfectly captures a new way of looking at the barrio. As Guridy noted in our conversations about the choice of it, the swaying buildings represent the disruption of the "barrio" and the road through it could convey our desire to move "beyond" it.

We are especially grateful for the generous feedback offered by the anonymous reviewers of the manuscript and are indebted to a number of senior scholars who have provided sustained intellectual and emotional support, encouragement, and wisdom over the years. Working with New York University Press has been an incredibly rewarding experience. Our thanks to Eric Zinner for first believing in the project and for countless conversations about it, as well as to Ciara McLaughlin, Despina Papazoglou Gimbel, and Robert Swanson for their guidance and patience at various stages in the process of completing the manuscript. We also offer heartfelt thanks to colleagues and friends at Oberlin College, the University of Texas, Austin and the University of Illinois for the support that made such a long-term project possible.

Finally, we are immeasurably indebted to our families who have offered us love, encouragement, and sustained intellectual engagement over the years. Our lives have been enriched by our children (Antonio, Pablo, Lucia, Zaya, Miranda, and Julia) who continue to inspire us to do what we can to build a better world. But none of this would have been possible without the indefatigable support, love, and patience of our partners, Baron, Deborah and Dolly. We humbly dedicate this book to them.

Introduction

GINA M. PÉREZ, FRANK A. GURIDY,

AND ADRIAN BURGOS, JR.

In *The Souls of Black Folk,* W. E. B. Du Bois notes that a persistent, yet unasked question between him and "the other world" is "How does it feel to be a problem?" A similar question might be posed to contemporary America's Latina/o populations, who recently have emerged simultaneously as a possible solution to America's race problem, as well as a pernicious symbol of the nation's enduring dilemma of citizenship, race, legality, and social membership. Thus the question Latinas/os face today is a similar one posed by Du Bois more than one hundred years ago, about not only the feelings of being defined as a problem, but also the strange experience of looking at oneself and one's communities "through the eyes of others."[1] For many Latinas/os, media images and popular cultural renderings of their families and communities mirror the anxieties as well as the expectations and hopes of mainstream America, rather than the complex realities characterizing Latina/o lives. Ironically, at a moment in which Latinas/os are increasingly visible in U.S. popular culture, media, public discourse, and community struggles, the material conditions and actual experiences of U.S. Latinas/os are largely unexplored, misunderstood, and frequently trapped in racialized stereotypes.

This interdisciplinary volume intervenes in public discourse about Latina/o communities by featuring scholarship that critically interrogates both how Latinas/os are portrayed in media, public policy, and popular culture, as well as the material conditions in which different Latina/o groups build meaningful communities. In the chapters that follow, the authors illustrate how despite the hypervisibility of Latinas/os and Latin American immigrants in recent political debates and popular culture, the daily lives of America's new "majority minority"—their efforts to build community with other racial, ethnic, and sexual communities; their attempts to lay claim to full citizenship rights; their community activism; their rich array of cultural production—remain largely invisible and, perhaps more important, mischaracterized. Indeed, while dominant political and popular discourses about Latinas/os offer up foreboding images of threat, invasion, and contamination, there is a simultaneous move by some politicians, writers, and marketers to advance a vision of Latinas/os embodying quintessentially American values and behaviors. Anthropologist Arlene Dávila refers to this latter trend as "Latino spin," which she defines as the "selective dominance" of sanitized and marketable Latina/o representations that are "central to the national conversation about the future of Latinos."[2] While these marketable discourses frequently emerge as important correctives to negative depictions of Latina/o communities, they often do so at the expense of empirical evidence as well as those groups whose marginal economic and social standing are attributed to individual failures and moral shortcomings. These contradictory representations are deeply political constructs that conveniently elide the lived experiences of Latinas/os. They also play a critical role in contemporary politics of exclusion. Moreover, as Dávila observes, "as a group that is at once both living and socially imagined, Latinos continue to occupy a marginal position in society, even when they are joining the ranks of mainstream culture."[3]

This anthology moves beyond these dominant representations to offer, instead, nuanced portraits of Latina/o life. In the chapters that follow, writers explore the complexity and diversity of Latina/o communities, both past and present, and provide analyses that not only defy stubborn stereotypes, but also present novel narratives of Latina/o communities that do not necessarily fit within recognizable categories, units of analysis, or topics of research that can, unwittingly, reify and reproduce static images of U.S. Latinas/os. In other words, these chapters help us to move "beyond el barrio": beyond stereotypes, assumptions, and stigmatizing tropes, as well as nostalgic, reified, and uncritical portraits of complex and heterogeneous Latina/o lives. As we argue in the following section, we recognize "el barrio" to be a fraught material and ideological space that can both sustain and marginalize those associated with it. Thus our intention is not to deny the existence of barrios, nor is it to diminish their importance as a cultural, political, social, and ideological space. Rather, the authors in this anthology invite readers to expand contemporary understandings and representations that can narrowly define, homogenize, mischaracterize, and stigmatize Latina/o lives. The writers do so with research that challenges enduring tropes of Latina/o identities and affiliations; interrogates assumptions about the racialized spatial locations of Latina/o communities; recovers and rethinks community histories and memories; and highlights the creative activism and cultural production emerging from various Latina/o populations.

Beyond El Barrio engages with these questions by identifying three arenas of daily existence that significantly structure the lives of U.S. Latinas/os, namely citizenship and nationalism; gender and sexuality; and community activism and memory. Not surprisingly, citizenship, sexuality, and activism also constitute key sites of misunderstanding that are steeped in racialized notions of difference. The ongoing battles about immigration, for example, often focus on the alleged divided loyalties of Latin American immigrants, who demand full citizenship rights while they simultaneously display affinities for their countries of origin. Similarly, Latina/o sexuality is deeply racialized both in popular culture and policy debates, including the unquestioned assumption of Latina/o homophobia and machismo. Latina/o communities are also persistently characterized as docile, disorganized, and unrooted. The writers in this anthology explore these issues by employing multiple methodological approaches and interdisciplinary frameworks in order to explore the multiple intersections of Latina/o life in the United States.

El Barrio as Place, Space, and Metaphor

If, as Chicano literary scholar Raúl Villa notes, "the barrio is a complex and contradictory social space for its residents," it is an equally vexing and contested concept for scholars, artists, activists, and policy makers alike.[4] As a spatial formation, barrios emerge out of histories of segregation, marginalization, and exclusion-based race, class, ethnicity, and citizenship, that vary regionally but share what anthropologist Diego Vigil describes as the experience of being inferior places "spatially separate and socially distanced from the dominant majority group."[5] Thus Puerto Ricans and Dominicans residing in Manhattan neighborhoods like El Barrio (East Harlem or Spanish Harlem) and Washington Heights share much with Chicanas/os, Salvadorans, and Guatemalans in barrios in Los Angeles, Houston, Chicago, and Washington DC in their experiences of displacement, marginalization, and land loss. For Puerto Ricans, for example, twentieth-century displacement and migration to *colonias* in New York City was the result of consolidated U.S. agrarian capitalism following occupation in 1898, as well as the island's industrialization program and state-sanctioned migration program. These migrants eventually settled in neighborhoods like El Barrio, which provided cheap housing for Puerto Rican newcomers, as it had for its earlier Jewish, Italian, and eastern European residents.[6] Similarly, Mexican barrios in Los Angeles emerged in the late nineteenth-century as a result of land loss in the wake of the Mexican American War of 1846–1848, and the transformation of

Los Angeles into an "Anglo city" through various public policy measures that racially stigmatized and isolated Mexican residents, relegating them to *colonias* in rural contexts and *barrios* in urban settings.[7] Both historically and today, barrio formations are the result of specific plans and policies on the local, state, and federal levels that have resulted in high levels of racial segregation, substandard and limited housing stock, poor schooling, and severely circumscribed economic mobility.[8]

These early barrios were—and continue to be—home to heterogeneous groupings of Latin American and Caribbean immigrants based on race, class, gender, sexuality, and national origin. They also served as important settlement communities for subsequent arrivals, such as Dominicans, Salvadorans, Guatemalans, Nicaraguans, and Cuban immigrants beginning in the 1960s. Thus, while racism and social, economic, and political marginalization have shaped the physical boundaries of barrios, the civic organizations, social networks, and economic and cultural resources within them have an important use value that has nurtured sentimental attachments to place.[9] As anthropologist Ana Aparicio notes (this volume), early waves of Dominican immigration played a critical role in contemporary political mobilization among Dominican youth that also includes African American and Puerto Rican activists and community workers. San Francisco's Mission District played a similar role for queer Latinas/os as well as Central American immigrants who benefited from—and contributed to—vibrant political, cultural, and social networks critical to their survival (Roque Ramírez and Cordova, this volume). Thus, while racism, segregation, uneven development, and urban policy help to create barrios, the residents within them often develop and sustain important place-based networks that also transcend local and national boundaries (see Burgos, Jr., and Guridy; and Fernández, this volume).

The structural forces shaping racialized urban space are an important part of what sociologist Andrés Torres refers to as the "mutual history" of Latina/o and African American experiences in American cities.[10] Barrios and ghettos emerge from this shared history of racism, segregation, poverty, social marginalization, and the struggle over urban space; and, despite social policies aimed at ameliorating the plight of the urban poor, these areas continue to be "permanent fixtures of American cities."[11] Like the extensive and influential research on African Americans, urban poverty, and "the ghetto," research on barrios, and the residents who live in them, has been an important, albeit controversial, area of urban sociology, anthropology, and Latina/o, Ethnic, and American Studies.[12] Anthropologist Oscar Lewis, for example, used his research among the Puerto Rican poor to develop the theory of an intergenerationally transmitted culture of poverty shared among impoverished residents in the San Juan and New York barrios. Similarly, studies characterizing Mexican immigrants as alien, docile, diseased, and deviant have been used to justify spatial segregation of Mexicans, as have urban renewal policies that have effectively threatened and destroyed barrios of great use value to their residents.[13] These characterizations of the barrio and ghetto poor are deeply gendered and rest on particular constructions of racialized gender, sexuality, and culture that allegedly render Puerto Rican, Mexican, and African American women as deviant and unfit mothers. According to historian Natalia Molina, contemporary discourses of excessive sexuality, fecundity, and the racialized threat this poses resonate with early twentieth-century racial anxieties and constructions of Mexican and other women of color as "sexually and morally aberrant."[14] Similarly, legal scholar Dorothy Roberts argues that powerful cultural constructions of black womanhood—as careless, matriarchal, unwed mothers and welfare queens—render them as unfit mothers in popular, scholarly, and policy discourse.[15] Feminist scholars of color have challenged these depictions of impoverished Latina/o and black women and their families and have advanced, instead, nuanced analyses of what Puerto Rican feminist writers identify as "cultural codes of rights and entitlements" in the face of diminishing federal resources and social support.[16]

While it is clear that race and class have shaped the livelihoods and residential patterns of Latinas/os and African Americans in U.S. cities, the analytic utility of the concepts "ghetto" and "barrio" is less clear, and they remain contested terms.[17] Some scholars argue that these terms are often used as metaphors for social isolation, disorganization, and moral decay, and as such are powerful ways of conceptualizing—and by extension, pathologizing—Latina/o and African American communities.[18] In this way, the metaphor of "el barrio" is part of a larger public discourse about Latinas/os and Latin American immigration that often employs metaphors of disease, contagion, and invasion, and which profoundly shapes public understandings of Latina/o communities and even elicits nativist responses.[19] Metaphors, therefore, are not neutral terms; they profoundly shape our understandings of the world.[20]

For many Latina/o Studies scholars and artists, however, the barrio remains a useful analytical tool for explaining the histories and contemporary realities of Latinas/os. The popularity of the term—in book titles, artistic production, scholarly journals, and public symposia—attests to the enduring importance of el barrio as a concept as well as a unit of analysis, although how it is used varies significantly. For some writers, el barrio is embraced and celebrated as a critical space nurturing cultural production, political mobilizations, and ethnic identity and solidarity.[21] For others, concerns about criminalization, marginalization, and social dislocation inform research about barrio residents that is meant to contextualize their lives and communities.[22] Alternative framings of el barrio also involve careful attention to the social construction of space, the commodification of place, and a transnational approach to conceptualizing barrio life and culture in various historical contexts.[23] Clearly, el barrio is simultaneously space, place, and metaphor, with deep cultural, material, and symbolic meanings for artists, activists, policy makers, and scholars. The chapters in this anthology engage with these various conceptualizations and attempt to build and move beyond them in order to explore new meanings, identities, and experiences of a diverse and dynamic Latina/o population in various communities throughout the United States.

Latina/o Demographics Inside and Outside the Academy

While scholarship on Latinas/os has existed for several decades, thanks to the efforts of pioneering scholars in the fields of Puerto Rican, Chicana/o, Cuban, and Dominican Studies it is only recently that Latina/o Studies has become increasingly influential in North American academic circles.[24] This is apparent in the proliferation of Latina/o topics at academic conferences, as well as the increased attention university and trade presses are giving to Latina/o Studies manuscripts. These intellectual developments reflect demographic shifts of Latina/o communities both in urban centers that have historically housed migrants from the Spanish-speaking Americas (such as New York, Chicago, Miami, and Los Angeles), but also in areas outside these historic communities, including Winston-Salem, North Carolina, Orlando, Florida, and Downers Grove, Illinois. These changes provide the backdrop for current debates and demand research to understand and explore the changing experiences of Latinas/os and how these demographic changes shape American life in the new millennium.

These demographic shifts inspire, in part, the title for this anthology. In order to recognize and interrogate how the global economy and transnational practices have transformed life in historic and new Latina/o communities throughout the United States, scholars are compelled to move beyond traditional frameworks and disciplines to develop new methodologies. Inspired by Chicana feminists and other feminists of color, moving "beyond el bar-

GINA M. PÉREZ, FRANK A. GURIDY, AND ADRIAN BURGOS, JR.

rio" is a political as well as an intellectual stance, challenging narrow understandings of Latina/o community life that are often framed within nationalist discourse.[25] As the authors of the edited anthology *Chicana Feminisms* note, Chicana feminist writings seek to "move discourse beyond binaries and toward intersectionality and hybridity," and to do so while contesting axes of inequality based on race, gender, sexuality, class, and nationality.[26] The notion of moving "beyond el barrio," therefore, is a reminder to Latina/o Studies (as well as to other) scholars to be attuned to how new social and spatial relations beyond the academy create new ways of knowing and being that can challenge the assumptions, questions, and frameworks we employ in our scholarly work.[27] As George Lipsitz notes, American Studies programs and scholarship emerged as a result of "the cultural and intellectual spaces opened up by the mass movements of the 1930s."[28] Similarly, Latina/o Studies emerged out of civil rights struggles, student protests, and community activism of the 1960s and 1970s. This anthology, therefore, contributes to burgeoning literature in Latina/o, American, and Ethnic Studies that moves beyond disciplinary as well as academic boundaries to explore "new epistemologies and new ontologies" within Latina/o communities, past and present.[29]

Despite the increased visibility and institutionalization of Latina/o Studies within the academy, particularly in the 1980s, the barrio remains an apt metaphor for understanding the location of Latina/o Studies within higher educational institutions. Indeed, these units have taken on a number of configurations within the academy: as centers, stand-alone programs, units within comparative race and ethnicity programs, and, most infrequently, as full-fledged departments with right to grant tenure.[30] These spaces have been invaluable for scholars examining the everyday experiences of Latinas/os in the United States and abroad, and are critical intellectual centers of the production of knowledge about Latinas/os. Like American barrios and their residents, however, Latina/o Studies units and their faculty often thrive despite limited institutional funding and support. As Latina/o Studies scholar Pedro Cabán notes, administrators often fund these units assuming, at least initially, that they would likely "never counter the institutional power of the discipline-based departments nor ever attain the academic rigor to challenge their epistemological moorings."[31] Moreover, as anthropologist Arlene Dávila argues, few Latina/o Studies programs have the ability to conduct tenure-track hires on their own—that is, without a partnering disciplinary department in a joint search. In this way, Latina/o Studies units undergo their own form of "barrioization" within academe, often left isolated and comparatively disenfranchised from the rest of campus academic units.[32] University administrators' decisions about how to fund or structure Latina/o Studies often consign these programs to the margins, making them dependent on disciplinary units to validate hiring and tenure decisions. This has been further exacerbated with the recent trend of consolidation of race and ethnic studies units into American Studies departments or the merging of Latina/o Studies units with Latin American Studies programs. In either scenario, Dávila explains, the ability of these units to formulate their own intellectual agenda and innovation is subordinate to the interests of the larger (read more intellectually rigorous) unit. That this is transpiring at precisely the moment when Latinas/os are now the nation's "majority minority" speaks to the ways the most vital centers of knowledge creation about Latinas/os within the academy remain subject to the vagaries of market forces and assumptions about the relevance of such knowledge to a transnational or global world.[33]

This anthology makes the argument for the importance and, indeed, necessity of Latina/o Studies scholarship precisely because it engages with both the challenges and opportunities emerging from an increasingly globalized world. One of the ways the essays in this anthology do this is by employing a transnational framework for apprehending the varied experiences of Latinas/os in multiple contexts. Since the early 1990s, transnational approaches to immigration research have highlighted the multiple networks, strands, and affiliations connecting communities of origin and settlement and have been critical in redirecting scholars' analytical focus to include a more complex rendering of immigrant life.[34] Within Latina/o Studies scholarship specifically, this approach has facilitated nuanced analyses of shifting gender ideologies and sexuality; flows of capital and their impact on local political economies; different household arrangements and family ideologies; and new forms of activism, community building, and place making.[35] Moreover, this body of work has deeply informed debates within American Studies, for example, that call for scholarly research that seriously attends to questions of transnationalism, globalization, and U.S. political-economic power.[36] This anthology offers key examples of how transnational frameworks challenge conventional understandings of Latina/o communities and, in so doing, build on and are in dialogue with scholars within African American, Asian American, Native American/Indigenous, and LGBTQ Studies as well.[37]

Methodologically, *Beyond El Barrio*'s contributors draw from their training in history, media studies, literature, American Studies, anthropology, and sociology to explore in an interdisciplinary way the complex experiences of Latinas/os within the context of evolving power relations based on race, class, sexuality, and nationality. *Beyond El Barrio*'s particular attention to racialized sexuality and power in U.S. cultural production, in news media, and within discourses of citizenship also builds on exciting new scholarship that considers these axes of power within a transnational frame. As literary scholar Lawrence La Fountain-Stokes notes, this work promises to transform the way we think of place, sexuality, and identity.[38] In the chapters that follow, the anthology's contributors build on the work of a number of important scholars whose attention to the changing notions of race and racialization projects have fundamentally challenged earlier notions of race, power, and citizenship.[39] This anthology's attention to popular culture, cultural production, and media studies makes invaluable methodological contributions by employing discourse analysis, ethnography, and oral history to explore the meanings and experiences of cultural production within Latina/o communities. These articles, therefore, contribute to the rapidly growing literature on Latina/o popular culture and representation.[40] Ethnography also figures prominently within the anthology with contributors exploring the meaning of citizenship, race, and belonging both within the contexts of new militarism in the United States, the evolving urban economy, and migrant social networks.[41]

Outline of the Book

The chapters that follow engage with important questions of citizenship, race, and nationalism; gender, sexuality, and the politics of memory and representation; and Latina/o activism and histories. The authors in this anthology employ a wide range of methods and sources to explore in careful detail the lived experiences of U.S. Latinas/os, both past and present, which often challenge conventional understandings of Latina/o communities. The essays in part I, for example, interrogate matters of citizenship and belonging not only in actual lived barrios, but also within mediated transnational spaces, such as listening publics, television, newspapers, and migrant networks. In her chapter, María Elena Cepeda focuses on the pro-immigrant marches in the spring of 2006 and the ways in which mainstream media focused on some features of Latina/o immigrants' organizing efforts, and how it often failed to consider a broader canvas of Latina/o popular culture that explores inter-Latino dynamics and notions of a (trans)national Latina/o *familia*. Designed as a response to what many viewed as draconian measures to halt undocumented immigration, the peaceful marches were notable for their skillful manipulation of the transnational popular media, particularly talk radio and music, as a key part of organizational efforts. Employing an interdisciplinary approach, Cepeda analyzes mainstream and ethnic media discourse regarding "Nuestro Himno," a Spanish-language paraphrasing of "The Star-Spangled Banner," performed by a group of U.S. Latina/o, Latin American, and Spanish recording artists, and pays particular attention to the role of language in the debates surrounding the recording. "Nuestro Himno," Cepeda notes, was actually part of the album *Somos Americanos* (*We Are Americans*), an important piece of cultural production that needs to be analyzed within a broader context of recent Latina/o cultural production, such as reggaetón recordings. Situated within the context of the ongoing legal, socioeconomic, and political struggles of recent Latina/o immigrants in particular, both the recording and the demonstrations constituted important symbolic gestures toward (re)claiming U.S. public space and the contested meanings of nation and belonging.

The focus on radio as a critical medium for cultural expression, political organizing, and creating a sense of belonging is the focus of Dolores Inés Casillas's chapter, where she notes that the fastest growing formats on the airwaves of U.S. radio are those broadcast in Spanish. Though just 67 Spanish-oriented radio stations existed in 1980, the number swelled to 390 by 1990. By 2000, the FCC identified nearly 600 Spanish-language radio stations in the United States. Casillas examines how U.S. Spanish-language radio successfully caters to a U.S. Latina/o listenership characterized largely by factors of language, race, and migration. This chapter leads attention away from the discussions of music play that crowd radio studies, focusing instead on the significance of the voice, specifically on-air *saludos* (shout-outs), long-distance dedications, and call-in shows. Through an analysis of radio vignettes, she demonstrates how Spanish-language radio mediates nostalgia for homelands while helping listeners navigate newfound residences and political structures, thereby showing how it provides an acoustic space for radio broadcasts and listeners to discursively map and locate the complexities of transnational Latina/o experiences.

Like Casillas, Lourdes Gutiérrez Nájera examines the various ways that migrants navigate new social relations, contexts, and political structures, and how they ultimately negotiate transnational membership and belonging. Drawing on ethnographic research in both Yalálag, México, and Los Angeles, Gutiérrez analyzes how Yalaltecos fostered a sense of belonging and membership in what may otherwise have been an alienating urban environment. It is not uncommon to hear of Yalaltecos returning to their natal community because "they couldn't find themselves" (*no se hayaban*) in Los Angeles. Ironically, there are many who remain in Los Angeles because they "no longer fit in" (*no se hayan*) back home. Gutiérrez explores Yalalteco expressions of displacement (*hayandose*) and the various creative ways they find to express membership and belonging, given their marginalized positions as indigenous immigrants and laborers in Los Angeles and a growing estrangement from the community they left behind. Given the marginal status of indigenous people within Mexico and the United States, Gutiérrez also poses critical questions about how indigenous migrants create spaces of inclusion and what practices are used to create a sense of belonging or community. In answering these questions, she focuses specifically on migrant credit associations and other cultural practices that bring Yalaltecans together and reproduce their ethnic identity.

Adrian Burgos and Frank Guridy's contribution examines contemporary Latino struggles for citizenship and belonging in the United States within the world of baseball. Their chapter highlights the anxieties generated by the specter of Latino success in a game that has been touted as "America's national pastime." They highlight the xenophobic reaction to the Rolando Paulino All Stars, a team from the Bronx, New York, comprising boys from Puerto Rican and Dominican backgrounds, which came within one game of the final round of the 2001 Little League World Series. While the sporting press celebrated the Paulino All Stars as the "Baby Bronx Bombers"—a reference to the nickname of professional baseball's most celebrated franchise, the New York Yankees—opponents accused the Bronx team of using ineligible players. Suspicions focused primarily on Danny Almonte, the star pitcher who was the driving force behind the team's success. Burgos and Guridy are interested in the results of these investigations and concerned with what perhaps kindled the suspicions of cheating. These allegations were driven not only by the racial and class backgrounds of the Paulino All Stars, but also by the fact that the team represented the Bronx, a historic African American and Latino barrio that occupies an ambivalent place in the U.S. national imaginary. Thus the authors show how the reaction to the Rolando Paulino All Stars was informed by racialized narratives that construct the Bronx as a community marked by a lost white ethnic innocence, symbolized by the Yankees, that was supplanted by black and brown poverty and urban decay and violence.

The ways that gender, sexuality, race, and identity are remembered, reconfigured, and deployed by Latinas/os as well as the larger public is the subject of part II. These essays move beyond familiar community histories, geographic regions, and gendered cultural tropes of Latina/o families to consider nuanced portraits of struggle around memory, representation, community formation, and political-economic inclusion. Thus the authors illustrate the critical need for place-based historical research to excavate Latina/o lives that have been forgotten; but they also offer a cautionary tale about the ways that cultural practices and kin relations associated with barrio life are often reified and given too much explanatory power regarding Latina/o aspirations. Horacio Roque Ramírez's chapter, for example, addresses important questions about memory, archives, and sexuality in San Francisco's Latina/o communities. How do queer Latino lives enter historical consciousness in this new millennium, twenty-five years into the AIDS pandemic? What is "everyday life" like for simultaneously queer and racial ethnic subjects, always positioned in historical margins, amid the no-longer-seen crisis of AIDS? Roque Ramírez's chapter—a blend of research, remembrance, and manifesto—tackles the ongoing silences surrounding gay Latino life and history, and what we can refer to a "gay Latino album of the dead"—the record of life and death of over three hundred gay Latinos documented in the obituaries of San Francisco's *Bay Area Reporter* since the 1980s. By examining obituaries from the longest running gay weekly in the Bay Area, Roque Ramírez explore the possibilities for writing a history of sexual, gender, and racial intersections using what we can call queer archives of the dead.

Popular cultural renderings of death, absence, and memory are central to Deborah Paredez's chapter, which explores the function of the absent mother in recent popular depictions of young Latina aspiration. Paredez argues that one pervasive narrative in recent representations of Latinas in popular culture is the absent or dead Latina mother, whose very absence or loss operates as a central component in Latina aspirations for material gain, social visibility, and self-understanding. She explores the cultural function and implications of the absent mother trope in two works from different genres: the critically acclaimed coming-of-age film *Real Women Have Curves* (2002); and *Ugly Betty* (2006), the queer-camp U.S. version of the Colombian telenovela *Yo soy Betty, la fea*. Both works, released in the years since the much-touted "Latin Explosion" of the 1990s, are regularly regarded as affirming representations of young working-class Latinas. Despite the various pleasures and promises offered by these works, Paredez argues, they both share the same troubling narrative premise of the absent or dead Latina mother. Paredez explores how absent mothers function in these projects, and highlights the implications for prevailing ideas about Latina subjectivity that arise from their absence. She does so by situating her close readings within the recent sociopolitical moment during which Latinas/os, in light of their growing demographics, have gained increasing recognition as an important voting bloc, market base, and labor pool while struggling for recognition as citizens in the face of prevailing nativist sentiments and legislation. Examined within this context, Paredez persuasively demonstrates how the absent mother emerges not only as a key component in narratives of Latina aspiration, but also as a representational index of these recent anxieties and concerns of and about Latinas/os in the United States.

The final two chapters in this section reengage with important insights provided by Roque Ramírez and Paredez regarding memory, sexuality, and culture and explore how ideas of sexual respectability, cultural values, and gender inform Latina/o claims to full U.S. citizenship. Focusing on Lorain, Ohio—home to ten thousand Puerto Ricans, or about 15 percent of the city's inhabitants in 2000—Pablo Mitchell and Haley Pollack argue that although a significant number of Puerto Ricans had lived in Lorain since the late 1940s, academic scholars have largely ignored their presence. Their chapter begins to reconstruct the beginnings of the Puerto Rican community through an examination of the *Lorain Morning Journal*, the city's main daily newspaper, and highlights how Puerto Rican migrants and their families struggled mightily to assert full citizenship claims in the face of a social order that characteristically enforced racial division and strict codes of sexual respectability. Gina Pérez's contribution explores a contemporary example of Latinas/os' attempts to lay claim to social membership and citizenship by focusing on youth participation in the proliferating number of Junior Reserve Officer Training Corps (JROTC) programs in U.S. public high schools. While they have complicated reasons for joining JROTC, students consistently underscore the various benefits they receive by participating in a program that not only enjoys broad support from teachers, parents, administrators, and local civic groups, but one that also fosters a sense of meaningful belonging in local and even national communities. The rising number of Latina/o youth participating in JROTC within the past decade is concomitant with the U.S. Army's Spanish-language recruitment campaign targeting Latina/o and Latin American youth. "Yo soy el army" (I am the army) is the result of a carefully researched marketing strategy advanced by the Latina/o marketing agency Cartel Creativo, which draws on culturally specific understandings of family, motherhood, patriotism, and Latina/o identity to appeal to young Latinas/os for military enlistment. Using ethnographic methods as well as media analysis of Cartel Creativo's marketing campaign, Pérez demonstrates the various ways "Hispanic" values are identified to be similar to military culture and values that ultimately benefit the nation.

In the anthology's final section, scholars from American Studies, history, and anthropology take up the critical issue of Latina/o activism and histories, both locally and transnationally. These chapters contribute to rich scholarly and popular literature documenting Latina/o collective struggle and agency, which is often place-based; but like other writers in this anthology, they also point to the need to examine how these processes have also been rooted in transnational and global visions of shared struggle and history. John McKiernan-González's chapter provides an important challenge to Latina/o Studies scholars seeking various models of engaged, transformative, and empowering research. As a key collaborator in the Cuentos de mi Familia oral history project, McKiernan-González inquires about the forms of informal schooling that accompany the public crafting of Latina/o history at the turn of the century. How do Latina/o youth craft historical narratives amid this schooling? And how do students and their families transform the schooling that funds, supports, and advocates the public presentation of their histories under the Latina/o label? Participants in the Cuentos de mi Familia collaborative history project in Tampa, Florida, confronted these questions individually and as a collective. The Cuentos project asked selected rural and urban Latina/o middle school students to build a history of their favorite family member. Working with University of South Florida undergraduates and faculty as well as their fellow students, Cuentos participants used emblematic Chicana/o, Latina/o, and Puerto Rican biographical essays as initial models for their family narratives. Their finished project stepped past these models, and combined image and text to create artwork that spoke to their understanding of their favorite family member's life. McKiernan-González shows how the process of creating their *cuentos* led these students to confront deeply framing questions, such as why they were selected to be part of a university-based Latina/o outreach project; what parts of their family's biography they would share with their fellow students; how they would present their family research in a Latina/o-themed public history project; and finally, how their project would fit the expected narratives of Latina/o family life and how they would navigate these tensions.

This innovative strategy of producing alternative narratives of history in relation to Latina/o biographical histories speaks to other creative organizing, such Latina/o artists' political organizing in San Francisco in the 1970s and 1980s. Cary Cordova's contribution explores the different ways Latina/o cultural workers asserted their solidarity with the people of Nicaragua, regardless of whether they were of Nicaraguan origin. Pro-Sandinista sentiment flourished in San Francisco as a result of its large Nicaraguan immigrant community, the devastating 1972 earthquake in Managua, and the 1973 U.S.-engineered coup in Chile. As cultural workers organized to promote an alternate, socialist form of government in Nicaragua, they also stood in opposition to the diplomatic objectives of the U.S. government. These interactions, Cordova argues, had a profound impact on Latina/o artists who decided that their place was in Managua, both literally and figuratively. Using oral histories and careful archival research, Cordova explores the galvanizing impact of Central American movements on the aesthetics and cultural work of various Mission-based artists. Working with poems and images created during the existence of the Neighborhood Arts Program, Cordova argues that the wars in Central America expanded Latina/o artists' vision of themselves. Their efforts contributed to the success of the Sandinista revolution and merit examination, perhaps even more so now, as the language of U.S. patriotism attempts to extinguish such forms of activism.

Like Cordova, Lilia Fernández highlights the powerful role of community activism in laying claim to place and belonging in the face of powerful political and economic forces. By focusing on origins of Chicago's Mexican Pilsen barrio (also known as Eighteenth Street) in the 1960s and 1970s, Fernández challenges pernicious reifications of barrios as naturally given communities with little historical understanding of the structural conditions that led to their creation. Such communities, she argues, bear the traces of urban planning, public housing, and other raced, classed, and gendered socioeconomic policies that have shaped the life chances and residential possibilities of their residents. Rather than simply a casual congregation of people with a shared ethno-racial identity, the Pilsen barrio materialized as a result of mid-twentieth-century urban renewal policies, which displaced this population from the neighboring Near West Side. Fernández traces the history of the Mexican (and Puerto Rican) enclaves on the Near West Side in the 1940s and 1950s, and examines their efforts to recreate their community anew and claim Pilsen as their own. The author argues that as scholars of Latina/o Studies we must examine the origins of Latina/o barrios, the perspective of both community action and memory as well as the macro-level forces that have led to such social and spatial formations.

Finally, Ana Aparicio employs historical and ethnographic methods to explore what she identifies as "transglocal barrio politics." Over the past two decades, Dominican American activists working in the Manhattan neighborhood of Washington Heights have initiated projects that have reshaped their neighborhood and the local political landscape. In this process, Aparicio argues, they have established and utilized numerous networks that include and extend beyond local or transnational Dominican circles, including alliances with African Americans, Puerto Ricans, Cubans, and progressive whites. While these alliances are critical to Dominican organizing in Washington Heights, Aparicio demonstrates the need for rethinking the frameworks of community activism that privilege the local, and offers instead an approach that seriously considers the ways people identify with various populations and localities beyond their local communities. Aparicio draws on ethnographic and historical data to theorize the different ways in which Dominican activists have increasingly become "transglocal" in their organizing efforts to address challenges and problems in Washington Heights.

In significant ways, the essays in this anthology address many of the same questions the Cuentos students faced, namely how to represent the diversity of Latina/o communities and histories; the difficulties inherent in engaging with the realities and social constructions of Latina/o families, including gender relations and sexuality; and how to move beyond available models and tropes of Latina/o migration histories, narratives of citizenship, and political behavior that often obscure the complexities of Latina/o life. Our hope is that this anthology builds on and furthers important scholarly and activist efforts to engage, in a meaningful way, constructive dialogue about the challenges facing U.S. Latinas/os (as well as their active efforts to transform their material conditions), to remedy historical silences, and to offer, instead, models of hopeful and engaged research that move us all beyond static understandings of everyday life in Latina/o America.

NOTES

1. Du Bois 1903: 4. Anthropologist Arlene Dávila makes a similar argument about the ways that Latinas/os are simultaneously cast as a threat as well as solution to many of the nation's problems, particularly those involving race. She argues that while these seemingly paradoxical images of Latinas/os are not new, the various ways Latinas/os are "being characterized in a more marketable, sanitized, and compensatory way" is both new and "suggestive of Latinos' shifting place in the politics of race" (Dávila 2008: 1). Other important works documenting representations of Latinas/os and Latin American immigrants as threats to the nation include Hondagneu-Sotelo 1995; Perea 1997; Sánchez 1997; Santa Ana 2002; Fregoso 2003; Briggs 2003; Whalen 2001; Chavez 2001, 2008. Throughout this anthology, authors employ a variety of ways to refer to U.S. Latinas/os, including Latino, Latina, and Latinas/os. Given the lack of consensus within Latina/o Studies scholarship in how to navigate this tricky linguistic terrain, the editors have preserved each author's use of the term, recognizing that each has attempted to address these gendered linguistic concerns carefully.

2. Dávila 2008: 6–7.

3. Ibid.: 161.

4. Villa 2000: 8.

5. Vigil 2008: 366.

6. Sánchez Korrol 1994: 55–58. For more on the history of El Barrio, see Dávila 2004.

7. Molina 2004; Vigil 2007, 2008; Villa 2000.

8. Díaz 2005: 5.

9. Logan and Molotch 1987: 1, 17; Villa 2000: 10.

10. Torres 1995: 165.

11. Vigil 2008: 366.

12. Much of the early research on Mexican immigrants and their communities focused largely on rural and semirural *colonias,* which, as Vigil (2008) and Díaz (2005) note, eventually became *barrios* with urbanization and sprawl. See Moore and Pinderhughes 1993 (xx) for a discussion of early literature of Mexican rural and semirural communities in the Southwest. See also McWilliams 1949.

13. See Villa 2000, especially chapter 2; Molina 2004: 44; Ruiz 1999: 28–29.

14. Molina 2004: 185.

15. Roberts 1997.

16. Benmayor, Torruellas, and Jurabe 1997: 153. See also Souza 2000; Briggs 2003.

17. A 2008 issue of the sociological journal *City & Community* focused specifically on concept of "ghetto." See contributions by Monteiro and by Small for discussions of the concept as metaphor, as well as critiques of its analytic utility. Vigil's contribution provides an important analysis of the similarities and differences between barrios and ghettos. Gina Pérez would like to thank Greggor Mattson for bringing this volume of *City & Community* to her attention.

18. Monteiro 2008: 379; Freidenberg 2000: 208, 237.

19. See Leo Chavez's (2001, 2008) pioneering work in the areas of Mexican immigration, public discourse, and representations of Latin American immigration, as well as Fregoso 2003; Negrón-Muntaner 2004; and Chabram-Dernersesian 2007 for discussions of representations of Latinas/os in American popular culture.

20. Santa Ana 2002.

21. Recent examples of this work include Cammarota 2008; Freidenberg 2000; Gaspar de Alba 2003; Iber and Regalado 2007; Muñiz 1998; Nabhan-Warren 2005; Treviño 2006; Loza 1993. Our thanks to one of the press's anonymous reviewers for helping to typologize and think critically of the various conceptualizations of el barrio in recent scholarly work.

22. Díaz-Cotto 2006; Dohan 2003; Vigil 2007.

23. See, for example, Dávila 2004; Laó-Montes and Dávila 2001; García 2006; Villa 2000; Valle and Torres 2000.

24. Examples of pioneering work include History Task Force 1979; Rodriguez 1991; Flores 1993; Sánchez-Korrol 1994; Sánchez 1993; Zavella 1987; Behar 1995; García 1996; Guarnizo 1994; Hernández 2002; Pessar and Grasmuck 1991.

25. Critical contributions by Chicana, Puerto Rican, and Latina feminists include Anzaldúa 1987; Torre and Pesquera 1993; Moraga and Anzaldúa 1981; Pérez 1991; Zavella 1987; Torruellas, Benmayor, and Juarbe 1996; Ortiz 1996; López 1985; Souza 2000.

26. Arredondo et al. 2003: 2.

27. Thus moving "beyond el barrio" is not meant to suggest a notion of "post-barrio" that jettisons the barrio concept completely. As we have argued above, this fraught and contested term remains an important frame for Latina/o life. Rather, our call for moving beyond el barrio is to emphasize the need to challenge enduring tropes that often obscure, rather than illuminate, the complexities of Latina/o experiences, both in the United States and abroad. See Boyd 2008 for a discussion of these tensions in African American communities.

28. Lipsitz 2001: 21.

29. Ibid.: 8.

30. See Cabán 2003; and Dávila 2008 for critical discussions of the evolution of the field of Latina/o Studies and its place in the U.S. academy.

31. Cabán 2003: 8.

32. Here we draw on Villa's analytically useful framework of the dialectical relationship of "barrioization" and "barriology," the former term referring to powerful external forces that give shape to marginalized, and therefore inferior, spaces. See Villa 2000: 16.

33. Dávila 2008.

34. Glick Schiller et al. 1992; Rouse 1992.

35. Cantú's (2003) work on Mexican men, sexuality, and migration is an excellent example of this work, as is the work of Carrillo (2001). Zavella and Castañeda 2005; Torres 2007; and González-López 2005 focus on the experiences of women, sexuality, and migration. Important examples of transnational research in Latina/o Studies include Alicea 1997; Aranda 2007; Levitt 2001; Smith 2005; Mahler 1999; Mahler and Pessar 2001; Pessar 1999.

36. Fisher Fishkin 2005; Poblete 2003.

37. For Native American/Indigenous Studies, see Silva 2005; Smith 2005. For examples in Asian American Studies, see Hsu 2000; Das Gupta 2005.

38. La Fountain-Stokes 2005. Important scholarship in this area also includes Carrillo 2001; González-López 2005; Rodríguez 2003; Torres 2007; Cruz-Malavé and Manalansan 2002; Sandoval Sánchez 2005; Manalansan 2003.

39. See Almaguer 1994; Shah 2001; Guglielmo 2003.

40. For example, see Fregoso 2003; Habell-Pallán and Romero 2002; Gaspar de Alba 2003; Negrón-Muntaner 2004; Aparicio and Jaquez 2003; Chabram-Dernersesian 2007.

41. Examples of this work include Smith 2005; Lutz 2001; Levitt 2001; Dávila 2004.

REFERENCES

Alicea, Marixsa. 1997. "'A Chambered Nautilus': The Contradictory Nature of Puerto Rican Women's Role in the Social Construction of a Transnational Community." *Gender & Society* 11(5): 597–626.

Almaguer, Tomás. 1994. *Racial Fault Lines: The Historical Origins of White Supremacy.* Berkeley: University of California Press.

Anzaldúa, Gloria. 1987. *Borderlands/La Frontera: The New Mestiza.* San Francisco: Aunt Lute Books.

Aparicio, Frances, and Candida F. Jaquez, eds. 2003. *Musical Migrations: Transnationalism and Cultural Hybridity in Latin/o America.* New York: Palgrave Macmillan.

Aranda, Elizabeth. 2007. *Emotional Bridges to Puerto Rico: Migration, Return Migration, and the Struggles of Incorporation.* Lanham, MD: Rowman & Littlefield Publishers.

Arredondo, Gabriela F., Aída Hurtado, Norma Klahn, Olga Nájera-Ramírez, and Patricia Zavella. 2003. "Chicana Feminisms at the Crossroads: Disruptions in Dialogue." In *Chicana Feminisms.* Gabriela F. Arredondo, Aída Hurtado, Norma Klahn, Olga Nájera-Ramírez, and Patricia Zavella, eds. Durham: Duke University Press, 1–17.

Behar, Ruth, ed. 1995. *Bridges to Cuba = Puentes a Cuba.* Ann Arbor: University of Michigan Press.

Benmayor, Rina, Rosa L. Torruellas, and Ana M. Jurabe. 1997. "Claiming Cultural Citizenship in East Harlem: Si Esto Puede Ayudar a la Comunidad Mia." In *Latino Cultural Citizenship: Claiming Identity, Space, and Rights*. William V. Flores and Rina Benmayor, eds. Boston: Beacon Press, 152–209.

Boyd, Michelle R. 2008. *Jim Crow Nostalgia: Reconstructing Race in Bronzeville*. Minneapolis: University of Minnesota Press.

Briggs, Laura. 2003. *Reproducing Empire: Race, Sex, Science, and U.S. Imperialism in Puerto Rico*. Berkeley: University of California Press.

Cabán, Pedro. 2003. "Moving from the Margins to Where? Three Decades of Latino/a Studies." *Latino Studies* 1(1): 5–35.

Cammarota, Julio. 2008. *Sueños Americanos: Barrio Youth Negotiating Social and Cultural Identities*. Tucson: University of Arizona Press.

Cantú, Lionel. 2003. "A Place Called Home: A Queer Political Economy of Mexican Immigration." In *Perspectives on Las Américas: A Reader in Culture, History, and Representation*. Matthew C. Gutmann, Félix V. Matos Rodríguez, Lynn Stephen, and Patricia Zavella, eds. Malden, MA: Blackwell, 259–273.

Carrillo, Hector. 2001. *The Night Is Young: Sexuality in Mexico in the Time of AIDS*. Chicago: University of Chicago Press.

Chabram-Dernersesian, Angie, ed. 2007. *The Chicana/o Cultural Studies Forum: Critical and Ethnographic Practices*. New York: New York University Press.

Chan, Sucheng. 2006. *Chinese American Transnationalism: The Flow of People, Resources, and Ideas Between China and America During the Exclusion Era*. Philadelphia: Temple University Press.

Chavez, Leo. 2001. *Covering Immigration: Popular Images and the Politics of the Nation*. Berkeley: University of California Press.

———. 2008. *The Latino Threat: Constructing Immigrants, Citizens, and the Nation*. Stanford: Stanford University Press.

Cruz-Malavé, Arnaldo, and Martin Manalansan, eds. 2002. *Queer Globalizations: Citizenship and the Afterlife of Colonialism*. New York: New York University Press.

Das Gupta, Monisha. 2005. *Unruly Immigrants: Rights, Activism, and Transnational South Asian Politics in the United States*. Durham: Duke University Press.

Dávila, Arlene. 2004. *Barrio Dreams: Puerto Ricans, Latinos, and the Neoliberal City*. Berkeley: University of California Press.

———. 2008. *Latino Spin: Public Image and the Whitewashing of Race*. New York: New York University Press.

Díaz, David. 2005. *Barrio Urbanism: Chicanos, Planning, and American Cities*. New York: Routledge.

Díaz-Cotto, Juanita. 2006. *Chicana Lives and Criminal Justice: Voices from El Barrio*. Austin: University of Texas Press.

Dohan, Daniel. 2003. *The Price of Poverty: Money, Work, and Culture in the Mexican American Barrio*. Berkeley: University of California Press.

Du Bois, W. E. B. 1903 [2003]. *Souls of Black Folk*. New York: Modern Library.

Fisher Fishkin, Shelley. 2005. "Crossroads of Cultures: The Transnational Turn in American Studies: Presidential Address to the American Studies Association, November 12, 2004." *American Quarterly* 57(1): 17–57.

Flores, Juan. 1993. *Divided Borders: Essays on Puerto Rican Identity*. Houston: Arte Público Press.

Fregoso, Rosa Linda. 2003. *MeXicana Encounters: The Making of Social Identities on the Borderlands*. Berkeley: University of California Press.

Freidenberg, Judith Noemi. 2000. *Growing Old in El Barrio*. New York: New York University Press.

García, María Cristina. 1996. *Havana USA: Cuban Exiles and Cuban Americans in South Florida, 1959–1994*. Berkeley: University of California Press.

Gaspar de Alba, Alicia, ed. 2003. *Velvet Barrios: Popular Culture and Chicana/o Sexualities*. New York: Palgrave Macmillan.

Glick Schiller, Nina, Linda Basch, and Cristina Szanton Blanc, eds. 1992. *Towards a Transnational Perspective on Migration: Race, Class, Ethnicity, and Nationalism Reconsidered*. New York: New York Academy of Sciences.

González-López, Gloria. 2005. *Erotic Journeys: Mexican Immigrants and Their Sex Lives*. Berkeley: University of California Press.

Guarnizo, Luis. 1994. "Los Dominicanyorks: The Making of a Binational Society." *Annals of the American Academy of Political and Social Science* 530 (May): 70–86

Guglielmo, Thomas. 2003. *White on Arrival: Italians, Race, Color, and Power in Chicago*. New York: Oxford University Press.

Gutmann, Matthew, Félix Matos Rodríguez, Lynn Stephens, and Patricia Zavella, eds. 2003. *Perspectives on Las Américas: A Reader in Culture, History, and Representation*. Malden, MA: Blackwell.

Habell-Pallán, Michelle, and Mary Romero, eds. 2002. *Latina/o Popular Culture*. New York: New York University Press.

Hernández, Ramona. 2002. *The Mobility of Workers Under Advanced Capitalism: Dominican Migration to the United States*. New York: Columbia University Press.

History Task Force. 1979. *Labor Migration Under Capitalism: The Puerto Rican Experience*. New York: Monthly Review Press.

Hondagneu-Sotelo, Pierrette. 1995. "Women and Children First." *Socialist Review* 25:169–190.

Hsu, Madeline. 2000. *Dreaming of Gold, Dreaming of Home: Transnationalism and Migration Between the United States and South China, 1882–1943*. Stanford: Stanford University Press.

Iber, Jorge, and Samuel Octavio Regalado, eds. 2007. *Mexican American and Sports: A Reader on Athletics and Barrio Life*. College Station: Texas A&M University Press.

La Fountain-Stokes, Lawrence. 2005. "Cultures of the Puerto Rican Queer Diaspora." In *Passing Lines: Sexuality and Immigration*. Brad Epps, Keja Valens, and Bill Johnson González, eds. Cambridge: Harvard University Press, 275–309.

Laó-Montes, Agustín, and Arlene Dávila, eds. 2001. *Mambo Montage: The Latinization of New York*. New York: Columbia University Press.

Latina Feminist Group. 2001. *Telling to Live: Latina Feminist Testimonios*. Durham: Duke University Press.

Levitt, Peggy. 2001. *Transnational Villagers*. Berkeley: University of California Press.

Lipsitz, George. 2001. *American Studies in a Moment of Danger*. Minneapolis: University of Minnesota Press.

Logan, John R., and Harvey L. Molotch. 1987. *Urban Fortunes: The Political Economy of Place*. Berkeley: University of California Press.

López, Iris. 1985. Sterilization Among Puerto Rican Women: A Case Study in New York City. Ph.D. diss., Graduate School of Arts and Sciences.

Loza, Steven. 1993. *Barrio Rhythm: Mexican American Music in Los Angeles.* Urbana: University of Illinois Press.

Lutz, Catherine. 2001. *Homefront: A Military City and the American Twentieth Century.* Boston: Beacon Press.

Mahler, Sarah J. 1999. "Engendering Transnational Migration: A Case Study of Salvadorans." *American Behavioral Scientist* 42(4): 690–719.

Mahler, Sarah J., and Patricia Pessar. 2001. "Gendered Geographies of Power: Analyzing Gender Across Transnational Spaces." *Identities* 7(4): 441–459.

Manalansan, Martin. 2003. *Global Divas: Filipino Gay Men in the Diaspora.* Durham: Duke University Press.

McWilliams, Carey. 1949. *North from Mexico.* New York: J. B. Lippincott.

Molina, Natalia. 2004. *Fit To Be Citizens? Public Health and Race in Los Angeles, 1879–1939.* Berkeley: University of California Press.

Monteiro, Circe. 2008. "Enclaves, Condominiums, and Favelas: Where Are the Ghettos in Brazil?" *City & Community* 7(4): 378–383.

Moore, Joan, and Raquel Pinderhughes, eds. 1993. *In the Barrios: Latinos and the Underclass Debate.* New York: Russell Sage Foundation.

Moraga, Cherríe, and Gloria Anzaldúa, eds. 1981. *This Bridge Called My Back: Writings by Radical Women of Color.* Watertown, MA: Persephone Press.

Muñiz, Vicky. 1998. *Resisting Gentrification and Displacement: Voices of Puerto Rican Women of the Barrio.* New York: Routledge.

Nabhan-Warren, Kristy. 2005. *The Virgin of El Barrio: Marian Apparitions, Catholic Evangelizing, and Mexican American Activism.* New York: New York University Press.

Negrón-Muntaner, Frances. 2004. *Boricua Pop: Puerto Ricans and the Latinization of American Culture.* New York: New York University Press.

Ortiz, Altagracia, ed. 1996. *Puerto Rican Women and Work: Bridges in Transnational Labor.* Philadelphia: Temple University Press.

Perea, Juan, ed. 1997. *Immigrants Out! The New Nativism and the Anti-immigration Impulse in the United States.* New York: New York University Press.

Pérez, Emma. 1991. "Sexuality and Discourse: Notes from a Chicana Survivor." In *Chicana Lesbians: The Girls Our Mothers Warned Us About.* Carla Trujillo, ed. Berkeley: Third Woman Press, 159–184.

Pessar, Patricia. 1999. "Engendering Migration Studies: The Case of New Immigrants in the United States." *American Behavioral Scientist* 42(4): 577–600.

Pessar, Patricia, and Sherri Grasmuck. 1991. *Between Two Islands: Dominican International Migration.* Berkeley: University of California Press.

Poblete, Juan, ed. 2003. *Critical Latin American and Latino Studies.* Minneapolis: University of Minnesota Press.

Roberts, Dorothy. 1997. *Killing the Black Body: Race, Reproduction, and the Meaning of Liberty.* New York: Random House.

Rodriguez, Clara. 1991. *Puerto Ricans: Born in the U.S.A.* Boulder: Westview Press

Rodríguez, Juana María. 2003. *Queer Latinidad: Identity Practices, Discursive Spaces.* New York: New York University Press.

Rouse, Roger. 1992. "Making Sense of Settlement: Class Transformation, Cultural Struggle, and Transnationalism Among Mexican Migrants in the United States." *Annals of the New York Academy of Science* 645:25–52.

Ruiz, Vicki. 1999. *From Out of the Shadows: Mexican Women in Twentieth-Century America.* New York: Oxford University Press.

Sánchez, George. 1993. *Becoming Mexican American: Ethnicity, Culture, and Identity in Chicano Los Angeles, 1900–1945.* New York: Oxford University Press.

———. 1997. "Face the Nation: Race, Immigration, and the Rise of Nativism in Late Twentieth Century America." *International Migration Review* 31(4): 1009–30.

Sánchez-Korrol, Virginia. 1994. *From Colonia to Community: The History of Puerto Ricans in New York City.* 2nd ed. Berkeley: University of California Press.

Sandoval Sánchez, Alberto. 2005. "Politicizing Abjection: Towards the Articulation of a Latino AIDS Queer Identity." In *Passing Lines: Sexuality and Immigration.* Brad Epps, Keja Valens, and Bill Johnson González, eds. Cambridge: Harvard University Press, 275–310.

Santa Ana, Otto. 2002. *Brown Tide Rising: Metaphors of Latinos in Contemporary American Public Discourse.* Austin: University of Texas Press.

Shah, Nayan. 2001. *Contagious Divides: Epidemics and Race in San Francisco's Chinatown.* Berkeley: University of California Press.

Silva, Noenoe. 2005. *Aloha Betrayed: Native Hawaiian Resistance to American Colonialism.* Durham: Duke University Press.

Small, Mario Luis. 2008. "Four Reasons to Abandon the Idea of 'The Ghetto.'" *City & Community* 7(4): 389–395.

Smith, Andrea. 2005. *Conquest: Sexual Violence and American Indian Genocide.* Boston: South End Press.

Smith, Robert. 2005. *Mexican New York: Transnational Lives of New Immigrants.* Berkeley: University of California Press.

Souza, Caridad. 2000. "Welfare Debates and Puerto Rican Teenage Mothers in New York City." *Economic and Political Weekly* 35(20–21): L24–32.

Torre, Adela de la, and Denise Pesquera, eds. 1993. *Building with Our Hands: New Directions in Chicana Studies.* Berkeley: University of California Press.

Torres, Andrés. 1995. *From Melting Pot to Mosaic: African Americans and Puerto Ricans in the New York Political Economy.* Philadelphia: Temple University Press.

Torres, Lourdes. 2007. "Boricua Lesbians: Sexuality, Nationality, and the Politics of Passing." *CENTRO Journal: Journal of the Center for Puerto Rican Studies* 19(1): 231–249

Torruellas, Rosa, Rina Benmayor, and Ana Juarbe. 1996. "Negotiating Gender, Work, and Welfare: *Familia* as Productive Labor Among Puerto Rican Women in New York City." In *Puerto Rican Women and Work: Bridges in Transnational Labor.* Altagracia Ortiz, ed. Philadelphia: Temple University Press, 184–208.

Treviño, Roberto. 2006. *The Church in the Barrio: Mexican American Ethno-Catholicism in Houston.* Durham: University of North Carolina Press.

Valle, Victor M., and Rodolfo D. Torres. 2000. *Latino Metropolis.* Minneapolis: University of Minnesota Press.

Vigil, Diego. 2007. *The Projects: Gang and Non-gang Families in East Los Angeles.* Austin: University of Texas Press.

———. 2008. "Barrio Genealogy." *City & Community* 7(4): 366–371.

Villa, Raúl Homero. 2000. *Barrio-Logos: Space and Place in Urban Chicano Literature and Culture*. Austin: University of Texas Press.

Whalen, Carmen. 2001. *From Puerto Rico to Philadelphia: Puerto Rican Workers and Post-war Economies*. Philadelphia: Temple University Press.

Zavella, Patricia. 1987. *Women's Work and Chicano Families: Cannery Workers of the Santa Clara Valley*. Ithaca: Cornell University Press.

Zavella, Patricia, and Xóchitl Castañeda. 2005. "Sexuality and Risks: Gendered Discourses About Virginity and Disease Among Young Women of Mexican Origin." *Latino Studies* 3(2): 226–245.

Part I

Citizenship, Belonging, and
(the Limits of) Latina/o Inclusion

1

Singing the "Star-Spanglish Banner"

The Politics and Pathologization of Bilingualism
in U.S. Popular Media

MARÍA ELENA CEPEDA

Sus estrellas, sus franjas, / la libertad, somos iguales. / Somos hermanos. Es nuestro himno. / En el fiero combate en señal de victoria, / Fulgor de lucha / (Mi gente sigue luchando) / al paso de la libertad / (Ya es tiempo de romper las cadenas) / Por la noche decían: "¡Se va defiendiendo!" / ¡Oh decid! ¿Despliega aún su hermosura estrellada / sobre tierra de libres, / la bandera sagrada?
—"Nuestro Himno"[1]

The general argument about the importance of literacy in general (literacy in languages other than English by immigrant people is not discussed) has here been replaced by an argument that suggests that English itself is threatened by immigration. Somehow, then, the existence of people in America whose first language is not English has become a threat to English. And, even the sanctity of government in English is under threat.
—Alastair Pennycook, *English and the Discourses of Colonialism*

In the spring of 2006, U.S. residents of all political persuasions were witness to the largest pro-immigrant cross-country protests in the nation's history. Designed as a response to what many viewed as draconian measures to halt undocumented immigration,[2] the peaceful marches were notable for their strategic use of the transnational popular media, particularly radio, as a key part of organizational efforts. Significantly, mainstream (English-language) U.S. media focused almost exclusively on the critical role that Spanish-language media played in the protests, as well as widespread public reaction to the song "Nuestro Himno" ("Our Anthem"). During the apex of the pro-immigrant demonstrations—the May 2006 transnational celebration that grassroots organizers labeled "A Day Without Immigrants"—the single "Nuestro Himno," a Spanish-language paraphrasing of "The Star-Spangled Banner," was released. Performed by a cohort of U.S. Latina/o and Latin American recording artists, "Nuestro Himno" was part of a larger project, the album *Somos Americanos* (*We Are Americans*) (Associated Press 2006; Sanneh 2006; National Public Radio 2006; Various Artists 2006). Situated within the context of the ongoing legal, socioeconomic, and political struggles of recent Latino immigrants, both the recording and the demonstrations constituted important symbolic gestures toward the (re)claiming of U.S. public space and the contested meanings of nation and belonging.[3] Indeed, the case study of "Nuestro Himno" provokes particular concern, given the disproportionate impact that the historiographic configuration of more "commercial" Latino music has on our collective understanding of *all* Latino music as well as Latino cultural expression itself—despite many scholars' reluctance to view this music as a legitimate object of study.

Mainstream English-language media accounts of both Latino organizational efforts and "Nuestro Himno" underscored the contradictory tensions rooted in the escalation of transnationalism and the increased mobility of individuals, capital, and labor coupled with the impulse toward xenophobic re-entrenchment. Referred to as "open-" and "shut-door" immigration approaches, the strategies of "policies of ingestion and expellation" (Takacs 1999: 592, 595; Massey and Redstone Akresh 2006)—masked in the interest of preserving a commonsense notion of national identity and community— ultimately underscore undocumented workers' paradoxical relationship to the nation-state: that despite the vital role that they play in the economy, undocumented individuals' contributions to and de facto membership in U.S. society remain largely unrecognized (Varsanyi 2006). As Oboler observes, "The Latino/a experience attests [that] it is not citizenship per se but the lack of it that fuels political debates and conservative measures today" (2006: 22). This liminal status vis-à-vis the nation, or what Robinson (2007: 22) describes as the "*condition of [the] deportable*," in turn ensures the state's ability to exploit and dispose of unruly, potentially counter-hegemonic immigrant laborers should the need arise.

This chapter commences with a discussion of what I have termed the "musical imagi/nation" as it pertains to Latino popular music and concepts of the nation, followed by an examination of mainstream (English-language) Internet and print media discourse regarding the "Nuestro Himno" recording. Not intended as an analysis of its lyrical or musical content, my critique instead considers the specific historical and ideological circumstances surrounding the song's production and release. Throughout, my reading adheres to van Dijk's sociopolitical model of critical discourse analysis (CDA), which foregrounds the place of public discourse in the (re)creation of and challenges to societal dominance, or a "political critique of those responsible for [discourse's] perversion in the reproduction of dominance and inequality" (1993: 253). According to van Dijk's CDA model, discourse and dominance are linked along two primary axes: the invocation of dominance in text and speech, and (more indirectly) via the influence of discourse on others' minds. Differential patterns of access to everyday public discourse figure prominently in this relationship (249, 279; see also Santa Ana 2002).

My reading of "Nuestro Himno" and public reaction to the recording are conducted with an eye toward the roles of language, gender, class, and ethno-racial subjectivities as they pertain to contemporary constructions of the mainstream "American" and U.S. Latino body politics. As I posit here, while the numerous and largely unfavorable mainstream media responses to the "Nuestro Himno" recording may certainly be interpreted as evidence of the successful and ongoing racialization of both the Spanish language and U.S. Latina/os (a process that, as we shall see, possesses definitive historical roots), to categorize "Nuestro Himno" as a resolutely oppositional text proves simplistic at best. Indeed, many Latina/os, regardless of their political leanings or their relationship to Spanish, publicly expressed their distaste for "Nuestro Himno." Rather, I would argue that this particular representation of Latino patriotism and much of the popular media reaction to it are more aptly described in terms of their "competing tensions" (Báez 2006) and strategic historical erasures.

Conceptualizing the Musical ImagiNation

The "musical imagi/nation" refers to a transnational Latino community whose identity narratives are based on routes, as well as roots. In this context, Latino popular music is cast as a common space for imagining and enacting Latinidad outside traditional national borders, and in ways not so overtly shaped by the racism, classism, heterosexism, sexism, and xenophobia that many U.S. Latina/os confront on a daily basis.[4] This understanding of the musical imagi/nation draws on Appadurai's seminal work regarding the symbiotic relationship between new media and imagination in the globalized context. As Appadurai argues, present-day immigrants are intimately familiar with the mass-mediated imagery that shapes as much as it reflects their movements "homeward" and back. Further, he maintains that the imagination assumes a different function in today's deterritorialized "communities of sentiment": as an "organized field of social practices, a form of work (in the sense of both labor and culturally organized practice), and a form of negotiation between sites of agency (individuals) and globally defined fields of possibility . . . the imagination is now central to all forms of agency, is itself a social fact, and is the key component of the new global order" (1996: 6, 8, 31). Despite the lesser importance ascribed to the traditional nation-state in this formulation, however, its ongoing role in the lives of transmigrants is not to be underestimated, as the numerous critiques with regard to this aspect of Appadurai's work attest (e.g., Alvarez 2005; Glick Schiller and Fouron 2001; Smith and Guarnizo 1998; Manalansan 2003; Ong 1999).

Understood, if not explicitly expressed, as both noun and verb, and as a collective activity embedded in a definitive sense of place(lessness), the Latino musical imagi/nation renders Latino popular music the locus for the "everyday social project" (Appadurai 1996: 4) of self-imagination and the construction of family, a powerful arbitrator of memory, identity, and nation among the diaspora. (One such example is the very title of "Nuestro Himno," which via its use of the possessive "our" disrupts traditional, monolithic notions of "American" identity.) In this regard, as a popular artifact "Nuestro Himno" highlights the inextricable links between U.S. Latino (popular) cultural and political phenomena, much like the spring of 2006's radio-based organizational efforts. Thus any nuanced reading of "Nuestro Himno" must favor a consideration of historical context as well as actual content.

"Nuestro Himno" and the Discourse(s) of National Belonging

Entities of power are dangerous when they are ascending and when they are declining and it is a moot point whether they are more dangerous in the second or the first moment. The first moment, they gobble up everybody and in the second moment they take everybody down with them. So when I say the decline or erosion of the nation-state, do not for a moment imagine that the nation-state is bowing off the stage of history. . . . It goes into an even deeper trough of defensive exclusionism.

—Stuart Hall, "The Local and the Global"

The original Spanish-language version of "Nuestro Himno" was released on May 1, 2006, with a remix including English lyrics released the following month. Both versions were marketed by Urban Box Office Records, a company that has also released recordings by several major reggaetón artists, many of which have been spearheaded by the producer Adam Kidron.[5] A wide range of performers, including Ivy Queen, Olga Tañón, Wyclef Jean, and Carlos Ponce, recorded the album in studios in New York, Puerto Rico, Miami, Mexico City, Los Angeles, and Madrid. One dollar from each sale was donated to the Washington DC–based National Capital Immigrant Coalition and the Latin War Veterans (Associated Press 2006; Clark 2006; Ratner-Arías 2006). Within a broader historical context, the media backlash against "Nuestro Himno" brings to mind a long history of ambivalently received contemporary rewritings of "The Star-Spangled Banner," despite the fact that, as a May 4, 2006 *Washington Post* editorial noted, "converting national symbols into new art forms is an American tradition." Notably, rewritten versions were realized by artists of color such as José Feliciano (1968), Jimi Hendrix (1969), Marvin Gaye (1983), and R. Kelly (2005). As exemplified by Feliciano's poorly received rendition, which he performed in Detroit's Tiger Stadium during the height of the anti–Vietnam War protests and in the aftermath of the 1967 Detroit race riots (Block October 27, 2006; Teepen 2006), most of these performances have occurred during historic moments in which U.S. communities of color and other marginalized peoples were openly challenging existing hierarchies of power. For example, a mere ten months following Feliciano's performance in Detroit, guitarist Jimi Hendrix unveiled his legendary instrumental version of "The Star-Spangled Banner" at Woodstock. Yet without exception, these earlier renderings of the national anthem constituted individual, as opposed to collective, instances of subaltern expression—a significant difference that casts the collective nature of the "Nuestro Himno" project, and the recent pro-immigrant marches themselves, in another light.

In response to the recording, and amid a hard-fought congressional and White House battle over his proposals regarding immigration policy, President George W. Bush was quick to criticize the content of "Nuestro Himno," stating, "One of the important things here is that we not lose our national soul" (Liasson 2006). Bush further clarified that "The Star-Spangled Banner" simply does not possess the same *value* in Spanish as in English, and that to become a U.S. citizen one must learn English (Rutenberg 2006; emphasis mine). These statements prove provocative on several counts, both in terms of their public policy implications as well their symbolic connotations. Among these is Bush's own well-documented usage of Spanish throughout his political career, both on the campaign trail and perhaps most notably in the first-ever presidential radio address entirely in Spanish, delivered during the 2001 Cinco de Mayo celebration. While the president's strategic deployment of Spanish has been referred to in some mainstream media outlets as one of his administration's "convenient little fictions" due to the limited nature of his Spanish-speaking skills (Froomkin 2006), his usage of Spanish has also been welcomed by many Latina/os as a positive sign of cross-cultural exchange and mainstream acceptance. Nevertheless, it is important that we contextualize Bush's use of Spanish within the United States's historic tendency toward differential bilingualism.[6]

According to Aparicio's (1998) notion of differential bilingualism, the study of Spanish in the contemporary United States must be understood as a commodity readily available to privileged Anglos in search of improved employment opportunities in the globalized marketplace, just as native Spanish speakers are systematically discouraged from maintaining, reclaiming, or building on existing Spanish-language skills within both the U.S. educational system and society at large. Within this hierarchical framework, any usage of Spanish on the part of an upper-class, Anglo president is hailed as a sign of cosmopolitanism, whereas Latino linguistic practices are deemed unsophisticated and "ethnically safe" only within the contained, deliberately scripted contexts of ethnic festivals, print media, and the like (Urciuoli 1996: 35). (I would add to that list the highly gendered domestic/private sphere.) Conversely, the "unscripted" public deployment of languages other than English is indexed as an affront to English's authority (Urciuoli 1996: 37–38) and "white public space," or what Hill (1999: 682) describes as "a morally significant set of contexts that are the most important sites of the practices of a racializing hegemony, in which Whites are visibly normal, and in which racialized populations are visibly marginal and the objects of monitoring range from individual judgment to Official English legislation." Indeed, as one Michigan journalist wryly noted, "What's really behind the ruckus [over "Nuestro Himno"] is power—the power to control and the power to define" (Hardiman 2006).

Moreover, the material and symbolic struggles over this power—and more specifically, the struggles over the quotidian linguistic practices to which it is attached—emerged from a distinct historical context. Significantly, the commonsense linkages between language, race, and "American" identity that persist today only came to light in the late nineteenth century in response to the influx of new immigrants from eastern and southern Europe. Tied to Romantic beliefs about the construction of national identities as not only political and cultural but racial as well (and hence linguistic), the "inextricable" relationship between language and ethno-racial identity became noticeable features of the era's public documents. By the 1950s, however, these southern and eastern European immigrants and their offspring had been recast as "ethnic" as opposed to "colored" Americans (Leeman 2004: 516–517, 520–521).

The product of more than a century of linguistic and racial ideologies, Bush's statements regarding "Nuestro Himno" mirror the linguistic "shorthand" of public discourse, in which "immigrant," "illegal," "alien," "ESL," and "bilingual education" all become code for "Latino" (Zentella 2002). Within this racialized discourse, who is the (unspoken yet patently clear) "we" to whom Bush refers in his pronouncement regarding "our" national soul? Are we to understand his use of the possessive here as an inclusive gesture, or as a mere repetition of the monolithic "Americanness" historically endemic to U.S. assimilationist rhetoric? Moreover, Bush's assertion of the English-language anthem's inherently superior "value" recalls the discourse of family values that permeated the Bush administration and U.S. conservative factions as a whole. This language has proven central to the construction and maintenance of a U.S. national identity in which the patriarchal family serves as a privileged metaphor (Takacs 1999: 594). According to this ideology, the nation is conceptualized as a spontaneous entity, created and existing in a historical vacuum, and untouched by economic or political forces—or an ideological system in which certain individuals or communities are cast as "naturally" belonging to the nation (i.e., those possessing "unmarked bodies"). As Anderson asserts, "In everything 'natural' there is always something unchosen," hence the struggle for "others" (the immigrants, the "aliens," or the "marked bodies") to be "invited into" the imagined community, or to become "naturalized" (1991: 143, 145; Takacs 1999: 596–598). With the advent of "fourth wave" immigration as well as the successes of the civil rights movements of the 1960s and 1970s, these gender-, class-, and race-based categorizations persist, as evinced in the following web post in reaction to "Nuestro Himno":

It is apparent that the hate of some people can never be under estimated [sic] . . . Many attack the president over his opinion of how our Nation [sic] Anthem should be sung. People in this blog have painted him as a scourge on the earth. The amazing part is he is the strongest voice of support for illegal immigrants. The left, socialists, communists, progressives, gays, lesbians, Hollywood types, hate our president no matter what he does or how congruent his position is with theirs. It's a mind set [sic] of hate, disrespect, and bullying as I have never seen in my 47 years in this country.

I employ my immigrants and have had a soft place in my heart and in my company for those trying to better their life. The pollution of America's National Anthem and the marching on our streets demanding rights by those that are not legal to be here *has nearly destroyed my feelings of compassion for Hispanic immigrants.* Before the slamming of me for making money off the backs of these poor uneducated immigrants keep in mind they start without experience at $14.00 per hour and after I train them I pay them from $18.00 to $24.00 per hour. *For this I owe them citizenship they have not earned?* (posted by "Charles" on May 8, 2006, in response to Liasson 2006; emphasis mine)

This post is noteworthy not only due to its content, which is generally representative of Internet commentary on the subject, but also for its form. Much like the U.S. government, Charles's recognition of undocumented workers' contributions to his own economic vitality, not to mention his own failure to observe the letter of the law (his preoccupation with the "illegal" status of his immigrant employees notwithstanding), proves selective. By framing the use of Spanish in the national anthem (and by extension, in the public arena) as a form of "pollution," the writer deems Spanish speakers "dirty" (read immoral) and therefore unfit to participate in the U.S. body politic. Ultimately, the U.S. business owner, much like the privileged, white, male land and slave owners of the past, considers himself fit to "bestow" citizenship on the less fortunate individuals in his employ. Indeed, the patronizing tone and particular use of the possessive ("my immigrants") recalls the failed "forty acres and a mule" policy extended to freed African American slaves in the Reconstruction era.

In the period immediately following the May 1, 2006, "Nuestro Himno" release, analogous examples appeared in newspaper editorials and letters to the editor across the country. Most of these items subscribed to a cultural and economic logic similar to that of the web posting above. As the *Augusta Chronicle* editorial page warned in its discussion of the "bastardization"[7] of "The Star-Spangled Banner": "You can't make a nation's anthem your own, especially in a land not your own, by stealing the words and changing them and putting them in another language. The title Our Hymn is patently vile and insulting. *It's not your hymn*" (Editorial, May 2, 2006; emphasis mine). Here, the editorial's emphatic and repeated use of the second person plural ("you") emerges in marked opposition to the (again unspoken yet clearly enunciated) "we/us" that stakes a discursive claim to the singularly "legitimate" expression of "The Star-Spangled Banner" and thus the land/nation-state itself. The use of the possessive ("It's not *your* hymn"), along with the use of the verb "steal" ("stealing the words") posits a sharp division between Spanish-speakers and Anglos, as it simultaneously casts into doubt the very legitimacy of Latino claims to U.S. public citizenship and belonging. Most notably, the editorial's words enact what Behdad describes as the United States's "historical amnesia towards immigration." As he asserts, the myth of immigrant America, which simplistically posits the United States as the benevolent champion of the global "huddled masses," "not only obscures the ideological underpinnings of national formation and the political economy of immigration but also disavows the importance of xenophobia in the founding of the United States" (2005: xv). Given the historical linkages constructed between race and language, which under the dictates of "new racism" have partially given way to a potent emphasis on the role of personal choice and individual responsibility (Schmidt 2002: 154; Leeman 2004), Spanish-speaking immigrants are frequently depicted as individuals who *willfully choose* not to learn English. As the *Augusta Chronicle* editorial illustrates, Spanish speakers (and by extension all other Latinos, regardless of their Spanish-language proficiency) are also repeatedly framed as perpetual foreigners in the U.S. popular imagination, as exemplified by the phrase "especially in a land not your own." In this context, language diversity is erroneously understood as an imported phenomenon (Wiley 2004: 322), despite the fact that Spanish and numerous Native American languages were spoken in the United States prior to the British colonists' arrival and that much of what is now the U.S. Southwest belonged to Mexico until the 1848 Treaty of Guadalupe Hidalgo.

In sum, the xenophobic reaction to "Nuestro Himno" cited here illuminates the myriad anxieties that converge around the contested terrain of voice, as well as the symbolic threats posed to mainstream national identity by the increased visibility of brown, working-class, undocumented bodies. As such, the public debate over "Nuestro Himno" might loosely be characterized as a struggle over *who* will speak, *what* will they say, and *in what language(s)* they will say it (Dorfman 2006; Takacs 1999: 592, 606, 608). Arguably, this discourse is designed to reaffirm the solidity and stability of national boundaries at the moment of their dissolution (Takacs 1999: 592), and is therefore reflective of a refashioned, if not unique, conflict over state-sanctioned notions of citizenship in the post-9/11 era.[8]

Contextualizing "Nuestro Himno" from the Inside Out

The meaning of the American Dream is in that record: the struggle for
freedom, opportunity, everything that *they* are trying to shut down on *us*.
—U.S.-Cuban rapper Pitbull (Armando Pérez),
commenting on "Nuestro Himno" (emphasis mine)

The tendency to frame the everyday linguistic practices and cultural
production of U.S. Latinos almost exclusively as mechanisms of resistance predominates in Cultural Studies literature. But the case of "Nuestro
Himno" necessitates a far more measured approach to the everyday politics
of language and cultural production that recognizes the possibility that not
all minoritarian expressive practices are necessarily purposefully resistant,
just as all dominant practices are not conscientiously manipulative. Indeed,
as the above epigraph by the popular U.S. Latino rapper Pitbull illustrates,
the tendency to subscribe to a monolithic, facile notion of the "American
Dream," or to express U.S. ethno-racial, class, gender, and cultural struggles in binary terms (us/them) is not unique to the nation's power brokers
and political elites, despite their differential access to public discourse.
The justifications of inequality embedded in the us/them binary entail the
positive representation of one's own community offered in contrast to the
negative representation of the Other(s). Explicitly framed as "typical," with
time the generalizations attached to these discursive frameworks acquire
commonsensical status (van Dijk 1993: 263–264). Nonetheless, perhaps the
more urgent question in this regard is: how does the construction of the
communal "we-ness" cited above compare to George W. Bush's reaction
to "Nuestro Himno"? In this respect, I posit that "Nuestro Himno," while
nominally advancing certain narrow conceptualizations of cultural citizenship and belonging under the guise of popular musical expression, ultimately underscores the political shortcomings of essentializing approaches
toward Latinidad.

As previously noted, the president's call for sameness via the privileging of the English-language "Star-Spangled Banner" elides the quotidian realities of a polyglot nation, and thereby highlights one of the key
shortcomings of rigid, state-sanctioned discourses regarding "American"
national identity. More specifically, the conflict over a singular national
identity versus multiculturalism, embodied in individual as well as official
reactions to popular texts like "Nuestro Himno," ultimately perpetuates,
if not constructs, a false dichotomy pitting U.S. political and economic

citizenship against multicultural identity—a dichotomy in which culture is intrinsically linked to difference, and in which, as Rosaldo (1989: 198) observes, "full citizenship and cultural visibility appear to be inversely related. When one increases, the other decreases. Full citizens lack culture, and those most culturally endowed lack full citizenship." In their aesthetic response to this flawed equation, the performers and producers of "Nuestro Himno" also manage to proactively address some of the chief misrepresentations about contemporary Latino popular music. Among the most noteworthy of these are the Spanish-language anthem's clear aesthetic debt to rhythm and blues and rap music, itself a means of reasserting the intimate historical, racial, and artistic relationships between Latinos and African Americans as well as the visibility and participation of Afro-Latinos in these networks. In addition, the use of code switching ("Spanglish"), as performed in the song by then-eleven-year-old female rapper P-Star, once more underscores the active role of urban Latinos, including young women, in the creation and dissemination of rap music and hip-hop in both English and Spanish. Nonetheless, the Spanish-language anthem's most noteworthy oppositional move—its association with the May 2006 pro-immigrant demonstrations—is resolutely detached from its aesthetic foundations. Purposeful or not, this aesthetic uncoupling arguably proved the most effective ideological weapon against "Nuestro Himno" and the marcher's calls for social justice and an expanded definition of U.S. citizenship and patriotism. In this respect, the successful media attacks leveled against the notion of Spanish-speakers as equal participants in the U.S. musical imagi/nation—and in a broader sense, the nation itself—highlighted the potent relationship between symbol and gesture.

Ironically, some of the most prominent public defenders of "Nuestro Himno" have ultimately, if unintentionally, perpetuated long-standing beliefs about the nature of the English language (and by extension, dominant Anglo-Saxon culture) as under constant threat from other languages, including Spanish (Leeman 2007: 3). The noted U.S.-Chilean writer and scholar Ariel Dorfman offers a case in point in his May 7, 2006, *Washington Post* editorial:

Spanish is not going to fade away like Norwegian or Italian or German did during previous assimilative waves. . . . I believe this is why "Nuestro Himno" has been received with such trepidation. By infiltrating one of the safest symbols of U.S. national identity with Spanish syllables, this version of "The Star-Spangled Banner" has crossed a line. It has inadvertently announced something many Americans have dreaded for years: that *their country is on its way to becoming a bilingual nation.* (emphasis mine)

While offering fervent support throughout his opinion piece of Latinos' right to bilingual, bicultural public expression, in this key passage Dorfman overlooks a well-documented reality of U.S. Latino linguistic life: that Latinos are experiencing an exceedingly rapid and absolute shift toward English monolingualism by the second generation (Portes and Hao 1998). Thus he unwittingly upholds a societal axiom that scholars of U.S. bilingual education and specifically differential bilingualism have long realized: that the right to maintain or achieve functional literacy in languages other than English is not in fact practiced or treated as a right, but rather as an elite privilege, as Dorfman's own autobiography, *Heading South, Looking North: A Bilingual Journey* (1999), attests.

In this light, while widely interpreted in the mainstream English-language press as a progressive social tool, the reconstituted anthem's highly gendered, generationally grounded portrayal of the "ideal" U.S. Latino citizen as a hard-working, uncomplaining, functionally bilingual adherent of the "American Dream" may at best be read as an exclusionary tool—as exemplified by its rather monolithic portrayal of "el pueblo latino" ("the [singular] Latino people") and Latinos' relationship to the Spanish language. At worst, this may be read as a dominant strategy of containment. As Behdad argues, the archetype of the "successful" U.S. immigrant (i.e., one who does not accept government aid) has historically been employed as a disciplinary mechanism aimed at internal minorities like Latinos, Native Americans, and African Americans. He notes that this strategy serves as a means of displacing culpability for the failings of the United States's supposed meritocracy from the dominant classes onto marginalized communities (2005: 13–14).

Indeed, the very existence of a Spanish-language "Star-Spangled Banner" is not unique. An earlier Spanish-language version of the "Star-Spangled Banner," simply titled "La Bandera de las Estrellas" ("The Flag of Stars"), has existed since 1919. Commissioned by the U.S. Department of Education, "La Bandera" boasts nearly identical lyrics to those that appear in "Nuestro Himno" eighty years later.[9] The Library of Congress possesses vintage versions of the "Star-Spangled Banner" in French, Polish, Italian, Armenian, and Portuguese, among others, with Internet versions in Yiddish and Samoan easily accessible as well. And in more recent years, the U.S. State Department website has offered translations of the Pledge of Allegiance, the U.S. Constitution, and other government documents into several languages, including French and Arabic (Feldman and Peralta 2006; Feran 2006; Goldstein 2006; Leo 2006; Montgomery 2006; Editorial, May 6, 2006; Shea 2006; Editorial, May 2, 2006).

As the highly visible and audible case of the 2006 "Nuestro Himno" recording evinces, the failure to embrace a more expanded definition or representation of "American" identity is not novel, and neither are its material impacts, as demonstrated by the long-standing socioeconomic, cultural, and educational marginalization of U.S. Latinos and other communities of color, both immigrant and native-born. The political project of U.S. national identity has historically depended on the relaxation of geopolitical borders and utilization of the subsequent immigrant presence as a key source of capital. Increased immigration has in turn fostered the need for more stringent gatekeeping measures such as stricter immigration and language policies, themselves ideological strategies designed to promote nationalist anxieties centered on "broken borders" and "waves of illegal immigrants." Indeed, the systematic oppression and dehumanization of the immigration labor force demands this discursive framework (Behdad 2005: 12; Robinson 2007: 22). Much like the "benign myth" of the United States's democratic roots and the refusal to acknowledge the role of conquest, labor exploitation, and colonialist annexation in the formation of the nation (Behdad 2005: 6), the historical erasure of these previous translations ultimately constitutes a violent discursive denial that successfully casts "Nuestro Himno," and by extension U.S. Latino public claims to cultural citizenship, as aberrations. As the retracing of the Spanish-language anthem's historical roots neatly illustrates, the doors of the greater U.S. musical imagi/nation "open" and "shut" on a situational basis, just as popular music and media continue to serve as vital sites for national conflicts over self-expression, nation, and belonging.

ACKNOWLEDGMENTS

Portions of this chapter appear in the essay "Whose Musical Imagi/nation?: Contradictory Discourses of Belonging in 'Nuestro Himno' and 'Reggaetón Latino'" (*Identities: Global Studies in Culture and Power* 16 [5], 2009, 548–572). Many thanks to Mari Castañeda and the Communications faculty of the University of Massachusetts, Amherst, for the opportunity to present an early draft of this piece. *Muchísimas gracias* to Carlos Alamo Pastrana, Rogelio Miñana, the editors of this volume, and the anonymous reviewers of New York University Press for their insightful suggestions, and to Jennifer Leeman for generously sharing her work. Finally, I would like to extend a very special thanks to Dolores Inés Casillas for her invaluable commentary. This essay would certainly not be the same were it not for her immensely critical, yet always *cariñoso*, eye.

NOTES

1. The most widely circulated translation of this verse of "Nuestro Himno" reads as follows: "Its stars, its stripes / liberty, we are equals. / We are brothers in our anthem. / In fierce combat, a symbol of victory / the glory of battle, / (My people fight on) / the march toward liberty. / (The time has come to break the chains.) / Throughout the night they proclaimed: "We will defend it!" / Tell me! Does its starry beauty still wave / above the land of the free, / the sacred flag?"

2. The protests of the spring of 2006 were largely in response to two specific pieces of legislation passed in December 2005 by the House of Representatives and in May 2006 by the Senate. The House legislation (HR4437, otherwise known as "The Border Protection, Antiterrorism, and Illegal Immigration Control Act") requested the following: the construction of a seven-hundred-mile wall along the U.S.-Mexico border; the right for state and local law enforcement to enforce federal immigration laws; legal changes that would allow individuals, organizations and religious factions to be criminally penalized for assisting undocumented immigrants; and that those undocumented immigrants residing in the United States be penalized as felons. The Senate version of this legislation (S2611) was nearly identical in content (U.S. Congress 2006).

3. As one Lancaster, Pennsylvania, newspaper editorial argued in 2006 with regard to the performance of the "Star-Spangled Banner" in any language other than English, "It sounds the best—and it *means* the most—when sung in English" (emphasis mine).

4. This is not to suggest, as I demonstrate below, that strict hierarchies of gender, race, culture, and class are not present in the Latino community's own self-renderings, or that the concept of the musical imagi/nation is employed in an exclusively symbolic or counter-hegemonic vein.

5. In defense of his record label's release of "Nuestro Himno," Kidron, a British-born U.S. resident for sixteen years, stated that "there's no attempt to usurp anything. The intent is to communicate. I wanted to show my thanks to these people who buy my records and listen to the music we release and do the jobs I don't want to do." While his remarks might initially be superficially read as a benign gesture of cross-cultural solidarity, on second glance Kidron's statement is nonetheless problematic. This is due to the way Kidron chooses not to emphasize the immigrant status that he shares with so many of reggaetón's consumers. Instead, he distances himself from the racialized, working-class individuals that he assumes compose his company's primary target audience. As such, Kidron's previous utterance ("I wanted to show my thanks to these people who buy my records . . . ") may be interpreted as disingenuous at best. Conversely, Kidron's connections lead one to wonder if at least some of the resentment toward "Nuestro Himno" might be attributed to the fact that many of its performers and its producer are connected to the reggaetón music scene, itself a target of race and class prejudice both within the music industry as well as among Latinos and non-Latinos alike.

6. Bush was not the only Washington DC politician to express his unequivocal disagreement with "Nuestro Himno." Shortly following the song's release, both the House and the Senate introduced resolutions "affirming that statements of national unity, including the National Anthem, should be recited or sung in English" (HR458; S458). Several state legislatures, including those of Oklahoma and Minnesota, considered similar measures (Talley 2006; Sweeney 2006).

7. In several print media outlets, among them the aforementioned *Augusta Chronicle* (Editorial, May 2, 2006) and the *Herald News* (Letter to the editor 2006), "Nuestro Himno" was characterized as a "bastardization" of the "Star-Spangled Banner." The lexical choice in these cases proves significant, particularly given the historic anxieties regarding cultural and racial miscegenation in the United States.

8. Indeed, the current struggles over citizenship are not unique to the present case, as evidenced by the Americanization programs of the late nineteenth and early twentieth centuries aimed at Native Americans and Chicanos, as well as the imposition of English within the Puerto Rican educational system in the post-1898 period.

9. Most media outlets cite 1919 as the year of publication for "La Bandera," with the exception of Woodard Maderazo (2006), who lists 1912 as the year of publication. Notably, the commissioning of this translation occurred during the same period as the infamous Americanization programs on the U.S. mainland and forced English instruction in Puerto Rico.

REFERENCES

Alvarez, Robert. 2005. *Mangos, Chiles, and Truckers: The Business of Transnationalism.* Minneapolis: University of Minnesota Press.

Anderson, Benedict. 1991 [1983]. *Imagined Communities: Reflections on the Origins and the Spread of Nationalism*, rev. ed. London: Verso.

Aparicio, Frances R. Spring 1998. Whose Spanish, whose language, whose power? An ethnographic inquiry into differential bilingualism. *Indiana Journal of Hispanic Literatures* 12:5–25.

Appadurai, Arjun. 1996. *Modernity at Large: Cultural Dimensions of Globalization.* Minneapolis: University of Minnesota Press.

Associated Press. April 28, 2006. Oh say can you see the national anthem in Spanish?

Báez, Jillian. 2006. "En mi imperio": Competing discourses of agency in Ivy Queen's reggaetón. *CENTRO: Journal of the Center for Puerto Rican Studies* 18 (11): 62–81.

Behdad, Ali. 2005. *A Forgetful Nation: On Immigration and Cultural Identity in the United States.* Durham: Duke University Press.

Block, Melissa. April 28, 2006. Album to showcase Spanish "Star-Spangled Banner." *All Things Considered*, National Public Radio.

———. October 27, 2006. Anthem singers test "the land of the free." *All Things Considered*, National Public Radio.

Clark, Lesley. April 29, 2006. Anthem song sparks debate in the "land of the free." *Miami Herald.*

Dorfman, Ariel. May 7, 2006. Waving the star-spanglish banner. *Washington Post.*

———. 1999. *Heading South, Looking North: A Bilingual Journey.* New York: Penguin.

Editorial. May 2, 2006. English should be spoken here: It seems that no barriers—even language—are keeping illegals out. *Augusta Chronicle* (Augusta, Georgia).

Editorial. May 2, 2006. It means the most when sung in English. *Lancaster New Era* (Lancaster, Pennsylvania).

Editorial. May 2, 2006. Spanish-language national anthem backers get boost. *Grand Rapids Press* (Grand Rapids, Michigan).

Editorial. May 4, 2006. Nuestro Himno: O nap s-ap neid mo an ke:k s'alig tonlig ta:gio? *Washington Post.*

Editorial. May 6, 2006. National anthem translation is old news. *Augusta Chronicle* (Augusta, Georgia).

Feldman, Claudia, and Eyder Peralta. May 4, 2006. Anthem angst: Despite Bush's English-only stance, Spanish is old tradition. *Houston Chronicle*.

Feran, Tom. May 5, 2006. Bush sings new tune about national anthem. *Plain Dealer* (Cleveland, Ohio).

Froomkin, Dan. May 5, 2006. No habla español. *Washington Post*.

Glick Schiller, Nina, and Georges Fouron. 2001. *Georges Woke Up Laughing: Long-Distance Nationalism and the Search for Home*. Durham: Duke University Press.

Goldstein, David. May 6, 2006. National anthem in other languages? Heard this before. *Seattle Times*.

Hall, Stuart. 1997. The local and the global: Globalization and ethnicity. In *Culture, Globalization, and the World-System: Contemporary Conditions for the Representation of Identity*. A. D. King, ed. Minneapolis: University of Minneapolis Press.

Hardiman, Clay. May 2, 2006. Where's the freedom if the anthem can't be in Spanish? *Muskegon Chronicle* (Muskegon, Michigan).

Hill, Jane H. 1999. Language, race, and white public space. *American Anthropologist* 100 (3): 680–689.

Leeman, Jennifer. 2004. Racializing language: A history of linguistic ideologies in the U.S. Census. *Journal of Language and Politics* 3 (3): 507–534.

———. September 2007. Nuestro Himno: Language, race, and nation in the national anthem debates. Presentation. Latin American Studies Association International Congress. Montreal, Quebec, Canada.

Leo, Peter. May 26, 2006. O say, can you sing? *Pittsburgh Post-Gazette*.

Letter to the editor. May 15, 2006. Resounding "no" to "Nuestro Himno." *Herald News* (Passaic County, New Jersey).

Liasson, Mara. May 1, 2006. With "banner" rhetoric, Bush sings a new tune. National Public Radio.

Manalansan, Martin F., IV. 2003. *Global Divas: Filipino Gay Men in the Diaspora*. Durham: Duke University Press.

Massey, Douglas S., and Ilana Redstone Akresh. 2006. Immigrant's intensions and mobility in a global economy: The attitudes and behavior of recently arrived U.S. immigrants. *Social Science Quarterly* 87 (5): 954–971.

Montgomery, David. May 7, 2006. Unfurling new glory: America's international anthem. *Washington Post*.

National Public Radio. April 28, 2006. A Spanish version of "The Star-Spangled Banner."

Oboler, Suzanne. 2006. Redefining citizenship as lived experience. In *Latinos and Citizenship: The Dilemma of Belonging*. Suzanne Oboler, ed. New York: Palgrave Macmillan.

Ong, Aiwa. 1999. *Flexible Citizenship: The Cultural Logics of Transnationalism*. Durham: Duke University Press.

Pennycook, Alastair. 1998. *English and the Discourses of Colonialism*. London: Routledge.

Portes, Alejandro, and Lingxin Hao. 1998. E pluribus unum: Bilingualism and language loss in the second generation. *Sociology of Education* 71 (4): 269–294.

Ratner-Arías, Sigal. May 31, 2006. Spanish-language anthem performed at Ellis Island. Associated Press State and Local Wire (New York, New York).

Robinson, William I. 2007. Why the immigrants rights struggle compels us to reconceptualize both Latin American and Latino/a Studies. *Latin American Studies Association Forum* 38 (2): 21–23.

Rosaldo, Renato. 1989. *Culture and Truth: The Remaking of Social Analysis*. Boston: Beacon Press.

Rutenberg, Jim. April 29, 2006. Bush enters anthem fight on language. *New York Times*.

Sanneh, Kelefa. May 1, 2006. A protest song of sorts, to a very familiar tune. *New York Times*.

Santa Ana, Otto. 2002. *Brown Tide Rising: Metaphors of Latinos in Contemporary America Public Discourse*. Austin: University of Texas Press.

Schmidt, Ronald, Sr. 2002. Racialization and language policy: The case of the U.S.A. *Multilingua* 21 (August): 141–161.

Shea, Christopher. May 7, 2006. Oy ve, can you see . . . : Translating—and tweaking— "The Star-Spangled Banner" is an American tradition almost as old as the anthem itself. *Boston Globe*.

Smith, Michael Peter, and Luis E. Guarnizo. 1998. *The Locations of Transnationalism*. In *Transnationalism from Below*. M. Smith and L. E. Guarnizo, eds. New Brunswick, NJ: Transaction Publishers.

Sweeney, Patrick. May 16, 2006. Bill would bar Spanish pledge in schools: Lawmaker upset after learning non-English version was being read at Lakeville school. *Pioneer Press* (St. Paul, Minnesota).

Talley, Tim. May 5, 2006. State House wants national anthem sung in English. Associated Press State and Local Wire (Oklahoma City, Oklahoma).

Takacs, Stacey. 1999. Alien-nation: Immigration, national identity, and transnationalism. *Cultural Studies* 13 (4): 591–620.

Teepen, Tom. May 2, 2006. Oh, say, can you see the point of this debate? *Times Union* (Albany, New York).

Urcioli, Bonnie. 1996. *Exposing Prejudice: Puerto Rican Experiences of Language, Race, and Class*. Boulder, CO: Westview Press.

———. 1991. The political topography of Spanish and English: The view from a New York Puerto Rican neighborhood. *American Ethnologist* 18 (2): 295–310.

U.S. Congress. 2006. Text of H.R. 4437 [109th]: Border Protection, Antiterrorism, and Illegal Immigration Control Act of 2005. http://www.govtrack.us/congress/billtext.xpd?bill=h109-4437 (accessed April 8, 2007).

Van Dijk, Teun A. 1993. Principles of discourse analysis. *Discourse and Society* 4 (2): 249–283.

Various Artists. 2006. "Nuestro Himno." *Somos Americanos (We Are Americans)*. Urban Box Office Records.

Varsanyi, Monica W. 2006. "Getting out the vote" in Los Angeles: The mobilization of undocumented immigrants in electoral politics. In *Latinos and Citizenship: The Dilemma of Belonging*. Suzanne Oboler, ed. New York: Palgrave Macmillan.

Wiley, Terrence G. 2004. Language planning, language policy, and the English-only movement. In *Language in the USA: Themes for the Twenty-first Century*. E. Finegan and J. R. Rickford, eds. Cambridge: Cambridge University Press.

Woodard Maderazo, Jennifer. May 4, 2006. Anthem translation is nothing new. *VivirLatino*, http://www.vivirlatino.com/2006/05/04/newsflash-anthem-translation-is-nothing-new.php/ (accessed November 25, 2006).

Zentella, Ana Celia. 2002. Latin@ languages and identities. In *Latinos: Remaking America*. M. Súarez-Orozco and M. Páez, eds. Berkeley: University of California Press.

2

"¡Puuurrrooo MÉXICO!"

Listening to Transnationalism on
U.S. Spanish-Language Radio

DOLORES INÉS CASILLAS

¡San Francisco! ¡San José! ¡San Leandro! ¡Oakland! ¡Toda la bahía de San Francisco es [en voz alta] puuurrrooo MÉXICO!

(San Francisco! San Jose! San Leandro! Oakland! The San Francisco Bay Area is [voice rises] reeeaallyy MEXICO!)[1]
—Estéreo Sol (KSOL, 98.9/99.1 FM) tagline

One of broadcasting's principal achievements lies in the way it links the "biography" of an occasion or event with the "geography of the situation" of its audiences.
—David Morley, *Home Territories*

The Spanish-language radio station Estéreo Sol broadcasts from northern California, nearly seven hundred miles north of the geographical U.S.-Mexico border. In the face of San Francisco's renowned foggy forecasts, Estéreo Sol broadcasts with a sunny, transnationalist disposition. For the twenty-two percent of San Francisco Bay Area residents that identify as Hispanic or Latino (U.S. Census Bureau, 2005), tuning into Estéreo Sol entails listening, and often singing along, to acoustic traces of "Mexico."[2] The station's parent company, Univisión, is the largest Spanish-language media company in the United States. Thirteen of Univisión's seventeen radio markets feature at least one radio station akin to Estéreo Sol. Each sister station drapes their individual call numbers and station name on an identical visual logo (which can be seen at http://www.univision.com/). Estéreo Sol's green-and-white logo showcases an eagle dangling a snake from its mouth, a not-so-subtle reference to the famed serpent that graces Mexico's national flag.

Each of their musical rotations, classified as "Mexican regional," offers tuba-fused bandas, accordion-laced norteños, and the dramatic bellows of rancheras. The genre's racial and working-class connotations are tersely described by Hispanic marketers as "foreign, niche, and old-fashioned," a distant second from the seemingly more ear-friendly sounds of Latin-tinged or spoon-fed salsa (Clemens, 2005). Despite these classed undertones, Mexican regional music accounts for over half of all U.S. Spanish-language record sales (Quiñones, 2005). Moreover, an astounding forty-four percent of all radio stations within the top fifty Hispanic-identified U.S. radio markets carry the Mexican regional format (Chambers, 2006). If, as Josh Kun (2005, 13) proposes, "all musical listening is a form of confrontation" where identities are "made self-aware," then Mexican Spanish-language radio listeners are turning up the volume and proudly flaunting their working-class aesthetics and immigrant sensibilities. The sounds of "Mexico"—both in music and talk form—occupy a prominent and profitable place within the U.S. airwaves.

The popularity of musical groups such as Los Tigres del Norte, whose lyrics testify to the border crossings of Mexicans, has recast the Mexican-specific genre as a transfrontera, transnational soundtrack (Saldívar, 1997; Kun, 2005).[3] To tune into "Mexico" vis-à-vis radio involves a series of acoustic border crossings where listeners are conversant in both Mexico and U.S. politics and popular culture. Two of Los Tigres del Norte's most admired songs are corridos aptly titled "El Mojado Acaudalado" (The Wealthy Wetback) and "Mis Dos Patrias" (My Two Countries). As corridos, or narrative ballads, these songs are lyrical testimonies of immigrants' experiences as undocumented ("mojado") and later legal citizens of two countries (the United States and Mexico). A line from "Mis Dos Patrias" depicts the sentiment of the transnational U.S.-Mexico moment: "caben dos patrias en el mismo corazón" (two nations fit within the same heart). In this case, "patrias" speaks not only to heartfelt national allegiance(s) but also to the legislative realities of the border. Many Latinos, for instance, are cognizant that border politics and anti-immigrant responses are not public attitudes geographically isolated on the U.S.-Mexico border but extend deep into the U.S. heartland and southern states.

Communications systems that cater to immigrant-based and ethnic communities have become sites for community building, nostalgia, and advocacy across national geographical boundaries (Castañeda, 2008). Bilingual and Spanish-language Latino listeners often turn to Spanish-language radio for public updates on key immigrant-related legislation. Listeners are familiar, for example, with on-air fund-raisers hosted on behalf of home countries recovering from natural catastrophes. In 2005, for instance, Latino listeners were briefed on the aftermath of Hurricane Katrina in New Orleans as well as the devastation left by Hurricane Wilma in Cancún, Mexico. Although both garnered air time, on-air fund-raising from three Los Angeles–based radio stations sent proceeds to victims affected by Hurricane Wilma. As one caller poignantly explained to fellow Estéreo Sol radio listeners, "México no tiene ningún FEMA, sino que tiene mexicanos en los EE.UU." (Mexico has no FEMA, but it does have Mexicans in the United States). Just as FEMA was held accountable for New Orleans evacuees, Mexican listeners living in the United States were regarded as the financial backbone to rebuilding the lesser-populated provinces outside tourist-friendly Cancún. Perhaps not so coincidentally, comedian George Lopez joked post-Katrina that FEMA, indeed, would help rebuild New Orleans, but that the acronym actually stood for "Find Every Mexican Available" (Ruíz, 2008). Mexicans in the United States have persistently carried "the cross of illegality even after having been sworn in as citizens" (Chabram-Dernersesian, 1999, 180). Nonetheless, as with both natural and bureaucratic disasters, the labor of Mexicans—as evidenced during post-hurricane radio—quite literally "shoulders the transnational economy" (Chabram-Dernersesian, 1999, 181).

This chapter argues that U.S. Spanish-language programming transgresses conventional ideas of home and homeland discursively across and despite physical national borders between the United States and Mexico. Spanish-language radio acts as companion to its legion listeners precisely because of the geographical and legislative realities of the border. In many ways, Spanish-language radio plays distinct roles as both acoustic ally and public advocate to a body of listeners distinguished by race, class, migration, and language (Casillas, 2006). In this chapter, I analyze selected on-air saludos (greetings), long-distance dedications, and other listener-turned-caller utterances heard on Estéreo Sol in San Francisco as well as its sister station located in Los Angeles.[4] Estéreo Sol exemplifies how the broader landscape of U.S. Spanish-language radio engages with a transnational listenership. In doing so, Spanish-language radio acoustically remaps national boundaries and national(ist) sentiments on the airwaves.[5] As David Morley (2000) maintains in this chapter's epigraph, one of broadcasting's chief roles lies in its ability to link and synchronize a biographical moment or experience across great geographical distances. Through these on-air saludos, the complexity of the transnational Latino experience materializes acoustically.

Given the commercial turn to computerized playlists and the diminishing role of the disc jockey, radio listeners are much more accustomed to radio host chatter during the morning commuting hours. Here, I make the case that such spontaneous greetings, provided by both radio hosts and listeners themselves, are transgressive, unscripted verbal addresses. In a similar vein, "shout-outs" within hip-hop and rap music gestures to verbal "recognitions or 'hellos' to a friend, posse, or neighborhood" (Keyes, 2004, 234). Arguably, both "shout-outs" and "saludos" voiced by communities of color represent a declaration and appropriation of public space.

Recognized as "space fillers" to deter from radio's dreaded "dead air," these verbal addresses are frequently heard outside designated talk-based radio programming, in between music play. Space fillers tend to dislodge the role of the DJ or radio host, where hosts traditionally take turns in conversation or their comment is met with either a canned laugh or audience track (Montgomery, 1986, 423). In contrast, on-air saludos bypass the confinement of the studio or microphone and enable callers to speak to the listening audience at large.

This chapter purposely disrupts the media's "gaze" and lends attention to the role of the voice and the work of the ear entailed within radio broadcasts and listening. In an effort to decouple and dethrone hierarchical notions between sight/vision and proof/knowledge, I contend—by evoking Michel de Certeau (1988)—that through sound, listeners metaphorically see "the voice" since it can "insinuate itself into the text as a mark or trace, an effect or metonymy of the body" (155). At a time when language and brown bodies are policed and surveilled through legally yet racially codified standards, the sounds of spoken and musical forms of Spanish permeate the public sphere.[6] While radio trade magazines credit population growth as the "cause" of Spanish-language radio's implausible growth, I argue elsewhere that immigration policies and public attitudes toward immigrants have played an influential role in its popularity (Casillas, 2006). For Latinos, audible Spanish constructs a type of "disembodied presence" (Hilmes, 1997). Often, Latinos are imagined as discorporate within the U.S. popular imagination, as simply units of labor, topics of public debate, not quite full-fledged citizens (Chavez, 2001). U.S. Spanish-language radio provides an acoustic space for radio broadcasts and listeners to discursively "locate" themselves over the air above state surveillance and without a material body.

Found in (Spanish-Language) Translation

With an airwave presence and history of on-air advocacy since the 1920s, Spanish-language radio experienced its first growth spurt in the 1950s as it surpassed fellow immigrant-based Polish and Yiddish broadcasting (Kelman, 2006). Coupled with Latino population growth, Mexican-based broadcasting companies shifted their attention to the diaspora of Mexican listeners in the United States. Given the Mexican ownership, Spanish-language radio attempted to deliver an "authentic" sound of Mexico through radio sets (Gutiérrez and Schement, 1979).

Media and advertising industries renewed their attention toward bilingual (Spanish-English) U.S. consumers in the 1980s during the much-touted and government-sponsored "Decade of the Hispanic" (Dávila, 2001). Though just 67 Spanish-oriented radio stations existed in 1980, the number swelled to 390 by 1990 (Warren, 1995; Petrozello, 1996; Castañeda Paredes, 2003). Many of these gains made within urban radio markets were heard on stronger, acoustically crisp FM bands rather than low-cost AM stations. The crossover from static AM to lucrative FM signaled the mainstreaming of Spanish-language radio programming in tandem, mind you, with the passage of the Immigrant Reform and Control Act (IRCA) of 1986. IRCA, referred to as the amnesty bill, provided legal permanence for nearly three million persons. This parallel crossover welcomed three million more listeners into the U.S. radio market (Casillas, 2006).

By 2000, the FCC identified nearly six hundred Spanish-language radio stations in the United States (Alfredo, 2006).[7] By then, Spanish-language radio had successfully dethroned English-language stations from their number one standings in many major radio markets, including Los Angeles, Houston, Miami, and New York City (Alfredo, 2006). Even up-and-coming Latino metropolises such as Salt Lake City, Utah; Raleigh, North Carolina; and Walla Walla, Washington, debuted Spanish-language radio programming (Castañeda Paredes, 2003). Whereas English-language radio expanded by ten percent between 1990 and 2000, Spanish-language radio experienced a much more substantial growth of 300 percent.

Today, at least fourteen different Spanish-language formats have flourished on the airwaves, from tejano, news/talk, and oldies to tropical (Chambers, 2006). In urban, suburban, and rural landscapes, radio listeners surfing for a station are bound—perhaps unintentionally—to stumble across a Spanish-language broadcast. Unsurprisingly, media and advertising industries argue that radio has proven to be the medium of choice for U.S. Latino consumers. When given the option of eliminating either the Internet or the radio in their households, 67 percent of Latinos surveyed in the United States chose to keep radio (Arbitron/Edison Media Research, 2005). Even with popular Internet offerings of Latino-tailored websites, such as iTunes Latino, and the availability of satellite dish services delivering Spanish-language television, Latinos continue to rely on broadcast radio—much more than their English-speaking peers—as a source for news and entertainment. In fact, Latinos account for ten percent of all U.S. radio listening and, according to industry reports, listen to the radio an average of three hours a week longer than the "general" (white, English-speaking) radio listener (Arbitron, 2006).

Many Spanish-language radio stations strategically target their listenership by advertising their call numbers and radio personalities at public transit stops. The public nature of most Spanish-language radio listening, found visually at bus stops and audibly at work sites, marks the listening experience as both communal and classed. This differs considerably from what I term "white-collar" modes of listening—the mostly solitary practices promoted by private car commutes, personal satellite radios, iPod use, and Internet broadcasts (Casillas, 2006). Symbolically, the public practice of Spanish-language radio listening carries an even greater political significance given the context of English-only policies and anti-immigrant attitudes.

Remapping Mexico

> ¡Saludos a todos de Michoacán que nos escuchan esta tarde desde San Leandro, California—bienvenidos!
> (Greetings to those from Michoacán who are tuning in this afternoon from San Leandro, California—welcome!)
> —Radio host afternoon greeting on Estéreo Sol (KSOL, 98.9/99.1 FM)

Routine station taglines and on-air saludos discursively link regional townships in northern California with specific provinces and pueblos in Mexico. Listeners fortunate enough to find themselves on the air, often "llamada número seis" (caller number six), frankly identify where they are from *and* where they are calling from. I make use of the "discursive," as well as the term "discourse," to indicate how language, and more specifically voices and sounds, function as more than expressive or descriptive statements. My analysis, rather, centers on how radio broadcasts and the voices of listeners and callers are articulated within existing power structures. As Michel Foucault (1980) asserts, relationships between language and power are dialogical and hold social and political repercussions. In this case, station identifications create "ways of belonging," or what Peggy Levitt and Nina Glick Schiller (2004, 597) distinguish as "practices that signal or enact an identity which demonstrates a conscious connection to a particular group . . . concrete, visible actions that mark belonging." Listening to such discursive gestures of belonging is politically significant for U.S. Latinos—specifically, Spanish-speaking Mexicans and Central Americans who populate the Southwest—given their history of and ongoing political and social disenfranchisement.

The tagline above demonstrates how on-air greetings identify listeners through two "homes": their place of origin (Michoacán, Mexico) and their current residence (San Leandro, California). Encased within quotation marks, "home" does not necessarily "signify a physical entity fixed in a particular place, but rather a mobile symbolic habitat, a performative way of life and of doing things in which one makes one's home while in movement" (Morley, 2000, 47). The combination of both Mexican and U.S. locations on the radio resonates with a listenership whose legal and social experiences of belonging have historically been complicated by migration, race, and language. The renewed emphasis on protecting national borders in the post-9/11 context of a "war on terror" has only intensified the legal vulnerability of undocumented peoples.

According to Hamid Naficy (1993), deterritorialized communities affected by geographical displacements often form strong attachments to popular culture. In many ways, Latino listeners' references to multiple "homes" normalizes, reterritorializes, or remaps the experience and bodies of Latino listeners. On-air acknowledgments given to listeners' two (or more) national, geographic homes help construct familiar relationships between radio stations and their listeners, thereby cementing listener loyalty and thus the commercial value of these stations. Conveniently, in addition to forging a consumer relationship, radio also plays the role of "acoustic ally" on behalf of a Spanish-dominated, transnational listenership.

Saludos (Shout-Outs) to Labor

> Saludos hoy a los pintores, construccionistas, todos los janitors y otros afuera trabajando abajo del solcito, pero con ganas, por el billete, pa' las cuentas, hombres, o simplemente por la remesa, ¿no?
>
> (Greetings today to painters, construction workers, all the janitors and others working outside in the sun, but with drive, for the [dollar] bill, man, for those bills, or simply for the remittance, right?)
>
> —Radio host afternoon greeting on Estéreo Sol (KSOL, 98.9/99.1 FM)

Radio sets provide a form of portable, cost-efficient companionship that attracts many working-class, immigrant Latinos. National demographic profiles of Hispanic radio listeners list their annual income as less than twenty-five thousand dollars (Arbitron, 2006). Situated as a mostly working-class listenership, radios often accompany Latinos to their jobs. Globalization's effect on labor has also influenced Latino listening patterns. Liza Catanzarite (2003) effectively calls attention to the cadre of "brown-collar" occupations— low-level service-sectors work—that are disproportionately performed by an immigrant workforce. These positions within construction, janitorial, agriculture, and manufacturing sectors comprise painters, field hands, and dishwashers. In urban centers such as Chicago, Los Angeles, New York City, and San Diego, immigrant Latinos constitute an overwhelming forty to seventy percent of this workforce (Catanzarite, 2003). Unmistakably, the sounds of Spanish-language programming are heard from the kitchens of restaurants and outside construction sites, rendering the presence of this brown-collar workforce acoustically "concrete."

In the afternoon airwave greeting above, the radio host does not refer to a geographical location but rather identifies listeners through brown-collar occupations: "pintores, construccionistas" (painters, construction workers). Aside from the explicit naming of multiple geographical homes, Estéreo Sol often situates listeners' U.S. locations within the contexts of labor, work, and ultimately earned income. The radio host locates her listeners discursively "afuera trabajando abajo del solecito" (outside working beneath the sun), understanding the environment in which her listeners are situated and recognizing the extra daily burden this type of labor entails.

Not only do work and workplace mentions frequent Estéreo Sol's airwaves, particularly during the early morning hours, but "work titles" of brown-collar occupations are referred to with esteem during host greetings. Morning salutations are extended to those driving taxis, washing dishes, grooming yards, or caring for other people's children—a gendered prompt to Latina listeners employed as nannies and babysitters. Aware of their distinct listenership, radio hosts foreground a collective immigration and working-class experience through these on-air shout-outs. The added assurance that listeners—assumed to be all Latino, immigrant, and employed in positions of manual labor—toil at work "con ganas" (with drive) validates the work ethic, value, and place of immigrants.

The manner in which U.S. politicians boast the strength of the global economy rarely accounts for the ways labor and immigration are intricately bound. According to Saskia Sassen (2000, 50), "Immigration is . . . a major process through which a new transnational economy is being constituted . . . even though it is not recognized or represented in mainstream accounts of the global economy." Despite numbering nearly thirty-five million in the United States (U.S. Census Bureau, 2005), many Latinos are often rendered as "invisible" laborers who are absent within larger discussions of U.S. politics (Romero, 1992; Chang, 2000; Marchevsky and Theoharis, 2006) and, as Sassen remarks, global economies. Yet within the mainstream English-language news media, Latinos are often framed as social welfare service predators or simply confined to stereotypical farm worker roles—both unproductive and limiting portrayals of U.S. Latinos that minimize their contributions to multiple national economies (Hondagneu-Sotelo, 1996). The paradox that presents itself is that while Latinos' bodies are instrumental to the productivity of U.S. labor and its political economy, they are ridiculed by U.S. public opinion, positioned as matters of debate for politicians, and generally isolated from U.S. public and political life.

Saskia Sassen's insistence, as noted above, that immigration be brought to the forefront of discussions on global capital reflects the tension framed by this short vignette. The radio host's focus on work is immediately followed by the acknowledgment of working: "el billete," a distinct (Spanglish) gesture toward the U.S. dollar bill and its economic weight in comparison to Latin American currencies. Perhaps more tellingly, the casual reference to "la remesa" (remittance), or the means of wiring or sending money abroad, stresses how such transactions and their significance to national economies have become "normalized" practices that serve simultaneously as both affective and economic ties.

Figures confirm that remittances to Mexico, Central America, and the Dominican Republic account for these countries' largest source of revenue. The business of wiring money across distances has been lucrative for corporate giants, not to mention frequent radio sponsor Western Union (Rawe, 2003; Singer, 2004). Mediating the migration of money, Spanish-language radio ads entice listeners to wire additional funds to an insinuated waiting or dependent family located miles away, asking listeners to envision "the extra room on that house" or "how pretty she'll look in that dress." Broadcast references to listeners' remesas, coupled with the prevalence of commercials that advertise sending money, further accentuate the importance of Latino and immigrant labor in the United States. During the Mother's Day season of 2006, for instance, radio listeners were assailed and reminded of the capitalist use of affect with the AT&T ad line "Mexico is only seven cents away." Immigrant listeners are made sentient through these commercials, reflecting their place in the geographical United States and the interests of those with family located across national borders.

Despite Latinos' contributions to U.S. society, they are persistently deemed as "foreign" and "Other." Given this broader political context, Estéreo Sol's visual and acoustic evocation of Mexico and its Latino listenership constructs a Spanish-language, immigrant, and ethnically (nonwhite) public sphere within the very confines of the geographical United States. Over the airwaves, Latinos (vis-à-vis listening) experience a sense of membership and cultural belonging.

Listening as (Cultural) Belonging

Tengo mis dos hermanas, viven las dos in Tijuana, en mis pensamientos; ojalá que esten bien.

(I am thinking of my two sisters, they both live in Tijuana; hopefully they are both well.)

—Elvira, listener-turned-caller, dedication

By and large, radio allows callers to phone-in, often via cell phone, with song requests, dedications, or to share the customary saludo or "shout-out." Here, both listeners and radio hosts maximize the reach of radio broadcasts to communicate messages to friends and loved ones and express opinions in a public sphere. While the on-air greeting is in itself a popular practice of all radio, Spanish-language radio stations send saludos over great distances in real time. Given the limitations of technology and communications policy, on-air saludos sent across state and national lines represent more symbolic gestures, since the technical capability to link listenerships across borders is not commonplace.[8] Nevertheless, the on-air citing by radio hosts or listeners of either an individual's name or hometown imparts audible public recognition.

Often, radio hosts will ask listeners to identify their calling location in an effort to boast the geographical span of their station's listener base. When listener-turned-caller Elvira, quoted above, called via cell phone in the evening to dedicate "cualquier canción de Juan Gabriel" (any song by [Mexican singer] Juan Gabriel) while en route to Tijuana, she explained: "Pues, ahora vivo en Modesto . . . apenas pase la ciudad de Fremont . . . me paré a comprar un café en McDonald's . . . me esperan en Tijuana" (I live in Modesto . . . I just passed Fremont . . . I stopped to buy a cup of coffee at McDonald's . . . my family is expecting me in Tijuana). Radio scholars Martin Montgomery (1986) and Paddy Scannell (1996) recognize the mapping of listeners' locations as a strategic move to craft a more intimate on-air meeting. Listeners cognitively "map" Elvira's travels vis-à-vis her descriptions. Unlike traditional notions of community building or community formation bound by and dependent on fixed parameters of space, for many Latinos this form of mapping via radio transcends official boundaries, as family and friends may be scattered outside the confines of and beyond el barrio. On Spanish-language radio, geographical mentions include actual sites of listening and often listeners' countries of origin, as evidenced in the chapter epigraph, demonstrating Estéreo Sol's geographical coupling of the San Francisco Bay Area with "puuurrrooo MÉXICO" (despite the seven-hundred-mile distance). Here, listeners accompany Elvira on her travels from Modesto's Highway 99 and presumably across Interstate 280 to the 580 before arriving in Fremont via the 680 as she makes her trek south across the border to Tijuana. The McDonald's pit stop for coffee reminds listeners that while it may be early evening, Elvira has a long night ahead of her, warranting the companionship of Juan Gabriel.

Although hosts and taglines blatantly interlace their station's identity with a particular national or regional identity, not all listeners interpret the references with explicit regard to Mexico. According to Ari Kelman (2006, 129): "Although we take the process of listening for granted . . . the ways in which we listen are deeply social . . . they change over time [and] they reveal significant characteristics about the particular social situations in which people are listening." My larger project on U.S. Spanish-language radio broadcasts and listening throughout the twentieth century unveiled the complexity behind space, place, and listening. While conducting focus groups with immigrant radio listeners, I found that many turned to radio for entertainment, companionship, and as a resource. Alma, one of the women interviewed and an avid Spanish-language radio listener, described to me (in Spanish) how such broadcasts signal more of a U.S.-based Mexican community: "I was so happy the first time I came across a Spanish-language [radio] station. It kind of reaffirmed my presence here or at least made me feel as if I was a part of a larger group . . . that we're all displaced somehow or at least lost . . . but together." Her comments focused on the familiarity of Spanish and revealed much more about her relationship to radio listening in the United States than about Mexico itself. While the majority of literature on the role of U.S. ethnic media dwells on broadcasting's nostalgic character, Alma's sense of geographical and cultural displacement is clearly not about nostalgia. Rather, Alma's sincerity reflects how listening to Spanish-language radio represents much more than a leisurely activity or mere window to her home country. Her candid characterization of her first acoustic encounter with U.S. Spanish-language radio reveals how U.S. ethnic media also configures newfound practices of community building and belonging.

Musical and linguistic nods to Mexico bear a different significance within a U.S. soundscape. Radio listeners tune into Spanish-language broadcast news and musical programming in the imagined company (Anderson, 1991) of fellow Latino radio listeners. Yet listening, for Alma and many other Latinos, also serves as a means of belonging, culturally and later politically. The significance of that belonging manifests when, as political scientists maintain, engendered feelings of belonging among immigrants and people of color, and desires of "wanting to participate," translate into higher rates of civic and political participation (Johnson, 2004).

Alma's comments are site-specific and socially bound, in that her listening practices are influenced by her migration to the United States and subsequently by her sense of cultural displacement. Spanish-language broadcasts signal Latino listenerships that, as seen in Alma's case, are brought together discursively. In many respects, the feelings of actively belonging via listening redirects the significance of listening away from what Kelman (2006) suggests are more passive connotations. In similar ways, Latinos "locate" themselves in the United States through listening to Spanish-language broadcasts; listening, in this sense, reconfigures the audience as part of larger, multiple communities.

Listening as (Political) Practice

We Hispanics do everything in this country. We clean the buildings. We clean the roads. We pick the crops. The only thing we don't do is vote.
—U.S. Spanish-language radio host,
quoted in Dan Baum, "On the Air, Arriba!"

¡Hoy marchamos, mañana votamos!
(Today we march, tomorrow we vote!)
—Popular rally cheer in spring 2006 pro-immigrant marches

For many, juxtaposing several of the aforementioned vignettes' patriotic and Mexican nationalist references with the public encouragement of radio show hosts to participate in U.S. electoral politics may seem inherently contradictory. The complexities of the Latino transnational experience, however, are reflected in the nostalgic sounds of one's homeland as well as the broadcast support to develop (newfound) spaces of home and belonging. On one hand, Spanish-language radio offers a Latino-directed, culturally familiar, Spanish-language (perhaps safe) space where Latinos retreat and deliberate "outside the surveillance of the dominant group" (Squires, 2000, 75). On the other hand, stations direct an acute awareness of both their popularity and influence among Latinos to help listeners navigate the tumultuous geopolitical terrain.

For Spanish-language programming, steering between U.S. and Mexican politics entails two different forms of politically oriented broadcasts. In the more traditional vein, Spanish-language radio invites politicians to join them on the air in often-interactive formats that invite listener dialogue. Spanish-language programming facilitates on-air discussions by playing the role of on-air linguistic and cultural translator between political institutions and listenerships. But Spanish-language radio has also redressed conventional notions of politics by assigning local resources and service agencies prominent positions within on-air broadcasts.

The on-air insistence typified by the radio host quoted above—that Latinos be a part of the electoral process—reflects the increasing programming emphasis on getting Latino listeners to vote or to adopt a greater political role in the United States. Because the concept of "transnational" is, at times, applied strictly at an abstract level, it is important to recognize the difference between symbolically "claiming rights" and "gaining rights" legally and electorally (Fox, 2005). In the summer of 2006, for example, the top-rated Spanish-language radio station, which is based in Los Angeles and broadcasts nationally, kicked off a "Votos por América" eleven-city voter registration bus tour. The tour reached out to Latinos by setting up live broadcasts outside Latino supermercados (supermarkets) in an effort to boost the number of registered Latino voters (Hendricks, 2006). At each stop, listeners were presented with the significance of either registering to vote (if they were legally able) or investigating their next steps toward acquiring U.S. citizenship, all the while maintaining allegiances to their homelands. The promotion of dual citizenship, albeit legally easier for specific Latin American countries than others, challenges traditional notions of civic duties. In many ways, the radio tour encouraged listeners to become not just politically active at the ballot box but also politicized in terms of immigration, living wages, and so forth.

During the tour, listeners tuning in at home were privy to live conversations on location. They overheard the excitement, for instance, of Ricardo, a Texas listener who had recently attained his U.S. citizenship, and the skepticism in María's voice as the radio hosts bantered with her about her responsibility to vote both in the United States and Mexico. The tour ended in Washington DC, where popular and influential radio hosts took the day to lobby on behalf of "la gente Latina" (Latino peoples). The tour not only showcased how U.S. Spanish-language radio takes their shows and politics "on the road," but also exemplified the public responsibility taken on by radio hosts to represent (in this case via lobbying) the political needs of their listenership.

Spanish-language radio's political role as "on-air organizer" was made most apparent in the spring of 2006 when millions of listeners attended record-breaking pro-immigrant rallies across the nation (Flaccus, 2006; Johnson and Spice, 2006).[9] These mass mobilizations—organized by grassroots organizations—served as powerful responses to a series of disconcerting pieces of anti-immigrant legislation.[10] Radio hosts across the nation, with the blessings of station management and network executives, used the airwaves as their public podiums in preparing listeners to join them on the streets. The slogan endorsed and used in the numerous marches—"¡Hoy marchamos, mañana votamos!" (Today we march, tomorrow we vote!)—set the stage for the subsequent bus tour discussed above. Many within the liberal English-language media were astounded by the record number of attendees. *Time* magazine columnist Joel Stein, for instance, coyly asked regarding the Los Angeles pro-immigrant rally: "500,000 people, and no one called me?" (Stein, 2006). His bafflement called attention to the unique relationship between Latinos and U.S. Spanish-language radio.

Aside from hosting on-location voter registration and citizenship drives, each major U.S. Spanish-language radio network prominently showcases an in-house attorney, a trusted doctor, or spokespeople from local service agencies during radio shows. Spanish-language radio, through both commercial and community-based programming, provides a regional (and depending on the strength of the network, national) public space for the Latino transnational experience. Health programs, for instance, encourage listeners to advocate for bicultural and bilingual health providers; pop psychologists counsel immigrant parents on the challenges of raising children in the United States; finance-related shows stress the benefits of setting up bank accounts; and guest attorneys offer live question-and-answer sessions with listeners. This access to immediate legal information, culturally specific health guidance, and local resources characterizes the political efficacy that defines these broadcasts (Casillas, 2006). For immigrants, access to health care and decoding the complexity of immigration law are all aspects of a transnational political experience as broadcast over Spanish-language radio.

During campaign seasons, politicians dispatch Spanish-speaking staff or conduct on-air interviews with translators to Spanish-language morning radio shows in the hopes of courting the votes of U.S. Latinos. Memorable on-air campaigning include: then New York mayoral candidate Michael Bloomberg speaking (in heavily accented Spanish) alongside salsa legend Willie Colón in staged campaign jingles; once-hopeful GOP presidential candidate Mitt Romney's son politely urging Florida radio listeners (in enunciated Honduran Spanish) to "vota por mi papá" (vote for my dad); and recently, then Democratic presidential candidate Barack Obama's campaign pledge to Los Angeles–based host El Piolín (live and via translation) that, if elected, he would indeed return to his morning show. Twenty-four hours later, Hillary Clinton (live and via translation) upped the ante and promised that, if elected, she would welcome El Piolín to broadcast *from* the White House. Both of the latter campaign pitches were met with canned studio applause and frenzied hoots from radio hosts. In each instance, politicians or their Spanish-speaking endorsers capitalized on their experience within U.S. Latino communities (Obama, Clinton) or time spent in Central or Latin American (Romney, Clinton, Bloomberg).

Civic politics aside, Spanish-language commercial programming continues to broadcast sexually laden and titillating broadcasts that arguably do much more to entertain than to educate. For many of the top-ranked U.S. Spanish-language radio stations, gender politics or the disconcerting on-air treatment of women remains woefully troubling (Casillas, 2008).

Sound Endings

Spanish-language programming has come to dominate U.S. radio with a force that supersedes its historically marginal status. Spanish-language formats populate not only the actual airwaves but also the visual landscape of bumper stickers and billboards that advertise call numbers and radio slogans in Spanish. Nurturing feelings of nostalgia with Mexican regional music, for instance, while simultaneously assisting in the betterment of listeners' lives in the United States, Spanish-language radio at times mediates the competing desires of transnational listeners. Politically oriented broadcasts "teach" listeners the political ropes of U.S. politics at the same time as they create a sentiment of imagined community. But unlike both Benedict Anderson's (1991) classic ideal and Los Tigres del Norte's lyrical "dos patrias," not all Spanish-language listeners are "citizens" of this nation-state.

Rather than romanticize transnationalism as a borderless or metaphorical site, this chapter highlighted how Spanish-language radio is a "site" where borders are acoustically remapped. With a large number of listeners disproportionately confined to service-sector levels of work, radio provides an acoustic "visibility" to working-class listeners not easily afforded elsewhere. It is precisely the discursive ability to locate and map Latino experiences through music, voices, and political actions that permits the construction of an acoustic transnational landscape for belonging.

ACKNOWLEDGMENTS

Mil gracias a mis colegas María Elena Cepeda, Deborah Paredez, Felicity Schaeffer-Grabiel, and Horacio Roque Ramírez for bringing a sense of clarity, gusto, and humor to the writing process.

NOTES

1. Translation note: English-language translations of Spanish-language broadcasts are mine. I do not italicize the Spanish out of a desire to refrain from marking Spanish, normalizing the English text, and sustaining U.S.-based class, racial, and linguistic hierarchies. For an exemplary discussion on language politics, see Anzaldúa (1987), Urciuoli (1998), Aparicio (1998), and Zentella (1997).

2. Because not all those who identify as Hispanic or Latino are nationally Mexican, the dominance of Mexican-centered radio stations contributes to the existing Mexican hegemony within U.S. Spanish-language popular culture.

To clarify the use of terms within this essay, "U.S. Latinos" refers to persons of any Latin American origin living within the geographical boundaries of the United States. I also interchange "U.S. Latino" with "Latino" and only use the label "Hispanic" when referencing a source that has done so.

3. The term "transfrontera," coined by José David Saldívar (1997), refers to the two-thousand-mile-long U.S.-Mexico border as a metaphorical site where "peoples geopolitically forced to separate themselves now negotiate with one another and manufacture new relations, hybrid cultures, and multiple-voiced aesthetics" (13–14).

Several academic studies have offered engaging analyses of Mexican- and Chicano-based music, and how such songs are musical testimonios of the political moment; see Saldívar (1997), Kun (2005), and Lipsitz (2007).

4. In the San Francisco Bay Area, Estéreo Sol's call numbers can be found on 98.1 and 99.1 FM, and in Los Angeles listeners go to sister station La Nueva at 101.9 FM. Both stations offer online streaming. Over the years, however, I have found listeners' voices online to appear much more staged and integrated within station commercials. As a result, I focused on listener-turned-caller remarks made live on the radio.

Methodologically, for the purposes of this chapter, radio broadcasts were recorded during the spring and summer of 2006. An average of ten afternoon hours and five evening hours were recorded per week from April to October. The spring months focused much more on Bay Area listening, while the latter months focused on the Los Angeles broadcasts. On occasion, if I heard an intriguing saludo while driving, I pulled over and jotted down the conversation. A combination of audio and note taking made up the bulk of this chapter's data.

5. Although this chapter focuses on mostly Mexican radio listeners and radio excerpts from San Francisco and Los Angeles, Caribbean-directed radio functions similarly. For instance, Spanish-language radio stations in Miami often reference Cuban politics and include parodies of Fidel Castro. In New York City, radio hosts lament the snowy cold winters by reminding Puerto Rican and Dominican listeners of the beauty and warmth of their patria. In each instance, a third geographical location or national figure is folded into the on-air conversation.

6. Robin D. G. Kelley's (1994) depictions of pre–Rosa Parks public transportation in the segregated South raise some interesting parallels. Kelley argues that despite the fact that African Americans could not physically cross the "color line," they often did so audibly by making noises, joking, cursing, and exercising other forms of "loud talking." I thank David Manuel Hernández for bringing this point to my attention.

7. The categorization of Spanish-language radio has shifted throughout the decades from "foreign-language," "ethnic," and "Mexican" to "Spanish" (Casillas, 2006).

8. An exception is the Fresno-based community radio station Radio Bilingüe, which hosts a daily talk-based public affairs program that broadcasts nationally and, as of 1992, transnationally to sister radio stations in Puerto Rico and Mexico.

9. These rallies took place in both Latino- and non-Latino-identified centers, including Miami, Charlotte, Milwaukee, Chicago, Nashville, Dallas, Houston, San Francisco, San Diego, and Los Angeles.

10. Two controversial pieces of legislation were passed in December 2005 (House of Representatives) and May 2006 (Senate). HR4437, the former, known as The Border Protection, Antiterrorism, and Illegal Immigration Control Act, asked, among other things: (1) that a seven-hundred-mile wall be constructed along the U.S.-Mexico border; (2) that state and local enforcement be authorized to enforce federal immigration law; (3) for changes in law so that individuals, organizations, and religious factions could be penalized criminally for assisting undocumented immigrants; and (4) that felony penalties be imposed on undocumented immigrants for residing in the United States. The latter, S2611, was largely a modified version of HR4437.

REFERENCES

Alfredo, Alonso. 2006. "Spanish Niche Formats: A Radio Gold Mine." *Billboard*, April 29.
Anderson, Benedict. 1991 [1983]. *Imagined Communities: Reflections on the Origin and Spread of Nationalism*. New York: Verso Books.
Anzaldúa, Gloria. 1987. "How to Tame a Wild Tongue." In *Borderlands/La Frontera: The New Mestiza*. San Francisco: Spinsters/Aunt Lute, 207–243.
Aparicio, Frances R. 1998. "Whose Spanish? Whose Language? Whose Power?: Testifying to Differential Bilingualism." *Indiana Journal of Hispanic Literatures* 12 (Spring): 5–25.
Arbitron. 2000, 2002, 2003, 2006. "Hispanic Radio Today: How America Listens to Radio" [information for broadcasters, agencies, and advertisers], all available at: http://www.arbitron.com/radio_stations/home.htm (accessed on 10 October 2006).
Arbitron/Edison Media Research. 2005. "Internet and Multimedia Research, 2005: The On-Demand Media Consumer." Report available at: http://www.arbitron.com/downloads/IM2005Study.pdf (accessed 30 September 2006).

Ballvé, Marcelo. 2004. "The Battle for Latino Media." *NACLA Report on the Americas* 37(4): 20–25.

Baum, Dan. 2006. "On the Air, Arriba! Getting out the Latino Vote." *New Yorker,* October 23.

Casillas, Dolores Inés. 2006. "Sounds of Belonging: A Cultural History of Spanish-Language Radio in the United States, 1922—2004." Ph.D. Diss: University of Michigan, Ann Arbor.

———. 2008. "A Morning Dose of Latino Masculinity: U.S. Spanish-Language Radio and the Politics of Gender." In *Latina/o Communication Studies Today*. Angharad Valdivía, ed. New York: Peter Lang, 161–186.

Castañeda, Mari. 2008. "The Importance of Spanish-Language and Latino Media." In *Latina/o Communication Studies Today*. Angharad Valdivía, ed. New York: Peter Lang, 51–68.

Castañeda Paredes, Mari. 2003. "The Transformation of Spanish-Language Radio." *Journal of Radio Studies* 10(1): 5–15.

Catanzarite, Liza. 2003. "Wage Penalties in Brown-Collar Occupations." *Latino Policy and Issues Brief* 8:1–4.

Chabram-Dernersesian, Angie. 1999. "Chicana/o Latina/o Cultural Studies: Transnational and Transdisciplinary Movements." *Cultural Studies* 13(2): 173–194.

Chambers, Todd. 2006. "The State of Spanish-Language Radio." *Journal of Radio Studies* 13(1): 34–50.

Chang, Grace. 2000. *Disposable Domestics: Immigrant Women Workers in the Global Economy*. Cambridge, MA: South End Press.

Chavez, Leo. 2001. *Covering Immigration: Popular Images and the Politics of the Nation*. Berkeley: University of California Press.

Clemens, Luis. 2005. "The Sound That Sells." *Marketing y Medios*, December 1.

Dávila, Arlene. 2001. *Latinos Inc.: The Marketing and Making of a People*. Berkeley: University of California.

de Certeau, Michel. 1988. *The Practice of Everyday Life*. Berkeley: University of California, 1988.

Flaccus, Gillian. 2006. "Spanish-Language Media Credited on Pro-immigrant Rallies." *Boston Globe*, March 29.

Foucault, Michel. 1980. *Power/Knowledge: Selected Interviews and Other Writings, 1972–1977*. Colin Gordon, ed. New York: Pantheon Books.

Fox, Jonathan. 2005. "Unpacking Transnational Citizenship." *Annual Review of Political Science* 8 (June): 171–201.

Gutiérrez, Félix, and Jorge Reina Schement. 1979. *Spanish-Language Radio in the Southwestern United States*. Austin: Center for Mexican American Studies, University of Texas at Austin.

Hendricks, Tyche. 2006. "Popular DJ Takes Registration Drive to Latino Voters." *San Francisco Chronicle*, August 1.

Hilmes, Michele. 1997. *Radio Voices: American Broadcasting, 1922—1952*. Minneapolis: University of Minnesota Press.

Hondagneu-Sotelo, Pierrette. 1996. "Unpacking 187: Targeting Mejicanas." In *Immigration and Ethnic Communities: A Focus on Latinos*. Refugio I. Rochin, ed. East Lansing, MI: Julian Samora Institute, 93–103.

Johnson, Kevin R. 2004. "The Continuing Latino Quest for Full Membership and Equal Citizenship: Legal Progress, Social Setbacks, and Political Promise." In *The Columbia History of Latinos in the United States Since 1960*. David Gutiérrez, ed. New York: Columbia University Press, 391–420.

Johnson, Mark, and Linda Spice. 2006. "Thousands Marched for Immigrants." *Milwaukee Journal Sentinel*, March 23.

Kelman, Ari Y. 2006. "The Acoustic Culture of Yiddish." *Shofar: An Interdisciplinary Journal of Jewish Studies* 25(1): 127–151.

Kelley, Robin D. G. 1994. *Race Rebels: Culture, Politics, and the Black Working Class*. New York: Free Press.

Keyes, Cheryl L. 2004. *Rap Music and Street Consciousness*. Champaign: University of Illinois Press.

Kun, Josh. 2005. *Audiotopia: Music, Race, and America*. Berkeley: University of California Press.

Lipsitz, George. 2007. *Footsteps in the Dark: The Hidden Histories of Pop Music*. Minneapolis: Minnesota University Press.

Levitt, Peggy, and Nina Glick-Schiller. 2004. "Conceptualizing Simultaneity: A Transnational Social Field Perspective on Society." *International Migration Review* 38(145): 595–629.

Marchevsky, Alejandra, and Jeanne Theoharis. 2006. *Not Working: Latina Immigrants, Low-Wage Jobs, and the Failure of Welfare Reform*. New York: New York University Press.

Montgomery, Martin. 1986. "DJ Talk." *Media, Culture, and Society* 8(4): 421–440.

Morley, David. 2000. *Home Territories: Media, Mobility, and Identity*. New York: Routledge.

Naficy, Hamid. 1993. *The Making of Exile Cultures: Iranian Television in Los Angeles*. Minneapolis: University of Minnesota Press.

Petrozello, Donna. 1996. "Audience Share Swells for Spanish Formats." *Broadcasting and Cable* 126(4): 122.

Quiñones, Ben. 2005. "¡Despiertese, Despiertese!" *LA Weekly*, March 25.

Rawe, Julie. 2003. "The Fastest Way to Make Money." *TIME*, June 23.

Romero, Mary. 1992. *Maid in the U.S.A.* New York: Routledge.

Ruíz, Vicki. 2008. "Citizen Restaurant: American Imaginaries, American Communities." *American Quarterly* 60(1): 1–21.

Saldívar, José David. 1997. *Border Matters: Remapping American Cultural Studies*. Berkeley: University of California Press.

Sassen, Saskia. 2000. "The Global City: Strategic Site/New Frontier." In *Democracy, Citizenship, and the Global City*. Engin F. Isin, ed. New York: Routledge, 48–61.

Scannell, Paddy. 1996. *Radio, Television, and Modern Life*. Malden, MA: Blackwell.

Singer, Linda. 2004. "Make Regular Remittance a Creditworthy Activity." *American Banker*, April 30.

Stein, Joel. 2006. "500,000 and No One Invited Me?" *TIME*, March 28.

Squires, Catherine. 2000. "Black Talk Radio: Defining Community Needs and Identity." *Harvard International Journal of Press and Politics* 5 (Spring): 73–96.

Urciuoli, Bonnie. 1998. *Exposing Prejudice: Puerto Rican Experiences of Language, Race, and Class*. Boulder, CO: Westview Press.

U.S. Census Bureau. 2005. "2005 American Community Survey," available at: http://factfinder.census.gov/home/saff/main.html?_lang=en (accessed 15 August 2006).

Warren, Susan. 1995. "Stations Change Tune to Woo Hispanics." *Wall Street Journal*, January 25.

Zentella, Ana Celia. 1997. *Growing Up Bilingual: Puerto Rican Children in New York*. Malden, MA: Blackwell.

3

Hayandose

Zapotec Migrant Expressions of
Membership and Belonging

LOURDES GUTIÉRREZ NÁJERA

The Wake

"Yiusll kumadr!" (Hello *comadre!*).[1] The words rang out as my friend
Marta and I walked up the driveway between the two buildings. Like Marta,
the speaker was a Zapotec woman from Yalálag, Oaxaca. She approached us
and accompanied us to several chairs nearby. Other people were already there
and a rosary was being recited by a group composed primarily of women.
A group of men sat in chairs across from us, talking among themselves. As
we sat down I felt awkward. The arrangement of the space unsettled me.
Between two residential buildings somewhere in the Koreatown district of
Los Angeles, a parking lot had been transformed into a temporary viewing
area for the body of a nineteen-year-old young man killed in a car accident.

The young man's open coffin stood under a blue tarp and over green plastic turf covering the pavement. Next to the viewing area, a table decorated
with marigolds, roses, and other flowers held a guest book and an offering
basket to help offset the costs of funerary arrangements and of transporting
the body back to Oaxaca. Keeping with cultural customs, they had placed
several glasses of water along with burning candles and incense on the green
turf just in front of the coffin to help guide the young man into the spirit
world. As guests filed through, they placed more flowers on the table and
lit candles to assist his journey. A picture of the young man had been positioned at the foot of the coffin, on a second table, reconnecting guests with
their memories of the once-vibrant young man.

The rosary recitation came to an end and I followed Marta into the
kitchen, where we greeted several women who were busy preparing chicken
tamales to be served to the guests later that evening. Her cousins were there
and we chatted with them in Spanish. Marta and I helped for a bit and then

returned outside to our seats. We noticed more guests trickling in, offering their respects to the young man and his family, as we sat and talked. Since we had been there several hours and the sun was beginning to set, we decided to leave. As Marta and I walked down the driveway, several Yalaltecos who were members of a brass band arrived to play funerary marches—commonly played at Oaxacan funerals—into the night.

Though this event took place in 1999, it has remained etched in my memory. Everything seemed surreal. The concrete buildings towering over the body, the parking lot converted into a parlor, Zapotec spoken in the heart of Koreatown, a dead Zapotec migrant waiting to be transported back to Oaxaca in a box on an airplane. There is something else about this story that captured my attention—the ways that these migrants organized to aid one another in times of crisis and the role that their identity as migrants from the town of Yalálag played in the process of creating belonging. Here, Yalaltecos provided not only financial assistance to the young man's family in Los Angeles, but perhaps more important, emotional support. As they came together as a group, they asserted their ties to family, friends, and their hometown of Yalálag, fostering a sense of belonging and membership in an otherwise alienating urban environment. This environment was a consequence of working lives, labor conditions, linguistic dissonance, racial discrimination, and residential isolation. Thus the transformation of an already ethnically marked space (i.e., Korean) into a space where Yalaltecos can claim membership, where they can recreate community, became a meaningful practice of belonging.

Hayandose: Creating Spaces of Belonging

Research suggests that there are between fifty thousand and seventy thousand Zapotecs living in Los Angeles County alone (Fox and Rivera-Salgado 2004). Zapotecs throughout Los Angeles County cluster demographically, forming enclaves. Relatives and friends tend to live in nearby residencies with others who have emigrated from a common town or region of origin. In Santa Monica, for example, there are many Zapotecs from Oaxaca's Central Valley, while in Los Angeles's Koreatown district many Zapotecs come from the Sierra Norte of Oaxaca, and Yalálag specifically. Altogether, Yalaltecos number roughly three thousand within the LA metropolitan area.[2]

Yalalteco migrants work as domestics, cooks, janitors, and day laborers—marginalized positions within Los Angeles's globalizing economy. The expanse of the urban landscape, the distance between people, and their working lives contribute to Yalaltecos commonly expressing feelings of displacement. It is not uncommon to hear of individuals returning to their natal home because "they couldn't find themselves" (*no se hayaban*) in Los Angeles. Yet at the same time, there are many who remain in Los Angeles because they no longer fit in or "cannot find themselves" (*no se hayan*) back home. In this chapter I analyze Yalalteco experiences of displacement (*hayandose*) and the various creative ways that Yalaltecos find to express membership and belonging despite their marginalized positions as indigenous migrants and laborers in Los Angeles and their growing estrangement from the place they left behind.

Specifically, this chapter explores the various ways that Yalalteco migrants express belonging and membership in Los Angeles. Given the marginal status of indigenous people both within Mexico and the United States, how do they create spaces of inclusion? What practices create a sense of community? How do they convey solidarity or belonging to a greater collective? To answer these questions, I look specifically at informal gatherings, migrant microcredit associations, and social dances that both bring migrants together and in the process reproduce their indigenous ethnic identity as Yalaltecos and Zapotecos. As evinced through these practices, such as the wake, Yalaltecos express deep emotional attachments to Yalálag, the place where their umbilical cords are buried.[3] Although there are multiple ways of expressing these sentiments, there is an enduring tendency to imagine themselves as belonging to a larger Yalalteco collective, no matter where they might live. I argue that such bonds and sentiments of belonging are critical to countering feelings of marginality.

Beyond the specific ethnographic case, this chapter is guided by a broader set of interests, specifically to locate indigenous migrants within the larger field of Latino Studies. Despite visionary discourses of inclusiveness, Latino Studies has been dominated by studies of national groups (e.g., Mexicans and Puerto Ricans) that tend to bypass discussions of race, ethnicity, and cultural differences within these broader groups. But such understandings of Latinos inadvertently homogenize experience. The recent recognition of indigenous transnational migrants' experiences in the United States (Fox and Rivera-Salgado 2004; Stephen 2007) suggests a growing recognition of the need to reconsider diversity among Latinos with regard to race, ethnicity, and class, demanding that we rethink these nationalized frameworks for understanding Latino experiences (cf. Oboler 1995, 2006). Yet, despite the growing presence of indigenous migrants in the United States, there remains little discussion of indigenous experiences within the broader field of Latino Studies. Through a focus on Zapotec migrants to Los Angeles, this chapter attempts to bring experiences of indigenous people from the margins to the center of the discipline. In this sense, we are creating a space where indigenous people may find a place for themselves—should they choose to claim a pan-ethnic Latino identity—within the discipline without erasing their unique ethnic identities. Thus the chapter contributes to the forging of a more inclusive disciplinary vision that does not overlook other national, racial, and ethnic groupings that exist within modern, complicated, heterogeneous nation-states.

My research is based on ethnographic methods—including participant-observation and interviews—among Yalaltecos in Los Angeles and Yalálag. I recorded migrant life histories; spoke with and interviewed Yalaltecos regarding their pueblo's history, traditions, and customs; and participated in social events like *fiestas* (social celebrations, parties) and *bailes* (social dances). I also took part in their everyday lives, accompanying people on errands and working in the fields with them. A majority of my time, though, was spent in people's homes. This angle provided particular insight into how Yalaltecos understood and experienced migration, and how various social and cultural practices allowed them to lay claim to ethnic forms of membership and belonging in an otherwise alienating environment.

Locating Yalaltecos Within the Broader Contours of Migration and Marginalization

Throughout the early to mid-twentieth century, Mexican migration to the United States was a process primarily associated with regions of northern México like Durango, Zacatecas, and Michoacán, in addition to the border states of Sonora and Chihuahua. By the 1970s and 1980s, there were well-established migration patterns between many locations in México and the United States. For example, in California and Illinois, there were settlements of migrants from Zacatecas and Durango. As early migrants facilitated and even encouraged other family and friends to migrate north, these settlements became more established. This pattern was elucidated in the 1980s by scholars of Mexican migration and subsequently verified by others (e.g., Cornelius 1988; Hondagneu-Sotelo 1994; Massey et al. 1990; Kearney 1986, 1996; Kearney and Nagengast 1989; Mines 1981; Rouse 1989, 1992; Smith 1994, 2006). By the 1990s, however, a new pattern began to emerge, that of migration from new regions within México, primarily from southern states like Guerrero, Oaxaca, Veracruz, and Chiapas (Fox and Rivera-Salgado 2004; Kearney 1995; Rouse 1989, 1992; Smith 1994, 2006; Zabin 1992; Zabin et al. 1993).

This recent trend has been unique not only in that it represents new regions being integrated into the migration process, but also because it has been increasingly indigenous in character. By the early 1990s indigenous migrants included Mixtecs and Zapotecs from Oaxaca, Maya from Yucatan, Purepechas from Michoacán, and Nahuas from Guerrero. In Oaxaca, a study produced jointly by the Colegio de la Frontera Norte and the Consejo Estatal de Población de Oaxaca in 1995 demonstrated the dramatic surges in migration from the various Oaxacan indigenous populations to the United States. These patterns were substantiated by both North American scholars (Corbett et al. 1992; Fox and Rivera-Salgado 2004; Kearney 1995; Klaver 1997; Mountz and Wright 1996; Zabin et al. 1993) and Mexican scholars alike (Guidi 1992; Ramos 1986, 1992).

Oaxaca boasts the most ethnically diverse population in Mexico, representing sixteen different groups of indigenous people. Among them, the Zapotec, who inhabit the Isthmus of Tehuantepec, the Central Valleys, and the Sierra, constitute the second largest ethnic group. Nestled in the Sierra Norte, just sixty kilometers northeast of the city of Oaxaca at an elevation of 3,854 feet, lies the Zapotec town of Yalálag. The town is the largest *municipio* (township) in the region, and its population of two thousand is distributed throughout four quarters.[4] Zapotec continues to be the primary language spoken by approximately 83 percent of the population, while Spanish and Mixe constitute secondary and tertiary languages.[5] Throughout most of the twentieth century, most Yalaltecos labored in subsistence agriculture and the production of leather goods. Today, they increasingly rely on migration to supplement their incomes, through remittances or by engaging in wage labor outside their town. Yalálag has a post office, a dental clinic, a medical clinic, telephone service that includes both public and private lines, and bus service to and from Oaxaca City several times daily. The village currently benefits from a running, potable water system (which delivers water from a nearby alpine aquifer), electricity, and a sewage system. During my research in 1998, the road between Oaxaca and Yalálag was made of packed dirt; today it is paved, cutting the driving time of five or six hours in half. Many of the services available to Yalaltecos are directly linked to resources acquired through migration, like the tower receivers for the satellite phone system, paid for by migrants living in Los Angeles.

Skyscrapers, asphalt pavement, crowded apartments, and the street life of Los Angeles stand in stark contrast to the Mexican countryside. Yet so many Oaxacan indigenous people have settled in LA that migrants and scholars alike call it Oaxacalifornia: the imaginary transnational space between places of origin and settlement (for original usage of term, see Kearney and Nagengast 1989; Nagengast and Kearney 1990). For Yalaltecos in Los Angeles, the formation of their well-established transnational networks began during the 1960s, when several people from the village found jobs in the LA service sector and settled in the city (Equipo Pueblo 1988). By 2000, more Yalaltecos were living in Los Angeles (3,000) than in Yalálag itself (1,799) (INEGI 2000).

Facilitated by family and friends, indigenous migrants have continued to find work in the Los Angeles service sector. Their experiences in the labor market have been largely gendered. Men have predominantly worked in restaurants as cooks and dishwashers, as janitors, and in small businesses (Cohen 2004). It is not surprising to find entire kitchen crews composed of indigenous *paisanos* (people from the same hometown or region), nor is it uncommon to find restaurants owned by indigenous migrants in Los Angeles (in fact, several of these restaurants are owned by families from Yalálag).[6] In contrast, women work primarily in homes as nannies and domestics for upper-middle-class families and LA's rich and famous. While economic opportunities for indigenous migrants are to be found in Los Angeles, most are paid very little, so it is common for both men and women to supplement their low wages by holding down two or more jobs. They may also supplement their incomes in other ways. Women, for example, sell home and beauty products for such companies as Avon, Mary Kay, and Tupperware.

In spite of working and residing several thousand miles from their natal communities in Oaxaca, indigenous migrants presently in Los Angeles actively participate in the economic, social, and political lives of their communities (Fox and Rivera-Salgado 2004). Yalaltecos living in Los Angeles continue to celebrate the festivities surrounding their main patron saints, crowding together in dance halls and people's backyards. They also celebrate life cycle events, such as deaths and marriages. Some Yalaltecos are deeply committed to maintaining their links to their natal communities and indigenous identities, while others seek to integrate themselves into U.S. culture. As Yalaltecos, part of the Oaxacalifornia experience, inhabiting a space that is neither fully Yalálag nor Angelinos, reflects the ambiguities they feel about belonging neither here nor there. But through participation in cultural events and practices such as those described in this chapter, Yalaltecos living in Los Angeles create a sense of belonging. Laying claim to a larger collective is instrumental to overcoming alienation and marginality in Southern California's urban environment.

Both within Mexico and the United States, Yalaltecos find themselves relatively marginalized. In Mexico, their indigenous status places them at the margins of the state. Indigenous people are continually subjected to the strong arm of the state, as the national government dictates terms for the future development of their communities. In fact, they are often denied social justice and are treated as second-class citizens (Bonfil Batalla 1989; Castellanos 2007; Díaz-Polanco 1979; Gutiérrez Nájera 2007; Kearney 1996; Knight 1999; Stavenhagen 1996). Indigenous communities are among the poorest in Mexico in terms of income distribution, health outcomes, and education. In Oaxaca, these conditions drive indigenous people from their places of origin. Paradoxically, it is only by leaving that many Oaxacans have been able to rally for social change in their towns of origin.

In Los Angeles, Yalaltecos' indigeneity is rendered invisible by their national status. In the process of migration, they are identified more broadly by others as Mexican or Latino. Yet this label belies their unique language, culture, religion, and customs, which differentiate their experiences of migration from those of other Mexican migrants. Among Mexican migrants, the differences between indigenous and mestizo do not go unnoticed. Mestizos often belittle indigenous migrants and accuse them of being "backward." Moreover, their perceived phenotypic differences as indigenous migrants fuel more discrimination. They are thought to have darker skin and shorter stature; a common complaint among Yalaltecos is that Mexican Americans call them "Oaxaquitos," a diminutive form of the word used to debase native Oaxacans. Within the broader context of Anglo-Mexican relations, indigenous migrants are also targets of abuse, being particularly susceptible because they may speak neither English nor Spanish. Many Anglos will assume that the Yalaltecos do not speak English and therefore will shout epithets directly in their faces. For example, while shopping in a store one day, an Anglo woman approached my friend and I and hurled English-language insults at us. When we replied to her in English, she looked befuddled, failing to acknowledge what we were saying and continuing to insult us until we walked away. Marta explained that this type of behavior is not uncommon. Because many Oaxacan migrants remain undocumented in the United States, they are vulnerable to employers and landlords who may use knowledge of their status to manipulate them by offering lower wages, making them work longer hours, withholding pay, and threatening deportation.

Intimate Gatherings: Contexts for Affirmations of Belonging

Many Yalaltecos invest in asserting their identity as a way of providing pleasure and understanding their situation in Los Angeles. Some social contexts under which they assert their belonging are more subtle than others. Assertion of an ethnic identity allows Yalaltecos to claim membership to a collective ultimately rooted in experiences within their natal hometown. Claims of Yalaltecanness, a sense of ethnic belonging, are possible even when national membership may not be attainable and are readily fostered through participation in life cycle events such as baptisms, weddings, and funerals. These occasions provide appropriate contexts for collective sharing of sentiments and information. As the following examples suggest, formalized events are critical for the maintenance and reproduction of community building processes, but everyday practices such as talking on the phone, intimate gatherings with relatives and friends, and collective viewing of videos are equally important.

I spent a lot of time with Agustín and his wife, Conchita, in the cream-colored stucco ranch home they own in South Central Los Angeles. They migrated from Yalálag over thirty years ago are both in their fifties. They are naturalized U.S. citizens and have two college-aged sons who were born in LA. Despite being longtime residents, they travel frequently to Yalálag to visit the family members they left behind. Their strong connections to their hometown are readily evident. Inside their home the walls are decorated with numerous photographs of Yalálag, alongside wedding pictures and various images of family members, and delicious Yalalteco-style food and pastries, coffee, chocolate, or other drinks are always available for their guests on the dining room table. I became accustomed to the constant flow of Yalalteco visitors, to whom I was always warmly introduced. One afternoon, at least fifty people came through their house. We oscillated between sitting on the back patio in white plastic lounge chairs under some fruit trees, and inside the house on the softly covered living room couch and chairs. As we moved around, the guests joked with one another, ate, shared gossip, and discussed Oaxacan politics (since one of the guests had just returned from southern Mexico).

One particular afternoon, Agustín invited his friend Pablo, a musician who plays in a local Yalalteco band and a longtime LA resident. Since I was interested in the development of Yalalteco networks in the city, Agustín assured me that Pablo could recount early experiences of migrants in Los Angeles. After several hours of talking and exchanging stories about people and experiences in Yalálag, Agustín announced that we should watch a video he had just received from another friend who had recently returned from their homeland. Indeed, video viewing becomes a way to mediate collective formation. This particular video, which ran for several hours, documented a recent fiesta in honor of one of the town's patron saints. It opened with footage from a *jaripeo* (rodeo). There was a large crowd of mostly men sitting along the wooden fence, which encircled the area where several local riders were taking turn riding a bull. The bull bucked each rider one by one until finally a man was able to stay on long enough to claim victory. In the background of this scenery played music typical of the region. The *jaripeo* lasted for about an hour, and then the video focused on the performance of several *danzas* (ritualized dances) by Yalalteco youth. Each *danza* enacted a story related to Mexico's colonial past and was elaborated with beautiful choreography and costuming. Finally, the video shows nighttime dancing and celebration. The *jaripeo* and *danzas* elicited nostalgic memories for Agustín and Pablo. But it was the nighttime celebration that spawned the most engaged conversations as we commented on people in the video. There were many migrants present and we talked and laughed as we saw people dancing around. They commented on topics from decorations of the place to dress, dance, and hair styles. As we finished watching the video, they continued to talk about people and places they had seen.[7]

Home gatherings are important community-building practices that, while spanning the distance between LA and Yalálag, also foster a sense of belonging. The act of collective formation relies on more subtle forms of community practices, such as the sharing of sentiments and memories that create bonds between people and places. The viewing of videos, sharing of photographs, and gossip mediate these affective responses that reaffirm their ethnic identity. After all, it is an identity as indigenous (Zapotec) people that is being reiterated through practice. It is commonplace for Yalaltecos to spend Saturdays and Sundays in the company of other *paisanos*. Through countless interactions and the sharing of food, stories, and videos, Yalaltecos perpetuate their communal and ethnic identities, maintaining connections and shared set of concerns with their counterparts in Oaxaca. At the same time that they are fostering social membership in the United States, the fact that they participate at a distance contributes to differentiating them further from the others living in the hometown, expressed through their anxieties about no longer finding themselves in Yalálag.

Tandas: Gendered Spaces of Belonging

In contrast to intimate home gatherings where men, women, and children participate to build communal and ethnic solidarities, other forms of belonging appear to be constructed along gendered axes. Participation in *tandas*, micro-credit associations common among Oaxacan migrants, is particularly illuminating for understanding the ways that women build on networks to create spaces of belonging.[8] For Yalaltecas, who often work alone either in their own homes or the homes of other Angelinos for whom they work, tandas offer a social environment through which to combat isolation and deprivation—the support is both financial and emotional.

On a Sunday afternoon while I was accompanying my friend Micah on her errands, we went to the home of another Yalalteca residing in a nearby neighborhood in Los Angeles. Micah was going to put in her share of money in a weekly tanda. A tanda is system whereby a group of people agrees to contribute an equal portion of money on a weekly basis, which is put into a generalized pool.[9] Each week, in turn, one member of the group takes the entire pool of money. Depending on the financial need of the people in the group, members may allow someone who needs the money to take their turn before the others. Also contingent on circumstances, migrants use the money to meet different needs: to send relatives in Oaxaca money; to buy appliances, furniture, or other household goods; to pay off loans; and even to reinvest in other tandas, since many people belong to multiple tandas at once. In Micah's case, this tanda (one of three she participates in) has roughly twenty participants and each contributes twenty dollars every week. Once every twenty weeks, Micah collects four hundred dollars. For many struggling migrants like Micah, the tanda represents a form of savings. At one point, for example, Micah was able to pay off a debt she had accrued. Beyond the savings potential, tandas offer a social space through which women, in particular, reassert their membership in a broader network. Within the context of migration, tandas help remedy the isolation experienced by many Yalalteca women living and working in Los Angeles.

I first encountered this practice in Yalálag when a friend of mine, Carmen, surprised me by asking me for a loan to pay for her tanda. Unfamiliar with the term, I asked her to explain. She responded that every month she put in money for her tanda. When I asked her how much money she put in, Carmen informed me that she put one hundred dollars (one thousand pesos) every month. I was surprised that she put in so much money. She laughed and confessed that she was part of several tandas, not just one. Sensing my interest, she asked me if I wanted to join one and suggested I accompany her that Sunday when she delivered her money to the person in charge so that I could get a better sense of how they worked. On Sunday afternoon, I went with Carmen to run her errands. Along the way, we would stop when she encountered a friend, with whom she would spend a few minutes exchanging the latest gossip and reporting it back to me. Time passed quickly, until she suddenly exclaimed that she was now late for her tanda. It was set for three o'clock in the afternoon. We quickened our pace and made our way along the dirt road that cuts across the middle of town, until we came to María's house.

María coordinated this particular tanda and it was the participants' duty to come to her house the last Sunday of every month to pay their share. As we approached the gate outside, we were greeted by another woman who was just leaving. We continued into the courtyard, where we were greeted by several other women who were standing around talking and gossiping with one another. Carmen gave her thousand pesos to María, who was busily collecting money from the women as she checked their names off a list. We stayed behind for a while to chat with the other women as we waited for the last person to check in for her monthly contribution. María then turned over the money to one of the women who had been chatting nearby. Afterward we returned to Carmen's home and she wanted to know if I would join the tanda now that I had seen how it operated.

For Francisca, a thirty-five-year-old Yalalteca living in Los Angeles, tandas offered a rare social space where she can speak Zapotec and relax. She migrated to Los Angeles with the goal of earning enough money so that she could build her own home in Yalálag. Yet more than five years later she still found herself in the United States. Francisca expressed feelings of isolation and longed to return to her hometown. On one occasion she confided, "No me hayo" (I cannot find myself), an expression used to describe a sense of not fitting in, an inability to adapt to the local environment. When I asked her what she found difficult about life in Southern California, she replied, "Everything. The food. The language. The way of life. Even though I live nearby other Yalaltecos, I do not see them." She worked as a nanny in West Los Angeles, commuting every day on local buses. Francisca left home early and returned late, too tired to socialize. She also still struggled with English and sometimes felt that her employer took advantage of that fact. Still, Francisca also confessed that despite the isolation, she liked the freedom she enjoyed in Los Angeles and wondered openly if she would be able to fit in—*hayarse* (to find herself)—when she returned to Yalálag, where as a woman her opportunities would be limited due to more rigidly defined gender roles. At the tanda she was relaxed and laughed with friends as she chatted in Zapotec. This is typical on Sunday afternoons for many women involved in tandas.

In Los Angeles, many of the women I accompanied to tandas were excluded from formalized forms of savings through institutional banking networks because of their undocumented status. When Bank of America began to work with the Mexican consulate in 1999 to open up bank accounts for migrants regardless of legal status in the United States, many feared an eventual backlash and refrained from participation. For these women, the tanda provides a way to safeguard their money until they need it. But tandas are about more than money; they are an important part of the social fabric among migrant Yalaltecas in Los Angeles. As women contribute to the weekly pool of money, they are helping one another out, asserting their bonds of friendship and trust. This was made evident when Angela received her tanda out of turn and Micah remarked, "How good it is that she receives the tanda. She really needs the money. She had a death in her family, and her husband is sick. Poor thing, she can really use the money." Further, the women use this practice to construct a sense of belonging. In Los Angeles, many of these same women work as domestics and nannies throughout the week. Some of them work as live-ins with only one or two days off. Given the isolated nature of their work, the weekly tandas also offer women a space to meet and come together. At the tandas, women are able to talk to one another and exchange enough gossip to sustain them for a week. During their verbal exchanges they often speak about their jobs and their bosses. These discussions are vital for the women, many of whom face another week of isolation ahead. As one woman claimed, "The only reason women participate in tandas is for the gossip, otherwise it doesn't make sense." Ultimately, tandas provide a sense of cohesion by bringing together women of different generations. The conversational exchange—the *chisme*—taking place at these gatherings is critical for creating cohesion, as these experiences contribute to cultural transmission and continuity. The exchange of money also fosters a sense of community by fostering economic and emotional interdependence between the women. Thus, within a broader context of marginalization, tandas offer a way for Yalaltecas to claim belonging to a wide social network.

Community Fiestas/Bailes:
Outward Expressions of Ethnic Belongings

Outward expressions of ethnic membership are facilitated through public community events. The *guelaguetza*, a pan-ethnic celebration showcasing folkloric dances from every Oaxacan indigenous ethnic group, has grown to such scale that it now takes places in the Staples Center, home of the LA Lakers. This fiesta allows migrants living in California to proudly claim their ethnic identities as Mixes, Zapotecos, Mixtecos, Chinantecos, and so forth. On a smaller scale, fiestas in celebration of hometown patron saints also provide spaces for the public display of ethnic belonging. Members of hometown associations and secular and religious committees, formed by migrants, typically organize these events, which are common in Los Angeles. Often taking place in dance halls around the city, the turnout for these events is always large and the halls fill quickly to capacity. Through participation in the fiestas, and in particular the dances that accompany these celebrations, Yalaltecos reaffirm their ethnic membership as the shared environment and the rhythms of the music connect them with their natal home.

On a Saturday night I drove my friend Irene and her uncle to a dance hall several miles from their home. Irene wore high heels and a sleeveless black dress that came slightly above the knees. Her uncle Felipe wore a new pair of black jeans, a dress shirt, and shoes. As we entered the dance hall we found adults, youth, and entire families already inside. The hall was dingy, dated, and dimly lit. Despite the décor, laughter and chatter filled the air. We arrived during an intermission, too late to enjoy traditional *danzas* performed by migrant dance groups, but just in time for a local band to play *sones* and *jarabes,* music and dance forms typical of Yalálag. Since my friends enjoy dancing, we sat at a table not too far from the dance floor with their acquaintances. As the band began to play, the room filled with excitement and the dance floor filled with men, women, and children. We watched as two young girls danced with one another to the rhythms of the music while mimicking the movements of adults on the dance floor. At the sound of the *jarabe* Yalalteco, the dance representing the hometown, Felipe turned to me and said, "It is like being transported to one's home. You know? To be Yalalteco is to dance." His comment, served as reminder that the body has a history, a memory that in this case is linked to his natal community. Still looking toward me, he raised his arms in the air and, giving a little hop (as Yalaltecos do when they dance *jarabes* from their hometown), took to the dance floor, remaining there for the better part of the night.

Beyond offering diversion for Yalaltecos, public dances provide social spaces for the affirmation of belonging to a wider community. As Yalaltecos dance to the music, they reassert their connections to their town—both physically, through dancing, as well as emotionally by sharing sentiments of belonging. Again, the music they dance to is typical of their region, though the particular dances, rhythms, and styles are unique to Yalálag. It is no surprise then that Felipe equates dancing with being Yalalteco. Ultimately, dancing provides a way to express ethnic identity. Sentiments of joy, sadness, and love shared with family, friends, and *paisanos* at public *bailes* reaffirm their collectivity. Within an urban context, where Yalaltecos are widely dispersed and often remain isolated from one another, *bailes* play a critical role in the affirmation of community. In the dance halls it is not citizenship or nationality that defines Yalaltecos, but the sharing of a common culture, language, and heritage.

Conclusion

While tandas, wakes, informal gatherings, and dances are also practiced in the town of origin, and offer similar opportunities for sharing economic, social, and emotional resources, they play a unique role in the lives and experiences of Yalalteco migrants living in Southern California. Among Oaxaqueños, ethnic identity becomes salient through the process of migration. This ethnic identity has been asserted in recent years to rally for indigenous rights and development of hometown communities in Oaxaca, as well as to organize in the United States around immigration legislation (Fox and River-Salgado 2004; Kearney 1996). Among Yalaltecos, there seems to be an understanding of marginalization that emerges in the migration circuit. Understanding that life can be figured otherwise, they develop a desire for change that fuels their activism (Gutiérrez Nájera 2007). This chapter suggests that cultural practices such as tandas, casual gatherings, life cycle events, and public fiestas play a critical role in fomenting ethnic forms of identification unique to the migrant community. Further, the chapter suggests that the formation of ethnic identifications is critical for the assertion of belonging among Yalalteco migrants. This form of belonging contrasts sharply with institutionalized norms that define membership at the national level. In the United States, citizenship and residential status define membership and belonging. For undocumented persons, this sort of belonging remains out of reach. Consequently, migrants retain a marginalized position that makes them vulnerable to abuse, prejudice, and discrimination. In Mexico, racial discrimination linked to nationalist ideologies often prevents indigenous people from achieving full rights as citizens. While in Los Angeles they are also multiply marginalized, as we have seen Yalaltecos participate in cultural practices and lay claim to ethnic and cultural memberships to combat vulnerability, depravation, and domination—even, as we saw in the opening vignette, in death.

As scholars interested in Latino Studies, a consideration of Yalalteco belonging begs us to question the place of indigenous migrants within the field. Certainly, the experiences of Yalalteco Zapotec migration are not unique today. In the face of increasing indigenous migration to the United States in the last two decades, we must rethink nationalized categories that tend to homogenize experience while erasing ethnic, racial, and cultural differences. The experiences of Yalaltecos described in this chapter suggest that ethnic and cultural forms of belonging often precede nationalized forms of identification and demand that we call attention to these differences. At risk is the continued alienation and marginalization of racial, ethnic, gender, and sexual minority groups who cannot easily claim the nationalized identities often privileged in Latino Studies.

ACKNOWLEDGMENTS

I want to extend sincere appreciation to Adrian Burgos, Frank Guridy, and Gina Pérez for inviting me to participate in this exciting project and for their valuable feedback. Also, thanks to Erica Lehrer, Ellen Moodie, and William Orchard for their insights and constructive comments on this chapter.

NOTES

1. This spelling is based on my own interpretation of the phonetic sounds in Zapotec. While there are new emerging orthographies from Yalálag, I am not familiar with them. The translation I have provided is an approximate equivalent of our standard greeting.

2. This number is an approximation based on both municipal records in Oaxaca as well as an ethnographic census conducted during 1998 Yalálag fieldwork that accounted for migrants living in the United States. The census information was further verified through a survey taken in Los Angeles among migrants.

3. It is common practice to bury the umbilical cord of an infant in the courtyard of the home where he or she was born. Yalaltecos often use this reference to their umbilical cord to speak of the deep sentiments they hold for their hometown.

4. This is reminiscent of the pre-Hispanic *altepetl* system of sociopolitical organization that divided communities into four sections to facilitate redistribution systems managed by the state. See James Lockhart (1992) for further discussion of *altepetls* and their functions within the larger Nahua cosmogony.

5. Mixe is an indigenous language spoken in Oaxaca. The Mixe people live in a neighboring region of the Sierra Norte.

6. The three restaurants in Los Angeles are El Danzante (established in 2000), Yalálag Restaurant (2002), and El Torito Oaxaqueño (2001) (López and Runsten 2004: 268–269). López and Runsten also provide a list of twenty-five other restaurants owned and operated by indigenous Oaxacan migrants.

7. Certainly, my own presence stimulated this conversation, but these types of interactions are common practice among Yalaltecos.

8. Though some men do participate in these tandas, they are predominantly run by women, and I never encountered a tanda that was run solely by men.

9. This type of practice is common around the world, although known by other names.

REFERENCES

Bonfil Batalla, Guillermo. 1989. *México profundo, una civilización negada.* 2nd ed. México D.F.: Consejo Nacional para la Cultura y las Artes/Editorial Grijalbo.
Castellanos, M. Bianet. 2007. "Constructing the Family: Mexican Migrant Households, Marriage, and the State." *Latin American Perspectives* 35(1): 64–77
Cohen, Jeffrey. 2004. *The Culture of Migration in Southern Mexico.* Austin: University of Texas Press.
Colegio de la Frontera Norte/Consejo Estatal de Población de Oaxaca. 1995. *La migración nacional e internacional de los Oaxaqueños.* Oaxaca, México: Consejo Estatal de Población de Oaxaca.
Corbett, Jack, et al. 1992. *Migración y etnicidad en Oaxaca.* Nashville: Vanderbilt University Publications in Anthropology, 43.
Cornelius, Wayne A. 1988. *The Changing Profile of Mexican Labor Migration to California in the 1980s.* La Jolla: Center for U.S.-Mexican Studies, University of California, San Diego.
Díaz-Polanco, Héctor. 1981 (1979). "La teoría indigenista y la integración." In *Indigenismo, modernización y marginalidad: Una revisión crítica,* Héctor Díaz-Polanco et al., eds. Mexico City: Juan Pablos/Centro de Investigación para la Integración Social, 9–45.
Equipo Pueblo. 1988. *Yalálag: Testimonios indígenas.* México D.F.: Equipo Pueblo.
Fox, Jonathan, and Gaspar Rivera-Salgado. 2004. *Indigenous Mexican Americans in the United States.* La Jolla: Center for U.S.-Mexican Studies and Center for Comparative Immigration Studies, University of California, San Diego.
Guidi, Marta. 1992. *Estigma y prestigio: La tradición de migrar en San Juan Mixtepec (Oaxaca, México).* Mundus Riehe Ethnologie. Amsterdam, Netherlands: Holos Verlag.
Gutiérrez Nájera, Lourdes. 2007. "Yalálag Is No Longer Just Yalálag: Circulating Conflict and Contesting Community Within a Transnational Migrant Circuit." Unpublished Ph.D. Dissertation. University of Michigan.
Hondagneu-Sotelo, Pierrette. 1994. *Gendered Transitions: Mexican Experiences of Migration.* Berkeley: University of California Press.
INEGI (Instituto Nacional de Estadísticas y Geografía). 2000. *XII censo general de población y vivienda (2000), estado de Oaxaca.* Aguascalientes: INEGI.
Kearney, Michael. 1986. "From the Invisible Hand to Visible Feet: Anthropological Studies of Migration and Development." *Annual Review of Anthropology* 15:331–361.
———. 1995. "The Local and Global: The Anthropology of Globalization and Transnationalism." *Annual Review of Anthropology* 24:547–565.

———. 1996. *Reconceptualizing the Peasantry: Anthropology in Global Perspective.* Boulder, CO: Westview Press.

Kearney, Michael, and Carole Nagengast. 1989. *Anthropological Perspectives on Transnational Communities in Rural California.* Davis: California Institute for Rural Studies.

Klaver, Jeanine. 1997. *From the Land of the Sun to the City of the Angels: The Migration Process of Zapotec Indians from Oaxaca, Mexico, to Los Angeles, California.* Amsterdam, Netherlands: Netherlands Geographical Studies, 228.

Knight, Allan. 1999. "Racism, Revolution, and Indigenismo: Mexico, 1910–1940." In *The Idea of Race in Latin America, 1870–1940*, Richard Graham, ed. Austin: University of Texas Press, 71–113.

Lockhart, James. 1992. *The Nahuas After the Conquest: A Social and Cultural History of the Indians of Central Mexico, Sixteenth Through Eighteenth Centuries.* Stanford: Stanford University Press.

López, Felipe, and David Runsten. 2004. "Mixtecs and Zapotecs Working in California: Rural and Urban Experiences." In *Indigenous Mexican Migrants in the United States*, Jonathan Fox and Gaspar Rivera-Salgado, eds. La Jolla, CA: Center for U.S.-Mexican Studies, UCSD/Center for Comparative Immigration Studies, 249–278.

Massey, Douglas, Rafael Alarcón, Jorge Durand, and Humberto González. 1990. *Return to Aztlan: The Social Process of International Migration from Western Mexico.* Berkeley: University of California Press.

Mines, Richard. 1981. *Developing a Community Tradition of Migration: A Field Study in Rural Zacatecas, Mexico, and California Settlement Areas.* La Jolla: Center for U.S.-Mexican Studies, University of California, San Diego.

Mountz, Allison, and Richard A. Wright. 1996. "Daily Life in the Transnational Migrant Community of San Agustin, Oaxaca, and Poughkeepsie, New York." *Diaspora* 5(3): 403–427.

Nagengast, Carole, and Michael Kearney. 1990. "Mixtec Ethnicity: Social Identity, Political Consciousness, and Political Activism." *Latin American Research Review* 25(2): 61–91.

Oboler, Suzanne. 1995. *Ethnic Labels, Latino Lives: Identity and the Politics of (Re)presentation in the United Status.* Minneapolis: University of Minnesota Press.

———, ed. 2006. *Latinos and Citizenship: The Dilemma of Belonging.* New York: Palgrave Macmillan.

Ramos, Donato Pioquinto. 1986. "Migración y transformación de la comunidad indígena de Zoogocho (1940–1980)." *México Indígena* 13(2): 38–41.

———. 1988. *Migración y sistema de cargos en la reproducción social de la comunidad campesina indígena de Zoogocho, Oaxaca de 1940 a 1987.* Tesis professional, Oaxaca, Universidad Autónoma Benito Juarez de Oaxaca, Facultad de Sociología.

———. 1992. "Factores que provocan la migración en la Sierra Norte." Asociación Mexicana de Población, México.

Rouse, Roger. 1989. "Mexican Migration to the U.S.: Family Relations in a Transnational Migrant Circuit." Unpublished Ph.D. Dissertation. Stanford University.

———. 1992. "Making Sense of Settlement: Class Transformation, Cultural Struggle, and Transnationalism Among Mexican Migrants in the United States." In *Towards a Transnational Perspective on Migration: Race, Class, Ethnicity, and Nationalism Reconsidered*, Glick Schiller et al., eds. New York: Annals of the New York Academy of Sciences, 25–52.

Smith, Robert C. 1994. "'Los Ausentes siempre presentes': The Imagining, Making, and Politics of a Transnational Community Between Ticuani, Puebla, Mexico, and New York City." Ph.D. Dissertation. Columbia University.

———. 2006. *Mexican New York: Transnational Lives of New Immigrants.* Berkeley: University of California Press.

Stavenhagen, Rodolfo. 1994. *Ethnic Conflicts and the Nation-State.* New York: St. Martin's Press.

Stephen, Lynn. 2007. *Transborder Lives: Indigenous Oaxacans in Mexico, California, and Oregon.* Durham: Duke University Press.

Zabin, Carol. 1992. *Mixtec Migrant Farm Workers in California Agriculture.* Davis: California Institute for Rural Studies.

———. 1993. *Mixtec Migrants in California Agriculture: A New Cycle of Poverty.* Davis: California Institute for Rural Studies.

4

Becoming Suspect in Usual Places

Latinos, Baseball, and Belonging in
El Barrio del Bronx

——— ADRIAN BURGOS, JR., AND FRANK A. GURIDY ———

On 25 August 2001, the Rolando Paulino All Stars from the Bronx, New York, faced off against the Apopka, Florida, team during the semifinal round of the Little League World Series (LLWS). Broadcast internationally on ESPN, the Paulino All Stars were the main attraction for countless viewers. The Bronx team was propelled by Dominican-born pitcher Danny Almonte, who frustrated his opponents and infuriated their parents with his blazing fastball. The team captured national and international attention. Comprising boys from working-class and impoverished Dominican and Puerto Rican backgrounds, including a number of players who could not speak English, the Bronx team battled its way to within a game of the LLWS championship. The team's stunning success led the sporting press to hail the team the "Baby Bronx Bombers," a reference to the nickname of the other famous baseball team from the Bronx: the New York Yankees.

The success of the Baby Bronx Bombers did not breed universal celebration. Accusations of cheating and using ineligible players followed the Paulino All Stars during their inexorable march through the Little League tournament that summer. Suspicions focused primarily on Danny Almonte, although other team members were also placed under a cloud of suspicion of being too old to participate. Unofficial and eventually official investigations were launched to verify their age eligibility.

Nationalist displays by fans throughout the Little League World Series exacerbated tensions, especially in the games between the United States teams. During the U.S. semifinal game between Apopka and Paulino All Stars, fans of the Florida team routinely waved U.S. flags, projecting the impression that the Bronx team was somehow un-American. In contrast, the fans in the Bronx team's cheering section waved Puerto Rican, Dominican, and U.S. flags, asserting their own expansive claims of national identity and belonging. Apopka's 8–2 triumph over the Bronx team, in a game in which Almonte did not pitch, ended the Paulino All Stars' run. But Apopka's victory did not eliminate the speculation or nationalist tensions. As the Apopka Little Leaguers celebrated their victory, the almost exclusively white fans in their cheering section triumphantly chanted "USA, USA, USA," in an effort to assert their definition of who the real "Americans" were in the contest.

Two months after the 2001 Little League World Series, Bronx baseball once again figured in the staging of U.S. national identity. On October 31, two months after the Little League tournament and about six weeks after the terrorist attacks of September 11, President George W. Bush threw out the ceremonial first pitch at the third game of the Major League World Series at Yankee Stadium in the Bronx. Bush received a thunderous ovation as he walked out onto the diamond that evening. After the president threw the first pitch, the sold out crowd of over fifty-five thousand spectators roared its approval and began to chant "USA, USA, USA."[1]

The story of the Rolando Paulino All-Stars' mercurial rise and its equally rapid demise elicits much broader questions about the perception of Latina/os, their acceptance within the U.S. public, and the ambivalent place of their communities. This chapter situates the xenophobic reaction to the Paulino All Stars during the summer of 2001 within a longer history of racialized anxieties surrounding Latinos in baseball as well as struggles over citizenship and belonging in U.S. society. It illuminates the ambivalent space of the Bronx as a historic black-and-brown "barrio" in the U.S. imagination. Indeed, baseball in the Bronx has been overdetermined by the New York Yankees, the most successful team in Major League Baseball, whose history has been cloaked in white racialized narratives of the team's and the Bronx's white ethnic past. An examination of the team's relationship with the Bronx illustrates the ways the borough's identity, like U.S. national identity, has been predicated on marking the Latino presence as foreign. This racialized imagination runs headlong into the changing transnational circulation of capital and labor that has led to the increase of Latinos in U.S. professional baseball starting in the second half of the twentieth century. As transnational subjects, Latino baseball players, like Latina/o migrants in general, have taken advantage of labor opportunities in the United States despite being subject to intensified scrutiny and policing. The influx of Latin American players parallels the increased presence and ambivalence about Latino migrants in the United States, including in urban communities such as the Bronx.

The tightening up of both the geographic and imaginative borders of the U.S. nation is one direct result of the shift toward homeland security in a post–September 11 United States. The context of increased surveillance of "the Other" has thus cast Latinos, regardless of national origins, under further suspicion within popular and hegemonic views of U.S. national identity. Interestingly, the baseball world has emerged as one of the more public sites for the unfolding of the post–September 11 heightened surveillance of the migratory movement and actions of Latinos to secure entry into the United States. In this sense, the Almonte case presaged more recent controversies within professional baseball (and U.S. society) about the manipulation of age, visa paperwork, and other official state documents, and of state laws or institutional rules to extract greater personal or financial gain. Suspicions of Danny Almonte and the Rolando Paulino All Stars were always about more than the on-field success of young boys; it reiterated suburban fears about urban (barrio) residents, as it projected the racialized suspicions and tensions about national belonging among adults onto the boys.

Complete with discourses that stress the diamond as a level playing field that rewards athletic achievement (merit), the baseball diamond is quite an appropriate setting for this drama about race, place, and national belonging. Often hailed as the U.S. national pastime, proponents have long viewed baseball as a site for the Americanization of immigrants. Advocates claimed that in addition to vigorous exercise baseball also taught important life lessons vital to individuals functioning as citizens within a democracy: teamwork, they contended, taught individuals to subordinate personal achievement for the larger goal of winning as a team, and this lesson mirrored how community members had to suppress individual desires for the greater good. The investment of such discursive ideals into the pastime is contrasted by the actual history of U.S. professional baseball, where a gentleman's agreement excluded blacks from the major leagues from the late 1880s until 1947. As for Latinos, they could only participate in organized baseball if they passed a racial litmus test administered by organized baseball executives to distinguish them from those perceived as having African ancestry. Upon close examination, one finds that organized baseball long operated as a social institution that abided by its own racialized understandings that affected opportunity. In this sense, the national pastime at its most elite level has existed as a laboratory for the testing of new understandings of race as members of different racialized communities were proposed for entry into the segregated institution—this too can be understood as a version of America's game with real economic and social stakes.[2]

Dominicans in particular have come under increased scrutiny when it comes to their very public success in baseball. One can easily connect the suspicions about Danny Almonte and the Paulino All-Stars to speculations about the extent to which Dominicans engage in what we refer to as "the age game" in seeking to land a contract with a Major League organization, or in other machinations on and off the playing field as seen in the organized baseball's steroids scandal. Part of what connects these stories at the amateur and professional levels is how just being successful as a Latino generally or Dominican specifically has come to raise some suspicion. This is most evident in popular forums such as sports talk radio or blogs where participants enjoy a degree of unanimity, remove some of the filters that normally govern regular discourse, and offer biting, racialized critiques of who is viewed as willing to cheat and why. Although analysis of such banter is beyond the purview of this chapter, which focuses on newspaper and national sports media coverage, the tone of these forums is nonetheless instructive. They reveal the existence of an undercurrent to the suspicion of "brown"/Latino players where their success renders them "suspect" and their actions are easily portrayed as those of the all-too-willing-to-cheat foreigner. What remains uninterrogated in the production of these suspicions and portrayals is both the racial gaze through which suspicion is often initially produced and how the systems that create different pathways to success are themselves agents of racialization.

For all the preoccupation with Dominican and other Latin American "foreigners," the polarizing reactions to Danny Almonte and the Paulino All Stars actually illustrate the anxieties prompted by Latinos who live *within* U.S. borders. What made the success of the Bronx team so threatening was precisely that they were a team from a racialized barrio that was on the verge of representing the United States in a sport historically known as "America's game." The rapid reversal of baseball in the Bronx from nonnational other to the staging ground for American patriotism during the summer and fall of 2001 illustrates the ways racialized areas of the United States such as the Bronx occupy ambivalent places in the U.S. national imaginary. This racialized ambivalence is clear upon an examination of the relationship between the New York Yankees and the black and brown people who inhabit the neighborhood that surrounds the team's famous stadium.

The Bombers and the Barrio

The outrage directed at the Paulino All Stars before and after the Almonte scandal broke was fueled in part by the fact that the team was from the Bronx, New York, a longtime symbol of urban poverty and violence. Much of the Bronx's baseball history is shaped by the borough's fraught relationship with the Yankees, the most successful franchise in U.S. professional baseball history. While deeply rooted in the borough's history (the Yankees have played their home games in the Bronx since 1923), the team has and continues to be an expression of the white ethnic nostalgia for the Bronx of yesteryear. The Yankees are the borough's last connection to the pre-white-flight Bronx, to the era when the Jews and the Irish lived on the Grand Concourse, the borough's famous boulevard that was modeled on Paris's Champs-Élysées, and when ballplayers and celebrities stayed at the Concourse Hotel a few blocks away.

White ethnic nostalgic narratives usually center on the 1940s, '50s, and early '60s, the years when the Yankees routinely appeared in the World Series, led by popular stars Joe DiMaggio, Yogi Berra, Whitey Ford, and Mickey Mantle. Baseball documentaries routinely wax poetic about DiMaggio and Mantle smacking line drives and home runs at "The Stadium." "Yankee Stadium was the only thing we had in the Bronx," recalled actress, director, and Bronx native Penny Marshall in her recent reflections on the closing of Yankee Stadium. Marshall's reminiscences were part of a series of recollections by celebrities published by the *New York Times* on the day of Yankee Stadium's last game (21 September 2008). The series, titled "Echoes in the Bronx," exhibited much of the white ethnic nostalgia narratives that dominate Yankee history. To many, especially to those who left the borough for the suburbs, the Bronx and its baseball cathedral operate as projection screens for an imagined past of simplicity and innocence before the influx of Latina/os and African Americans into the borough during the 1970s. The era of white ethnic innocence was supplanted by the urban decay and violence symbolized by the Hollywood film *Fort Apache, the Bronx* and by television sportscaster Howard Cosell's famous declaration "the Bronx is burning" during a telecast of the 1977 World Series.[3]

Such narratives gloss over the Yankees organization's long history of racial exclusion, not just against African American players but also Latinos. This period so fondly recalled in these narratives is marked by the particular absence of black and Latino players in the Yankees lineup. After Jackie Robinson officially broke baseball's color line in 1947 with the Brooklyn Dodgers, the Yankees were slow to integrate ballplayers of color. And once they did begin to appear, Latino and African American Yankees have either been completely excluded from histories of the Bronx Bombers or have been relegated to the background while its white stars have received more attention from team historians. A few prominent examples are Victor Pellot (Vic Power), the Puerto Rican first baseman who languished in the team's minor league system in the 1950s because he was black; Ed Figueroa, the Puerto Rican pitcher whose contributions to the Yankees championship teams of the late 1970s have been utterly overlooked; and Reggie Jackson, the team's first megastar of color, whose achievements have tended to be minimized by team historians.[4] It was not until the emergence of Bernabe "Bernie" Williams in the 1990s that the Bronx Bombers faithful fully embraced a Puerto Rican or Latino star. Subsequent years have seen the Yankees seeking to promote Latino culture to its fan base, even though few Latina/os inside and outside the Bronx are able to afford tickets to a game. In recent years, the team launched Latino food concession stands at the stadium sponsored by Goya Foods. Fans could munch on delicacies such as *alcapurrias*, empanadas, and rice and beans while watching Alex Rodríguez, their current Latino star, hit home runs. In September 2008, the Yankees honored Emilio Navarro, the centenarian who was the first Puerto Rican to play in the Negro leagues. With the emergence of Williams, Mariano Rivera, Jorge Posada, and Rodriguez, the Yankees at last featured Latino ballplayers.[5]

If the Yankees have only recently marketed their Latino stars, the team in concert with city politicians has continued to act in ways that disregard the vast majority of Latina/os who live in the shadow of their stadium. Beginning in the 1960s, the Bronx's racial demographics changed dramatically. The borough's African American and Latina/o population rose as the borough's white population declined. In 1960, 350,781 African Americans and Latina/os lived in the Bronx, constituting 24.6 percent of the total Bronx population. By 1980, the Bronx was predominantly black and Latina/o. African Americans and Latina/os grew to 745,099, or 63.7 percent the borough's population. Since the 1980s, the Latina/o population has varied as it came to include new immigrants, especially Dominicans.

The Bronx's changing demographics were at the heart of the city's effort to renovate Yankee Stadium in the early 1970s. New York City mayor John Lindsay successfully campaigned to renovate the stadium amid fears that the surrounding neighborhood was in decline. A project that was supposed to cost the city twenty-four million dollars ballooned to one hundred million dollars by the time the stadium reopened in April 1976.[6] As many critics at the time pointed out, the renovation project made little sense in a period when the city was undergoing the worst fiscal crisis in its history. Two decades later, the Yankees initiated calls for another new stadium, arguing that the then thirty-year-old facility did not allow them to compete in the baseball market, even though the team was generating unprecedented levels of revenue. In 2006, the city agreed to allow the team to build a new Yankee Stadium on the site of Macombs Dam Park (across the street from the old stadium), creatively financed by the Yankees through tax-free bonds and city funds that would pay for new parkland, new parking facilities, and the demolition of the old stadium. The decision generated protest from local residents who abhorred the thought of the team taking away one of the few parks that existed in the neighborhood. Their efforts were in vain as the team, with the support of the city government, constructed their new ballpark, which opened in April 2009.[7] It was into this history of peripheralization that the Rolando Paulino All Stars stepped during the summer of 2001. Their emergence threatened to disrupt the historical narrative of the Bronx as the space of white ethnic nostalgia layered on top of a more recent history of black and brown urban poverty. It was this prospect of disruption that partially fueled the public fascination with the Paulino All Stars and the frantic efforts to document Danny Almonte's age.

Searching for the Real Almonte

Investigative searches to establish Danny Almonte's "official" age retraced the transnational paths that tens of thousands of Dominicans and Puerto Ricans travel annually. A team from Staten Island, New York, launched the first investigation after having lost to the Paulino All Stars in a regional Little League tournament. Parents of Staten Island players spent ten thousand dollars on a private investigation to verify the age of Almonte and his teammates.[8] The private investigators hired by the Staten Island club searched official state documents (visas, birth certificates, etc.) in New York and in the Dominican Republic for proof that the Bronx team included cheaters. Although unsuccessful, the costly investigation effectively cast a cloud of suspicion over the Paulino All Stars as the team headed to Williamsport, Pennsylvania, for the Little League World Series. Rumors persisted throughout the championship tournament that Almonte and several teammates were much older than they claimed and that perhaps their supporting documents were forged. Thus, in addition to gaining vocal supporters because of the story line of underprivileged Bronx kids making it to the Little League World Series, the Paulino All Stars also developed an ardent group of dissenters who were convinced that the success of the team of brown-faced kids must be due to their cheating.

Continued suspicions prompted *Sports Illustrated* to launch its own independent investigation. "Tipped off" by a "concerned" fan, the sporting publication sent one of its sportswriters to the Dominican Republic in late

August to examine official records in local and national archival holdings. Traveling to Moca, the town where Almonte was actually born, the journalist discovered a dual set of birth certificates.[9] Each certificate listed a different birth date: one April 7, 1987, the other April 9, 1989. The multiple birth certificates uncovered, the Almonte matter was referred to the Dominican Electoral Committee, the national agency charged with maintaining most of the country's official records. On August 31 the Committee announced its official proclamation: the birth certificate with the 1987 date was official.[10] It was later found that Almonte's father had falsified his son's age in order for him to participate in the Little League competition, an act that opened up the team and the Almonte family to widespread ridicule.

The hiring of private investigators and money spent in investigating the cheating allegations is evidence of the broader stakes involved past just winning and losing. Money was at stake. While Little League baseball is primarily a middle-class pursuit, played on finely manicured fields in the suburbs, Little League Incorporated has undertaken special programs to help revive baseball in inner cities, which have been plagued by soaring insurance costs and often a lack of suitable playing fields. Suburban parents of Little Leaguers are much better positioned to invest thousands of dollars to purchase the finest equipment and to send their children to baseball camps for training. This investment in their children's athletics is envisioned as a way to facilitate success on the playing field and perhaps garner a collegiate college scholarship (or at worst a more well-rounded college application). Given what we refer to as the investment model of athletic success, expectations of performance are raised in relation to the amount of money spent on training, facilities, and equipment. Simply stated, if their children are attending the best baseball camps run by professional or collegiate coaches and are outfitted with the best equipment, then the expectation is that they should win. According to this logic, well-trained and well-equipped teams should not suffer defeat at the hands of inner-city teams comprising Dominican and Puerto Rican boys from working-class and impoverished backgrounds. This was what was partly at stake in the matchups between the Paulino All Stars and suburban teams—the ability of social class privilege to translate into competitive advantage and success.

Economic class not only affects the pursuit of athletic competition but also the perception of who can succeed. For some, success on the playing field is directly related to the amount of money invested into training and equipment (and not just athletic ability). Yet, as the controversy surrounding the Paulino All Stars reveals, success is also viewed through a highly racialized discourse of legality. This discourse has even infiltrated the playing field, resulting in an uneven suspicion of who is viewed as legitimately participating and what is the root cause of those who are successful. This was clearly at play as the Paulino All Stars plowed through their competition. With every win leading up to their showdown with Apopka, speculation grew: they must be cheating. Questions about Danny Almonte's age led to a maelstrom that made everyone on the team suspect: Are they overage? Are they legal? What about their parents? The questions turned to more pointed demands and queries: Show us your papers. Have these papers been falsified?

The 2001 LLWS controversy poignantly captures the unevenness of such speculation. Little League director of media relations Lance Van Auken's observation in August 2001 illustrated how not everyone was equally suspect. "There have been better pitchers here," Van Auken observed. "The difference is [that] most of them have been white. In some of the e-mails I get, the racism is thinly veiled: in others it's overt." A *Sports Illustrated* writer noted that e-mails to Van Auken revealed another layer of suspicion: "Most of [them] complained that [Paulino's team] should be playing for the Dominican Republic, where three of the 12 Paulino All-Stars were born."[11] Envy and racism drove suspicions about his team's success, according to Rolando Paulino. "Every time a Hispanic team, even though the majority of [the players] were born here, triumphs, people look for whatever way to take away what they've done," Paulino observed. "Most of those people are bad losers, poor sports. No other team, not even those from abroad, has been scrutinized like us. . . . With all the money people spend investigating us, they could have started a new league or helped the kids."[12]

Reactions to the performance of the Paulino All Stars on the field and of their supporters in the stands reiterated the politics of race and place and the social policing of U.S. national identity. The public inquisition into the background of the Paulino All Stars eventually produced falsified documents. The *Sports Illustrated* investigation and the Dominican government's finding concerning Danny Almonte's authentic birth certificate gave a sense of vindication to the Staten Island team and others who insisted the Bronx team cheated. The quest to prove their suspicion correct exposed a powerful class divide, one that represented the gulf between those who play on the (ever-vanishing) urban baseball diamonds and those who enjoy finely manicured suburban ballparks. Class-inflected difference not only shaped suspicion of the Paulino All Stars, but class also made it possible for the Staten Island team to pursue an investigation. Given the financial crisis faced by many urban Little League organizations, one can scarcely imagine league supporters spending ten thousand dollars on private investigators to check the eligibility of opposing players.

The 2001 Almonte scandal, moreover, captured tensions regarding not only the changing face of the sport long heralded as the U.S. national pastime but also the boundaries of national inclusion. The emergence of the controversy captures continuing questions about national belonging: Who is an American? Who is a legal/legitimate participant in U.S. society? Can Latinos fully become American in a U.S. national sense? The campaign to catch the suspected cheaters illuminates everyday acts of social policing within the U.S. body politic and, in particular, how individuals imbue themselves with the authority to question who belongs or who is legal. For parents of the kids on the Bronx team, the experience of living under suspicions, whether warranted or not, was all too familiar. They did not sit idly by during the games at Williamsport while others positioned them outside the nation. They too performed nation, waving American flags and asserting membership in the U.S. body politic. The fact that these issues emerged in baseball—a pastime shared between the United States, Puerto Rico, and the Dominican Republic—underscores the perceived stakes. After all, the Little League World Series was supposed to be little boys playing baseball, not a case of international intrigue. Falsifying documents, "age tampering," and other presumed illegalities on the part of the Bronx parents and the team's organizers are the stuff of professional baseball, where again Dominicans and other Latinos are viewed with suspicion as their presence in the major leagues continues to grow.

Latinos and the Transnational Economy of Baseball

The increased presence of Latinos throughout U.S. professional baseball no doubt buoys the big league dreams of Latino Little Leaguers. The ascendance of stars such as Pedro Martínez, Alex Rodríguez, and Albert Pujols along with the rags-to-riches stories of Sammy Sosa and Miguel Tejada have captivated the baseball world the last several decades. Their big league success is both inspiration and explanation for what Dominicans invest in their sons, knowing that even minor league contracts can provide greater social mobility than occasional wage employment in the Dominican Republic ever could.

The Almonte case and the big league aspirations of island-born Dominicans are by-products of the same global capital system that has reshaped relationships between Major League Baseball and Latin American countries. This reconfiguration has resulted in the Dominican Republic becoming the

highest per capita producer of major leaguers in the world. The incorporation of Dominican talent does not escape the economic realities of late capitalism. Dominicans are scouted as preteens and teenagers, and those deemed
prospects are then eligible to be signed at sixteen years old by major league
rules. Along with other Latin Americans—except for Puerto Ricans, who are
U.S. citizens—they enter organized baseball as amateur free agents, a status
that typically results in their receiving lower signing bonuses than what those
eligible for the amateur draft garner.[13]

Organized baseball's interest in scouting and acquiring talent in Latin
America was not motivated simply by the goal of locating the best prospects or an altruistic desire to provide individuals a chance to break into the
majors—two notions that permeate popular justifications for the difference
in signing bonuses paid and that fuel perceptions of foreign-born Latinos
as ungrateful when they seek better compensation. Much of this interest in
Latin America has been driven by what baseball executive Dick Balderson
labeled "a boatload mentality" popular among organizational developmental
personnel; baseball scholars such as Samuel Regalado refer to this mentality
as a desire to sign "Latin players on the cheap."[14]

The inequity created by the process of initial inclusion unveils an economic toll that foreign-born Latinos pay for their foreignness. First insti-
tuted in 1965, baseball's amateur draft was envisioned as a way to boost
competitive balance by distributing the sport's best amateur prospects in a
systematic fashion—organizations drafted in reverse order of the previous
season's win-loss records. The major leagues precluded foreign-born Latinos from participation in its amateur draft. Even Puerto Ricans were not
allowed to participate until 1989, the only group of U.S. citizens so excluded.
Conversely, all foreign-born Latinos were eligible to be signed as free agents
upon turning sixteen years old. Responding to protests about abuses, Major
League Baseball clarified its policy in 1984, raising the age to seventeen but
allowing organizations to sign a player who is sixteen if he turns seventeen
before the end of the relevant season or September 1, whichever is later.[15]
The signing bonuses paid to players selected through the amateur draft and
Latinos signed as undrafted amateur free agents are telling. In 1975, major
league organizations gave U.S.-born players chosen in the amateur draft an
average signing bonus of sixty thousand dollars, whereas signing bonuses for
foreign-born Latinos acquired as undrafted free agents averaged five thousand dollars.[16] The case of Dominican American superstar Alex Rodríguez
powerfully speaks to the continued disparity in signing bonuses. The first
pick of the 1993 amateur draft, the Seattle Mariners paid an eighteen-year-

old Rodríguez a $1.3 million signing bonus. Rodríguez recognized that this bonus far exceeded what he would have received as an undrafted free agent from the Dominican Republic. "I'm really grateful I was born and raised in the U.S. . . . . I'm sure I would have been a top prospect [in the Dominican Republic] but maybe I would have gotten $5,000 or $10,000. . . . The point is, it would have been a much tougher road."[17]

The privileging of U.S. citizenship within this system illustrates how racialization can transpire even within a process of inclusion. That racialization can accompany inclusion was evident in discussions about whether the "browning" of baseball would negatively affect the gate after Latinos became Major League Baseball's majority minority in 1997.[18] Political pundits, scholars, and everyday people have likewise speculated on the impact of Latina/os on social relations, racial dynamics, American (U.S.) culture, and the U.S. economy once Latina/os were declared the nation's new majority minority. In both contexts, discussions intimate a level of unease with the increased, and seemingly permanent, presence of Latinos in baseball and in wider U.S. society.

In organized baseball, Latino participation has continued to spiral upward in spite of tightened U.S. immigration procedures following September 11, 2001, and the quota the Immigration and Naturalization Service (now the U.S. Citizenship and Immigration Services, USCIS) set on the number of H2B visas assigned to each Major League organization from 1974 through 2006.[19] Herein lies a connection between the professional baseball world and the 2001 Almonte scandal. Ever since September 11, the closer scrutiny of all visa applications and supporting documents by the USCIS and Homeland Security officials reveals that Danny Almonte's family was not alone in engaging in manipulating their papers in order to secure a better chance at gaining entry into the United States.

The Age Game in the Post-9/11 Climate

Major league organizations have become even more aggressive in scouting the Dominican Republic. This further involvement remains rooted in the maintenance of a different pathway for the acquisition of amateur players from Latin America. Discussions of a worldwide amateur draft as part of a new collective bargaining agreement between major league owners and the MLB Players Association have stalled due in part to the equal footing on which this system would put all amateur players, regardless of national origins. A worldwide amateur draft would end major league organizations access to Latin America as an unfettered market, and likewise eliminate the economic advantage that U.S. and Canadian citizens receive at the initial point of entry into organized baseball. In contrast to major league organizations' preference for young, foreign-born Latino prospects, the trend in its amateur draft has been to select college-experienced, U.S.-born players. In the short span from 2000 to 2004, the percentage of drafted players who signed with major league clubs with college or junior college experience increased from 71.6 to 81.7 percent. In short, as baseball scholars Arturo Marcano and David Fidler note, drafted players are "older, more mature, and better educated than draftees in the early years of the draft."[20]

The continued preference for younger Latino prospects has motivated late bloomers to manipulate their age by signing contracts under a relative's name, falsifying a birth certificate, or entering into an agreement with an organization's scout to list a younger age in exchange for a cut of the (larger) signing bonus. Javier Rodriguez, a scout for agent Joe Cubas, summed up what inspired participating in the "age game": "An 18-year-old player in the Dominican is not worth anything . . . If you have a lot of ability and you were worth $100,000 or $200,000, at 18 they'd give you $3,000. A year can go by in a flash, and [then] you're worth nothing."[21] This drives individuals to subtract anywhere from a few months to five or more years from a player's actual age, a practice that further fuels the perception of Dominicans specifically and Latinos in general as suspect participants in U.S. professional baseball.

The international and political ramifications of Major League Baseball's lax enforcement of its rules came to the fore after the September 11 terrorist attacks. Thereafter, U.S. federal authorities required all major league organizations applying for work visas to provide authentic documentation of their applicants' ages. Scrutiny of visa applications most immediately affected players from the Dominican Republic and Venezuela, the two largest groups of non-U.S. citizens in organized baseball. Those who had provided false information met swift repercussions. The Texas Rangers immediately released second baseman Marcus Agramonte after learning that their "young" nineteen-year-old Dominican prospect was in actuality twenty-five years old. Miguel Richardson met a similar fate when the Seattle Mariners discovered that the supposedly twenty-two-year-old Dominican was six years older. Investigations into the ages of foreign-born players found that 126 players had initially given erroneous information about their age. But contrary to claims by major league organizations about being the unwitting victims of underage prospects who understated their age, over 95 percent of the 126 players turned out to be older, not younger, than what they had originally claimed.[22]

Organized baseball's increasingly global reach and the continuation of a visa system for all foreign-born minor leaguers (who until 2006 were classified as H2B) have exacerbated the pressure for Dominican ballplayers to succeed. Nonetheless, while scrutiny of visa applications has brought much attention to actions of individual actors who manipulate their age for a chance to achieve their American dream, much less focus has been placed on the economic relationship forged between the United States and the Dominican Republic over the last several decades, and how it has become manifest in the professional baseball world. The Dominican Republic has become increasingly dependent on remittances from Dominicans working in the States, including hundreds of Dominicans playing at all levels of professional baseball. Organized baseball has likewise become increasingly dependent on young Dominican players as a cost-effective strategy in talent procurement in the era of multimillion-dollar contracts for established players. Interestingly, the quotas in place until 2006 set an artificial limit on the number of foreign-born Latinos in the minors. Major league organizations responded to this limitation in two ways. Most organizations have invested resources in the Dominican Republic, establishing training complexes that operate as baseball academies. The sixteen-year-old prospects hosted at these facilities not only receive baseball training but are provided room and board along with nutrition counseling and English-language instruction. In addition, major league teams have created a Dominican Summer League, an extension of its minor league system. The young Dominicans, along with Venezuelan prospects in these newly created (or updated) facilities, literally compete for a chance to play in the United States.

A number of recent controversies reveal that the "age game" is not strictly the domain of Dominican prospects and their interested supporters. In March 2009, the Washington Nationals learned that their "prized" Dominican prospect Esmailyn "Smiley" González was actually Carlos Alvarez and five years older than claimed at the 2007 signing when he received a $1.3 million bonus. The Nationals general manager Jim Bowden resigned under a cloud of suspicion, since the team had earlier fired José Rijo, a special assistant in the Dominican Republic and former major leaguer.[23] Washington's troubles came on the heels of other major league officials working in the Dominican Republic coming under scrutiny from U.S. federal law enforcement officials for their possible participation in bonus skimming—team officials overinflating a prospect's value to take a sizable chunk of the bonus for themselves as unreported income. The previous three years the Boston Red Sox, Chicago White Sox, and New York Yankees had all fired team personnel involved in the Dominican Republic. Importantly, the firings and resignations unveil a wider cast of actors involved in the "age game," and that it is not just impoverished barrio residents angling for a bigger payoff.

The ramifications of tightened national security, heightened concern about immigration, and the increased presence of Latinos have been played out across the United States in professional baseball circles. In this very public arena, Americans have become intimately familiar with the changing face of America's game arising from the increased presence of Latinos. For many popular observers, the rapid increase in Latino participation is testament to the ability of U.S. institutions to absorb new people and to see beyond race. Others, however, are perturbed by the Latino influx. Fearing the loss of the national game (read nation) to outsiders, they engage in a vigilant watch that extends from the professional baseball diamonds to the Little League fields and the streets of "El Bronx," which can render the very presence of poor and working-class Latinos as suspicious or intrusive.

The Bronx Bombers Strike Again

A parallel with the U.S. government's intensified (official) policing of black and brown ballplayers from Latin America and the Caribbean since September 11 can be seen in the process by which corporations and local politicians have erected racialized borders between the rich and poor in cities across the country. Indeed, the treatment of African American and Latina/o residents of the Bronx serves as a microcosm for what's happening on the national stage when it comes to the active redefining of who belongs within the national body politic. This was vividly enacted in the construction of the new Yankee Stadium in the Bronx, which exemplifies the processes of race- and class-inflected gentrification that has come to mark the lives of Latina/os in countless urban neighborhoods where corporate interests and political officials collaborated in sparking their renewal.

On August 16, 2006, state and local officials, including then governor George Pataki, Mayor Michael Bloomberg, and Bronx borough president Adolfo Carrion; and representatives of the New York Yankees, including owner George Steinbrenner, team president Randy Levine, legend Yogi Berra, and celebrity fan Billy Crystal, participated in the groundbreaking ceremony for the new Yankee Stadium in Macombs Dam Park. The ceremony took place within shouting distance of a demonstration organized by a local group called Save Our Parks, warded off by police barricades to take them as far away from the proceedings as possible. Mayor Bloomberg dismissed critics who highlighted the $450 million of public funds that contributed to a stadium project that was supposedly privately financed by the Yankees. Meanwhile, Steinbrenner communicated his satisfaction to spectators by saying that he was "happy that we're able to do this for the Yankees and happy to do it for you people."[24] Steinbrenner's reference to "you people" could have been an inadvertent admission of the team's attitude toward the local community.

Since the groundbreaking ceremony the team has attempted to stave off criticism by going out of its way to emphasize its imagined connections to the surrounding neighborhood. On 8 November 2008, the team assembled a group of local black and brown "youths" and former Yankee players to bring home plate and infield dirt from the old to the new stadium. But as the team trots out nameless "youths" for good public relations, their usurping of the neighborhood's only major parkland took away a significant part of the precious few recreational spaces that existed for these youth, a park that had included a number of baseball diamonds. While the new stadium project originally included the construction of new parks on top of the new parking garages the city plans to construct for the Yankees, officials predictably reported that increased stadium-related expenses will force the city to postpone the building of the parks until 2011. Thus, as Major League Baseball continues its effort to promote baseball among kids in the "inner city," the construction of the new Yankee Stadium actually takes away recreational spaces where young people have played baseball in the very neighborhood of the sport's most celebrated franchise.[25]

The bitter history of exclusion that marks the team's history with the surrounding community has not prevented some residents from being spectators at Yankee games. An article in the New York Times from 18 July 2008 highlighted the ways residents in the buildings of Gerard Avenue, one block away from the stadium, have experienced Yankee games from their windows and rooftops. The buildings are perched on a hill that is raised high enough for residents to see parts of the field over the outfield wall that separates the stadium from River Avenue. Some could see parts of the field from their rooftops, while others saw from their windows the narrow slats of the famous frieze at the top of the outfield wall. The attempts at spectatorship by residents on Gerard Avenue serve as a metaphor for the dynamics of racial and class exclusion that define the team's relationship with the larger neighborhood. Residents were close enough to get fleeting glimpses of the action on the diamond through their obstructed views, but few could scarcely afford to actually attend a game at the old stadium (much less the new one). Families who live in the stadium's congressional district have a median household income of $21,088, with 40 percent of the residents living below the poverty line. Guiomar Camano, a twelve-year-old boy who lived with his family at 845 Gerard Avenue, informed the *Times* that he had never seen a game at the nearby stadium.[26]

The construction of the new stadium ended the limited sight lines that nearby residents had of Yankee games and took away the neighborhood's major parkland, leaving local boys and girls to enact their own baseball fantasies playing catch in the lobbies of the buildings on Gerard Avenue, a practice that will no doubt increase with the absence of nearby Macombs Dam Park. Such is life in el Barrio del Bronx and such are the cruel ironies embedded in the relationship between the Yankees and the neighborhood where the team plays its games. The Bronx hosts a sparkling new stadium with all the amenities built into its design for middle- and upper-class fans to enjoy. Yet few of the nearby residents can afford to enter its portals and witness the exploits of the increasing numbers of Latinos who now star in the game. Such is the often fraught relationship between Latinos and those who vigilantly stand guard over the next generation of performers in U.S. professional baseball, that when aspiring boys from the Bronx like those on the Rolando Paulino All Stars outperform teams produced from the well-manicured suburban parks, they are rendered suspect and told to resign themselves to living in their usual places.

NOTES

1. *New York Times* (hereafter *NYT*), 31 October 2001.

2. See Burgos, *Playing America's Game: Baseball, Latinos, and the Color Line* (Berkeley and Los Angeles: University of California Press, 2007).

3. Cosell made his famous remarks during the second game of the World Series as television cameras showed a building on fire in another part of the borough. "The Bronx is burning" came to symbolize the borough's history during the 1970s when a wave of arson fires burned down much of the South Bronx. Jill Jonnes, *South Bronx Rising: The Rise, Fall, and Resurrection of an American City* (New York: Fordham University Press, 2002), 231–345; and Jonathan Mahler, *Ladies and Gentlemen, the Bronx Is Burning: Baseball, Politics, and the Battle for the Soul of the City* (New York: Farrar, Straus and Giroux, 2005).

4. On the Yankees' refusal to bring Power up to the major leagues, see Burgos, *Playing America's Game*, 204–7.

5. On the Yankees' tribute to Navarro, see *NYT*, 18 September 2008.

6. On the politics of the renovation of Yankee Stadium, see Neil J. Sullivan, *The Diamond in the Bronx: Yankee Stadium and the Politics of New York* (Oxford: Oxford University Press, 2001), 97–162; and Jonnes, *South Bronx Rising*, 286–7.

7. *NYT*, 6 April 2006; and 17 August 2006.

8. Other reports noted that the Pequannock, New Jersey, Little League team had also hired a private investigator to check into the age eligibility of Almonte and his teammates. Ian Thomson and Luis Fernando Llosa, "One for the Ages." *Sports Illustrated*, 27 August 2001, http://sportsillustrated.cnn.com/features/cover/news/2001/08/27/llwseries/. Accessed 1 October 2001.

9. Associated Press, "Little League Investigating: SI Uncovers Document That Disputes Almonte's Age." *Sports Illustrated*, August 28, 2001, http://sportsillustrated.cnn.com/features/cover/news/2001/08/28/llwseries/. Accessed 1 October 2001.

10. "He's 14: Almonte's Team Forfeits LLWS Victories." *Sports Illustrated*, 1 September 2001, http://sportsillustrated.cnn.com/features/cover/news/2001/09/01/llwseries/. Accessed 1 October 2001.

11. Thomson and Llosa, "One for the Ages."

12. Ibid. Paulino was not entirely innocent in making these charges, having already been banned from coaching Little League baseball in the Dominican Republic for using ineligible players.

13. The legal and financial significance between inclusion in the amateur draft or signing as undrafted free agents is palpable. Players chosen in the amateur draft are fully protected under the formalized guidelines of the major league rules, can have legal representation, and can seek legal relief to become a free agent if an organization fails to abide by the rules.

14. Regalado, "Latin Players on the Cheap: Professional Baseball Recruitment in Latin America and the Neocolonialist Tradition," *Indiana Journal of Global Legal Studies* 8(1): 9–20.

15. Michael Oleksak and Mary Adams Oleksak, *Beisbol: Latin Americans and the Grand Old Game* (Grand Rapids, MI: Masters Press, 1996), 142; Arturo Marcano and David Fidler, *Stealing Lives: The Globalization of Baseball and the Tragic Story of Alexis Quiroz* (Bloomington: Indiana University Press, 2002), 32.

16. Regalado, "Latin Players on the Cheap."

17. Elliott Almond and Lupe Gervas, "A Cultural Curveball." *San Jose Mercury News* and *Nuevo Mundo,* 23 July 2003; and Marcos Bretón, *Away Games: The Life and Times of a Latin Baseball Player* (New York: Simon and Schuster, 1999), 39.

18. Their respective participation rates have continued to widen. By the 2009 season, U.S. and foreign-born Latinos accounted for 47 percent of all players within organized baseball and filled over a quarter of all Major League roster spots, while African Americans represented approximately 9 percent. Ozzie González, "Latinos in the Major Leagues: The 1999 Breakdown." Latino Legends in Sports, April 1999, http://www.latinosportslegends.com/LatinsinMLB.htm. Accessed 22 May 2004.

19. Dan Klores, "Viva Baseball," aired 23 September 2005, Spike TV; and Major League Baseball press release, "29.2 Percent of Major League Baseball Players Born Outside the U.S.," posted 7 April 2005, http://mlb.mlb.com/news/press_releases/press_release. jsp?ymd=20050407&content_id=1003066&vkey=pr_mlb_int&fext=.jsp&c_id=mlb. Accessed 24 August 2005. On tightened immigration restrictions on quotas, see Kevin Baxter, "Teams Scramble to Secure Work Visas," *Miami Herald,* 9 October 2004. On the history of immigration restrictions in organized baseball, see Milton Jamail, *Venezuelan Bust, Baseball Boon: Andrés Reiner and Scouting on the New Frontier* (Lincoln: University of Nebraska Press, 2008), 157–60.

20. Marcano and Fidler, *Stealing Lives,* 27.

21. *Chicago Sun-Times*, 2 September 2001.

22. "Dawn of a New Age." Baseball America, 13 May 2002, http://www.baseballamerica.com/today/features/agechart.html. Accessed 13 May 2002.

23. *NYT*, 1 March 2009.

24. See Ian O'Connor's commentary on Steinbrenner's comments and the groundbreaking ceremony in *USA Today*, 16 August 2001.

25. On the team's public relations efforts, see http://newyork.yankees.mlb.com/news/press_releases/press_release.jsp?ymd=20081108&content_id=3671689&vkey=pr_nyy&fext=.jsp&c_id=nyy. Accessed 1 March 2009.

26. *NYT*, 18 July 2008.

Part II

Gender, Sexuality, and the Politics of Memory and Representation

5

Gay Latino Histories/
Dying to Be Remembered

AIDS Obituaries, Public Memory, and
the Queer Latino Archive

HORACIO N. ROQUE RAMÍREZ

In early 1991, in the months prior to beginning to stop repressing my gay sexuality, I remember browsing surreptitiously the free gay weekly magazines my then roommate René brought into our shared apartment in West Los Angeles. Because he himself had only recently acknowledged his gay sexuality to me, these glossy English-language "rags" did not lie around freely and openly all over our place. I cannot recall if he actually left the door to his room open on occasion before heading out to UCLA for classes, allowing me to view the magazines lying carelessly on the floor just inside, or if I, repressed yet nervously inquisitive young homosexual that I was becoming, compromised his privacy to flip quickly through the white- and yellow-colored pages of his issues of *Frontiers Magazine*. My emotional, psychic, and erotic reactions to what I saw and read in these slick publications of gay public culture are still quite present almost two decades later. I recall distinctly the simultaneous attraction and recoil at my viewing: the fit and almost-always masculine white bodies that graced the covers; the yellow-page middle section with hundreds of masseurs, escorts, and other personal ads that often included suggestive images of crotches alongside written descriptions of dimensions, abilities, and prices; and, all over the magazine, ads about medical care, drug trials, pharmaceutical products, testing locations, and support groups related to HIV and AIDS. For me, all these new queer and medical discourses were inseparable, exciting, and anxiety-producing. To be part of such a visible gay LA culture, I was discovering still in silence and isolation, also required engaging the ever-growing discourses of HIV and AIDS, of death and desire intertwined, even in my longing for denial of either.

How do queer Latinos, both the living and the dead, enter historical consciousness in this new millennium, almost thirty years into the ongoing AIDS pandemic? What was the public record of life and death for simultaneously queer and racial/ethnic subjects like myself in the early 1990s, or other gay Latinos in the 1980s positioned in historical margins, or today amid the no-longer-seen-as-crisis age of AIDS? This chapter tackles the ongoing silences surrounding gay Latino life and history in relation to a particular form of archival evidence or trace: the record of life and death documented in AIDS obituaries, what might be called a "gay Latino album of the dead." Focusing on an existing record of AIDS-related deaths, recognized since 1981 in San Francisco's biweekly *Bay Area Reporter* (*BAR*), I consider questions of historical identification with the dead and how the historical legacy and politics of AIDS shapes gay Latino consciousness today.

By examining obituaries of Latinos in a ten-year period in the longest running gay weekly in San Francisco, I explore the possibilities for writing a history of sexual, gender, and racial intersections using such a queer archives of the dead. I discuss the relationship between public memory, archives, and queer feelings specifically within the *BAR*'s gay *Latino* album of the dead from 1984 to 1993. In addition, I address the multilayered narratives of life and death embedded in these gay Latino obituaries, portraying national, racial, gender, and erotic histories within but also beyond San Francisco's heavily Latino barrio of the Mission District. Using these unseen and underused archives as primary sources allows me to ground the history not only of queer Latino everyday *life* in the United States but also of everyday *death*. While scholars, authors, and activists queering Latin@ Studies have written about the many struggles, triumphs, and gains made on behalf of queer Latinas and Latinos, we have yet to write more critically about how patriarchal and heteronormative *latinidades*, in addition to racism, misogyny, and class oppression, figure in the lives and deaths of these queer bodies. And while el barrio has historically functioned in a presumably heteronormative frame, these hundreds of lives represented in these deaths demonstrate that it has been quite a queer barrio as well.

Archives, Feelings, and Memory

My interest in exploring the politics and practice of queer Latino archiving began through the ethnohistorical work of oral history research. As I began to record audio narratives of queer Latino and Latina community life and loss in San Francisco in the mid-1990s, I encountered material bits and pieces of individual collections of cultural, historical, and political artifacts from as far back as the 1940s. Although these represented a unique record of queer Latina life, labor, activism, and pleasure, none of these small and large personal collections had either a permanent or easily accessible home. It typically required gaining the trust of a community member before gaining access to these materials, at times eventually agreeing to keep them myself for later archiving in a permanent place.[1] My entry into the archives of the living and of the dead—specifically gay Latino albums of the dead— stems from the lack of recognition and general neglect of these histories and archives, my commitment to and encounter with these traces of queer evidence, including those of the history of AIDS in (gay) Latino communities.

To conjure the practice of queer archives opens up exciting epistemological possibilities, such as queering the Latina archive or racializing the queer archive. Also, however, queer archiving practices stir a host of theoretical debates, with empirical claims for historical knowledge production receiving postmodern critiques of the hegemonic, essentialist, and exclusionary practices in history writing, museum collections, and archival repositories. Simply put, some bodies and their representations—white, male, middle-class, heterosexual, and Anglo—have been much more present than all others in the official halls, drawers, and pages of "evidence." Yet despite these critiques of what counts as history, evidence, and archival importance, there have also been activist and academic movements for recognizing precisely the missing, neglected, and largely undocumented cultures, bodies, and histories of entire communities, usually within the same logics of historical rendition and archival practices.[2]

The queer archives of the dead, and specifically those dying from complications from AIDS since the early 1980s, suggest yet more complicated questions and logics. Given the close discursive, political, and epidemiological link between this medical condition and a stigmatized male homosexual/ gay population in the United States, to remember and to mourn the queer body today runs the risk of a historical "cleansing" whereby the gay body and its queer specificities are generalized and reduced to simply people who died from AIDS, or "AIDS victims." Writing about "queer trauma" and its manifestation in the AIDS crisis, Ann Cvetkovich alerts us to the differential mechanism through which some deaths and their memories—and the feelings associated with these—are archived more than others. "The AIDS crisis," she commented, "offered clear evidence that some deaths were more important than others and that homophobia and, significantly, racism could affect how trauma was publicly recognized."[3] Cvetkovich's work as an oral historian of lesbian activists (including herself) within ACT-UP was to dig through the individual and collective meanings they gained within a traumatic historical moment of homophobia, as well as the queer reaction and challenge against it. Her ethnohistorical project generated more mourning documents and historical sources—the oral histories and their respective transcripts, a new queer archive—to make further claims that (queer) AIDS deaths mattered then and still matter today. Memories of the dead, thus, do not carry the same valences for all the living. In the oral history interview with an aging male-to-female transgender Latina, in the one existing flyer about the Latino bar where many now-deceased gay Latino men used to congregate, and in the surviving archives of migration and family life for a Chicana lesbian no longer willing to remember—in these and similar deposits of human recollection, memory holds a distinct function for accessing life and loss.

A Gay Latino Album of the Dead: The Partial Public Memory of AIDS

You can't take from the living to give to the dead.[4]

A great deal of silence, discrimination, stigma, and uncertainty typified community and media acknowledgment about gay Latino deaths from AIDS, in English and in Spanish.[5] Often it was the tactical use of code words and phrases such as "cancer," "pneumonia," "unknown causes," or "long-term illness" that signaled yet obfuscated AIDS-related death. Grassroots nonprofit HIV agencies began to make the syndrome more visible in the mid to late 1980s and into the 1990s. Yet historical, biomedical, and demographic factors silenced and masked HIV and AIDS beginning in the mid-1990s, preventing an accurate appreciation of the ongoing seriousness of AIDS among queer, Latino, *and* queer Latino populations. Specifically, since the closing of the last century, a distinct historical and discursive roadblock emerged: because HIV treatment via protease inhibitors curtailed the rates of death from AIDS for particular demographic sectors (the middle and upper classes, typically white and male but not exclusively), HIV and AIDS were no longer seen as important political and cultural struggles. For the poor, women, and people of color—as well as the queer, whose access to health care is compromised and whose rates of death had not slowed down but actually increased in this period—the muted AIDS discourse reinscribed the silence of the 1980s. Such discriminating silences remain. David Román deems this historical moment and rhetoric the "not-about-AIDS" discourse. As he detailed, three factors facilitated this not-about-AIDS moment: the international AIDS community's declaration of the success of protease inhibitors in 1996 at the International AIDS Conference in Vancouver; the exaggerated, hopeful claims of "the end of AIDS" in mainstream national media; and so-called post-AIDS identities and cultures invoked by white gay commentators. These overly optimistic claims redirected national efforts away from HIV prevention and more toward same-sex marriage and gays in the military as the two primary struggles reflected in mainstream gay and lesbian media. Román argues that "both the 'end-of-AIDS' and the post-AIDS discourse participate in a larger social phenomenon that encourages us to believe that the immediate concerns facing contemporary American culture, including queer culture, are not-about-AIDS."[6]

From the position of an openly gay Latino professor teaching LGBT Latino community history since the mid-2000s, I would further argue that the not-about-AIDS discourse is a convenient denial mechanism for a younger queer male generation today (teens and twenty-somethings, though not restricted to them), similar to the varieties of denial among gay Latinos in the 1980s when the disease was conveniently cast as white. What is unique about denial today, I believe, is that it is also a rejection of being historically linked to an AIDS culture that intertwined queer history, desire, and death. For many queers today, the close historical link between gay male culture and HIV is tiresome, however real that conflation continues to be. Nevertheless, the ongoing not-about-AIDS moment, institutionalized or individualized, is dangerous and incorrect, especially for those of us in communities where it's quite still about HIV and AIDS. As a 2004 joint publication by AIDS Project Los Angeles and New York's Gay Men's Health Crisis pointed out, "HIV seroprevalence [was] estimated to be between 20% and 32% for some gay and bisexual men of color."[7] In 2005 in California, roughly 70 percent of adult AIDS cases involved "men who have sex with men," an undeniable link between AIDS and queer men, Latinos included.[8] With these rates of infection, queer men cannot afford the convenient luxury of entertaining a "post-AIDS" historical consciousness. Such rejections of the reality of AIDS are articulated at the expense of all the newly infected, the long-term survivors, the ongoing collective and individual efforts to remain seronegative, and the tens of thousands of dead to be remembered. For these dead, the San Francisco *BAR* is one of the existing windows through which we can peer back at those queer Latino documents of our dead.

While not-about-AIDS arguments render the ongoing AIDS and related crystal methamphetamine drug crises more invisible, they also cover up earlier histories of AIDS, especially those that are barely beginning to find documentation and analysis. These histories include the multiple gay Latino albums of the dead across the nation, some better documented than others, and some transnational. Yet there is not one single memoir of this generation to reflect on the impact of the disease.[9] Many of us know about individuals passing, including relatives and lovers, how and when they died from "a disease," typically as bits and pieces of queer Latino death shared through family memories by nephews, nieces, and others. For example, in the first queer Latino community history class many of my students take at the University California, Santa Barbara, there are always "coming out" stories about recognizing the late queer uncle. Overall, there is little historical documentation of how the disease has affected the Latino (queer) community (one of the exceptions being the ongoing "The Wall/Las Memories" nonprofit project in East Los Angeles).

The portraits that emerge from the *BAR*'s obituaries map geographies of birth, and some of the reasons for moving to San Francisco for those not native to the city. They reveal a queer migration for personal "sexile" from their places of origin, and who and what were left when death came: among family and community, in relation to both blood and queer kinships, or in relative silence with little reference to historical origins, as was the case for a great many.[10] Certainly, AIDS obituaries—and gay Latino ones in particular—are a different form of media frame, rich sources for understanding cultural, political, and social values, going beyond what we may find in more mainstream obituaries and what Janice Hume argues are the four typical framing categories used therein: "name and occupation of the diseased, cause of death, personal attributes of the diseased, and funeral arrangements."[11] The frames Hume identifies, arguably derived from the privileged histories of middle-class white bodies in death, do not function similarly for gay Latinos dying from AIDS. Socioeconomic position, (im)migrant roots, the queer gender expressions and desires of the diseased, and the stigma surrounding AIDS can each or in any intersecting combination complicate the seemingly neutral space of the obituary for the queer Latino body after death.[12]

In reviewing the publication for the ten-year period from 1984 to 1993, arguably the period of greatest loss from AIDS, there were about 350 San Francisco Bay Area obituaries of gay and bisexual Latinos, with AIDS being the most common reference as the cause of death. As I discuss below, 1984 is the first year there appears an obituary for a Latino in relation to AIDS in the *BAR*.[13] To claim "about" 350 Latino obituaries recognizes that it is not always clear whether Spanish surnames are always those of men of Latino descent. Latino identification is direct and full in most of the obituaries, such as the one for Alfredo Aguilera, who passed on 14 July 1987, which explained that "he was born in Santa Barbara, Chihuahua, Mexico, where he grew up, received his education, trained for the job which later became his career in business administration and banking."[14] Aguilera then moved to El Paso and relocated to San Francisco in 1977, part of a long-standing Chicano/Mexicano queer migration route from Texas to the gay city by the bay. In other obituaries, however, there is not enough background information to determine whether "La Marca," "Santoyo," or "Del Pozzo"—all of which *could* be Latino surnames—were actually those of Italians, Spanish, Portuguese, or other national groups.[15]

Further content analysis reveals that the overwhelming majority of obituaries making reference to a significant other or lover left behind marked same-sex (gay) relationships, but a few (including some of the former) also acknowledged a previous wife or children. Latino male bisexualities thus emerge—though weakly—in this Latino album of the dead, destabilizing the rigid either/or polarization of heterosexuality versus homosexuality. That this Latino bisexuality emerges within the stigmatized context of AIDS, however, would support the belief—with epidemiological substantiation—in the Latino community that it was bisexual men's simultaneous sexual relations with women and men (assumed not to be disclosed to either) that put unsuspecting Latinas at risk. On the question of AIDS as cause of death, more than two-thirds of the identified obituaries made direct reference to AIDS-related complications, although this should not be surprising as the *BAR* early on emerged as the city's "informal" public record of how the disease was progressing in the gay community. Thus, for someone's obituary to be included within its pages likely meant that the person responsible for penning and submitting the obituary and (usually) accompanying photo knew what this inclusion entailed. AIDS as the cause of death in a *BAR* obituary was more likely an assumed and expected rather than surprising feature for any one obituary. For many of those that did *not* overtly mention AIDS as a cause, requesting that donations be made in memory of the diseased to the Hospice AIDS Home Care or the San Francisco AIDS Foundation (SFAF) further placed AIDS centrally in the brief narrative. Finally, it is the presence of black-and-white photographs for the great majority of the obituaries that made the *BAR* a particularly useful record for marking gay Latino histories visually, of literally putting faces to the stigma, silence, and otherwise unmarked passing of such a large proportion of San Francisco's gay Latino community.

The First Public Records of the Gay Latino Dead

The very first San Francisco gay Latino AIDS death in the *BAR* seems to have appeared not in the obituaries section but in the letters section. "Whiteboy" Jim from the Mission District may have given us the first published entry into gay Latino AIDS deaths in the city's barrio. In an open letter in the *BAR*'s 9 February 1984 issue, Jim reflects "On a Friend's Death," that of his late roommate Ronaldo Cisneros, who died on 29 January 1984 at the age of twenty-eight. While the letter likely made reference to death resulting from AIDS (then still little understood), the narrative opens up a larger context for appreciating multiracial gay community life. Addressing the life he and Ronaldo shared in the Latino district and the intersecting cultural and political geographies of the Mission and the Castro for both of them, Jim writes in 1984 about Ron's illness, with no explicit name for his condition:

> I remember that day last summer when we had our very first sidewalk sale: We both had out-grown or out-used much of our clothes by then and the sale was a way to get rid of those items. Your sister Yolanda had contributed some of her outfits from by-gone days and what fun we had going through those many-paisley-ed and geometric prints that could have done Cher proud in her "hippy" era. . . . I knew you weren't feeling well so I was glad to make most of those trips up and down the stairs while you stayed below and arranged things on the tables. The sun was shining bright and those last few sun-burnt days of late summer seemed like magical times, didn't they?[16]

Jim's letter then turns to a discussion of his (white) desire to live in the Mission over Ronaldo's apprehensions, and the activist role his late Latino roommate played in "gay functions," not naming these explicitly:

> You were always so sweet to help me in bargaining with those elderly Mexican women from our neighborhood. They were tough to deal with and you knew that they were well accustomed to bargaining in those open-air markets of their homeland and that I, a "whiteboy" from Indiana, was out of my element. You had to leave that afternoon to push paper on the corner of Castro and 18th and that was fine. I knew you considered that a very important part of your life and I was always impressed that you could give so much of your time to those causes; causes which you really never got paid for, but which I knew gave you much satisfaction to be part of. . . . I

remember that you really didn't want to live in the Mission, claiming that you were trying to get "away from all that," but you ceded to my wishes, because you knew how much I loved living there. You were afraid that I might get beaten up by a gang of Latinos or something like that even though I assured you that I would be O.K. You even game me a "rape" whistle. . . . Thank you for living in the Mission with me.[17]

It is likely that this young gay Latino's death, at this historical juncture in the city, was the result of AIDS complications, suggested by his not feeling well six months earlier. Other details mark the negotiated positions Jim and Ronaldo had as roommates and the ongoing tense relations and assumptions about gay life in the city, gay safety in the barrio, and the attendant assumptions and realities of Latino youth gang violence. Despite his not feeling well, Ronaldo ventured to the gay Castro "to push paper" for "those causes." This gay activism appears almost in opposition to what Jim recalls being Ronaldo's desire to get "away from all that," in reference to the Latino district. Despite this rejection of what is presumed to be Latino culture or the Latino barrio, Ronaldo acquiesced to Jim's attraction to the Mission, for the "whiteboy's" desire for Latino culture (Latino men?), even at the implied risk (believed by Ronaldo, not Jim, according to the latter) of potential antigay violence from Latino youth gangs.[18]

As we see in the case of Jim's writing about Ronaldo's life and death, the portrait of AIDS deaths for gay Latinos in the *BAR* was often filtered or mediated by other non-Latinos, in this case a white man. Without Ronaldo's ability to narrate his own life, his relationship to the (hetero) barrio *and* the gay ghetto (the Castro, predominantly white), and his intersecting identity as a gay Latino in both, we are necessarily dependent on an outsider's memory. In Jim's recollection of Ronaldo, there is an explicit juxtaposition of the gay ghetto and the (straight) Latino barrio, suggesting the (positive) political "causes" of the former, but the presumed dangers of the latter ("all that," "a gang of Latinos," and "a 'rape' whistle"). The dangers and violence of racism and discrimination in the gay ghetto are left unsaid yet assumed.

This indirect public representation of life after death is always the case for obituaries, authored by and the results of the mourning needs of others. Still, as I argue here, AIDS obituaries in particular offer a wealth of opportunities for reading through narratives of life and death. These generally brief vignettes, between one hundred and two hundred words, are rich sources of national origins; ethnic generational roots in the United States and abroad; social and political organizing cultures; blood and queer kinships in life and death; and the ages, personalities, and wishes of the diseased. Mexico, Cuba, El Salvador, Costa Rica, Colombia, and other Latin American nations are represented. As Cary Cordova tells us in her contribution to this volume, the barrio's pan-Latino cultural and artistic expressions moved transnationally, challenging assumptions of their origin stories. There are also sizeable internal migrations joining natives in the queer mecca, from Los Angeles, Texas, New Mexico, New York, and elsewhere. The ages at the moment of death tell us also about the generational waves into the city: from pre–gay liberation moves in the 1960s; to the huge migration of the liberation-inflected 1970s; to more recent arrivals in the 1980s and 1990s, already into the AIDS epidemic. The chronological ages at the time of death range from that of World War II veteran Arthur Moreno at fifty-nine, to Colorado-native Cipriano Torres at twenty-three, with the overwhelming majority passing in their late twenties and early thirties.

In the painful context of overwhelming AIDS deaths that were the 1980s and early 1990s, obituaries served many purposes: to document, to make visible, to mourn, to remember, to celebrate, sometimes in terms of intimate, personal commitments to the loved one who passed, other times with deep political convictions to mark the gay Latino body and AIDS in a public forum. Indeed, AIDS obituaries in a gay publication like the *BAR* became an interactive medium through which living gay men struggled with larger cultures of silence and censorship against gay consciousness and visibility. In a 1991 *BAR* article titled "Obituary Cruising Rules," playful with its juxtaposition of the records of AIDS death with gay men's long-established culture of sexual cruising, the author describes his own entry into this practice of searching in the obituaries: "Rooting out closeted AIDS obituaries is a gruesome practice I fell into shortly A.D. [after diagnosis]). Angry at the enforced invisibility of HIVers, I found that 'obit outing' helped me resist my sense of isolation and reaffirm reality—that AIDS is having a major impact on our entire society that only constant, subtle censorship conceals."[19] For queer Latinos in the Bay Area in 1991, it had only been a few years since the first gay grassroots community effort—CURAS (Comunidad Unida en Respuesta al AIDS/SIDA, Community United in Response to AIDS/SIDA) and the Latino AIDS Coalition, for example—had been trying to make HIV infections and AIDS diagnoses among gay Latinos a less stigmatizing affair. It was also already several years into the epidemic when mainstream AIDS organizations such as the SFAF sought to address the culturally specific needs of "minority" gay men, such as through its Client Services, or when they were headed by gay Chicanos themselves, as was the case with the late Henry "Hank" Tavera, who did so from 1986 through 1989.[20] Still, with no

Felix Velarde-Munoz

Felix Velarde-Munoz, 33, died of AIDS-related causes Nov. 8 at Presbyterian Hospital.

Felix graduated from UC Berkeley in 1973 with a B.A. in Rhetoric and from Harvard Law School in 1977. In his most recent employment at the State Bar of California, Felix investigated malpractice charges against licensed attorneys.

Felix was a member of the Board of Directors of the Legal Aid Society of San Francisco, a member of the California State Bar Committee for Persons with Special Needs, and a Consultant for the National Endowment for the Humanities, Humanities and the Law Program.

Memorial services will be private; a gathering of friends to celebrate Felix and his life will be held Saturday, Nov. 17 at 7:30 p.m. at 1446 Waller, San Francisco. Contributions in Felix's memory should be sent to Shanti Project, 890 Hayes St., San Francisco, CA 94117.

Felix had been tenaciously fighting AIDS-related diseases for at least three years. He will be sadly missed and lovingly remembered by his family and his many friends.

5.1. Obituary for Felix Velarde-Muñoz. *Bay Area Reporter* 14, no. 46 (15 November 1984), 13.

Latino-specific record of who died from AIDS, dying gay Latinos more often made it into the white-dominated pages of the *BAR*.

Focusing now on two telling obituaries, I turn to the meanings emerging from these obituaries to illuminate gay Latino desire, community, and death. A "complete" analysis of the hundreds of obituaries identified would likely still not get us to the "entire" picture of AIDS and gay Latino community life in the region. The obituaries, of course, reflect a particular set of AIDS Latino deaths made public in one particular English-language gay publication. Further, even the seemingly more accurate—but less visible— city and county surveillance reports of AIDS covering the same period of analysis underreported the number of (gay) Latinos affected by AIDS, especially deaths within the undocumented population.[21] But the obituaries we do have access to suggest facets of these lives to account for our queer dead in the historical record. They are openings into larger histories of gay Latino culture, queer male desires, and intersecting histories of race, sexuality, and culture through regional and national gay Latino memory.

The first Latino death from AIDS complications that appeared in a *BAR* obituary was that of Felix Velarde-Muñoz, which appeared in the 15 November 1984 issue (figure 5.1). Besides his hyphenated last names in Spanish, there is no direct indication that he identified as Latino, Chicano, Hispanic, or any distinct Latino American national marker. With no reference to a surviving lover or partner, there is also no explicit suggestion of his sexuality. Besides indicating the place of his death at age thirty-three at Presbyterian Hospital, the focus of the obituary is on his professional accomplishments, which included graduating from UC Berkeley in 1973 with a BA in rhetoric, and from Harvard Law School in 1977. The obituary ends with the routine and hopeful declaration that "he will be missed and lovingly remembered by his family and his many friends," though there is no actual indication where these family and friends reside.[22] Felix's obituary appears between two other AIDS-related obituaries, which provide more detail about geographic roots and same-sex partnerships. Felix Velarde-Muñoz's name and life is thus documented as an AIDS death, yet with little biographical and historical background; no picture of him is printed either. Finally, there is no record of who penned this obituary, information that sometimes offers clues about family and community at the time of passing.

The possibilities for using the Internet as a research tool *and* an archive proved useful for pushing further back into the larger memory for and documentation of the death of Velarde-Muñoz. Despite useful cautionary arguments about the use of the Internet as an archival source, as a continuously living but also dying (silently disappearing) archive, it can still be a practical starting point for further research into the lives and deaths of others.[23] For Velarde-Muñoz, the Internet supplemented the scant information provided in his photo-less *BAR* obituary. Starting from the obituary and working my way through the labyrinthine promises of the World Wide Web led to the rich though brief life of an influential gay Chicano activist lawyer and civil rights advocate.[24] An Internet search using his hyphenated last names led to several hits listing the Felix Velarde-Muñoz (FVM) Fellowship for law school student graduates, many of them now employed throughout the country. According to Christopher Ho, a former Velarde-Muñoz Fellow and current employee at San Francisco's Legal Aid Society–Employment Law Center (LAS-ELC), the "Felix," as the fellowship was known at the LAS-ELC, was founded to honor Velarde-Muñoz at a time when "there were just a small handful of fellowships (maybe half a dozen at most) for people coming straight out of law school who wanted to go into public interest law. Without such fellowships, most students who wanted to devote themselves to social justice work would have a hard time finding jobs, which usually required several years of experience. In that context, the FVM was one of the few vehicles a recent law graduate could use to break into the public interest law field."[25] LAS-ELC's executive director (ED), Joan Graff, offered yet more background to appreciate the life marked too briefly in the *BAR* obituary. A former ED of the LAS-ELC, Felix, whom Graff remembered as "remarkable, warm, and totally dedicated to civil rights," became ill around 1981, when there was simply little-to-no information about his worsening illness or how it could be transmitted. Developing AIDS over the coming years, Felix, Graff recalled, was firm about making the decision of leaving his position as ED, concerned that his debilitating condition would prevent him from putting in all the effort necessary to keep the LAS-ELC moving forward.[26]

Benefiting from this knowledge, what can "beyond el barrio" mean for someone like Felix Velarde-Muñoz? What could this phrase have meant for him in 1969, when he left his Southern California suburban hometown of Gardena for UC Berkeley, moving yet farther from Aztlán (the Southwest) to Harvard in 1974 for his law degree, and returning to Northern California after graduation to begin his career in public interest law? How could the Chicano Movement of the late 1960s and 1970s—but also the Women's and Gay and Lesbian Movements—have affected a young (gay) Chicano like Felix, and how did he in turn influence the visions for structural change espoused in Chicano Movement rhetoric? And, most important for my discussion, how did his gay sexuality, his erotic desires, intersect in the public and professional lives he led? The professional and the grassroots converged in Velarde-Muñoz's life; his professional training became the foundation for his civil rights advocacy. But we're left with little knowledge of his gay erotic life, and only indirectly at best.[27] As we can appreciate through the Velarde-Muñoz archival dig, a seemingly empty historical obituary can be but just enough of an opening to find our way into larger histories and memories. That Velarde-Muñoz was an accomplished professional graduating from elite educational institutions and a well-known lawyer and civil rights leader made his life more archivable. For others, less institutionally and politically positioned and educated gay Latinos, obituaries do not take us much further. For other gay Latino obituary images presented in this chapter, such as those for Felipe Madrea, Jesse Anthony Maldonado, and Asel J. Sanchez and Enrique Perez (figures 5.2, 5.3, and 5.4, respectively), a similar cyber-archival hunt leads to nothing further about their lives.[28]

Unlike Felix's brief documented death, or the barely mentioned passing of those like Felipe Madrea and Jesse Anthony Maldonado, there

Felipe Madrea

Our friend and companion Felipe Madrea passed away on Nov. 2 at 4:50 p.m. at home with his family. He will be missed very much. Felipe battled with AIDS for almost one year and was very sick. He was always doing something for someone or helping someone. He was a true friend to all of us.

Felipe moved to S.F. in 1983 from Reno. That is where I met him and became good friends. Felipe was a bank teller at Continental Savings & Loan for two years.

Although Felipe is no longer with us, he will live in our hearts and minds forever. May God grant him peace.

Friendship is a priceless gift that can't be bought or sold. But its value is far greater than a mountain of gold. So when you ask God for a gift, be thankful that he sends no diamonds, pearls or riches but the love of true friendship.

Love,
The Lynn family

Jesse Anthony Maldonado

On Oct. 23, at 0030 hours, Sgt. Jesse Anthony Maldonado, 28, passed on to join other friends in a new life within the eternal light.

Bor Nov. 18, 1958, he was raised in Los Angeles. At the age of 18 he joined the U.S. Army.

During his 18 weeks of battling AIDS, Jesse won his greatest victories. Among

the physicians on staff at Letterman Army Hospital his courage, optimism and vitality amazed all. Among other patients he was caring and supportive of them, loving unconditionally.

At the time of his passing he was surrounded and cared for by his longtime friend and companion Rocco Brateman; his friend Hanalei Ofalia; parents, wife; brothers and sisters and his special family and all who were a part of 10 East Letterman Army Hospital.

Jesse was laid to rest with full military honors on Oct. 30 at Oakdale Cemetary in Glendora, CA.

He specifically requested any contributions be made in his memory to the AIDS Mastery: Northern Lights, 449 Dellbrook Ave., San Francisco, CA 94131.   ●

5.2. Obituary for Felipe Madrea. *Bay Area Reporter* 16, no. 46 (13 November 1986), 18.

5.3. Obituary for Jesse Anthony Maldonado. *Bay Area Reporter* 17, no. 46 (12 November 1987), 18.

California Mortgage Bankers Association and a member of the Press Club.

A Memorial Mass will be celebrated at 11 a.m. on Saturday, Jan. 2 at St. Dominick's Church, Bush and Steiner, S.F. In lieu of flowers, donations may be made to the Emergency Fund, AIDS Project of the East Bay, 400 40th Street, Oakland, CA 94609. ●

Asel J. Sanchez
4/20/64-12/6/87

Asel died peacefully of pneumocystis pneumonia in the arms of his lover on Dec. 6, at Davies Medical Center, after only being diagnosed on Nov. 25.

He will always be remembered as a proud, quiet, independent man, and a hard worker. He was also a very sensitive, loving, caring person. He had a quick wit and loved to have fun. He was a fighter and was determined that he was going to beat AIDS. He fought as hard as he could to live.

Asel came to San Francisco in January 1985 from Española, New Mexico. He attended the University of New Mexico, majoring in electrical engineering. He worked here in management at Wendy's on Market Street, and then joined Foodmaker's, Inc. in management.

He leaves behind his loving family, parents Theresa and Johnny; brothers Eric and Zack; grandmother Rosa; his

devoted lover and friend, Jim Hemphill; his close friend, Ken Pugh; and many other friends and relatives.

Funeral services and internment were held in Española, New Mexico on Dec. 10. Memorial services were held here at St. Francis Lutheran Church on December 11.

God bless you until we meet again. I miss you and will always love you, baby. Jim. ●

Enrique Perez

Enrique was taken from his many friends and family on Dec. 5. Burial services were held in Bakersfield, CA on Dec. 8.

He was born on Nov. 14, 1952 in Corpus Christi, TX, later moved to Bakersfield and finally to San Francisco. He is survived by his mother and three brothers. We will all miss him very much. Donations can be sent in his memory to: The Open Hand, 1668 Bush St., San Francisco, CA 94109. ●

5.4. Obituaries for Asel J. Sanchez and Enrique Perez. *Bay Area Reporter* 17, no. 53 (31 December 1987), 13.

were a few gay Latinos whose obituaries detailed leadership in the gay and AIDS education movements. One of these was for Paul Castro, who lived with and fought AIDS for twenty-seven months before passing on the 8 June 1985. Under the headline "He Put the 'People' in PWA [People with AIDS]," the twenty-paragraph report/obituary in the *BAR* written by Bill Bradley is a telling entry into racial and sexual intersections, AIDS phobia, and individual queer courage (figure 5.5). The first three of these paragraphs give a sense of how Castro was positioned racially and sexually:

> Paul was born and raised in Houston. He was a cute, little Mexican boy determined to make it in an Anglo culture. As a cheerleader at Southwest Texas State University, he was voted All Campus Favorite, a role he was to duplicate often, for Paul loved to be loved. After college, he settled in Houston and threw himself into its baroque Gay social scene. A series of trips to San Francisco in the late seventies showed him there was a world outside the Montrose. After a visit in 1981, he told himself, "Honey, if you wake up at 40 wishing you had moved to SF, you'll be sorry." So he packed his 501's and marabou pumps and jumped into the city as many had before.[29] [Castro lived to 31 years of age.]

The rest of the article highlights Paul's charismatic spirit, and how his life changed after February 1983 when he was diagnosed with Kaposi's sarcoma, the dark purple skin lesions that typically marked and visibly stigmatized a person with AIDS into the early 1990s. In an incident that became national news because of its AIDS phobia, the article explained, technicians from the ABC network's San Francisco affiliate KGO-TV refused to place a microphone on his body; this discriminatory incident prompted Castro to dedicate his life to AIDS education. He became active in the SFAF as a volunteer and board member, showing up at a board reception in a showgirl outfit, sequins, feathers, and pumps. At San Francisco General Hospital's AIDS Ward 86, he "lit up everybody's day with a smile, a joke or a rude comment." The article highlights Castro's love for his family, his last trip home to Houston for Christmas in 1984, and the fact that his mother, Faye Castro, flew to be at his bedside in San Francisco for two months until his death. In a *BAR* article Castro himself authored seven months before his death titled "Coming Out as a Person with AIDS," he explained the difficulty of addressing both his gay sexuality and the diagnosis at the same time to his parents:

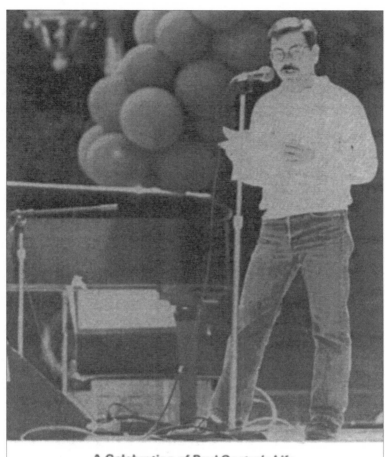

A Celebration of Paul Castro's Life
Monday June 17, 1985
7 - 9 P.M.
Valencia Rose
Showgirls, Cheerleaders and Sweaty Softball Players encouraged

5.5. Section from article on Paul Castro's life and death. *Bay Area Reporter* 15, no. 24 (13 June 1985), 3.

Telling my parents I had AIDS was particularly hard. I was close to Mom and Dad but, I had never come out to them as a Gay man. Did I tell them I had AIDS or that I was Gay or both at the same time? To top it off, at the same time I was diagnosed, no one with AIDS had experienced a way to do it, so this one was up to me. . . . With frequent communication, support from Parents and Friends of Gays, and time, we've been able to deal with my diagnosis and my homosexuality.[30]

Much can be said about both the long obituary for Castro and his own writing before his death. We know he was a popular figure in college, already transgressing gender to some degree by becoming a male cheerleader and joining Houston's gay social scene. Knowing more about the racial and class composition of Southwest Texas State University around 1970–1972 would help us consider what it would mean for someone like Castro to play such a visible sport-related, though queered, role in his school. Knowing more about the "Baroque" public gay scene in Houston could also tell us something about the intersecting racial, class, and sexual grounds he navigated, and which he eventually left for the lure of San Francisco.

The reference to Castro as "a cute, little Mexican boy determined to make it in an Anglo culture" *could* be part endearment, perhaps a "playful" cross-racial understanding Paul had with what seems to be a majority of white gay men in his close social circles. Regardless, as the phrase stands penned by what is likely a white author (based on his name), it comes off as a racist, paternalistic, and exoticizing framing of the Latino body—"cute, little Mexican boy" related to the "houseboy" discourse in dominant white gay culture, especially in the personal sexual want ads, a relic from the 1970s and alive and well today. These constructions of minority sexual and ethnic bodies were not necessarily only one-way, white-onto-other constructions; Asian, Latino, and African American men also participated actively, although from a numerically and economically inferior position, in their responses to and needs for white gay men and one another. My point here is that obituary pieces like the one for Castro are useful for what they tell us not only about AIDS, but also about the racial and sexual cultural compositions and expectations in the region at least since the 1970s.

It is probably not a coincidence that the obituary for Castro is not brief and picture-less (like Felix's), but rather a full-length article, with a picture of Castro making a speech on a stage; he was someone who in the new politics of death from AIDS remained tied to Anglo culture, determined "to make it," but also not entirely divorced from his Mexican family roots in Houston. Ending the obituary with the invitation of "Showgirls, Cheerleaders and Sweaty Softball Players" to the celebration of Castro's life reminds us that this is a queer context after all—that even in death, gender-bending gay culture was alive and well with camp as a rhetorical tool and a community resource for mourning, celebration, and commemoration, including the remembrance of the body of a gay Latino dying from AIDS.

In both Felix's and Paul's examples, we can see that obituaries are useful for what they say and what they leave out. Their obituaries, and those about people dying from AIDS generally, are especially tricky historical documents to use given several factors. Who writes them, who edits them, what information is available at the time of writing, and what the policies of the publication are all determine what we see (or don't see) in AIDS obituaries. In September 1984, the *BAR*'s "Death Notices Policy" explained that it published them free of charge as a public service, requesting from those submitting them "to include information about the person's job, club or activity associations, or other information to further describe his or her life."[31] Four years later, noting the "unfortunately large number of obituaries, *Bay Area Reporter* has been forced to change its obituary policy. We must now restrict obits to 200 words. And please, no poetry."[32] The *BAR*'s own collection of obituary pictures at the end of 1989—eight pages of over six hundred photographs of men and few women, most of whom had died from AIDS between October 1988 and November 1989—graphically portrayed the overwhelming impact the syndrome was having in the community, including its impact on gay Latino residents (figure 5.6).

Conclusion: To Claim the Gay Latino Living and the Dead

In his discussion of the 1998 production of the theatrical play *Quinceañera*, what he described as "A Latino Queer and Transcultural Party for AIDS," the gay Puerto Rican theater scholar Alberto Sandoval-Sánchez, writing as a gay Latino living with AIDS, declared that "the dead must be named because they have been silenced in the national official history of AIDS. . . . By naming, and even listing, the causes of AIDS, *Quinceañera* recovers and memorializes a Latino AIDS history."[33] Obituaries too are dramatic bio-*testimonios*, narrated by those left behind but still committed to an anti-silence for historicizing the bodily markings of AIDS. I would argue that the images and the obituaries discussed here are part of a revision of who counts in the national memory of AIDS, a national *Latino* memory. They register what these bodies meant when they were alive, and what their individual histories can tell

Walter **Leonard** **Larry**

Doug **Luis** **Jacob**

5.6. Sample of the collective portrait of men (and several women) who had died from AIDS. *Bay Area Reporter* 19, no. 46 (16 November 1989), 18.

about gay Latino life in the context of a still devastating epidemic. As we know, silences don't just happen; they just "aren't." In the intimacies of our erotic connections, our various families, or our roles with different media— we are active producers of silence, of not recognizing the living and the dead faithfully in all our complexity. To recognize the records of the dead we have, especially of those bodies racially and sexually stigmatized and shamed in life and in death, begins to challenge those silences. Obituaries thus serve as performative instances of historical memory, useful and challenging, not giving an easy or full bio-historical narrative, but also not allowing us to get away with not recognizing some of our dead.

It is of course a deep historiographical irony that with AIDS, and the obituary archival records it created through its ongoing waves of death, we could know more about gay Latino community history *after* the passing of thousands of its members than when they were alive. Writing in a period when archives-based and oral history–grounded research in both Latino and queer studies are not too popular, I cannot help but note what has been obvious to me for the past several years: there are quite a number of queer Latina and Latino histories dying to be remembered, literally and figuratively. As I have learned through my own ethnohistorical project on San Francisco's LGBT Latina and Latino community life since the 1960s, not all of these histories are always accessible.[34] As a gay Latino, Latina lesbian histories are a greater challenge for me to access than are those of queer men. Yet these methodological, political, and personal challenges should not prevent me from at least trying to devise creative and critical strategies to approach the numerous historical subjects in our communities, within and beyond el (queer) barrio.

Unlike Sandoval-Sánchez, I first wrote this chapter with a relative distance from AIDS as someone who struggled in multiple ways to remain HIV seronegative since 1991. This was of course a "queer distance" that involved fears of seroconversion and semi-rehearsed safer sexual practices with a relative serenity about the potential risks and their meanings, which I share with men in and out of our barrios through the erotic needs for one another.

AIDS marked gay in 1980s and early 1990s San Francisco (and vice versa), including the city's gay Latino population. In this conflation of disease and desire, obituaries offer historical anchors to reconsider some of that period's historical losses, to untangle carefully that conflation, but also to appreciate the routes of queer Latino desires. For me to speak with those dead today— to speak through them, even—surely is in part what David Román has described as a "narcissistic performance of survival," because yes, I do want to remain as healthy and alive as I can.[35] For me to do so—within the decade-long not-about-AIDS mainstream discourse and relative communal silence among queer colleagues, friends, and allies about the ongoing challenges to our collective sexual and political health—I cannot deny the desperate need to reach back and invoke the dead, to remember them and mourn them, as they continue to be the historical markers I need in order to remind myself where I am and where I can continue to be.

What does a queer archive of the dead do to our knowledge of ourselves? At the most basic level, it reminds us to remember, challenging us not to fall into the enticing everyday practice of forgetting, of not looking back. I have argued that the archive of the dead can return us to a living, dynamic memory. As the obituaries I have examined demonstrate, the hidden, unexpected documents we unearth and make visible, however intelligible, can help us understand el barrio's multigender and multisexual reality, and that the Latina experience is hardly just a discretely heterosexual one. To appreciate everyday life in Latina America, we have to be courageous enough to look critically at our everyday death. While these obituaries are about queer Latino history and memory, they also make public queer death while racializing and gendering the AIDS epidemic both domestically and transnationally. To belong and to claim space in the transnational Latina body, the AIDS body, and the queer body, the dead can indeed help us appreciate our lives and desires yet more deeply.

ACKNOWLEDGMENTS

A 2003–2006 University of California Office of the President Postdoctoral Research Fund administered through the Chicana and Chicano Studies Department, and a 2007–2008 Faculty Career Development Award at the University of California, Santa Barbara, facilitated completion of the research and writing for this chapter. My thanks to my then Department Chair Chela Sandoval, Acting Chair Claudine Michel, the Department's staff (Diane Mercado, Diana Almaraz, and Kristine Fernandez), and Associate Vice Chancellor María Herrera-Sobek for support of my research. I thank Eddy F. Alvarez, Jr., William A. Calvo, Cynthia Cifuentes, Sean Dubberke, and especially Elisa L. Cisneros Alvarado for research assistance; the editors for their invitation to contribute to this volume and their comments; the *Bay Area Reporter* for granting permission to use the images herein; the ONE National Gay and Lesbian Archives for access to their collections; and *mis colegas* Dolores Inés Casillas, Ofelia Ortiz Cuevas, Erualdo R. González, David Manuel Hernández, Denise M. Sandoval, and Tomás Summers-Sandoval for their writing support.

NOTES

   1. Luis Alberto Campos de la Garza, then staff member at UC Berkeley's former Chicano Studies Library, was pivotal in entrusting me access to the archival collection belonging to and willed to him by the late Rodrigo Reyes, who died from AIDS complications in early 1992. See Luis Alberto de la Garza and Horacio N. Roque Ramírez, "Community History and the Evidence of Desire: The Archivo Rodrigo Reyes, a Gay and Lesbian Latino Archive," in *The Power of Language/El Poder de la Palabra: Selected Papers from the 2nd Annual REFORMA National Conference*, ed. Lillian Castillo-Speed and the REFORMA National Conference Publications Committee (Englewood, CO: Libraries Unlimited, 2000), 181–198.
   2. Examples of these grassroots projects to recapture and make accessible missing histories are San Francisco's GLBT Historical Society (http://www.glbthistory.org/); Los Angeles's ONE National Gay and Lesbian Archives (http://www.onearchives.org/); New York's Lesbian Herstory Archives (http://www.lesbianherstoryarchives.org/); and the ACT-UP (AIDS Coalition to Unleash Power) Oral History Project (http://www.actuporal-history.org/). Antoinette Burton discusses the power relationships embedded in archival sources while acknowledging the wealth of materials that *do* and *can* exist without assuming a totalizing, single importance in their contents. See Burton, "Introduction: Archive

Fever, Archive Stories," in *Archive Stories: Facts, Fictions, and the Writing of History*, ed. Antoinette Burton (Durham: Duke University Press, 2005), 6.

3. Ann Cvetkovich, *An Archive of Feelings: Trauma, Sexuality, and Lesbian Public Cultures* (Durham: Duke University Press, 2003), 5.

4. Spoken by East Los Angeles, Lincoln Heights Neighborhood Council member Mary Luz Pacheco in 2003, protesting the location of the AIDS Monument by "The Wall/ Las Memorias," a non–gay specific (though quite queer), nonprofit organization providing HIV and drug use education and awareness services. The Wall has been mired in controversy throughout its history, including public opposition from homeowners like Pacheco not wanting to have an "AIDS monument" in Lincoln Park, near their homes. See http://www.thewalllasmemorias.org/ and http://www.thebody.com/cdc/news_updates_archive/2003/mar25_03/la_aids_memorial.html, accessed on 9 March 2007. Pitting heterosexually framed barrio family values via the strategic invocation of children against what she likely understood to be a gay-and-AIDS—and thus *not* barrio—public memory project, Pacheco additionally declared that "you cannot take the park away from the children." For an insightful analysis of a cross-racial alliance to protest the admission of schoolchildren with AIDS in the mid-1980s, see Jennifer Brier, "'Save Or Kids, Keep AIDS Out:' Anti-AIDS Activism and the Legacy of Community Control in Queens, New York," *Journal of Social History* 39, no. 4 (summer 2006), 965–987.

5. For gay/queer (in)visibility and AIDS silences in Latino contexts, see "AIDS in the Barrio: Eso No Me Pasa A Mí," produced by Alba Martinez and Frances Negrón, directed by Peter Biella and Frances Negrón, AIDS Film Initiative in collaboration with Documentary Film, video, 30 min. (Cinema Guild, 1988); "Eyes that Fail to See = Ojos Que No Ven," Instituto Familiar de la Raza, video. 52 min. (San Francisco, 1988); Ana María Alonso and María Teresa Koreck, "Silences: 'Hispanics,' AIDS, and Sexual Practices," *differences* 1, no. 1 (winter 1989), 101–124; Ray Navarro, "Eso Me Está Pasando," in *Chicanos and Film: Representation and Resistance*, ed. Chon H. Noriega (Minneapolis: University of Minnesota Press, 1992), 312–315; Rafael M. Díaz, *Latino Gay Men and HIV: Culture, Sexuality, and Risk Behavior* (New York: Routledge, 1998); and "Los Hijos del Silencio," directed by Mario Balcita, Samuel Bañales, and Craig Martinez, produced by STOP AIDS San Francisco, video, 35 min. (San Francisco, 2003).

6. David Román, "Not-About-AIDS," *GLQ: A Journal of Lesbian and Gay Studies* 6, no. 1 (2000), 6.

7. "Executive Summary," in George Ayala, Claire E. Husted, and Andrew Spieldenner, *Holding Space Open: Re-tooling and Re-imagining HIV Prevention for Gay and Bisexual Men of Color* (Los Angeles and New York: Institute for Gay Men's Health, 2004), xiii.

8. As of 30 September 2006, according to the San Francisco Department of Public Health, the cumulative percentage of total adult AIDS cases in San Francisco by the "exposure category" of "MSM" (men who have sex with men) since 1981 was 74 percent; an additional 14 percent involved the combined MSM/IDU (injection drug use). Total adult AIDS case percentages for the years 1987, 1992, 1997, 2002, and 2005 in California from the *combined* MSM and MSM/IDU categories were 90 percent, 80 percent, 66 percent, 62 percent, and 70 percent, respectively, suggesting the epidemic's relative decline in the 1990s and rise among gay men at the beginning of the new century. See San Francisco AIDS Foundation, "HIV and AIDS Transmission," http://www.sfaf.org/aidsinfo/statistics/transmission.html#1, accessed on 20 March 2007.

9. In addition to Navarro's essay cited above, there are several autobiographical essays about living with AIDS, including those of the late gay Chicano author Gil Cuadros in his *City of God* (San Francisco: City Lights, 1994); one from the late gay Puerto Rican writer Manuel Ramos Otero, "The Untelling," translated from the Spanish by Rod Lauren, in *The Portable Lower East Side* 5, nos. 1–2 (1988), 85–111; and several by the gay Puerto Rican author and scholar Alberto Sandoval-Sánchez, including "An AIDS Testimonial: It's a Broken Record/*Ese Disco Se Rayó*," in *Technofuturos: Critical Interventions in Latina/o Studies*, ed. Nancy Raquel Mirabal and Agustín Laó-Motes (Lanham, MD: Lexington Books/Rowman and Littlefield, 2007), 297–310. Perhaps the one full-fledged memoir by someone living with AIDS is that from the late gay Cuban refugee Reinaldo Arenas, first appearing in English in 1993 as *Before Night Falls: A Memoir* (New York: Viking). See also the analysis of an important play written and produced from the context of the experiences of queer people of color and AIDS in 1990s San Francisco, José Esteban Muñoz, "Feeling Brown: Ethnicity and Affect in Ricardo Bracho's *The Sweetest Hangover (and Other STDs)*," *Theatre Journal* 52, no. 1 (March 2000), 67–79. I thank Ricardo Abreu Bracho for bringing some of these works to my attention.

10. I first encountered the notion of the "sexile" in Manuel Guzmán's "'Pa' La Escuelita con Mucho Cuidaó y por la Orillita': A Journey Through the Contested Terrains of the Nation and Sexual Orientation," in *Puerto Rican Jam: Rethinking Colonialism and Nationalism*, ed. Frances Negrón-Muntaner and Ramón Grosfoguel (Minneapolis: University of Minnesota Press, 1997), 209–228. For further elaborations on the relationship between queer/LGBT sexualities and (im)migrations, see Eithne Luibhéid and Lionel Cantú, Jr., eds., *Queer Migrations: Sexuality, U.S. Citizenship, and Border Crossings* (Minneapolis: University of Minnesota Press, 2005); and the "Queer/Migration" issue edited by Luibhéid, *GLQ: A Journal of Lesbian and Gay Studies* 14, nos. 2–3 (January 2008).

11. Janice Hume, *Obituaries in American Culture* (Jackson: University Press of Mississippi, 2000), 23.

12. A. Odasuo Alali, "The Disposition of AIDS Imagery in *New York Times'* Obituaries," *OMEGA: Journal of Death and Dying* 29, no. 4 (1994), 273–289; Charles Winick, "AIDS Obituaries in the *New York Times*," *AIDS and Public Policy Journal* 11, no. 3 (fall 1996), 148–152; and Peter M. Nardi, "AIDS and Obituaries: The Perpetuation of Stigma in the Press," in *Culture and AIDS*, ed. Douglas A. Feldman (New York: Praeger, 1990), 159–168.

13. While the *BAR* did not document (gay) Latino deaths prior to this date, Latinos were represented in the very first casualties of the disease in San Francisco, although media representations of the first men afflicted involved gay white men. See Randy Shilts, *And the Band Played On: Politics, People, and the AIDS Epidemic* (New York: St. Martin's Press, 1987), 98. However useful Shilts's six-hundred-plus-page tome was for bringing awareness to the AIDS epidemic nationally, his exposé fit well within mainstream homophobic fantasies and fears of infected gay men rampantly spreading disease. See Douglas Crimp, "Randy Shilts's Miserable Failure," in *A Queer World: The Center for Lesbian and Gay Studies Reader*, ed. Martin Duberman (New York: New York University Press, 1997), 641–648.

14. "DEATHS: Alfredo Aguilera," *Bay Area Reporter* 17, no. 30 (23 July 1987), 23.

15. Christina Lindan, Norman Hearst, James A. Singleton, Alan I. Trachtenberg, Noreen M. Riordan, Diane A. Tokagawa, and George S. Chu, "Underreporting of Minority AIDS Deaths in San Francisco Bay Area, 1985–1986," *Public Health Reports* 105, no. 4 (July–August 1990), 400–404.

16. Jim, "On a Friend's Death," *Bay Area Reporter* 14, no. 6 (9 February 1984), 6.

17. Ibid.

18. The racial, sexual, and cultural dynamics suggested in Jim's brief public recollection of Ronaldo are quite similar to those that emerged in an incident sparked by the public writings of Tim Speck, another gay white man living in the Mission in 1982, who argued that San Francisco's Gay Latino Alliance (GALA) was hypocritical in its political work and rhetoric. Speck's claim sparked a significant counter-discourse from GALA and other gays of color in the city. I discuss this episode in "'That's *My* Place': Negotiating Racial, Sexual, and Gender Politics in San Francisco's Gay Latino Alliance, 1975–1983," *Journal of the History of Sexuality* 12, no. 2 (April 2003), 248–251.

19. Michael C. Botkin, "Obituary Cruising Rules," *Bay Area Reporter* 21, no. 32 (8 August 1991), 20.

20. Henry "Hank" Tavera, oral history interview by author, audio tape recording, San Francisco, California, 19 May 1995.

21. See Lindan et al., "Underreporting of Minority AIDS Deaths in San Francisco Bay Area."

22. "DEATHS: Felix Velarde-Muñoz," *Bay Area Reporter* 14, no. 46 (15 November 1984), 13.

23. Renée M. Sentilles, "Toiling in the Archives of Cyberspace," in Burton, *Archive Stories*, 136–156.

24. "Felix Velarde-Muñoz" is also a subject entry in the "Records, 1968–2002" of the Mexican American Legal Defense and Education Fund (MALDEF) at Stanford University's Special Collections.

25. Christopher Ho, personal electronic communication, 2 March 2007. I thank Ho for providing this historical context for the Velarde-Muñoz Fellowship, Pauline T. Kim and Eugene Pak for responding to my initial inquiry, and Joan Graff for contextualizing further the life and death of the late Velarde-Muñoz.

26. Joan Graff, telephone communication, 5 March 2007.

27. Velarde-Muñoz is one of two gay Latinos appearing in Shilts's *And the Band Played On*. Velarde-Muñoz, described as "a wonderful Mexican-American lawyer," appears in the lengthy narrative indirectly as "the romantic interest of summer 1980" of the San Francisco gay activist Cleve Jones, who was a student intern in 1978 in city hall when the city's first openly gay supervisor, Harvey Milk, was assassinated (along with Mayor George Moscone).

28. "DEATHS: Felipe Madrea," *Bay Area Reporter* 16, no. 46 (13 November 1986), 18; "DEATHS: Jesse Anthony Maldonado," *Bay Area Reporter* 17, no. 46 (12 November 1987), 18; "DEATHS: Asel J. Sanchez. Enrique Perez," *Bay Area Reporter* 17, no. 53 (31 December 1987), 13.

29. Bill Bradley, "He Put the 'People' in PWA: Paul Castro's Long Fight Ends," *Bay Area Reporter* 15, no. 24 (13 June 1985), 3.

30. Paul Castro, "Coming Out as a Person with AIDS," *Bay Area Reporter* 14, no 46 (15 November 1984), 11. PFLAG (Parents, Families, and Friends of Lesbians and Gays) was established in 1973 in New York City, and now includes several Spanish-language programs and chapters throughout the United States and Latin America.

31. "Death Notices Policy," *Bay Area Reporter* 14, no. 39 (27 September 1984), 14.

32. "Obituary Policy," *Bay Area Reporter* 18, no. 5 (10 November 1988), 18.

33. Alberto Sandoval-Sánchez, "Quinceañera: A Latino Queer and Transcultural Party for AIDS," in *The Color of Theatre: Race, Culture, and Contemporary Performance*, ed. Roberta Uno with Lucy Mae San Pablo Burns (New York: Continuum, 2002), 307.

34. I argue for more oral history– and archives-based public history and public memory projects in "Memory and Mourning: Living Oral History with Queer Latinos in San Francisco," in *Oral History and Public Memories*, ed. Paula Hamilton and Linda Shopes (Philadelphia: Temple University Press, 2008), 165–186; and "Borderlands, Diasporas, and Transnational Crossings: Teaching LGBT Latina and Latino Community Histories," in *Teaching American History in a Global Context*, ed. Carl Guarneri and Jim Davis (Armonk, NY: M. E. Sharpe, 2008), 267–270.

35. David Román, "Speaking with the Dead," in *AIDS and the National Body*, ed. Thomas E. Yingling (Durham: Duke University Press, 1997), 130.

6

All About My (Absent) Mother

Young Latina Aspirations in Real Women
Have Curves *and* Ugly Betty

DEBORAH PAREDEZ

In the critically acclaimed coming-of-age film *Real Women Have Curves* (2002), Ana Garcia, a first-generation Chicana teenager from East Los Angeles, aspires to attend Columbia University but first must reckon with her mother's traditional views about gender roles within the Mexican American family. Set in the summer months bridging high school graduation and the fall semester during which Ana was hoping to begin college, the film chronicles the mother-daughter conflicts that arise when Ana must fulfill her familial responsibility by working along with her mother at her sister's garment factory. When Ana eventually leaves for college at summer's end, her mother refuses to support her decision, remaining conspicuously absent from Ana's *despedida*, or farewell scene, that marks the beginnings of Ana's new life as an aspiring, independent woman.

This narrative journey—in which the daughter's fulfilled aspirations require the absence of the mother—is a strikingly familiar one, not simply for what many regard as its heart-wrenchingly realistic depiction of Latina mother-daughter acrimony, but also for its status as a recurring trope in popular representations of young female heroines. From Nancy Drew to Buffy the Vampire Slayer, absent or dead mothers frequently serve as key narrative features in tales of intrepid teenage girls who venture beyond the traditional feminine roles of the domestic realm to embrace adventure or embark on journeys of self-realization. Throughout these stories, as Ilana Nash and others have noted, the girl's bond with her father (or a surrogate father figure) ultimately serves as the relational path through which she attains and negotiates a sense of authority and selfhood in the public realm.[1] Thus, in spite of—or perhaps precisely because of—the feminist impulses that guide these representations of female self-reliance, Naomi Scheman argues, "The message to a woman is clear: within the systems of male privilege neither

her appropriately feminine sexual identity nor her ability to assume public power is compatible with her being her mother's daughter."[2]

While the absent mother trope in *Real Women Have Curves* aligns the film within these broader canons of female bildungsromans and action heroine tales, it also links the film to a trend within recent cinematic and televisual representations of Latinas. During the past decade, Latinas have emerged in popular culture as icons of posthumous worship, "It" girls of show business, and (sex) symbols for the emerging assertions and aspirations of all Latina/os.[3] And yet, despite the enduring popular fascination with the hypersexualized Latina body, recent representations have not entirely circumscribed Latinas within the frames of spicy, heavily accented otherness that marked Latina visibility in Hollywood films of the 1930s and 1940s.[4] In fact, as Jillian Báez observes, cinematic portrayals of Latinas in recent years have often depicted "*Latinidades feministas*—moments of female agency among and between Latinas."[5] But a disturbingly common narrative feature shared by these otherwise progressive depictions of Latinas is the absent or dead mother. Across a range of genres—from coming-of-age tales to epic family dramas to campy *telenovelas*—Latina mothers are frequently sidelined in the service of promoting (often unlikely and invariably Oedipal) father-daughter bonds, such as in *Selena* (1997) or *Crash* (2004), or are willfully disengaged from a young Latina's emergence into womanhood, as in *Real Women Have Curves*. More commonly, the premise of many plotlines chronicling the Latina/o family conspicuously include a dead Latina mother, as in the films *Girlfight* (2000), *Tortilla Soup* (2001), *Raising Victor Vargas* (2002), and the television shows *Resurrection Boulevard* (Showtime 2000), *American Family* (PBS 2002), and *Ugly Betty* (ABC 2006). This pervasive trend provokes the guiding question of this chapter: why is it that in order to make young women cinematically legible as U.S. Latinas their mothers must be absent or dead?

This chapter examines the absent mother trope in tales of young Latina aspiration depicted in *Real Women Have Curves* and *Ugly Betty*. Both works, released in the years since the much-touted "Latin Explosion" of the 1990s, are regularly regarded as affirming representations of young working-class Latinas. A critically and commercially successful independent film that secured wide distribution after winning awards at the Sundance Film Festival, *Real Women* is classified as a coming-of-age film, while *Ugly Betty* marks a new genre that I refer to as a queer U.S. *Latinovela*. Written and directed by Latina/o artists, both works feature the same lead actress (Honduran American America Ferrera) and are adaptations (of a U.S. Latina play and a Colombian telenovela, respectively). Despite the various pleasures and promises offered by these works, they share the same troubling narrative premise: the absent or dead Latina mother whose very absence or loss operates as a central component in Latina aspirations for material gain, social agency, and gendered self-understanding. This chapter explores how absent mothers function in these works and highlights the implications for prevailing ideas about Latina subjectivity that arise from their absence. While the absent mother trope may lend itself easily and fruitfully to a psychoanalytic or, more specifically, an Oedipal reading,[6] I am interested instead in situating my close readings of these works within the recent sociopolitical moment during which Latina/os, in light of their growing demographics, have gained increasing recognition as an important voting bloc, market base, and labor pool while struggling for recognition as citizens in the face of prevailing nativist sentiments and legislation. Examined within this context, the absent mother emerges not only as a key component in narratives of Latina aspiration but also serves as a representational index of these recent anxieties and concerns of and about Latina/os in the United States. Moreover, the absent or dead mother also serves as a representational sign of the continued legacy of the reproductive policing of Latina bodies throughout the Americas.[7]

Real Women Without Mothers

Lauded for its feminist emphasis on female body image, gendered labor practices, and young Latina agency, *Real Women Have Curves* is an adaptation of Josefina López's 1994 play of the same name. The screenplay, which won the prestigious 2002 Humanitas Prize (an award that honors film and television writing), was cowritten by López and George LaVoo. Directed by Colombian filmmaker Patricia Cardoso, the film was distributed by HBO and won the Dramatic Audience Award and Special Acting Awards for lead actresses America Ferrera and Lupe Ontiveros at the Sundance Film Festival. Ferrera portrays the young protagonist, Ana Garcia, and Ontiveros plays the role of Ana's traditional mother, Carmen. While the film focuses on the fraught encounters between Ana and Carmen, it also devotes substantial screen time to establishing the ways in which Ana's interactions with male figures ultimately serve to empower her.

Throughout the film, Ana's bonds with her father, paternal grandfather, and male Latino English teacher secure her path toward social and sexual liberation. Indeed, her mother is cinematically absent from the scenes wherein Ana seeks or attains social, sexual, or intellectual affirmation. For example, it is Ana's teacher, Mr. Guzmán (George López), who encourages

Ana to apply for college, makes visits to her home to urge her parents to permit her to pursue higher education, and helps her with her application. Ana's father, Raúl (Jorge Cervera, Jr.), and grandfather, "Abuelito" (Felipe de Alba), are also supportive of her educational dreams, even while they initially defer to Carmen's wishes. The scenes Ana shares with her father and grandfather explicitly facilitate her financial and sexual aspirations. Early in the film, Ana joins her father and grandfather on the patio of their home while her mother and aunt remain in the kitchen. The scene begins with a shot of the grandfather's hands lifting slices of glistening red tuna, or cactus apple/prickly pear, from a plate and announcing, "Estan deliciosas—si es como me gustan" [They are delicious—just how I like them], as Ana's father nods in agreement. The grandfather then tells Ana, "Tú eres un tesoro" [You are a treasure], and she smiles bashfully, saying, "Abuelito." The camera then cuts to Ana's hands on a cutting board, where the deep fuchsia curled skins of one tuna fruit rest alongside another tuna that she is slicing open. As the two men eat the tuna Ana has sliced, her grandfather launches into a legend about a cave filled with gold in his old village in Mexico. He ends the tale by saying to Ana, "Tú eres mi oro. Ahora yo quiere que tú encuentres el tuyo" [You are my (pot of) gold. And now I wish for you to find yours].

This scene features a clear slippage between allusions of financial and sexual treasure. The references to gold in Abuelito's story and his final benediction for Ana point toward the ways the film affirms Ana's aspirations of social and economic mobility through her male connections, which transpire outside the confines of domestic spaces. For example, later in the film, Ana secures a loan from her father (for her sister's business) at his workplace, which, given his position as a landscaper, takes place outside on the verdant grounds of a fancy home. When Ana repays the loan she again meets her father at this lush outdoor site, and it is here that he offers her his blessing to pursue her dreams of attending college. These outdoor scenes, saturated with imagery of treasure, wealth, and (grand)father-daughter bonding, equate financial "independence" and freedom with male affiliation in the public sphere. In the patio scene, the tale of a cave filled with treasures and the reference to the pot of gold not only evoke aspirations for financial fortune, but along with the glistening red fruit, serve as visual and discursive markers of Ana's blossoming sexuality. The preparation, exchange, and consumption of the tuna among Ana and the men also suggests the heterosexual economy into which Ana is being disciplined to enter as she approaches womanhood, and underscores the symbolic (public, male) world she must inhabit in order to attain sexual acknowledgment and affirmation.

Throughout the film, Abuelito literally and figuratively acts as Ana's paternal guide and coconspirator in her illicit romantic adventures with Jimmy, a white boy she met in her English class. When, for example, Ana plans her first date with Jimmy, she and her grandfather leave the house alone pretending that the two of them are spending the evening together at a movie. Later in the film, Ana's decision to become sexually active with Jimmy is revealed in a scene in the corner drugstore where Ana is running an errand for her grandfather. Ana approaches the pharmacy counter and says to the cashier, "A cigar for my grandpa, please." The clerk responds, "I know what kind he likes," and begins to ring up the purchase but is interrupted by Ana's request, "Um, can I get some condoms, too?" The explicit linking of, indeed the fungibility between, Ana's sexual awakening with the well-worn phallic imagery associated with her grandfather further reinforces the film's insistence that patrilineal alliance and devotion will bring about sexual freedom.

This equation of financial and sexual affirmation with the male public domain is reinforced by the fraught encounters Ana shares with her mother. In a representative scene, Carmen tells the family what happened on the episode of the Brazilian telenovela *Las Pobres Llorran Más* [The Poor Cry More] she had watched that evening. Ana quips, "Mom, I don't watch Spanish soap operas." Disregarding Ana's comment, Carmen proceeds to recount the plotline that involves a "cross-eyed daughter" who becomes pregnant from an encounter with a "handsome, dark stranger" and attempts to run away with him, "betray[ing] her mother's wishes." Amid her escape—and in fanciful telenovela style—the daughter dies after being decapitated by a bus. Throughout the story, Ana and her male cousins snicker and, by the story's end, openly laugh, deriding its far-fetched and blatantly cautionary tale. Ana scoffs, "Mom, that's the stupidest thing I've ever heard," to which Carmen replies, "Ana, you better listen. That's what happens to people who don't listen to their mothers!" Ana then retreats to her bedroom to make an illicit phone call to Jimmy.

While the scene operates on one level as a moment of comic relief, it also undeniably positions Ana's mother and the gendered spectatorship of telenovelas squarely within the easily ridiculed, Spanish-speaking (read unassimilated), financially and culturally impoverished (*The Poor Cry More*, with its hyperbolic storyline), outmoded ways of the immigrant's "old country." Jillian Báez observes, "Carmen serves as a vision of the 'Old World' . . . Given that Ana's mother reinforces patriarchy, traditions of the 'Old World' are gendered feminine, while her father's, grandfather's, and teacher's support of her pursuit of higher education genders the progress of the 'New

World' as masculine. As such, tradition is signified as located in women and modernity in men."[8] This scene solidifies Carmen as the antagonistic foil against the men in the film—including Jimmy, who ultimately affirms Ana's body and sexuality throughout their ensuing courtship and in a touching postcoital scene.

Such stark gendered divisions between the male world of financial and sexual freedom and the repressive female world wherein "the poor cry more" is remarkable considering the thrust and focus of the play on which the film is based. Drawing from Josefina López's experiences as a Mexican immigrant working alongside her mother in a Los Angeles sweatshop, the play's action unfolds exclusively within the realm of the garment factory over a five-day period during which Carmen, Ana, and Ana's sister, Estela (along with two other Latina workers) labor to meet a deadline. On the film's official website, López reflects, "My play was about five women and a radio in a sewing factory, fearful every second of an INS raid."[9] While some of the women in the play have already secured their legalization papers, Ana and Estela are revealed to be undocumented immigrants. When they meet their deadline, Estela offers the workers their checks, but the women collectively decide to pool their wages and return them to Estela to help cover the costs of her factory-related debts and the legal fees for her legalization papers. The play concludes with Estela opening her own boutique that specializes in clothing for women with "curves," and with her fellow laborers parading across the stage modeling Estela's original designs. While throughout the play Carmen does berate Ana about her appearance and aspirations, she is clearly not the antagonist she becomes in the film.[10]

Carmen's emergence as the film's antagonist—and eventual status as an absent mother—was due largely to the prevailing realism of the film medium, which, according to López, necessitated narrative shifts that foreclosed the possibilities for a woman-centered world that the play emphasized. López states:

> The main plot in the play was the whole immigration paranoia, which would not work in the movie. . . . Also, the mother in the play is funny and annoying, but she is not the antagonist. In the movie we needed a better antagonist since we were losing the whole immigration antagonist forcing things to happen. So the mother became the antagonist and the symbol of tradition and culture. . . . Since we had to open up the story and take women out of the factory, we had to add men. I loved the play for not having them, but we had to add them.[11]

In light of these script changes, the function of the castigating and ulti-mately absent mother antagonist in the film is to deflect attention and blame from the more common antagonist in young Latina efforts toward social and economic mobility: structural, legal, and institutional forces like the INS (now the USCIS). Here, the obstacles to young Latina aspiration are not attributed to a capricious and draconian system within the borders of the United States, but are relocated onto the body of the mother(land). With the Latina mother supplanting *la migra* as the antagonist, *Real Women Have Curves* is no longer about young Latina struggles to attain citizenship in an era of regressive immigration reform, as the play suggests, but rather about the terms of having achieved such status. The film suggests that the break from the Latina mother, and her subsequent cinematic absence, is the cost that aspiring young Latinas must pay as newly recognized citizens.

Carmen's position as the absent mother is most fully realized in the clos-ing moments of film when Ana prepares to leave for college. The scene begins with Ana washing her face and pausing for a moment as she catches her reflection in the mirror. The camera cuts immediately to Carmen's face looking distressed as she lies in bed. As Ana leaves her bedroom and enters the kitchen, her sister tells her that she will be unable to accompany them to the airport because she must rush off to the factory. Left alone and disap-pointed in the wake of her sister's unexpected departure, Ana turns toward her mother's closed bedroom door, twisting the doorknob of the locked door and pleading with her to come out to say a proper good-bye and to offer her blessing. Carmen moves toward the door, but retreats, standing before her dresser mirror, shifting her gaze from her own reflection to a photo of Ana tucked into the corner of the mirror. When Carmen does not emerge from the locked bedroom, Ana joins her father and grandfather outside and bids farewell to her male cousins before climbing into her father's truck. The bittersweet resignation and promise of the scene is heightened at this moment when Lila Downs's song "La Niña" [The Girl], an evocative homage to women laborers, begins to play with increasing volume over the remain-der of the scene. As the truck door slams and begins to pull away, Carmen makes her way through the house, parting the curtains in the living room window to peer at the receding truck just as Ana turns back to peer through the back window of the truck's cab. The women are unable to see each other. Ana turns her face away from the rear window and faces forward, and Car-men releases the curtain and exits the camera's frame.

At the airport, as Ana bids good-bye to her father and grandfather just before she boards her plane, she looks back one last time at the two men who stand close together, not unlike a romantic couple, one of her father's arms curled around her grandfather as they wave goodbye. The screen then flashes black for a moment as the galloping rhythm of Lila Downs's *cumbia* gives way to the sound of an accelerating subway train. In the film's final scene, Ana is ascending a flight of stairs framed by two male pedestrians as she emerges from the subway station in New York City's Times Square. She strides confidently down the sidewalk as the camera pans to a wider shot, establishing her securely within this new milieu. She turns the corner and exits the frame.

The framing of Ana and Carmen within mirrors and windows in these closing scenes visually links the two women, if only to mark the mother's banishment from the daughter's world. Each woman's recognition of her reflection within her respective mirror results ultimately in the acknowledgment of herself as undeniably and utterly separated from the other, thereby triggering her grief over this split.[12] Carmen acknowledges this loss when she dolefully shifts from her own reflection to the photo of Ana. The women gaze into their reflections within these pools of loss and thereby mark Ana's passage into womanhood. Carmen remains within the world of the past and of domesticity (although she works outside the home, she is symbolically linked to a traditional feminine role within the domestic sphere), while Ana joins her male relatives in the public realm. Once securely positioned in these separate worlds, Ana can no longer "see" or acknowledge her mother. Ana turns away from the truck's rear window, toward the road that stretches before her, and Carmen seals herself behind drawn curtains, eventually absent from the camera's frame.

And yet, while Ana and Carmen are cinematically unable to bridge the chasm between them, the film's soundtrack works against this visual narrative. In its lyrical tribute to Latina laborers, Lila Downs's "La Niña" sonically links the women and offers a hope for (eventual) connection. The song, which is "dedicada a todas las mujeres trabadoras" [dedicated to all women workers], shifts in tempo from plaintive lament into upbeat *cumbia* as it recounts the story of "la niña," Rosa María, a maquiladora worker:

> Desde temprano, la niña reza, pa' que su día no sea tan largo
> y con la luz de madrugada, hace limpieza de sus encargos
> \<tempo shift to *cumbia*>
> cierra los ojos pa' no mirarse, que en el espejo se va notando
> que su trabajo la está acabando y es que su santo está en descanso
> todo los días, todas las horas, en esa espuma de sus tristezas,
> uñas y carne, sudor y fuerzas, todo su empeño, todos sus sueños,
> se van quedando en sus recuerdos, en la memoria de sus anhelos

chorus:
Ay! melana negra carita triste, Rosa María
buscando vives tus días y noches una salida
que un domingo libra este infierno tuyo por tu alegría

Maquiladora solo un recuerdo será algún día
y la cosecha tu propio fruto será algún día,
y la desaparecida le hagan justicia,
será algún día, un día, un día

[Early in the morning, the girl prays, so that her day won't last too long
and in the dawn's light, she cleans and does her job
she closes her eyes, to not see herself, because in the mirror she sees
her job is making her older, because her patron saint is on vacation,
every day, every hour, in that soapy water of her sadness,
nails and flesh, sweat and strength, all her determination, all her
    dreams
are left behind, in her memories, in the memory of her yearning

Ay! Long black hair, sad little face, Rosa María,
every day and every night you look for a way out for your happiness,
only Sundays liberate you from this hell

The day will come when the maquiladora is only a memory
and one day the crop will be your own fruit
and there will be justice for the desaparecidas
the day will come, one day, one day][13]

The song's non-diegetic entrance in the moment of Ana's departure from the interior of the house serves at once to lament the relational loss between Latina mother and daughter and to implicate the political and economic forces (rather than the mother's intractable nature) that have brought about this loss. The song's reference to Rosa María, who, like Ana and Carmen, looks into her mirror with grief, links the song's protagonist to both women. In its depiction of Rosa María's laboring body and her yearning for "a way out for her happiness," the song honors both Carmen's status as a laborer and Ana's wish for the freedom from this fate. By recontextualizing the women within the workings of global capital, the song also underscores how transnational, gendered labor practices are the more likely culprits preventing young Latina aspirations for economic gain. By implicating these structural forces, the song works against their elision in the visual economy of the film. In its accelerating tempo and its echoing refrain, "the day will come, one day, one day," the song also suggests the possibility of a future free of exploitative labor for Latinas, a future where women like Ana and Carmen can achieve equality not only with "everyone else" but also with one another. The day will come when another antagonist can be recognized and when the disappeared—from the murdered maquila workers along the border to the absent Latina mothers just beyond the cinematic frame—will find justice.

Until that day, the Latina mother must remain absent from the daughter's aspirational journey. In fact, in *Real Women*'s final moments, the film no longer positions Ana's father and grandfather as narrative foils to Ana's mother, but as her replacements—as suggested by the men's final feminized pose and by Carmen's visual absence from the scene. It is within this male-centered world (the film's logic does not even allow Ana's sister to occupy a space) of social and economic opportunity that Ana is reborn. In the closing shot, Ana literally ascends into the scene, landing on the streets of New York—the city that serves in popular imagination as the culminating destination of immigrant and aspiring working-girl journeys. Cinematically linked to the men who flank her on the stairs, Ana is delivered from the surrogate womb of the subway station onto the expansive sidewalks leading to her college-bound, sexually liberated future. She has arrived—independent, unfettered, and motherless.

In Memory of Betty's Mother

Ugly Betty chronicles the triumphs and travails of Betty Suarez, a young, college-educated, unglamorous-yet-endearing Latina who secures employment and endures countless challenges at *Mode*, a high-fashion magazine in Manhattan. As Betty pursues her dreams for economic, romantic, and creative success, she continues to live with her father, sister, and nephew in the working-class Queens neighborhood where she was raised. Not unlike the protagonists in films like *The Devil Wears Prada* or *Working Girl*, Betty struggles to keep her integrity intact as she negotiates her coworkers' cutthroat antics and her crush on a fellow *Mode* outcast, Henry Grubstick (Christopher Gorham). The series, which premiered on ABC on 28 September 2006, is an adaptation of the transnational telenovela sensation *Yo Soy Betty la Fea* [I am Betty, the Ugly One], which originated in Colombia, drew eighty million viewers across Latin America, and spawned culturally specific versions in countries across the globe (from Mexico to India and eventually to the United States).[14] In the original, Beatriz, or Betty, is a brilliant but physically and socially awkward woman with a graduate degree in finance who lives at home with her parents, and who, along with her cohort of working-class girl-friends (*el cuartel de las feas*—the ugly ones), overcomes regular discrimination and humiliation in her job at a chic fashion magazine.

Betty la Fea's transformation into *Ugly Betty* for a major network in the U.S. market was effected by Cuban American writer Silvio Horta and by Mexican actress Salma Hayek's production company, Ventanarosa. The U.S.-born Betty is portrayed by America Ferrera, whose star-text no doubt imbues the role with memories of her portrayal of Ana Garcia from *Real Women Have Curves*. In some ways, as a recent college graduate in New York, Betty represents a future version of Ana. The legacy of Ana Garcia also emerges in another important way within *Ugly Betty*. In its transformation from Latin American telenovela to a U.S. Latina/o show, Betty's mother suffered the fate of many mothers of comic heroines: she died before the cameras started rolling, confirming Lucy Fischer's observation that often within the comic genre, "the figure of the mother is largely absent, suppressed, violated, or replaced."[15] Gone too are Betty's *cuartel de las feas*; within the adaptation, Betty is the only aspiring young Latina we ever encounter at her workplace.

Horta's clever and frequently touching rendition of *Betty* blurs generic boundaries. Categorized by the network as a "dramedy," the show combines queer Latina/o camp self-reflexivity with the indulgently outlandish high drama of the Latin American telenovela form, in many ways revealing the stylistic and affective commonalities between the two.[16] The result is what I call a queer U.S. *Latinovela*, an explicitly U.S. cultural product that embraces its queer and Latina/o *chusmeria*: tackiness, shamelessness, and above all, sincerity. Populated by characters such as a transgender *Mode* executive named Alexis (Rebecca Romijn) and Mark (Michael Urie), Betty's ever-catty gay male office mate, and shot in a campy, color-saturated style, *Ugly Betty* is unmistakably queer in many ways (although its progressive queer vision is limited by the fact that the only lesbian characters featured are prison inmates or escapees). But certainly the most talked about queer element in the series is the characterization of Betty's young proto-queer nephew, Justin (Mark Indelicato). In fact, it is through Justin's story that the show plays out a queer Latina/o wish fulfillment narrative of loving acceptance within the Latino family.[17] These explicitly queer stylistic and plot directions are often reined in by the Betty/Henry romance. While the couple could certainly be read as queer—outcasts who inhabit unconventional gender roles and bond over their love of Broadway musicals—they are often positioned as the central heterosexual couple with whom the audience is encouraged to identify.

The unconventional composition of Betty's family—a loving father, two single and self-possessed daughters, and a proto-queer grandson—can also be understood as a queering of the traditional Latino family that does not assert an investment in a masculinist patrilineal legacy. And yet this (potentially) queer depiction of the Latino family conspicuously excludes the presence of the Latina mother—which is especially striking given that in the original iteration of Betty, her mother was alive and supportive of Betty's choices. In some ways, the dead Latina mother trope within *Ugly Betty*, not unlike within the representation of the Latina/o family in the television family drama *American Family*, sets up the protagonist to act as surrogate caretaker for the Latino father. This narrative framing occurs within the show's pilot episode during a scene in which Betty advocates for her father in a frustrating telephone argument with his HMO. After Betty hangs up the phone, her father, Ignacio (Tony Plana), turns to her and says, "You're always so good to me, so strong, determined, optimistic. Just like your mother was." This scene establishes Betty as a caring Latina daughter bound to familial duty even as she strives for personal financial, romantic, and creative success.

Betty's conflicting loyalties to both her familial and work duties, and the role of her absent mother within this struggle, are revealed in a pivotal scene from the show's pilot. Arriving home late from an arduous day at work, Betty discovers that she has missed her father's birthday party and is chastised by her sister, Hilda (Ana Ortiz): "You know that this is the first time since Mom died that we haven't all been together on his birthday?" Betty responds, "Yes, I realize that, and I'm sorry—but I was working." Hilda retorts, "That's fine, Betty. I just hope it's all worth it." Defeated, Betty slumps resignedly onto the family's sofa. The camera lingers for a moment on this image of Betty as she is framed by a woven Mexican blanket spread across the top of the sofa, lace curtains in the window behind her, and a fringed red pillow to her left. She turns her head, and her gaze falls on an old photo of her and her mother, taken when Betty was a child. After a moment of gazing longingly at the photo, inspiration alights in Betty's face. She turns away from the photo, reaches into her purse, and pulls out a notepad on which she writes, "Work Ideas."

This scene establishes Betty as a Latina by framing her among visual signifiers of legible Latinidad (Latina/o identity): a Mexican blanket, bright colors, excessive fringe accessories, and Spanish-style lace curtains. As a young Latina protagonist torn between familial duties and career aspirations, Betty turns toward the memory of her dead mother for comfort and resolution. Within this narrative dilemma, the absent Latina mother fulfills a complicated role as both marker of and salve for bicultural Latina struggles, and as the engine for Latina creative inspiration. In this way, unlike in other comic heroine tales wherein "the absence of even the memory of a mother is a necessary part of the identity these women embrace," the memory of the Latina mother does not inhibit the heroine's progress but helps ensure it.[18] It is ironically within the domestic realm, within the memory of the lost mother, that "work ideas" are generated. But it is only though memory, through the feeling of grief for the absent Latina mother, and not through embodied connection with her in the present, that creative inspiration is sparked. This image of young Latina longing thereby reinscribes prevailing depictions of Latina/os as inevitably, naturally grieving subjects that have marked U.S. popular culture since the 1990s.[19]

Betty's sister, Hilda, does portray a Latina single mother, but it is important to note that she is the mother of a young son and that her aspirations (at least after two seasons) fail to take her "beyond el barrio." While the relationship between Hilda and her son, Justin, is an undeniably refreshing take on Latina/o family representations, it continues to further reinforce the absence of Latina mother-daughter relations. Moreover, when considered alongside Betty's Manhattan-bound aspirations, Hilda's perpetual financial and emotional struggles within the Queens context suggest that the successful aspiring young Latina must not only be motherless, but not a mother herself. Here, Hilda as the aspiring young Latina *mother* is kept within the material and symbolic confines of the barrio. While her childless sister finds romantic fulfillment beyond the barrio, Hilda ultimately is framed within a tragic barrio narrative when the father of her child is killed in a bodega robbery in the season 1 finale.

The memory of her absent mother serves Betty's career aspirations throughout her struggle for success at *Mode*. In the culminating scene of the pilot, Daniel and Betty present an advertising layout, based on Betty's absent-mother-inspired idea, to *Mode's* disgruntled cosmetic mogul client Fabia (played with delicious camp by Gina Gershon), who has rejected the magazine's previous layout proposal. Betty projects snapshots of herself and her mother—including the photo that provoked Betty's moment of creative inspiration in the living room scene. Daniel says, "In order to show the softer side of Fabia cosmetics, we're going to use the concept of mothers and daughters, focusing on the small special moments that are usually taken for granted. The theme being, it's not the big events, but the little moments that matter." Throughout Daniel's presentation, Betty stares wistfully and proudly at the photos rather than looking directly at Fabia. When Fabia asks them to justify how exactly the ad campaign would appeal to her customers, Betty turns her gaze from the photos to Fabia, clears her throat, and begins, "Well, if I may, I do have statistics here. Though one may assume that your demographic is very young, in fact there's been tremendous brand loyalty since you've launched, which means that the people who were teenagers when they began using your cosmetics, well, now, like you, they are beginning to settle down and have children—fifty-eight percent to be exact." Fabia, impressed by both Betty's concept and market savvy, approves the idea, and Daniel and Betty successfully secure their positions with the magazine.

Within this scene, the memory of the dead Latina mother once again generates and secures creative and economic success for the young Latina daughter within the public realm, offering an ironic twist on Stanley Cavell's observation that "the price of the woman's happiness [in comedy] is the absence of her mother."[20] Betty's use of the memory of her mother within her display of financial acumen also reveals the ways in which the dead Latina mother functions here to categorize Latina/os as reliable guides for consumption and thereby to reinscribe Latina/os within the realm of the marketplace.[21] Indeed, the commodified memory of Betty's dead Latina mother provides a symbol of Latina/o market savvy: they know how to transform pain into product.

The memory of and longing for her dead mother continues to shape Betty's aspirations throughout the first season. (In fact, yearning for lost parents emerges as a recurring theme throughout the series.) As the show's first season progresses, two of the major story lines converge at the site of the memory of the absent mother. The first concerns Betty's father, Ignacio, whom we discover is an undocumented immigrant who must return to Mexico to renew his visa. The other story line is Betty and Henry's attempted romance, which, true to the show's telenovela origins, is thwarted by the appearance of his former girlfriend, with whom he reunites and who is now pregnant with his child. Betty resigns herself to let Henry go and redirects all of her attention onto her family woes. The romance plot intersects with the family plot through the absent mother narrative when Betty travels to Mexico with her family to accompany her father on his quest for a visa. The result is that the young Latina's return to the "motherland" and quest for her missing mother ultimately serves as the guiding force in her journey toward self-fulfillment.

In the penultimate episode of the season, "A Tree Grows in Guadalajara," Betty tries to fill out the missing branches on her family tree on the flight to Mexico, only to discover "there's no one on [her] mom's side of the chart."

The family arrives in Mexico and is surrounded by numerous relatives at Betty's Aunt Milta's house, where a *curandera* [healer] approaches Betty with a foreboding message in Spanish. She informs Betty that she is stuck in her life and will not be able to move forward until she looks back. She continues, remarking that the answer for Betty lies behind a tree with missing branches. Confused, Betty leaves the room, but awakens the next morning with a revelation: "I know what the *curandera* meant. The tree, it's the family tree, and the empty branches, that's Mom's side of the family. It's, like, so obvious. She wants me to fill in Mom's side of the tree."

Betty soon discovers that her grandmother on her mother's side, Yolanda Salazar, is not dead after all, but simply estranged from the family. Betty's mother, Rosa, had not wanted her children to know about their grandmother because Yolanda had disowned Rosa after disapproving of Rosa's decision to run off with Betty's father. Despite this news, Betty remains resolved to seek out and meet Yolanda. On her quest, Betty begins seeing visions of Henry rushing past her on a motor scooter; these visions eventually lead her to her grandmother's house. Betty enters and comes upon an elderly woman sitting in a rocking chair, saying: "Hello? Hi, Yolanda Salazar? *Hola, yo soy Betty, Rosa's hija, tu nieta.* [Hi, I'm Betty, Rosa's daughter, your granddaughter.] Uh, you have no idea how much I wanted to meet you. *Mucho.* Can you understand me?" Another woman, clearly the older woman's caretaker, enters with a tray of food and speaks: "She won't talk to you. Her mind is, no longer—I'm sorry." Betty pauses for a moment and then starts again: "I'm sorry to barge in like this. I didn't mean to disturb you. Is it OK if I just—I just—I want to say good-bye." At Betty's last sentence, the grandmother's face lights up and she approaches Betty, thinking that Betty is her own daughter, Rosa:

> YOLANDA: Rosa, mi niña, regresaste. [Rosa, my daughter, you've returned.]
> BETTY: No, no, I'm not Rosa.
> YOLANDA: Perdoname, todas las cosas feas que yo te dije anoche. Siempre trae en mi corazon. Tú eres me hija. Yo te quiero. Ay Dios mio, gracias por esto sugundo oportunidad. [Forgive me, all of the horrible things I said to you last night. I've always carried you in my heart. You are my daughter. I love you. Oh my God, thank you for this second chance.]

Yolanda turns toward the armoire in the room and retrieves several dresses, one of them a wedding dress, and continues: "Se t'olvido algo. . . . Rosa, yo estaba equivocada. Vete con Ignacio. Porque la mujer tiene que esta a lado del hombre que ama. No importa que tenga que dejar la familia" [You forgot something. . . . Rosa, I was wrong. Go with Ignacio. A woman must be with the man she loves. Even if it means she must leave her family]. At this moment, Betty's father, Ignacio, enters the house and speaks to Betty: "Did you understand what she said?" Betty nods her head as Yolanda approaches closer, cupping Betty's head in her hands, saying: "Tú eres fuerte, mi Rosa. Lucha por el hombre que amas" [You are strong, my Rosa. Fight for the man you love]. Betty replies, "I will," as the show cuts to a commercial break.

In the closing scene of the episode, Betty stands on the outskirts of the village watching an eagle land on a motor scooter in the distance; it is same scooter she saw in her vision of Henry. Her father approaches and she says to him, "I'm gonna fight for Henry. If I don't, I'll regret it for the rest of my life." Ignacio affirms her choice and then delivers some bad news to Betty, informing her that he will not be able to return to the United States with them, as his visa was not approved. Betty insists that they all stay behind with him, to which Ignacio states firmly, "Oh, no, you are going home, Betty. This is your future. I left my family once, too. Don't be afraid. You're strong, *m'ija*. Just like your mother." They embrace, tearfully, and the camera pans from their bodies to a shot of the eagle taking flight overhead.

This sequence of scenes depicts the longing for the absent mother and the actual return to the motherland as necessary steps in the young Latina protagonist's quest for romantic fulfillment. The interplay between heterosexual romantic desire and matrilineal ties is clear: Betty's desire for and pursuit of (her vision of) Henry leads her to a moment of connection with her grandmother, which in turn provides her with a directive that strengthens her resolve to "fight for" her romantic desire. But this resolution is possible only because Betty assumes the place of her mother (and not simply in the overt Oedipal ways the ending of the scene suggests). In the scene between Yolanda and Betty, both granddaughter and grandmother unite by replaying and revising a memory of the missing mother; the redemption and insight the women gain from this shared memory relies on, indeed requires, Rosa's absence. While the young Latina daughter and aging Latina grandmother can move forward as a result of this exchange, Rosa must remain, to echo the *curandera*'s prediction, "stuck" in the realm of memory.

Betty's grandmother emerges here not simply as someone who benefits, like Betty, from the memory of Rosa, but as the originary absent mother, having severed ties with her daughter when Rosa sought out her own romantic dreams with Betty's father in the United States. As such, these scenes establish Betty (and *Ugly Betty*) as the product of a legacy of absent mothers. Even after the scene with Yolanda, Betty continues to "act out" the story of her mother, leaving her family behind to fight for the man she loves. Much like Ana Garcia in *Real Women*, Betty seeks to fulfill her aspirations with the blessings of her father. She returns home, crossing the border toward her "future," like the eagle soaring across and beyond the camera's frame. And like Rosa before her, she arrives, fettered only by newfound resolve and the memory of her mother.

Absent Latinas, Aspiring Latinas

Why must young Latinas have absent or dead mothers to be legible within cinematic and televisual spheres? How and why might this trend have emerged? Given recent attention to young Latinas as the fastest growing segments of the teenage and female markets in the United States,[22] the absent mother trope can be understood as an expression of anxiety among the Latino establishment and dominant culture about the possibilities of Latinas' increasing economic power. How else to explain that Ana's transformation from undocumented immigrant theatrical protagonist to college-bound U.S. Latina or Betty's emergence as a plucky and resourceful U.S. Latina conspicuously required the absence or death of their respective mothers? Inasmuch as the absent mother leaves a young Latina isolated, encourages her to forge male-identified alliances, or requires her to be a surrogate for her own family's maternal needs, the absent mother mitigates the threat (to Latino and mainstream patriarchy) of young Latina financial independence. Moreover, especially in light of the 2000 census results that revealed burgeoning Latino demographic numbers exceeding calculated projections, the refusal to represent the Latina mother also reflects anxieties about the rapidly growing U.S. Latino population. A telling subplot in *Real Women Have Curves* conveys these anxieties. Convinced she may be pregnant, Carmen seeks out her doctor, who informs her that, in fact, she is going through menopause. This discovery causes her great dismay as she feels her womanhood is passing her by. Set within the story of young Latina aspiration, this specter of the barren mother who will soon exit the frame into representational absence serves to contain the possibilities for collective Latina agency and to manage the potential threats of Latina reproduction.

While works like *Real Women Have Curves* and *Ugly Betty* undeniably provide affirming and unprecedented roles for Latino men, wherein they may maneuver beyond prevailing notions of Latino machismo, this representational freedom comes at great cost for Latina mothers.[23] This trend reflects, as Jillian Báez notes, the ways that films like *Real Women* are channeled within "a problematic narrative in which men are positioned as more feminist than women and in turn [decenter] women within feminism."[24] Ultimately then, Latino and young Latina liberation comes at the cost of the Latina mother's appearance within the camera's frame or, more commonly, at the cost of her life. But in their depictions of the future promise of Latinas, *Real Women* and *Ugly Betty* also suggest, however feebly, that working-class Latina aspiration may some-day come at the cost of no other woman. *Será algún día, un día, un día.*

ACKNOWLEDGMENTS

Many thanks to María Elena Cepeda, Marcela Peacock, and the students at Williams College for offering me the opportunity to present some of the ideas in this chapter as part of their Latina/o Speaker Series in November 2006. Thank you also to Carrie Kaplan, Mary Celeste Kearney, and Stacy Wolf for directing me to pertinent scholarship on motherless heroines. Thanks also to Frank Guridy and the NYU Press anonymous reviewer for their helpful feedback.

NOTES

1. Nash writes, "Mothers were seen as a restraining force whose apron strings bound the child to home and hearth, while fathers . . . bridge their children's journey from the confines of the home into worldly accomplishment." Ilana Nash, *American Sweethearts: Teenage Girls in Twentieth-Century Popular Culture* (Bloomington: University of Indiana Press, 2006), 36. See also Melanie Rehak, *Girl Sleuth: Nancy Drew and the Women Who Created Her* (Orlando: Harcourt, 2005); Deborah Siegel, "Nancy Drew as New Girl Wonder: Solving It All for the 1930s," *Nancy Drew and Company: Culture, Gender, and Girls' Series*, ed. Sherrie Inness (Bowling Green, OH: Bowling Green State University Press, 1997), 159–182; and J. P. Williams, "Choosing Your Own Mother: Mother-Daughter Conflicts in *Buffy*," *Fighting the Forces: What's at Stake in Buffy the Vampire Slayer*, eds. Rhonda V. Wilcox and David Lavery (Lanham, MD: Rowman and Littlefield, 2002), 61–72.

2. Naomi Scheman, "Missing Mothers/Desiring Daughters: Framing the Sight of Women," *Critical Inquiry* 15.1 (1988): 73. While Scheman's article is focused primarily on comic heroines, her observation is apt for considering women in coming-of-age stories as well.

3. See, for example, María Elena Cepeda, "Shakira as the Idealized Transnational Citizen: A Case Study of Colombianidad in Transition," *Latino Studies* 1.2 (2003): 211–232; Chris Holmlund, *Impossible Bodies: Masculinity and Femininity at the Movies* (New York: Routledge, 2002), 109–122; Myra Mendible, ed., *From Bananas to Buttocks: The Latina Body in Popular Film and Culture* (Austin: University of Texas Press, 2007); Deborah Paredez, *Selenidad: Selena, Latinos, and the Performance of Memory* (Durham: Duke University Press, 2009); and Angharad N. Valdivia, *A Latina in the Land of Hollywood, and Other Essays on Media Culture* (Tucson: University of Arizona Press, 2000).

4. For an analysis of Latina representation in the 1930s and 1940s, see Ana López, "Are All Latins from Manhattan?: Hollywood, Ethnography, and Cultural Colonialism," *Unspeakable Images*, ed. L. Friedman (Chicago: University of Illinois Press, 1991), 404–425.

5. Jillian M. Báez, "Towards a *Latinidad Feminista*: The Multiplicities of Latinidad and Feminism in Contemporary Cinema," *Popular Communication* 5.2 (2007): 112.

6. For an astute psychoanalytic reading of the film *Selena*, see Emma Pérez, *The Decolonial Imaginary: Writing Chicanas into History* (Bloomington: Indiana University Press, 1999).

7. For more on the reproductive policing and forced sterilization of Latina bodies, see Laura Briggs, *Reproducing Empire: Race, Sex, Science, and U.S. Imperialism in Puerto Rico* (Berkeley: University of California Press, 2002), 109–161; Elena Gutierrez, "Policing 'Pregnant Pilgrims': Welfare, Health Care, and the Control of Mexican-Origin Women's Fertility," *Women, Health, and Nation: Canada and the United States Since 1945*, eds. Georgina Feldberg, Molly Ladd-Taylor, Alison Li, and Katherine McPherson (Montreal: McGill-Queens University Press, 2003), 379–403; *La Operación*, dir. Anna María Garcia, 1982; Natalia Molina, *Fit to Be Citizens: Public Health and Race in Los Angeles, 1879–1939* (Berkeley: University of California Press, 2006), 75–156; and Alexandra Minna Stern, *Eugenic Nation: Faults and Frontiers of Better Breeding in Modern America* (Berkeley: University of California Press, 2005).

8. Báez "Towards a *Latinidad Feminista*," 121.

9. http://www.itshboinepicdetail.com/films/realwomen/. Accessed 19 April 2010.

10. For an analysis of the play, see María Figueroa, "Resisting 'Beauty' and *Real Women Have Curves*," *Velvet Barrios: Popular Culture and Chicana/o Sexualities*, ed. Alicia Gaspar de Alba (New York: Palgrave Macmillan, 2003), 265–282.

11. http://www.josefinalopez.com/.

12. Clearly this scene is also evocative of the Lacanian mirror stage, wherein the child's recognition of his/her selfhood in a mirror provokes a sense of loss resulting from the recognition that he/she is separate from the mother. For a scholarly treatment of Lacan and film studies, see Sheila Kunkle and Todd McGowan, eds., *Lacan and Contemporary Film* (New York: Other Press, 2004).

13. Lyric translations are my own. Lila Downs, "La Niña," *Real Women Have Curves* [soundtrack], Jellybean Records, 2002.

14. For more on *Yo Soy Betty la Fea*, See Yeidy Rivero, "The Performance and Reception of Televisual 'Ugliness' in *Yo soy Betty la fea*," *Feminist Media Studies* 3.1 (2003): 65–81.

15. Lucy Fischer, "Sometimes I Feel Like a Motherless Child: Comedy and Matricide," *Comedy/Cinema/Theory*, ed. Andrew Horton (Berkeley: University of California Press, 1991), 64.

16. For more on telenovelas, see Ana López, "Our Welcomed Guests: Telenovela in Latin America," *To Be Continued . . . Soap Operas Around the World*, ed. Robert Allen (London: Routledge, 1995), 256–284.

17. This narrative is tellingly showcased in a famous mid-season episode, "Derailed," when Justin gains his macho Latino father's acceptance in a poignant subway scene wherein Justin sings songs from the musical *Hairspray*.

18. Scheman "Missing Mothers/Desiring Daughters," 73.

19. For more on the ways that Latinos have been overdetermined as grieving subjects, see Paredez, *Selenidad*.

20. Stanley Cavell, "Psychoanalysis and the Cinema: The Melodrama of the Unknown Woman," *Images in Our Souls: Cavell, Psychoanalysis, and Cinema*, ed. Joseph H. Smith and William Kerrigan (Baltimore: Johns Hopkins University Press, 1987), 17.

21. For more on Latina/os as a category of capital, see Arlene Dávila, *Latinos Inc.: The Marketing and Making of a People* (Berkeley: University of California Press, 2001).

22. Leila Cobo, "Latin Biz Sets Sights on Teens New," *Billboard*, 2 October 2004, 1, 24; and Teresa Puente, "Culture Clash Complicates Latina Teen Years," *Chicago Tribune*, 28 February 1999, A1.

23. Josefina López notes: "George [LaVoo] and I felt it was important not to make [the men in *Real Women Have Curves*] the center of attention, because it wasn't about them, so we made them supportive. I liked that because my father was tired of being the antagonist. I also liked that it was a step forward for Latino men and their representation." http://www.josefinalopez.com/.

24. Báez, "Towards a *Latinidad Feminista*," 123. Báez's insight draws from Tania Modleski's *Feminism Without Women: Culture and Criticism in a "Postfeminist" Age* (New York: Routledge, 1991).

7

Making "The International City" Home

Latinos in Twentieth-Century Lorain, Ohio

PABLO MITCHELL AND HALEY POLLACK

Lorain, Ohio, along Lake Erie thirty miles west of Cleveland, is at present the home of 14,000 Latinos, about twenty percent of the population in a city of 68,000. Puerto Ricans are the largest majority, with over 10,000 citizens, while almost 2,500 residents are identified as Mexicans. African Americans currently represent an additional fifteen percent of the city population. Latinos first settled in "The International City" (as Lorain city boosters dubbed it) in significant numbers in the 1920s when ethnic Mexicans migrated from Texas and other borderlands regions. Drawn by jobs in the steel industry, 1,300 men, according to one account, arrived to work in the steel mills in 1923 and 1924. The men settled in South Lorain, within walking distance of the steel mills and surrounded by other immigrant communities, largely from southern and eastern Europe.[1] Twenty years later, the *Lorain Morning Journal* reported the arrival of "26 Puerto Ricans" to Lorain; they joined a Puerto Rican community that by the early 1950s had grown to 3,700, some seven percent of Lorain's 50,000 residents.

This chapter examines two critical periods in the history of Latinos in Lorain: the 1920s and the immediate postwar period of the late 1940s and the early 1950s. Through the use of newspaper accounts, court documents such as naturalization records and civil cases, and U.S. census enumerations, this chapter describes multiple aspects of the lives of Latinos in Lorain, including marriage patterns, residential geography, and community formation.[2] Carving out spaces of their own, Latinos in Lorain created a community distinct but not wholly separate from the town's white and African American citizens. Latinos negotiated their status among Lorain's other inhabitants with whom they often lived, married, and worked, making cross-racial and cross-cultural connections.

In examining overlooked locations like Lorain, Ohio, scholars can begin to fill in gaps in the history of Latinos in the United States, expanding past major urban centers and the U.S.-Mexico borderlands. The chapter broadens the field of Latino studies, and Latino history in particular, by focusing on sexuality. In what follows, we argue that thr key to Latinos' ability to claim citizenship and civic respectability in Lorain may have been their ability to present themselves as sexually proper. Though significant numbers of Latinos lived in Lorain during both periods, it was only in the 1940s and 1950s that they appeared in the popular press as respectable citizens. Unlike the earlier period, where the Latino community was predominantly male and childless, there were far more Latino families in the postwar era. Thus sexual respectability, always a key component of citizenship, was far easier for postwar Latinos to claim than for those arriving in the 1920s and 1930s. The study of sexuality, in this case is whether domestic lives are portrayed as marital and reproductive or non-normative and "queer," helps explain the increasing acceptance of Latinos in mid-century Lorain

Latinos in Lorain

Few historians have focused on the history of Latinos in Lorain. In fact, some of the most valuable sources of information on early twentieth-century settlements are sociological accounts. In 1926, George Edson's study of Lorain was one of several dozen investigations of Mexican communities in the Midwest and on the East Coast that he produced in the 1920s, including "Mexicans in Sioux City, Iowa," "Mexicans in Pittsburgh," "Mexicans in New York City," and "Mexicans in Saginaw." Fifteen years later, Herbert Krauss's 1941 master's thesis, "Immigrant Organizations in Lorain, Ohio," included brief comments on "the seven Mexican organizations existing in the Mexican quarter of South Lorain," as well as noting an "Honorary Commission" organized by the Mexican consul's office in Cleveland.[3]

More recently, historians have begun to examine the arrival of Latinos in Lorain. In 1981, Frank Jacinto published a valuable, though brief, overview in his "Mexican Community in Lorain, Ohio." Jacinto notes that "the first Mexicans, consisting of two or three families, to settle in Lorain, arrived about 1921," and that they had likely been workers of the B&O Railroad Company. Quoting another sociological study from 1931, he describes the "Mexican racial stock in 1930 as: Indians 23%, White 3%, and Mestizo 74%." Perhaps the most important contribution of Jacinto's work is his detailed description of the development and maintenance of early community organizations in

Lorain.[4] Zaragosa Vargas also includes a handful of descriptions of the Mexican community in Lorain in his study of Mexican immigration to the Midwest. At the National Tube Company, a major steel factory, the one thousand Mexicans recruited from Texas found "steady work at good wages," at least in the early years. According to Vargas, "Turnover of Mexicans at National Tube remained low, about 13 percent." Employees at National Tube and their families constituted about "half of the 500 parishioners" at the Mexican parish in Lorain, which was established in 1926 from "a converted auto paint shop purchased through individual contributions and monthly pledges." Vargas also notes, however, that a priest complained that "National Tube's Mexican steelworkers chose to pass their leisure time playing cards, thronging to weekend dances, or haunting the pool halls." Others also attended movies and "often preferred spending several hours at a Sunday matinee than being lulled to sleep at mass by the droning of a priest." After the onset of the Great Depression, Mexican workers who had been laid off from the National Tube Company turned to agricultural work in the Great Plains. They "enlisted," he notes, "for beet work in Kansas and Nebraska."[5]

The 1930 U.S. manuscript census schedule contains further basic information on Lorain's interwar Latino community. Of the 3,300 people that lived in one neighborhood adjacent to the steel mills, about 450 were of Spanish or Latin American descent. Of these, the majority, 382, were of Mexican descent—they or both their parents had been born in Mexico. Another seventy were born in Spain, three were from Puerto Rico, three from Cuba, two from the region described as "South America," and one from Peru. An additional three men appeared in the census with Spanish surnames: Domingo Rivera, Louis Langaria, and Ramon Martin had been born in New Mexico and Texas, to parents also born in New Mexico and Texas. The census also included almost one thousand African Americans and ten "Orientals." The remainder of Lorain's forty-five thousand people were either native-born whites (sixteen thousand) or whites of recent foreign descent (twenty-nine thousand).[6]

Sources indicate that the neighborhood around the steel mills had a reputation as a place of danger and criminal excess. "It was a rough town in those days," one man recalled. "There were so many single men living in crowded boarding houses—in the rooms, attics, and cellars." "There were only about four things," the man continued, "a man could do in the evening for entertainment." Besides church attendance and immigrant social clubs, according to the man, men could either gamble or visit prostitutes. "There was the Red Light District," he reported. "It was mostly on Broadway [in downtown

Lorain, several miles from the steel mills], but women walked the streets, too. And they used to send over a carload of women from Cleveland every pay day."[7]

Census records confirm the largely working-class and male nature of the Mexican community. The majority of Mexicans in Lorain were single men who worked as "laborers" in the city's steel mills. In the household of Isidro Flores, for instance, all thirteen members were Mexican men employed in Lorain's steel mills. Twelve of the thirteen were "laborers" in the mills, while thirty-seven-year-old Severando Maldonado was a "furnace man." Census records also reveal that most Mexicans had arrived recently in the United States. The Flores example was typical; all thirteen members were listed under the census category as "Aliens" and had arrived in the United States between 1923 and 1929.[8]

Like the Flores household, most Mexicans appearing in the census were listed as individuals, not as members of a separate household. Of the nearly four hundred individuals of Mexican descent in the district, the majority were men living in rooming or boarding houses. Moreover, most Mexicans tended to live in rooming houses owned or operated by non-Mexicans, mainly European immigrant families. In one rooming house on East Twenty-eighth Street, near the steel factories, John and Mary Triffa, from Romania and Yugoslavia respectively, operated a nearly twenty-person rooming house that included four single Mexican men, as well as single men from Russia, Greece, Austria, Romania, and Poland. In another house, on South Twenty-ninth Street, the Italian-born family of Dominick and Viola Armille ran a ten-person house with only Mexicans as boarders. The men, all laborers in the steel mills, were largely in their twenties, with the exception of one thirty-five-year-old and one thirteen-year-old. Two nearby rooming houses followed a similar pattern, operated by Italian families and populated by Mexicans. In one interesting case, the household of Frank and Manuela Tolea included an intermarried couple, Fidel Gude of Spain and Mary Gude of Ohio, and five roomers: two from Spain, one from Mexico, one from Puerto Rico, and one from Cuba.[9]

While most Mexicans in 1930 Lorain were individual men living in rooming houses, a significant number of Mexicans, even those living in rooming houses, were listed in the census as married. In the above household of Isidro Flores, seven of the thirteen men were in fact married. Most had been married over four years and one, Tomas Besarra, had been married for nineteen years. Other married Mexicans lived in Lorain with their spouses. In the eighteen months between June 1929 and December 1930, twenty-eight individuals or couples with Spanish surnames filed marriage documents in the Lorain County court-house at the county seat in nearby Elyria. The marriages represented less than three percent of the over one thousand marriages during the period, but they offer important insight into multiple aspects of the Latino community. It is notable, for instance, that over half the marriages involved couples where the wife and husband had Spanish surnames. In fifteen of the twenty-eight marriages, both spouses had Spanish surnames. In twelve marriages, the wife had a non-Spanish surname and the husband had a Spanish surname.[10]

Census records similarly suggest that a significant number of Latinos in Lorain had either intermarried or were involved in cross-cultural sexual liaisons. Nine of the households appearing in the 1930 census included individuals of mixed Latino heritage, direct evidence of cross-cultural sexual intimacy involving men and women of Spanish or Latin American descent. In seven of these nine households, the individual's fathers were from Spain or Latin America. In five cases, the father was Mexican while the mother hailed from inside the United States, including the states of Michigan, Ohio, and Louisiana. In one of these five homes, the family of Joseph and Mary Brambila, the father was Mexican while the mother, though born in Ohio, had parents born in Yugoslavia and spoke Slovenian as a child. Married four years, Mary and Joseph had two children in 1930, Mary, two years old, and newly born Cirilo. Another intermarried woman was Frances Sylvanos, sixteen in 1930. She had been born in Louisiana to Texan parents and in 1929 married Richard Sylvanos, an eighteen-year-old native of Mexico who had moved to the United States six years earlier. In 1930, the couple had a son, Manuel, and Richard Sylvanos worked in the steel mills. They lived on East Twenty-eighth Street in the heart of Lorain's Latino community. In two other households, the fathers were from Spain and the mothers were from Florida and Ohio.[11]

Only two households, on the other hand, had mothers of Spanish or Latin American descent. In one family, Dolores Orlanski, born in Spain to Spanish-born parents, was married to John Orlanski, a native of Poland. The Orlanski family (John was a barber) included three daughters, Elizabeth, Carmen, and Lena, and a son, Edward. The family lived next door to another intermarried couple, Laura Sanchez, a native of West Virginia, and Manuel Sanchez, a steelworker in the mills. Other households, though without children of mixed heritage, were also clearly intermarriages. Felix and Martha Aretta, for instance, lived at 1815 South Twenty-ninth Street with five-year-old Jean Siprish and three-year-old Mary Lou Siprish, Martha's daughters and Felix's stepdaughters. Martha Aretta was born in Pennsylvania to a father from Yugoslavia and an American-born mother. Felix, according to the census, had been born in "South America," while both his parents were from Spain. The couple had recently married and Felix Aretta worked, like so many others, as a laborer in the steel mills.[12]

The lives of intermarried Latinas and Latinos offer an especially clear view of sustained and at times intimate relations between Latinos and other communities in Lorain. Despite such interactions, Latinos remained largely invisible within broader public discourse and thus generally unrecognized as members of the city's body politic. Lorain's primary newspaper, the *Lorain Morning Journal (LMJ)*, contained only the thinnest mention of Latinos in 1930, the same year that the U.S. census documented the presence of hundreds of Latinos living in one neighborhood in south Lorain. In the first three months of 1930, for instance, the daily editions of the *LMJ* only sparingly mentioned Latinos. The paper covered two raids in early March in which thirteen men were arrested on charges of violating immigration laws. According to one article, of the thirteen arrested, "nine of those taken gave their nationalities as Spanish," while "one said he was Hungarian." John Gyuicalk described paying three hundred dollars to be smuggled from Hungary into what he had believed to be the United States. Arriving instead in Cuba, he reportedly "worked his way to Lorain and has been here for the past five years." The remaining men, though named with the location of their arrest also provided, remained silent in the articles, their stories of arriving in the country and migrating to Lorain left unrecorded.[13]

Slightly more detailed was the notice for Altagracia Orozco's funeral services. According to the notice, "Funeral services for Miss Altagracia Orozco, 55, who died at her home, 1653 E. 29th Street early Saturday following a nine-month illness with heart disease, were held today from Our Lady of Guadalupe Church, Rev. David Ramos officiating." The brief notice differed little from announcements of the deaths and funeral ceremonies of other Lorainites, and even struck a note of sympathy for the long-suffering "Miss" Orozco. The piece also recognized the presence in the community of Our Lady of Guadalupe Church and the presumably Latino, "Rev. David Ramos." Nonetheless, it is perhaps telling that the death notice appeared at the very bottom of the page, directly beneath an article describing the annual meeting nearby Orozco's home in South Lorain of the city's "Americanization Board," where "Miss Eleanor Ayres, superintendent," planned to deliver the group's annual report recommending expanding educational programming.[14]

In March 1930, the newspaper reported the arrest of "Jesus Barragan, late of Madrid, Spain, but now of 131 E. 30th Street" on charges of driving while intoxicated. This brief article was prominently placed at the top of page two, and despite its lighthearted tone made a crucial distinction between Barragan and the arresting officer, "Capt. H.J. Reilly." The article's headline announced, "Reilly's Cold to 'Spanish' Custom." Referring to Barragan's reckless driving, Reilly was quoted as saying, "It might be an old Spanish custom, but it doesn't get by the U.S.A." Purportedly "American" and foreign "old Spanish" customs are juxtaposed in the piece, with Barragan's poor driving and inebriated state described as "Spanish," as is implicitly the Spanish authorities' alleged indulgence of such activities. In contrast Officer Reilly appears to represent "the U.S.A.," where such recklessness "doesn't get by." A final article reported the arrest of four men on gambling charges, including a man named Candido Moreno."[15]

Like Latinos, relatively small populations of African Americans and Native Americans lived in Lorain and were rarely mentioned in local news stories. Unlike Latinos, however, the *LMJ* contained numerous articles drawn from national sources about "Negroes" and "Indians." The articles made clear that both groups were distinctly non-white and thus far removed from full civic inclusion either on a national scale, or by implication, in Lorain as well. In late March, the newspaper followed a murder trial from Buffalo where two Native American women were charged with the death of Clotilde Marquand. According to the series of articles, which were laced with descriptions of the "squaw" women and "witches," Lila Jimerson ("the red lilac") convinced Nancy Brown ("who has seen 44 harvest moons redden ripening corn") to murder Marquand, the wife of Henri Marquand, an artist with whom Jimerson had fallen in love. Accounts of the trial highlighted the distance between "whites" and Native Americans, associating "Indians" with superstition, "hexes," life on a reservation, and lack of familiarity with "the strange talk of the white man's court." Less sensational, though similarly divisive, was an account from Washington, DC, where "Oscar De Priest, the only negro in Congress," presented to his colleagues "two members of his race, both past the age of 80." With the headline, "Introduces Two Veteran Colored Solons in House," the article repeatedly noted the racial differences between De Priest and his visitors and others in Congress. "They happen to be gentlemen of the racial group with which I identify," De Priest was quoted as saying, "so I am not alone."[16]

Other recent newcomers to the United States received similar treatment. An editorial addressing efforts to bar Filipino immigration to the US mainland noted that Hawaiians viewed such restrictions with alarm, fearing that "they themselves will be in danger of such treatment." According to the editorial, "the acquisition of foreign territory brings Uncle Sam one problem after another," and it concludes noting, "He may have to be a little more consider-ate of his insular children, to keep peace in the family." In February, the *LMJ* reached a nadir of racialized discourse when it published a short account of the arrival and departure from Lorain of a "Chinaboy." Written entirely in nonstandard English, the article was titled, "No Ketchee Ride, Chinaboy Hafta Walk to San Francisco." "Lotay people laugh at Chinaboy," the article reported, "all dressed in red, who hike west along Erie ave." "Lorain no good town," the man commented, "Me like San Francisco better." The article con-cluded stating, "Chinaboy keep on heading west."[17]

Latinos and Latino culture were fortunate to be largely spared such vit-riol from their local paper. When the Spanish club of the local high school presented a play in Spanish at its weekly assembly, the newspaper described the production, including the names of the participants (none with Span-ish surnames) under the heading "Habla Espanol? Then You Could Enjoy High School Play." Noting that the play followed "the experiences of a group of American tourists who spoke Spanish poorly, trying to make themselves understood in a Spanish railroad station," the article, and the perhaps the play as well, distanced native Spanish-speakers from "Americans" and located issues of linguistic divide and translation in a faraway land, rather than within the confines of Lorain itself. Nevertheless, speaking Spanish appears in the piece as a worthy practice and, by not translating the headline "Habla Espanol?," the article suggests, if only slightly, that some readers of the newspaper may be fluent, even native, speakers of Spanish.[18]

By contrast, far less ambiguity was suggested by descriptions of other public performances involving racial others. When Lorain junior high school students staged "The Pioneer's Papoose," the newspaper celebrated their achievement with a larger than normal headline, "Longfellow Students Make Big 'Whoopee' in Indian Fashion." The "war dance" especially caught the writer's attention, as "they pranced and they whooped and they howled, and then they pranced some more." "The Blackfeet themselves," the article continued, "could not have done any better." Two months later, the news-paper described another school performance, "a musical comedy with mili-tary and minstrel flavor" presented by the "Famous Sambos of Cleveland." "Lorain audiences for the past six years have seen and heard the Sambos each St. Patrick's night," the article reported, "and a large crowd is expected here tonight." That the "Sambos To 'Strut Stuff,'" as the headline announced, on St. Patrick's Day is suggestive of both the role of demeaning representations of African Americans in clarifying the whiteness of ethnic groups like the Irish and the enduring "otherness" of African Americans themselves.[19]

While dodging the brunt of racialized discourse, Latinos nonetheless found little inclusion within respectable Lorain society. Marriage announcements, engagements, obituaries, and notices of outings by social clubs and civic organization were common features of the *LMJ*. Yet Spanish-surnamed individuals were largely excluded from such pages of society. Historian Nayan Shah has observed, from the vantage point of San Francisco's Chinatown, that rooming houses and bachelor living situations in general drew criticism both from within immigrant communities and from the broader society. Immigrant communities, especially those eager to proclaim their own fitness for full inclusion in the American nation, frequently attempted to demonstrate to a wider American public the healthy and non-threatening domestic lives of their members and thus often described bachelor quarters as sexually aberrant and outside the realm of normal behavior. Within broader society, single immigrant men were demonized on multiple levels for their supposed sexual aberrance, such as a purported desire to seduce, rape, and murder white girls and women.[20]

Lorain, of course, was a long way from San Francisco and thus far archival sources have revealed little in the way of similar demonization of single Latino men either from within the Latino community or from the city at large. Nonetheless, the Latino community could claim few of the requisites of full civic membership, including sexual propriety, in the form of heterosexual, marital, reproductive family lives. Framed as foreigners and with little purchase on heteronormativity, Latinos faced multiple and converging forms of exclusion in Lorain. Able to dodge the most grotesque racial rhetoric, Latinos seemed incapable of claiming broader public visibility and civic legitimacy.

Two decades later much had changed for Latinos in Lorain with the apparent broadening of the city's ethnic Mexican community. Herbert Krauss described several Mexican organizations in Lorain in the 1940s, including the "Mexican Mutual Club," "Club Ideal" (which was formed after members of a baseball club "got the idea of organizing a club to help each other") and a "Mexican Young Man's Club," where "15 young Mexican men had been going for over two years" and the "young men speak largely English at their meetings." Krauss also described a women's mutual aid society and the Mexican Damsel's Club ("Doncellas Mehicanos") where "about 15 young Mexican girls meet weekly" and where "the girls have made their own club uniforms consisting of black skirts and blue jackets."[21] Krauss ends his discussion with a lengthy description of two visits to Mexican social events in the early 1940s: an evening "banquet" and a Sunday afternoon Cinco de Mayo celebration.

Amid sociological comments about "the Mexican people" ("the writer found them one of the most interesting and enjoyable groups in the city" and "they are distinctive as a group in their quest for more education, their pleasure in reading one book after another, and in trying to better themselves") are rare and valuable first-hand accounts of life in mid-century Lorain. Krauss describes, for instance, his meal at the banquet: "Mexican style fried chicken with rice, peas, tomatoes, hard-boiled eggs and fried potatoes, dishes of hot chili sauce and lettuce salad, jello and beer" and the interiors of the social halls "decorated with red, white and green crepe paper...flanked by long sheets of unrolled white wrapping paper" and the "advertisements of drug-gists, doctors and stores painted on the stage curtain." He notes that "about 200 to 250 people were present, some few of them not Mexicans" at the Cinco de Mayo celebration. "The younger women and some of the girls with long hair," he adds "had permanent waves in their hair," while other girls "had red or white ribbons in their hair."[22]

Like Mexicans, the arrival of Puerto Ricans to the city in the postwar era was also significant. Historian Eugenio Rivera describes the recruitment of Puerto Ricans to work in steel factories in Lorain in the late 1940s as "the first experiment in the country of contracting labor for heavy industry." In 1947 and 1948, the S.G. Friedman Labor Agency facilitated the migration of an estimated one thousand Puerto Rican men and their families to Lorain. By 1951, Rivera notes, one hundred Puerto Ricans were arriving per week to the city.[23]

Newspaper accounts illustrate the role of the steel mills in the lives of Latinos in Lorain. Newspaper articles, for instance, often noted that Latinos worked in the steel industry. Even those individuals associated with crimes or criminal activity could be described as "steelworkers." An article from May 1949 described a victim of a stabbing during a late-night "brawl" in South Lorain. "A thirty-three-year-old steelworker," the article began, "with a stab wound was in surgery at St. Joseph's hospital at noon today." "Francisco R. Gonzales, 33, 28th street barracks," it continued, "was brought to the hospital by friends at 9 a.m., but reportedly was stabbed at 3 a.m. today in a brawl on 28th near Pearl av." Another article reported that Joseph Diaz and Francisco Garcia were accused of "trying to obtain drivers licenses by fraud" in nearby Fairview, Ohio. The two men were described in the article as "two Lorain steelworkers."[24]

While most Latinos worked in the steel factories, other Latinos worked for local railroad companies. A child support claim, for instance, filed in New York City by Felicita Rivera Cruz against her husband, Cristobal Cruz Coto, listed Coto's employer as Nickel Plate Railroad in Lorain. Cruz's petition added that she and her husband had married in 1949 in Cidra, Puerto Rico, and that he had last paid child support a year earlier in the amount of thirty dollars. In 1954, Pedro Mejia sued his employer, the Lake Terminal Railroad Company. Mejia asked Lorain County Common Pleas judges to award him more than fifty thousand dollars in compensation for two accidents that occurred while Mejia working as a trackman for the railroad. In August 1951, a railroad tie fell on Mejia's right hand while he was operating a push car. According to his petition to the court, the accident caused "injury to the muscle, nerves, ligaments, tendons, vessels and bones of the right hand, particularly in the region of the right thumb, causing pain suffering, and permanent injury." As a result, Mejia contended, "his earning capacity as a laborer in the future" had been placed in significant jeopardy. Two years later, while replacing railroad ties, Mejia suffered another accident. A piece of steel struck him in the left eye while his was loosening ground with a pick near a set of old railroad ties. Mejia suffered "a complete loss of vision" in the eye and asked for a judgment of forty thousand dollars from his employer in this second cause of action (he had asked for fifteen thousand dollars for the injury to his hand).[25]

While most Latino settlers in Lorain in the postwar era hailed directly from Puerto Rico, others arrived from elsewhere in the United States and Latin America. Cristobal Cruz Coto and Francisco González Viera, for instance, were both born in Puerto Rico, but moved to Lorain from New York City. A Lorain newspaper article described deportation hearings against two Mexican men, Raul Diaz-Torres and Manuel Perez-Espejo, in Cleveland. The "two job-seeking Mexicans," the article noted, had been arrested earlier in the week in Lorain. Diaz-Torres, the article added, told immigration officials that he had "entered the country last February by swimming the Rio Grande river near Laredo, Texas," while Perez-Espejo had reportedly "come to the United States illegally on three occasions."[26]

The spatial dimensions of Latinos' lives in Lorain and the surrounding county are also worth noting. Traditionally, the south side of Lorain has been the center of the Latino community. Eugenio Rivera notes that in the early 1950s "South Lorain, the neighborhood across the street from the steel mill, became the home for 2,235 of the 3,700 members" of the Puerto Rican community. Despite poor housing conditions and high rents, according to Rivera, "the colony began to establish institutions to meet their cultural, social, religious and political needs." In 1952, La Capilla del Sagrado Corazón de Jesús opened its doors, joining a Pentecostal church, El Templo Bethel, in the neighborhood. Early social service organizations in South Lorain included the short-lived Puerto Rican Welfare League and El Club Benéfico, as well as El Hogar Puertorriqueño, which in 1957 would relocate to a new home on Vine Avenue in South Lorain. According to Rivera, El Hogar quickly became a center for Puerto Rican life, "the scene of baptism parties, quinceaneras, weddings, and wakes." While most Latinos lived in South Lorain, a handful lived elsewhere in Lorain County. In his 1953 declaration of intention to become an American citizen, Pedro Suarez Tovar, a twenty-eight-year-old native of Mexico, listed his home address as 202 West Thirteenth Street, on the west side of Lorain. Raymundo Rodriquez de la Pena, a thirty-year-old Mexican native, listed a home address in Elyria in his petition for citizenship in 1955.[27]

Like Latinos throughout the history of Lorain, Puerto Rican newcomers faced myriad challenges, including uncertain employment opportunities, poor housing, and language barriers. Like other members of Lorain's Latino community, they also faced a governing power structure, exemplified by the popular press and newspapers such as the *LMJ*, determined to portray Lorain as a city of racial and sexual order, where whiteness was unthreatened by unruly racial others and where sexual misconduct was swiftly and severely punished. Lorain's postwar Latino community positioned themselves within the emerging discourses of white racial supremacy and sexual respectability. As seen in newspaper accounts, Latinos managed to construct competing narratives of proper citizenship that celebrated the community's civic virtue and stable home life.

The most prominent targets of narratives of racial "otherness" in Lorain's main newspaper were African Americans. Although African Americans constituted only a small percentage of Lorain's population at mid-century, crimes committed by African Americans received special attention in the press. Most newspaper articles also took care to mention the race ("colored") of the individuals identified in the story, further distinguishing African Americans from unmarked "white" Lorainites. In February 1947, for example, the newspaper reported that "a man giving his name as George Washington, 38, colored, of Lorain" had surrendered to Cincinnati police and confessed to shooting "Mrs. Sally Washington, 32, his divorced wife, as she walked from her Cincinnati home on her way to work." The article added that the woman had been walking with "her male companion" and that her condition was critical after the shooting. The story concluded by noting that "the Lorain directory listed no George Washington and Lorain police said they have no record of him."[28]

In 1949 another story, accompanied by a photo of the accused man, reported that a man named "Sam Oliver" had been arrested in Lorain "several weeks ago as an alleged molester of a Lorain woman." After "seven weeks of intensive work by Lorain police," FBI fingerprints revealed that in addition to the assault charge in Lorain "the man was wanted in the deaths of a man and a woman in 1946 in New York." Oliver, who apparently also used the alias "Frank Hooks" and had worked for two years in Lorain as construction worker, was to be transported to New York City to face the murder charges. Several days later another article reported that Lorain authorities had dropped the "charges of assault and battery against Sam Oliver, alias Frank Hooks," and that New York City police officers planned to take Oliver to the city for arraignment. Though Oliver had been accused of "molesting a girl on a South Lorain street," he was being released "to stand trial on the more serious charge." The story concluded by noting that Oliver "denied both the local assault and the murder charges."[29]

Like depictions of African Americans, media representations of Native Americans stood in stark contrast to most descriptions of Latinos. Articles involving Indians emphasized both the cultural and the temporal divide separating Indian peoples from readers of the *LMJ*. A November 1950 article, "Four 'Tribes' of Indians Take Over Garfield School," recounts a final project of third-grade students at Garfield Elementary, the "climax to about five weeks of work and study on Indian life all over the United States." Likely timed to coincide with Thanksgiving, the presentation lasted an entire afternoon and included elaborate costumes made by the students, painting of faces ("faces smeared with 'war paint'"), a "large 'tepee'" made of paper, and "Indian songs and an Indian dance." Throughout the piece, the distance between Indian communities, on the one hand, and the students "playing Indian" is highlighted. Themes of military conquest and territorial expansion that were made explicit, though satirical, in the headline continue in the first sentence of the article. "Garfield school," the author winks, "was 'given back to the Indians' yesterday." Indian land loss and military defeat are racialized in the next sentence, which speaks of "four 'tribes' of red skins . . . beating the toms-toms and letting out war whoops." The author links Indian peoples ("tribes") to physical characteristics ("skin") and embodied actions ("beating" drums and issuing loud "whoops" from their mouths).[30]

At the same time that the article reinforces the distinction between Native Americans and "whites" in Lorain, there is a clear appreciation of the supposed lessons to be learned from Indian peoples. Both the writer of the article and the teacher, Miss Zakarakes, make clear that students in the class learned a great deal from their section on Indians in the United States. The children, their teacher said, "learned Indian signs and designs and it was all correlated with other studies, such as English, writing, music, reading, and art." The accompanying illustration to the article suggests a further, more subtle lesson. The text of the article mentions only four children by name, all of them boys. The boys are listed by name and their titles as "chiefs" of the four groups ("Red Cloud" of the Comanche, "Chief Cocheese" of the Apache, "Chief Swift Eagle" of the Navajo, and "Chief Hiawatha" of the Kickapoos). The accompanying illustration, however, includes the following: "'Squaw' Judy Horn seated cross-legged on floor in front of the 'tepee' surrounded by the four 'chiefs.'" Historians have recently noted that gender distinctions are an important aspect of "playing Indian." Since the turn of the twentieth century, organizations such as the Boy Scouts and the Girl Scouts emphasized proper, that is, patriarchal, gender norms—girls learning to recognize different baby's cries and to make several soups; boys engaging in "manly" activities like mock warfare, swimming, fishing, and mountaineering. For students of Garfield Elementary, a similar lesson (boys as "chiefs," girls as "squaws") seems to have been imparted along with the Indian crafts and "war whoops."[31]

Elaborations of racial difference and inferiority in the *LMJ* were mirrored by accounts of sexual misconduct and deviance. A front-page story from 1950 described a police raid on a "vice den" reputedly the center of a "Midwestern vice ring." Accompanied by a four-column-wide map and a photo insert of the "brothel," the article detailed the career of John Roberts, aka "Rocky River," and his apparently thriving prostitution business. The "joint" was, according to the article, a popular destination for "customers" from throughout northeast Ohio, especially teenagers, who "comprise a large percentage of the clientele." "Cautious customers" were assured by the management that they were unlikely to be arrested and were "shown certificates proving the girls had health examinations recently." The female prostitutes at the brothel were reportedly "brought here from Cleveland, Detroit, Canton, and Youngstown."[32] An article two days later noted that the establishment was "darkened and locked for the first weekend in months," though "at least one taxi and several automobiles were seen to call . . . only to leave immediately." Likewise, "one man knocked on the door unsuccessfully at 4am Sunday, a time when the spot normally is busy." The article added comments by Sheriff Carl Finnega, who reassured readers that with the suspension of operations at the brothel, "he was aware of no other places 'operating now.'" He pointed out that two other "vice spots" had recently been closed down, in one case because "its woman operator was sent to Marysville reformatory."[33]

In May 1947, a similar police raid in Lorain led to the arrest of two women on prostitution charges. Reportedly, a "male customer had complained to the police he had been cheated out of some money" at the location known as "the Incubator at 1922 E. 28th st." Another article reported that "Jean Martin, 32," had pleaded guilty after being arrested on a prostitution charge in Lorain and had been sentenced to three months in jail. Martin had been arrested several days earlier "at a South Lorain rooming house last Monday when the landlady complained she was having intimate relations with a 22-year-old man who resided there." While the paper does not identify the man, mentioning only that he was "fined $50 and costs on a morals charge," the piece adds that before the judge sentenced Martin to jail, it was revealed that "the results of her medical examination by the county health board were negative."[34]

Another set of prostitution charges were leveled at "2 Elyria women who admitted frequenting taverns in Lorain for purposes of prostitution." According to the reports from the "police vice squad," the women, identified as "Maxine Vanderson, 22, 215 Bonsaire av., and Mrs. William Brown, 32, Oberlin rd.," signed statements admitting "visiting drinking places to make 'pick-up dates.'" Both women were forced to report to the "county board of health for medical examination." The article concluded noting that "police continued to question a 25-year-old man held on suspicion of procuring women for prostitution."[35]

Accusations of other forms of sexual misconduct by both women and men were similarly highlighted in the *LMJ*. In 1947, a sodomy charge from nearby Elyria was reported under the headline "Sentence Elyrian on Morals Charge." Elmer Nelson, a sixty-three-year-old former city councilman from Elyria, had been sentenced to the Lima State Hospital for the Criminal Insane after undergoing a psychiatric examination. According to the results of the exam, Nelson was "a psychopathic case and needed mental care." The article added that if Nelson were discharged from the Lima institution prior to serving twenty years, he would complete the remainder of his sentence at the Ohio penitentiary in Columbus. The article is silent on other aspects of the case, including the nature of the "sodomy" charge and details of the arrest and trial.[36] A year later, in April 1948, the *LMJ* reported the arrest of an unnamed "58-year-old resident of Ridgeville township" on charges of a "morals offense." The incident involved a "seven-year-old girl" who as a "child ward of the Lorain co. child welfare board" had been placed in the man's home by a caseworker.[37]

Latinos seeking civic acceptance in mid-century Lorain thus faced twin perils from press accounts: racial denigration of the sort targeting African Americans and Native Americans as well as a press eager to publicize a range of sexual violations. Presented with such threats, Latino community leaders managed to present an alternative discourse of respectability and civic virtue. One article from 1949 described an "outing" to be held by the officers of the "Club Puertoricana," [sic] during which the members of the organization planned to vote for "permanent officers." According to "Mrs. Elia F. Collizo," who announced the meeting to the newspaper, two hundred people were likely to attend "the picnic," and foremost on the agenda would be determining a "meeting place where Puerto Ricans [could] gather for parties and other social events, a place with social space and room for a library."[38]

In March 1947, the *LMJ* similarly reported a "social gathering in their club rooms" of Lorain's Mexican American community in honor of Jose Infante, an editorial staff member of "one of Mexico's leading magazines, *Asi*," which planned to devote an entire issue to Mexicans living in Ohio. Presided over by master of ceremonies "Rasael [sic] Jimenez," the festivities included the presentation of a gift to Infante, "group singing of Mexican folk songs," and the attendance of honored guests like the mayor of Lorain, the president of the "Steelworkers CIO," and "J. Heskamp, Spanish instructor at Lorain High school," as well as "Dr. L Bustamante and Dr. J Zapata, both of Mexico, who are studying in City hospital, Cleveland." In both articles, Latinos managed to present themselves as respectable ("*Mrs.* Elia F. Collizo"), well-organized, committed to settlement in Lorain ("permanent officers"), democratically-inclined, interested in education ("room for a library"), and worthy of civic acceptance (a "leading" Mexican magazine's interest in Mexican Americans in Ohio, the appearance of the mayor and a union president at their social events)."[39]

Announcements of weddings and engagements offered Latinos another opportunity to present themselves as proper members of the community. In June 1950, the *LMJ* reported, "Dolores Sanchez Weds in All White Ceremony." The article announced that Sanchez, "the daughter of Mr. and Mrs. Anacleto Razo, 1648 E. 30th st, became the bride of Jimmy Soto of Lorain," who was the son of "Mr. and Mrs. A. Soto of Fort Worth, Texas." Like the four other, non-Latino weddings described in similar detail on the same page, the bride's dress and accessories received special attention. Sanchez was, according to the paper, "attired in a gown of French imported lace, its bustle back and portrait neckline studded with seed pearls and beading. The full skirt fell into a short train. Her fingertip illusion veil was gathering to a crown of matching lace, and she carried a bouquet of calla lilies centered with a single white orchid. Her only jewelry was a single strand of pearls, the gift of the bridegroom." "Miss Margaret Segovia," the piece added, served as maid of honor, while "Misses Elvira and Josephine Silva" were bridesmaids and "Judy Smith was flower girl." The attendants reportedly wore "identical ankle-length gowns of white net over satin with off-shoulder neckline and bouffant skirt trimmed with white satin bows," as well as "white net bonnets."[40]

Another example of the respectful treatment of Latinos in the press emerges in reports of the deaths of Lorain County residents. In February 1949, a tragedy striking the Martinez family of Lorain drew the attention of the newspaper. "Infant Stricken; Funeral Monday," the headline read, and the article proceeded to announce the death of "the [unnamed] one-month-old daughter of Mr. and Mrs. Leonides Martinez, 2158 E. 28 st." "Aside from her parents," the notice added, "she is survived by a brother, Reinaldo, at home." The piece concluded by noting that funeral services would be held at the Reidy and Scanlon Funeral Home "at 2 pm Monday with Rev. Fr. Joseph Conlon, acting pastor at St. John's church officiating," and that "burial [would] be in Calvary cemetery."[41]

Latinos who were perceived as victims of criminal activities could at times also be treated by the press with sympathy and relative concern. "Mrs. Julio Arredondo," for instance, was the target of a particularly brutal assault in downtown Lorain in October 1949. Arredondo reportedly suffered a "throat-slashing knife attack," and, according to witnesses, her "windpipe was severed by the blade of a knife wielded by one of the men [currently] in custody of the police." The account thus identifies the Spanish-surnamed victim with a deferential title ("Mrs.") that also signals Arredondo's elevated civic status as a married woman. Latino community leaders likely would have approved of both the dignified press treatment accorded a seriously injured Latina (and the absence of jokes or criticism of her behavior) and the apparent quick response of police officers in apprehending her attacker.[42]

Conclusion

Newspaper accounts of Latino life in Lorain reveal important continuities and discontinuities between two critical periods of settlement and community formation in Lorain. Latinos' ability, or simple good fortune, to dodge the most virulent racist rhetoric is consistent in both eras, as is the marginal and racially-marked status of African Americans and Native Americans. More notable, however, are the discontinuities in popular discourse. Latinos in the late 1940s and early 1950s appeared more frequently in the press and were accorded far more respect and dignity than the earlier era. While many factors certainly had a hand in this development, this chapter suggests that mid-century Latinos' ability to present themselves as sexually-normative may have been a critical factor in their increased acceptance within broader Lorain public life.

Clearly, much more research is needed to uncover the history of Latinos in Lorain. Such research includes an analysis of newspaper accounts comparable to those from the 1940s and 1950s that address racial and sexual differences in Lorain in the 1920s. Marriage records from postwar Lorain could offer similar forms of comparison, as could more detailed investigations of Latino residential and cultural geography throughout Lorain and Lorain County. As Latino Studies broadens and expands, locations like the "The International City" and subjects like the Latinos who made that their home are an important next step. Furthering research of Lorain, Ohio, and geographical locations similar to it, will begin to create a fuller picture of the history of Latinos in the United States. More than simply recovering a narrative, a geographically broad story will help to illuminate a more inclusive and complete history.

NOTES

1. Herbert M. Krauss, "Immigrant Organizations in Lorain, Ohio," Master's Thesis, Oberlin College, 1941, 10; http://lorain.areaconnect.com/statistics.htm

2. *Lorain Morning Journal*, February 6, 1948, 2; Eugenio Rivera, "The Puerto Rican Colony of Lorain, Ohio," *Centro Journal* 2, no. 1 (Spring 1987), 12.

3. Krauss, "Immigrant Organizations in Lorain, Ohio," 210.

4. Frank Jacinto, *The Mexican Community in Lorain* (Avon, Ohio: Privately Printed, 1981), 1, 3.

5. Zaragosa Vargas, *Proletarians of the North: A History of Mexican Industrial Workers in Detroit and the Midwest, 1917–1933* (Berkeley: University of California Press, 1993), 31, 45, 144, 146. See also Gloria Alvarez, "Assimilation of Second Mexican-Americans in Lorain, Ohio," Master's Thesis, Oberlin College, 1952; and Dennis Nodín Valdés, *Barrios Norteños: St. Paul and Midwestern Mexican Communities in the Twentieth Century* (Austin: University of Texas Press, 2000).

6. U.S. Bureau of the Census, 1930, Lorain County, Ohio. The 1930 census for the entire city of Lorain included "Mexican" as a racial category and listed a total of two hundred "Mexicans."

7. Krauss, "Immigrant Organizations in Lorain, Ohio," 12.

8. U.S. Bureau of the Census, 1930, Lorain County, Ohio.

9. Ibid.

10. Lorain County Marriage Docket, Lorain County Courthouse, Elyria, Ohio. The remaining couple is difficult to decipher. The marriage register lists Fermina Ortiz marrying a man named Manuel Razuia. "Manuel," of course, is a common given name for Latinos, and the 1930 census listed over a dozen men named Manuel born in either Mexico or Spain living in Lorain County. Further, marriage clerks were hardly infallible when transcribing the names of their subjects (Ruiz or Ramirez, for instance, could have been misheard and miswritten as Razuia). The census, however, also listed a number of men named Manuel who were clearly not Latinos. Fifty-year-old junk dealer Manuel

Babich, for instance, had been born in Russia of Russian parents, while Manuel Baker was a thirty-two-year-old Ohio native of German descent.

11. U.S. Bureau of the Census, 1930, Lorain County, Ohio.

12. Ibid.

13. *Lorain Morning Journal*, March 5, 1930, 1; *Lorain Morning Journal*, March 13, 1930, 1.

14. *Lorain Morning Journal*, January 20, 1930, 5.

15. *Lorain Morning Journal*, March 26, 1930, 2; Lorain Journal, January 5, 1.

16. *Lorain Morning Journal*, March 20, 1930, 9; *Lorain Morning Journal*, March 29, 1930, 2; *Lorain Morning Journal*, March 2, 1930, 5.

17. *Lorain Morning Journal*, March 1, 1930, 4; *Lorain Morning Journal*, February 26, 1930, 1.

18. *Lorain Morning Journal*, March 25, 9.

19. *Lorain Morning Journal*, January 17, 1930, 1.

20. Nayan Shah, *Contagious Divides: Epidemics and Race in San Francisco's Chinatown* (Berkeley: University of California Press, 2001).

21. Krauss, "Immigrant Organizations in Lorain, Ohio," 199-206.

22. Ibid., 210, 213.

23. Rivera, "The Puerto Rican Colony of Lorain, Ohio," 11, 13.

24. *Lorain Morning Journal*, May 18, 1949, 1; *Lorain Morning Journal*, November 9, 1950, 1.

25. Felicita Rivera Cruz vs. Cristobal Cruz Coto, Lorain County Civil Case, No. 57582; Pedro Mejia vs. The Lake Terminal Railroad Company, Lorain County Court of Common Pleas, No. 57714.

26. Felicita Rivera Cruz vs. Cristobal Cruz Coto, Lorain County Civil Case, No. 57582; Candida Gonzalez vs. Francisco Gonzalez, Lorain County Civil Case, No. 57583; *Lorain Morning Journal*, January 27, 1950, 24.

27. Rivera, "Puerto Rican Colony of Lorain," 14, 16, 18; Declaration of Intention, No. 13401, Pedro Suarez Tovar; Declaration of Intention, No. 13412, Raymundo Rodriguez de la Pena.

28. *Lorain Morning Journal*, February 18, 1947, 2.

29. *Lorain Morning Journal*, January 8, 1949, 2; *Lorain Morning Journal*, January 13, 1949, 1.

30. *Lorain Morning Journal*, November 22, 1950, 16.

31. Ibid.; see also Phil Deloria, *Playing Indian* (New Haven: Yale University Press, 1998).

32. *Lorain Morning Journal*, November 11, 1950, 1, 2.

33. *Lorain Morning Journal*, November 13, 1950, 1.

34. *Lorain Morning Journal*, August 30, 1947, 2.

35. *Lorain Morning Journal*, January 10, 1947, 12. Notice the specificity with which the newspaper identifies the women accused, but not yet convicted, of prostitution. Such detailed reporting commonly occurred in the *LMJ* in the late 1940s and early 1950s, regardless of the severity of the incident under investigation. Even victims of car accidents at times appeared in the reports with full names and addresses.

36. *Lorain Morning Journal*, April 7, 1947, 9.

37. *Lorain Morning Journal*, April 2, 1948, 11.

38. *Lorain Morning Journal*, July 28, 1949, 17.

39. *Lorain Morning Journal*, March 3, 1947, 2.

40. *Lorain Morning Journal*, June 24, 1950, 6.

41. *Lorain Morning Journal*, February 5, 1949, 12.

42. *Lorain Morning Journal*, October 18, 1949, 1.

8

Hispanic Values, Military Values

Gender, Culture, and the Militarization
of Latina/o Youth

GINA M. PÉREZ

As the media consistently reminds us, we find ourselves at a critical and potentially dangerous time. A defining feature of this dangerous location, I would argue, is what conservative historian Andrew Bacevich (2005, 2) refers to as the new American militarism, which he defines as "a romanticized view of soldiers, a tendency to see military power as the truest measure of national greatness, and outsized expectations regarding the efficacy of force. To a degree without precedent in U.S. history, Americans have come to define the nation's strength and well-being in terms of military preparedness, military action, and the fostering of (or nostalgia for) military ideal." This chapter focuses on how Latina/o youth and Latin American immigrants are located within this new American militarism and how understandings of citizenship and belonging are shaped in this context. For many Latinas/os, enlisting in the military is both a literal and figurative move "beyond el barrio," although, as I will demonstrate below, advertising agencies, Latina/o civic organizations, military officials, and Latina/o families themselves frequently invoke and advance varied notions of "barrio life" in their discussions of Latina/o (or "Hispanic") culture, gender roles, and kin relations. This anthology's emphasis on the shifting meanings of citizenship, the wide range of lived experiences of Latinas/os, and their attempts to lay claim to belonging in both local and transnational contexts, offers a special opportunity to consider not only the limits, barriers, and exclusions im/migrants, communities of color, and other marginalized groups face today, but also to reflect on the creative strategies communities employ to navigate this dangerous time. Here I focus on how an examination of the military recruitment of Latinas/os and their participation in Junior Reserve Officer Training Corps programs (JRTOC) reveals a great deal about citizenship and belonging for marginalized communities throughout the United States.

Recent media, popular, and policy attention to Latinas/os as the new majority minority has fueled two interrelated and seemingly contradictory responses: attention from military recruiters eager to meet recruiting goals; and vicious nativist backlash that defines Latinas/os as not only outside the nation, but also as, following anthropologist Leo Chávez's (2008) argument, "the Latino threat." This nativist backlash takes many forms, including the rise of the Minuteman Project, an organized citizen militia aimed at controlling illegal immigration across the U.S.-Mexico border; as well as new legislative attempts to control immigrant labor, settlement, and reproduction through a proposed guest worker program, the construction of the seven-hundred-mile wall along the U.S.-Mexican border, and a well-funded assault on "birthright citizenship" and the Fourteenth Amendment (Chávez 2008, 92). Thus, while military recruiters seek to include U.S. Latinas/os and Latin American immigrants in the responsibilities and privileges of U.S. citizenship, policy makers, conservative policy analysts, and citizen groups vigorously resist and seek to exclude and regulate Latin American immigrant incorporation in the United States. These tensions and contradictions are not lost on Latina/o youth, who candidly discuss both their decisions to participate in their high schools' JROTC programs, as well as their concerns about the marginal economic, political, and social position of Latinas/os in the United States.

In what follows I explore these moments of Latina/o inclusion and exclusion in order to map out the political economic context in which Latina/o youth are increasingly implicated in a militarized world. By focusing on Latina/o youth participation in JROTC programs in American public high schools, as well as the ways the U.S. military employs notions of gender, culture, and family in its attempts to recruit young Latinas/os into its ranks, this analysis helps to illuminate what anthropologist Arlene Dávila (2008, 18) describes as "the politics and exclusions that are increasingly involved in the contemporary production, circulation, and consumption of Latinidad." The U.S. military is an especially important institution to examine regarding these moments of inclusion and exclusion, not only because it symbolizes a vision of citizenship that rests on sacrifice, honor, and patriotism, but also because it is a invaluable vehicle for economic mobility for many working-class families. Attention to the material conditions in which Latina/o youth and their families make decisions about their relationships to the military reveals a great deal about the price Latinas/os and other marginalized groups in the United States potentially pay for full citizenship rights, as well as the provisional nature of citizenship claims based on notions of culture, values, and performances of patriotism.

Yo Soy el Army

Political theorist Judith Shklar (1991, 2) argues that American citizenship "has never been just a matter of agency and empowerment, but also of social standing." Rather, American citizenship has historically been characterized by exclusion, and by the "prolonged struggle" for inclusion by women and men who have been denied key attributes of full citizenship rights (15). Like other scholars from marginalized communities, Latina/o Studies scholars have documented myriad examples of these historic and contemporary exclusions and have theorized various meanings of citizenship (cultural citizenship, for example) and struggles for full citizenship rights (Oropeza 2005; Mariscal 2004; Pulido 2006; Whalen 2001; Ramos-Zayas 2004; Rocco 2006). Given that the citizen-soldier is located at the pinnacle of citizenship hierarchy, one way marginalized communities of color have laid claim to full citizenship rights is precisely through military service and the performance of patriotism and loyalty. While race, class, gender, and sexuality are key axes for exclusion, military service promises to redeem those who possess what anthropologist Ana Yolanda Ramos-Zayas labels "deficient citizenship," by imbuing them with the Machiavellian virtues of patriotism, selflessness, and a willingness to sacrifice oneself for the "military glory" of the nation (Ramos-Zayas 2004; Shklar 1991, 31). Not surprisingly, many young Latinas/os have regarded their participation in the military as a one pathway to first-class citizenship. These realities are not lost on the Pentagon and military recruiters, who have increased funding for recruiting Latina/o youth with a clear understanding of the transnational contexts in which these potential soldiers live. The U.S. Army's recent bilingual recruitment is one example of how military officials understand and navigate the transnational, bilingual, and bicultural lives of many Latina/o residents.

In July 2000, the U.S. Army hired Chicago-based advertising firm Leo Burnett to develop a new series of recruiting materials to replace the Army's "Be All You Can Be" campaign of the 1980s and 1990s. Leo Burnett's slogan, "An Army of One," quickly circulated and featured slick pamphlets, interactive media, and online games in an effort to reach out and meet the new challenges in recruiting youth into the all-volunteer force in the post–cold war era. In order to ensure its reach into Latino and African American communities, Leo Burnett subcontracted Hispanic-owned Cartel Creativo and African American–owned IMAGES USA as part of its four-year advertising and marketing strategy.[1] Drawing on notions of Latino culture and emotion, Cartel Creativo developed the Spanish-language slogan *Yo soy el Army*, or "I am the Army," a phrase Cartel Creativo CEO Victoria Varela Hudson noted recognizes the bilingual lives of today's Latina/o youth. In an interview with the *Los Angeles Times*, Varela Hudson observed, "Un ejército de Uno [An Army of One] simply doesn't work en español. It had to be in Spanglish or bilingual. That's the way the majority of these kids speak. They say 'Army.'" By using the Spanglish word "Army" rather than "ejército," Cartel Creativo also addresses perhaps an even greater challenge to the military recruitment of Latina/o youth—namely, many Latin American immigrants' distrust of the military due to the histories of military violence and war in their countries of origin. According to Varela Hudson, "You need to address [cultural] perceptions about what this *ejército* is—and among many of these parents, the perception of the Army isn't necessarily something positive," especially for those immigrant parents who "grew up under Castro, Somoza and others" (Johnson 2001). These "cultural perceptions," however, are deeply embedded in experiences of brutal state violence enacted by Latin American security officials, supported and trained by the U.S. military personnel in the name of American empire. As anthropologist Lesley Gill powerfully demonstrates, this internationalized state-sponsored violence has "shattered the social bonds of those who survived the repression" (2004, 13).

The slogan *Yo soy el Army* sufficiently distances *patriotic* U.S. military service in a democratic society from its allegedly corrupt, despotic, and distinctively Latin American counterpart in order to assuage immigrant parents' fears regarding their children's decision to join the Army. More important, however, it does so by relying on notions of culturally specific kin relations centered around the dominant Latina mother. Major General Dennis D. Cavin, for example, noted that attracting more Latinas/os into the Army's ranks requires the understanding that "the mother is a dominant influence in Latino families in terms of big decisions" (Johnson 2001). And while Latino families are not unique in their susceptibility to various "influencers" (trusted people—such as school counselors, teachers, parents, siblings— who can inspire and advise young people regarding post–high school plans), they are reportedly distinctive in their extraordinary patriotism and bravery. Varela Hudson asserts that not only have Latinos earned more Medals of Honor than any other group on a per capita basis, but they have also "traditionally shown a passion for the Army, for being in the trenches. There is an incredible level of patriotism" (Johnson 2001).

This widely held sentiment about the distinctiveness of Latina/o patriotism is shared by prominent military officials and civic leaders, who regularly point to Latinos' loyalty and patriotism as models of American citizenship.

For example, former Secretary of the Army Louis Caldera noted that Latinos "make great soldiers," and that "Hispanic youth have the highest interest in military service . . . the highest success rate among soldiers and they have the highest re-enlistment rate" (Talerico 2000). Similarly, Lieutenant General Ricardo Sanchez, military commander in Iraq until 2004, noted, "When I became a soldier the ethics and the value system of the military profession fit almost perfectly with my own heritage. It made it very easy for me to adapt to the military value system" (Mariscal 2004, 46). Love of one's family and nation, self-sacrifice, and loyalty are the shared values binding Hispanic heritage and the military. This notion was further underscored during Hispanic Heritage Month in 2005, when the Department of Defense partnered with *Latina Style* magazine to honor Latinas in the military. In honoring Latina soldiers like Colonel Angie Salinas of the U.S. Marine Corps, the president and CEO of *Latina Style* observed that these women exemplified how "living the military life is a testament to Hispanic resilience and service to country. . . . And nobody can question that the Marine Corps is the service that can reinforce the principles that make this country great—the same principles that are found in many Hispanic homes" (Ayalin 2005).

This equation of "Hispanic values" with American (and, in this case, specifically military) values is echoed in political discourse as well. Arlene Dávila argues that these powerful narratives of Latina/o "communality, hard work, and family" infuse political campaigns and are increasingly advanced by "pundits, advocates, and scholars who insist and provide proof that Latinos are not a social liability; that they are moving up and contributing; and that, in fact, their values make them more American than 'the Americans'" (2008, 61, 63). These favorable representations, she argues, simultaneously obscure the realities that Latinas/os face and are used to denigrate African Americans and other marginalized groups, against whom Latinas/os are implicitly compared. This "spinning" of Latina/o experiences also serves to sanitize and ultimately whiten U.S. Latina/os, thus making them more "marketable" to a broader American public invested in "distinguishing the 'good' from the 'bad' Latino" (6–7). Thus, while dominant discourse continues to frame Latinas/os as a "threat" to the nation, "Latino spin" advances a vision of properly ordered Latina/o communities and families grounded in purportedly distinctive American values of hard work and family. As noted Univsión news anchor Jorge Ramos notes, "A nation that emphasizes Latinos' morals and family values while maintaining the prevailing U.S. political and economic processes would, without a doubt, be a healthier and more humane society" (in Dávila 2008, 2). Such an argument inverts the assimilation logic by demonstrating not only the ways that Latinas/os have indeed assimilated, but also how they have allegedly surpassed the morally dubious American mainstream. Like dominant discourses characterizing the American military, U.S. Latinas/os are praised for the ways they embody superior moral values that American civilians would do well to emulate.

These characterizations of U.S. Latinas/os, as well as the demographic reality of their population growth, inform the military recruitment of Latinas/os in specific geographic locations throughout the United States. According to the U.S. Army Recruiting Command's "Strategic Partnership Plan for 2002–2007," Latinas/os are projected to constitute 25 percent of the U.S. population by 2025; in order to capitalize on this expected growth, recruitment priority areas like Los Angeles and San Antonio exist "primarily as the cross section of weak labor opportunities and college-age population as determined by both [the] general and Hispanic population" (Mariscal 2004, 46). The Department of Defense has enlisted the research efforts of entities such as the RAND Corporation and the Center for Naval Analysis to identify the factors affecting Latina/o military enlistment. Both studies emphasize, for example, the youth of the U.S. Latina/o population (Latinas/os currently constitute 12 percent of the general U.S. population but nearly 18 percent of the eighteen- to twenty-four-year-old population); Latinas/os' positive attitudes toward the military compared to African American and white youth; and their higher "active duty propensity (i.e. they say they are interested in joining the military) than non-Hispanic youth" (Hattiangadi et al. 2004, 1; Asch et al. 2005). These trends are especially evident in the U.S. Marine Corps, where Latina/o recruits increasingly swell the ranks and are "more likely than recruits of other races and ethnicities to complete bootcamp and the first term of service" (ibid.).[2] Notwithstanding these positive signs, however, Latinas/os account for less than 10 percent of active-duty forces (Bilmes 2005; Pew Hispanic Center 2003). According to these and other studies, the military will need to address serious challenges in the areas of education, language fluency, and citizenship status if they hope to increase the number of Latina/o recruits in the years to come (Hattiangadi et al. 2004, 2; Asch et al. 2005).

The irony here, of course, is that the military has identified precisely those areas of Latinas/os' economic and social lives that progressive activists and scholars, as well as mainstream policy makers and Hispanic business and civic organizations, have consistently highlighted. *Hispanic Business* magazine, for example, noted the enduring labor market gap, with Latinas/os indexing higher unemployment rates than the population as a whole, and

Latinas experiencing higher unemployment rates than Latinos, even despite their higher levels of educational attainment (Lehman 2005). And a series of reports by the Pew Hispanic Center have focused on the widening wealth gap, occupational divide, and educational attainment levels between Hispanic and non-Hispanic whites in the past decade. A recent study detailing Latina/o occupational status notes, for example, that "the occupations in which Hispanics are concentrated rank low in wages, educational requirements and other indicators of socioeconomic status," and that even as unemployment declined for all racial and ethnic groups, "structural shifts in employment across industries contributed to a greater division in the occupational status of Hispanics and whites" (Pew Hispanic Center 2005). According to the 2000 census, nearly a third of all Latina/o workers are located in construction and production work, and 46 percent are employed in service and sales occupations.[3] As a result of Latinas/os' concentration in low-wage employment, more than 11 percent of Latino workers are poor.[4] Latino unemployment is also nearly twice that of non-Hispanic whites.[5]

In the area of education, Latinas/os continue to have high dropout rates in high school, with 15 percent of U.S.-born Latinos dropping out of high school, compared to 7 percent of whites and 44 percent of immigrant children (Pew Hispanic Center 2002b). Despite these high dropout rates, Latinas/os have increased their numbers in college enrollments, although they are half as likely to finish a bachelor's degree as non-Hispanic whites.[6] For those Latinas/os who remain in American public schools, they increasingly find themselves enmeshed in what Pauline Lipman has identified as "stratified academic programs," whereby African American and Latina/o high school students attend schools with "limited offerings of advanced courses and new vocational academies, basic skills transitional high schools" (or public military academies), rather than the "new academically selective magnet schools and programs, mainly located in largely white upper-income and/ or gentrifying neighborhoods" (Lipman 2003, 81).[7] These economic, social, and educational realities are not lost on military recruiters, who highlight the myriad ways in which military service can provide economic security and occupational training for all enlistees, as well as expedited naturalization for noncitizen soldiers. As literary scholar and Vietnam veteran Jorge Mariscal notes, "For all working-class youth with limited horizons, these appear as powerfully seductive messages" (Mariscal 2004, 49).

If, as Cynthia Enloe (2000, 245) argues, military service is often regarded as "the path to full citizenship status" and "first class citizenship," current Latina/o military recruitment serves as an important mechanism of Latina/o inclusion in the nation.[8] These militarized notions of inclusion for Latina/o citizen-soldiers, however, are contested, provisional, and, as Enloe notes, require "decisions, many decisions, decisions made by both civilians and people in uniform" (289). Interestingly, at precisely the same moment in which Latina/o citizen-soldiers attempt to lay claim to first-class citizenship through military service, citizen groups, policy makers, and prominent scholars challenge these claims, highlighting instead the alleged economic, social, and cultural burden of Latin American—specifically Mexican—immigrants on the nation. In April 2005, for example, the Minuteman Project commenced, mobilizing civilian patrols along the U.S.-Mexico border to draw attention to "the chaotic neglect by members of our local, state and federal governments charged with applying U.S. immigration law."[9] Throughout the month of April, approximately nine hundred people participated in the Minuteman border patrols, and while they did not have the power to arrest those suspected of crossing the border illegally, their presence—and the subsequent proliferation of Minuteman organizations throughout the United States—highlighted, once again, the powerful anti-immigrant sentiments that facilitated the passage of Proposition 187 and Proposition 227 in California in the late 1990s.[10] Recent legislative attempts to eliminate "birthright citizenship" and to implement a guest worker program underscore the enduring attempts of U.S. officials to encourage labor migration—with legal measures to control and regulate workers through the contract labor system reminiscent of the Bracero program from 1942 to 1964—but to discourage migrant settlement and immigrant communities.

Samuel Huntington's recent writings provide ideological support for such movements. High levels of Latin American—and specifically Mexican—immigration, he argues, have contributed to the erosion of Anglo-Protestant culture and values, which are the cornerstone of the American Dream. Unlike previous immigrant groups, contemporary Mexican/Latino immigrants have failed to assimilate into "mainstream U.S. culture" and have, instead, formed "political and ethnic enclaves" that threaten to erode a distinctive American national identity (Huntington 2004a, 2004b). While many scholars, advocacy groups, and progressive writers have effectively demonstrated the fallacies in Huntington's arguments, his fears resonate with anti-immigrant groups like the Minuteman Project, who point not only to the alleged economic costs of illegal immigration, but who increasingly employ the language of culture to explain their concerns. The Minuteman Project, for example, encourages volunteers to enlist in their struggle by warning that if they fail to do so, "future generations will inherit a tangle of rancorous, unassimilated, squabbling cultures with no common bond to hold them together, and a certain guarantee of the death of this nation as a harmonious 'melting pot.'"[11] What is particularly striking about Huntington's argument, though, is its seductiveness in turning to culture as terrain on which to fight for America's identity and soul. This strategy, of course, is not new. As Micaela di Leonardo eloquently argues, the culture wars of the 1990s employed similar rhetoric and alarmist imagery, and even those debates have roots that extend back to the 1960s and white ethnic reaction to the gains made by women, African Americans, Latinas/os, Asian American, and LGBT populations (di Leonardo 2000). For my purposes here, however, I am interested in how concern with "culture" and "values" shapes the lives of working-class and poor Latina/o youth and their families. Huntington (2004a, 2) notes, for example, that while Americans have focused on "the economic costs and benefits of immigration," they have ignored its social and cultural consequences.

Interestingly, academic research on Latinas/os in the military has found that military service is positively associated with Latina/o acculturation. In a study focusing on the acculturation of Latino veterans, political scientist David Leal finds that "Latino veterans had more friendships with Anglos, spoke more English at home, and reported more discrimination." Given that many researchers acknowledge Latinas/os' slow acculturation process and political incorporation, he concludes that "any factor that increases it should be of interest to scholars," and that his findings suggest "military service, either voluntarily or involuntarily, likely promotes this process" (Leal 2003, 207). Latinas/os' precarious economic position, their allegedly shared cultural values with the military, and the military's acculturating influence are all powerful forces that do not overly determine the educational experiences and career choices of Latina/o youth; but these factors certainly do shape the range of opportunities available to them as they make decisions and strategize in conditions not of their own choosing.

Latina/o Youth and JROTC

In addition to military's active recruitment of Latinas/os, their participation in the growing number of JROTC programs in American public schools provides another way to explore the various meanings of citizenship, and Latina/o communities' attempts to lay claim to full citizenship rights and belonging. Established in 1916, JROTC emphasizes the notion that "citizenship takes practice."[12] The program is regarded by some as a critical feature of revitalizing American military power by focusing on civilians and military personnel alike. As anthropologist Catherine Lutz notes, "preparedness movement" advocates of the early twentieth century advanced the idea that military conscription and training would "solve the problem they saw of American manhood gone soft" (2001, 33). In the early twentieth century, as now, these notions of citizenship, preparedness, and masculinity were forged in a context of increased anxiety as a result of high levels of immigration.

In Chicago—where more than a quarter of the population is Latina/o—JROTC has enjoyed unprecedented expansion in the public schools, with more than ten thousand students, largely Latina/o and African American, participating in some form of the program. While students have numerous reasons for joining JRTOC—the appeal of extracurricular activities; the possibility of receiving class credit; opting out of PE, to name a few—I will focus on a recurring theme in my work with JROTC cadets, namely their fascination with the military uniform they are issued and are required to wear. In Chicago and in Lorain, Ohio (where I am currently engaged in research), students spend a great deal of time talking about the cadet uniform. Almost all the students I interviewed and spoke with informally at Chicago's Bellow Academy[13] cited "being treated with respect" (especially while wearing the cadet uniform) both as a reason for joining as well as one of the greatest advantages of participating in JROTC. Students' concern with respect is no small matter since most reside in poor and working-class (and, often, slowly gentrifying) neighborhoods regarded in local media as dangerous, and are enmeshed in racialized policing practices aimed at containing suspect youth.[14] Latina/o and African American youth are also painfully aware of how their bodies are read—how the color of their skin, their manner of dress, and where they the live elicit suspicion and fear from law enforcement, business owners, and even their neighbors (López 2003, 37; Pérez 2004, 147). These transgressions of norms of dress, class, and ethnicity, Dwight Conquergood (1992, 135) observed, "legitimize official systems of surveillance, reform, enforcement and demolition."

Wearing a military uniform is one way of negotiating the racialized systems of surveillance that operate not only within their neighborhoods but also within their own schools. Some scholars have argued that the proliferation of JRTOC programs is only one example of a broader pattern of school security initiatives that justify zero tolerance discipline policies and reflect "a rising culture of 'law and order' that pervades popular culture, educational discourse, foreign policy, and language" (Saltman 2003, 21). Indeed, the emphasis of Chicago's school reform law on "accountability, high-stakes tests, standards, and centralized regulation of schools" has enabled administrators and elected officials to regulate teachers and students, and to "'crack down' on African American and Latino youth who are seen as largely superfluous in Chicago's restructured, informational economy and dangerous in the racialized social landscape of the city" (Lipman 2003, 81, 82).[15]

When I asked students participating in JROTC how they became interested in the program, almost everyone described a particular event that sparked their initial curiosity. Sixteen-year-old Letty, who was moved to Chicago from Acapulco, Mexico, when she was four months old, recalled seeing another girl wearing a military uniform on the bus and how she told her about JROTC. This conversation intrigued her, and when I asked her why, she responded, "They show you how to be a leader . . . I was mostly used to being a follower. So I wanted to learn how it was to be a leader." When I asked how JROTC teaches her to be a leader, she explained in detail how as squad leader, she organizes the cadets in lines and makes sure her squad is in order, and how she can continue to "get rank . . . depending on your behavior and your commitment to RO." She continued:

> Well, I am in Color Guard. And in the mornings, I don't miss a day in the mornings. And I'm always going, if there is an event going on, I'm always a part of it . . . I've always been the kind of girl that I can't stay and not do nothing. And I always have to do something and right now, they are giving me the opportunity to do something, so I'll just do it.

Letty explained also how she has remained in school because of JROTC: "It's because of ROTC that I am here. Because all of the responsibilities that we have, it makes us want to come to school so we can finish it. And because of ROTC, it makes us come to school." Many other students shared Letty's emphasis on leadership skills, on the value of the responsibilities she is given in JROTC, and on the way the program motivates students to stay in school. Marisol, a young Puerto Rican cadet whose father was a Marine, described how JROTC helped her to develop skills critical for college:

> I want to go to college and I want to get my degree in history. I want to be an archaeologist. I like to study things about the past and stuff. I would like to go away for college . . . and they [JROTC] teach you to focus. It teaches you to prepare for anything. It teaches you to take responsibility for what you want to happen in your life. It teaches you to stand your own ground.

Being a leader, learning how to focus, and being able to manage and get others to follow were skills the students not only valued in the context of their schools, but also ones they believed would help them get into college. Marisol also explained that being in JROTC made her more disciplined and taught her how to "take charge." These are important qualities that others now admire in her. Since joining JROTC, she regularly wakes up early to go to drill before classes begin in the morning and she does more physical exercise; despite her mother's initial resistance to her participation in JROTC, Marisol's mother now praises her for being more responsible. Wearing the uniform is particularly important for Marisol, and is a profound connection she shares with her uncle. When I asked if she liked wearing the uniform, she answered emphatically: "Yes. I don't know, it just . . . [it just] shows people that I'm trying to do something with my life. I'm in JROTC."

Many students talked at length about the uniform—how they preferred the Marines' uniforms over all other military dress, how wearing it made them feel like they were "somebody," and how being in JROTC made them feel proud. Lorena explained that she enjoyed excelling in JROTC because it made her feel proud: "I really want to be proud of myself, to show other people that I can do something." When I asked if there were other things that she was proud of, she quickly added: "I'm proud of myself because my grades are very good. My GPA is 3.0. So I'm very proud of that. I'm proud of my family, you know, because they're all very successful. My dad owns a company . . . and I want to follow in their footsteps."

Students connect wearing the cadet uniform not only with the respect they receive but also with discipline. This connection is reinforced by the JROTC commanders as well as their fellow cadets each week. Once a week, students wear their cadet uniform and are inspected by their company commander and the chain of command of their company. At Erie Shores High School in Lorain, Ohio, these inspections and the requirement of wearing the uniform weekly make up part of the final grade of the JROTC course. Uniforms are issued at the start of the school year, and as a student gains rank and participates in community service and other activities, he or she is awarded ribbons, medals, braids, and pins that adorn the uniform. New cadets, with little experience and opportunity to earn awards, often look admiringly at older cadets whose uniforms display rank and status in the school battalion. On inspection day, students spend a great deal of time fixing their uniforms, helping each other with proper placement of ribbons and pins, and eventually are marched by the company commander outside or in the school hallway, cafeteria, or auditorium for inspection. Inspection involves the company commander and the chain of command walking in front of each cadet and stopping to see if the cadet conforms to a list of at least ten items of proper uniform etiquette—hair length, cleanliness and condition of the uniform, placement of regalia, proper socks and shined shoes, even a look to see if the brass belt buckle is properly shined. When I ask why they take time to do this, the JROTC instructors reply that this is a required part of the program. They also explain that it is another example of how to reinforce the important values of discipline in JROTC. Students often seem nervous while being inspected, and they often giggle when six inches away from the inspecting officer. When I ask them about this process and about their uniforms, though, they all say that they really enjoy that part of the JROTC experience. Several young women noted that in their first year, they did not do well in JROTC because they were embarrassed to wear the uniform to school. This year, though, it is different, and they explain how they now wear their uniform with pride.

As uniformed students walk in the hallways—especially while they are marching and drilling—non-JROTC students often look at them, sometimes mocking, but other times they imitate them by saluting, walking beside them, and standing very tall. School security guards, on the other hand, are always very respectful of JROTC cadets, especially while they are in uniform. They often salute them as they walk by, offer their own versions of cadence songs, and frequently express approval with knowing nods and raised eyebrows. The JROTC commanders are very clear about how important it is for students to conduct themselves in a special way while wearing the dress uniforms. These are the only times they are not required to do push-ups if they are late to class; they also are told they will be severely punished if they allow non-JROTC students to wear parts of their uniforms. Students take this responsibility seriously and are constantly reminded how much the Army is investing in them by issuing them new uniforms each year. When they wear their uniforms both in school and at extracurricular events, students describe feeling proud and admired and respected by others. And the response they receive, not only from their peers, but perhaps more importantly from their families, veterans' groups, and other community members, is significant. At one event in which the JROTC Color Guard attended and honored POW/MIAs at a local AMVETS post, the host thanked the Erie Shores Color Guard for attending, commenting that looking at them in those uniforms and looking "so sharp" instilled a sense of pride for them and for the entire community. Commanding such respect is no small matter, especially for young people of color navigating the urban landscape and for young Latinas/os who are increasingly aware of the ways in which they are regarded as dangerous, unappealing, and increasingly superfluous to the local political economy. Wearing the uniform is one way of managing these perceptions; it is also a unique and important opportunity to receive positive attention by participating in community events and by practicing, as they are encouraged daily in their JROTC classrooms, good citizenship in their communities.

Conclusion

As many scholars remind us today, the contemporary seduction of the military has a long history in Puerto Rican, Chicana/o, African American, Native American, LGBTQ, and other marginalized communities. The military is successful in seducing young people into its ranks precisely because it is seen as an important avenue for social mobility and for full citizenship rights. American citizenship, as historian Lorena Oropeza (2005, 7) reminds us, is inextricably linked with race, respectability, and manhood (although I would also argue for new attention to the ways that femininity and being a "good daughter" are also mobilized within the rhetoric of military service among young women). Thus, when military leaders, politicians, and civic organizations appeal to Hispanic values and traditions as precisely the same values that characterize the U.S. military, the most respected American institution today, it is not surprising that many Latinas/os would feel proud and encourage such positive comparisons, especially given the anti-immigrant and racist political and social climate in which many live, work, and raise their families. It is also not surprising that young Latinas/os and African Americans would turn to JROTC programs that provide not only possibilities for respectability, but also enable them to access social capital otherwise unavailable to them. These are reasonable strategies among a shrinking number of opportunities facing all working-class youth.

The problem, however, is that there is a cost to this kind of inclusion; and given the ongoing wars in Iraq and Afghanistan, the cost is very high. Posthumous citizenship, disrupted education when a student's reserve unit is called for active duty, and the ironies of fighting for rights that continue to elude them are not lost on young Latinas/os contemplating their futures. One young woman participating in JROTC in Chicago remarked with pride regarding Latinas/os' patriotism. But she also noted that even though noncitizen Latina/o soldiers demonstrate tremendous patriotism by serving in the military, they still lacked equal rights with other Americans: "[Latinos] are patriotic. Even though they might not be given the same rights [as Americans]. Even though they're actually fighting for that in *this* country, which I still think is crazy, that some of them can't vote because they're not citizens. But they're still fighting." While such critical insights are hopeful in that they are reminiscent of the tensions characterizing Chicana/o, Puerto Rican, and African American protest and activism in the 1960s and 1970s, they emerge during a distinctive neoliberal moment that increasingly defines the role of government as the ability to create "a good business climate rather than look to the needs and well-being of the population at large" (Harvey 2005, 48). These neoliberal visions shape people's active attempts to lay claim to first-class citizenship, but they also exact a high price for respectability and belonging. The dreams of social mobility, economic advancement, and educational attainment are often what animate young people to consider military service. These dreams, however, may also obscure the cost of laying claim to first-class citizenship by enlisting in the military. For Latina/o youth, in particular, aspirations for moving "beyond el barrio" are simultaneously bound up with long, fraught histories of racial exclusion as well as moments of profound ethnic pride. With limited economic, social, and educational opportunities, many young Latinas/os will continue to turn to military service as a way beyond el barrio.

NOTES

1. Like Cartel Creativo, IMAGES USA specializes in "multicultural marketing" in order to connect its clients with the "viable and diverse African American, Hispanic/ Latino, and Asian markets." See http://www.imagesusa.net/about.html, accessed January 2006. My thanks to Miriam Lakes, whose seminar paper (2004) provided important sources and analysis of the Army's *Yo Soy el Army* campaign.

2. According to the CNA report, Hispanic recruits in the Marine Corps have outnumbered African American recruits since 2000. See Hattiangadi et al. 2004.

3. Pew Hispanic Center 2005, 2–3. The report also notes the declining representation of Latinas/os in managerial and professional occupations (16 percent in 2000) compared to whites (34 percent) and Asian workers (42 percent).

4. This compares with 10.2 percent and 4.0 percent of black and white workers, respectively. National Council of La Raza 2001.

5. The unemployment rate for Hispanics is 8 percent. See Pew Hispanic Center 2002a.

6. Interestingly, while Latinos are enrolling in college in higher numbers than ever before, their enrollments in four-year universities lag behind those of white students in those states with large Latino populations, such as California, Arizona, New Jersey, and New York. Thus, while Latina/o enrollments are "spread across both four-year and two-year colleges . . . the increase in enrollments among whites tilted in the direction of four-year colleges" (Fry 2005).

7. Elsewhere I discuss Chicago Public Schools' expanding JROTC programs and the increasing number of Latinas and Latinos who participate. See Pérez 2006.

8. Enloe critically interrogates this notion, as well as the attempts by some feminists and feminist organizations to argue that since military service is the "sine qua non of American citizenship," all groups should have equal access to full military participation. Her powerful critique of masculinity, militarism, and power challenges these attempts at full equality to highlight, instead, the need to question the pervasiveness of militarized values that "creep into ordinary daily routines" (Enloe 2000, 365, 3).

9. http://www.minutemanhq.com/, accessed February 2006. See also Chávez's (2008, chap. 4) powerful account of the Minuteman Project as spectacle.

10. Proposition 187 passed in 1994 and eliminated health care and educational services for undocumented residents. In 1998, Proposition 227 ended bilingual programs in California public schools. According to some estimates, there are currently forty Minuteman groups in at least a dozen states. See Knickerbocker 2006. The Minuteman website not only seeks to recruit more volunteers into its ranks, but it also features a column titled "From the States," detailing the group's activities across the country. See http://www.minutemanhq.com/hq/index.php. According to a report commissioned by the Congressional Immigration Reform Caucus (2005, 4), "The Minutemen Project demonstrated that with realistic and immediate manpower increases illegal immigration to America's southern border would be dramatically reduced if not virtually eliminated compared to current levels of illegal crossings."

11. http://www.minutemanhq.com/, accessed February 2006.

12. Poster in JROTC classroom, September 2006.

13. A pseudonym. All names and places have been changed to protect the anonymity of participants in the study.

14. Elsewhere (Pérez 2004) I have documented how Latina/o youth (especially those in rapidly gentrifying neighborhoods) are implicated in the policing of urban space aimed at curbing, for example, gang activity. Although Chicago's anti-loitering ordinance was declared unconstitutional in 1999, some scholars and activists have highlighted the "ongoing attempts to legalize harassment and street sweeps of youth," and particularly youth of color, who are regarded as dangerous and who allegedly "need to be locked up or removed from public space" (Lipman 2003, 95).

15. Lipman also notes, for example, how Chicago's 1995 school reform law not only gave Mayor Richard Daley control of the schools, but it also allowed Chicago Public School CEO Paul Vallas to establish "a corporatist regime focused on accountability, high-stakes testing, standards, and centralized regulation of schools" that has resulted in the retention of thousands of Latino and black youth, as well as their being sent "to mandatory remedial programs and basic education transition high schools" (2003, 81). The result has been not only a deepening stratification of academic programs, but also stronger centralized control over local school districts.

REFERENCES

Abu-Lughod, Janet L. 1999. *New York, Chicago, Los Angeles: America's Global Cities.* Minneapolis: University of Minnesota Press.

Asch, Beth, Christopher Buck, Jacob Alex Klerman, Meredith Kleykamp, and David S. Loughran. 2005. "What Factors Affect the Military Enlistment of Hispanic Youth? A Look at Enlistment Qualifications." Report Prepared for the Office of the Secretary of Defense in RAND National Defense Research Institute. Santa Monica, CA: RAND Corporation.

Ayalin, March. 2005. "Marine Colonel Honored by *Latina Style* Magazine." September 9. http://www.usmc.mil/marinelink/mcn2000.nsf/0/f94a2de8d450631a85257083000fb89 5?O, accessed February 2006.

Bacevich, Andrew. 2005. *The New American Militarism: How Americans Are Seduced By War.* New York: Oxford University Press.

Berlowitz, Marvin J., and Nathan A. Long. 2003. "The Proliferation of JROTC: Education Reform or Militarization." In *Education as Enforcement: The Militarization and Corporatization of Schools,* Kenneth J. Saltman and David A. Gabbard, eds. New York: RoutledgeFalmer, 163–174.

Betancur, John J., Teresa Cordova, and María de los Angeles Torres. 1993. "Economic Restructuring and the Process of Incorporation of Latinos into the Chicago Economy." In *Latinos in a Changing U.S. Economy,* Rebecca Morales and Frank Bonilla, eds. New York: Sage Publications, 109–132.

Bilmes, Linda. 2005. "Uncle Sam Really Wants Usted." *Los Angeles Times,* August 21.

Chávez, Leo. 2008. *The Latino Threat: Constructing Immigrants, Citizens, and the Nation.* Stanford: Stanford University Press.

Congressional Immigration Reform Caucus. 2005. "Results and Implications of the Minuteman Project." May 19.

Conquergood, Dwight. 1992. "Life in Big Red." In *Structuring Diversity,* Louise Lamphere, ed. Chicago: University of Chicago Press, 95–144.

Cordova, Teresa. 1991. "Community Intervention Efforts to Oppose Gentrification." In *Challenging Uneven Development: An Urban Agenda for the 1990s,* Philip W. Nyden and Wim Wiewel, eds. New Brunswick: Rutgers University Press, 25–48.

Dávila, Arlene. 2008. *Latino Spin: Public Image and the Whitewashing of Race.* New York: New York University Press.

di Leonardo, Micaela. 2000. *Exotics at Home: Anthropologies, Others, and American Modernity.* Chicago: University of Chicago Press.

Enloe, Cynthia. 2000. *Maneuvers: The International Politics of Militarizing Women's Lives.* Berkeley: University of California Press.

Flores-Gonzalez, Nilda. 2002. *School Kids/Street Kids: Identity Development in Latino Students.* New York: Teachers College Press.

Fry, Richard. 2005. "Recent Changes in the Entry of Hispanic and White Youth into College." *Report for the Pew Hispanic Center,* November 1.

Gill, Lesley. 2004. *The School of the Americas: Military Training and Political Violence in the Americas.* Durham: Duke University Press.

Harvey, David. 2005. *A Brief History of Neoliberalism.* New York: Oxford University Press.

Hattiangadi, Anita, Gary Lee, and Aline Quester. 2004. *Recruiting Hispanics: The Marine Corps Experience.* Alexandria, VA: Center for Naval Analysis.

Huntington, Samuel. 2004a. "The Hispanic Challenge." *Foreign Policy,* March/April.

———. 2004b. *Who Are We? Challenges to America's National Identity.* New York: Simon and Schuster.

Johnson, Greg. 2001. "Enlisting Spanish to Recruit the Troops." *Los Angeles Times,* March 1.

Knickerbocker, Brad. 2006. "Across the Country, Many Mobilize Against Illegal Immigration." *Christian Science Monitor,* January 23.

Lakes, Miriam. 2004. "Enlisting in Citizenship: An Analysis of the Current U.S. Military Recruitment of Latinos." Paper submitted for seminar, Militarization of American Daily Life, Oberlin College, May 20.

Latino Institute. 1994. *A Profile of Nine Latino Groups in Chicago.* Chicago: Latino Institute.

———. 1995. *Facts on Chicago's Puerto Rican Population.* Chicago: Latino Institute.

Leal, David L. 2003. "The Multicultural Military: Military Service and the Acculturation of Latinos and Anglos." *Armed Forces and Society* 29(2): 205–226.

Lehman, Andrea. 2005. "Hispanic Labor Market Gap Continues." *Hispanic Business*, October. http://www.hispanicbusiness.com/news/news_print.asp?id=25892, accessed February 2006.

Lipman, Pauline. 2003. "Cracking Down: Chicago School Policy and the Regulation of Black and Latino Youth." In *Education as Enforcement: The Militarization and Corporatization of Schools*, Kenneth J. Saltman and David A. Gabbard, eds. New York: Routledge-Falmer, 81–101.

López, Nancy. 2003. *Hopeful Girls, Troubled Boys: Race and Gender Disparity in Urban Education.* New York: Routledge.

Lutz, Catherine. 2001. *Homefront: A Military City and the American Twentieth Century.* Boston: Beacon Press.

Lutz, Catherine, and Lesley Bartlett. 1995. *Making Soldiers in the Public Schools.* Philadelphia: American Friends Service Committee.

Mariscal, George. 2004. "No Where To Go: Latino Youth and the Poverty Draft." *Public Affairs Magazine*, November.

National Council of La Raza. 2001. "NCLR Statement on the Economic Status of Latino Families." October 8. http://www.nclr.org/content/news/detail/2211/, accessed February 2006.

Oropeza, Lorena. 2005. *Raza Sí! Guerra No!: Chicano Protest and Patriotism During the Vietnam War Era.* Berkeley: University of California Press.

Pérez, Gina. 2004. *The Near Northwest Side Story: Migration, Displacement, and Puerto Rican Families.* Berkeley: University of California Press.

———. 2006. "How a Scholarship Girl Becomes a Soldier: The Militarization of Latina/o Youth in Chicago Public Schools." *Identities* 13:53–72.

Pew Hispanic Center. 2002a. "Educational Attainment: Better Than Meets the Eye, but Large Challenges Remain." January.

———. 2002b. "Hispanic Economic Prospects Depend on Education and a Strong Economy." January 1.

———. 2003. "Hispanics in the Military." March 27.

———. 2005. "The Occupational Status and Mobility of Hispanics." December 15.

Pulido, Laura. 2006. *Black, Brown, Yellow, and Left: Radical Activism in Los Angeles.* Berkeley: University of California Press.

Ramos-Zayas, Ana Yolanda. 2004. "Delinquent Citizenship, National Performances: Racialization, Surveillance, and the Politics of 'Worthiness' in Puerto Rican Chicago." *Latino Studies* 2:26–44.

Ranney, David C., and William Cecil. 1993. *Transnational Investment, and Job Loss in Chicago: Impacts on Women, African-Americans, and Latinos.* Chicago: Center for Urban Economic Development, University of Illinois at Chicago.

Rocco, Raymond. 2006. "Transforming Citizenship: Membership, Strategies of Containment, and the Public Sphere in Latino Communities." In *Latinos and Citizenship: The Dilemma of Belonging,* Suzanne Oboler, ed. New York: Palgrave Macmillan, 301–328.

Saltman, Kenneth J. 2003. "Introduction." In *Education as Enforcement: The Militarization and Corporatization of Schools,* Kenneth J. Saltman and David A. Gabbard, eds. New York: RoutledgeFalmer, 1–23.

Sassen, Saskia. 1998. *Globalization and Its Discontents.* New York: New Press.

Shklar, Judith. 1991. *American Citizenship: The Quest for Inclusion.* Cambridge: Harvard University Press.

Talerico, Teresa. "Hispanic-Owned Firm Wins U.S. Army Contract." *Hispanic Business,* October 6. http://www.hispanicbusiness.com/news/news_print.asp?id=1710, accessed January 2006.

Whalen, Carmen. 2001. *From Puerto Rico to Philadelphia: Puerto Rican Workers and Post-war Economies.* Philadelphia: Temple University Press.

Part III

Latina/o Activisms and Histories

9

Going Public?

*Tampa Youth, Racial Schooling, and Public
History in the Cuentos de mi Familia Project*

JOHN MCKIERNAN-GONZÁLEZ

"History": A word I don't hear very often. I am doing history on
my mother. Doing history on my mother will let me get closer
to her and I will get to know her a little bit better.
—Rocío Lopez Padilla, October 2002

The biggest challenge in the Cuentos de mi Familia project was getting middle school students to commit to writing a biography of one of their
family members. One student, Rocío Lopez Padilla, understood that writing
and sharing a family biography could change her relationship to her mother.
Other middle school students in the Cuentos project were more wary of the
risks involved in a public history project that centered their families' lives.
They may have had concerns about the sudden visibility of their families'
lives. The students who did risk public visibility in the Cuentos project
demonstrated the challenge Latino diversity poses to the existing history of
Latino communities in Greater Tampa.

The Cuentos project embraced the narrative challenge of increasing
Latino diversity. Historical accounts of Latinidad in Florida begin with the
politics among Cuban and West Indian cigar workers in Tampa at the turn of
the twentieth century, the tensions between *marielitos* and *balseros* in Miami,
and the transformation of Cuban exile politics.[1] The difficulties of Nicaraguan and Haitian communities, the large settlement of Puerto Ricans in Central Florida, and the creative organizing among Mexican, Guatemalan, and
Haitian workers in Immokalee have at times made their way past a Miami-
Cuban frame for Latinos in Florida. The Cuentos project bears witness that
the Cuban inflection of Latinidad in Tampa is undergoing drastic changes.
Only two of the thirty-two Greater Tampa students completed a Cuba-based

project in Cuentos. Eight of the thirty-two Latino biographies in the Cuentos de mi Familia project started in Texas. Migrant farm worker children were the only Cuentos students born in Hillsborough County. Moreover, Tejano, Mexican, and Puerto Rican students were the majority of Cuentos students. The diversity of Latino working-class life in Greater Tampa challenged established ways of writing the history of Latinos in Florida. The students in the Cuentos project confronted shallow Latino scripts in middle schools and popular culture as well as in the Cuentos de mi Familia project.[2] The historical narratives that Cuentos students put together emphasized high levels of geographic mobility across the United States as well as Latin America. The stories about their favorite family member also exposed limiting assumptions about class, gender, and place-bound identity that initially structured the Cuentos project.

This middle-school-based public history project should force a public reconsideration of the relationship of a Cuban-dominant Latino history in Tampa and in Florida as a whole. Collectively, the students' history projects complicated the regional contexts, exposed the variety of national origins, and underlined the importance of women in the everyday life of Latino/a America. As they constructed genres that fit the life outlines of their favorite family member, the Cuentos students circumvented the barrio-based narratives that provided the historical models for the Cuentos de mi Familia project. These Latino middle school students present a different Florida to scholarly understandings of Latinidad. They highlight the complications of narrating a life in the face of unrecognized Latino diversity. Through the process of creating a biography that would make sense to their fellow Latino classmates, the students transformed the narrowly American frameworks I built into the project, and sidestepped the immediate racial schooling they faced in Southern public schools. The Cuentos project used short, barrio-based biographical essays by Piri Thomas, Mandalit del Barco, Pat Mora, and Patricia Preciado Martin as models for writing about a family member. Middle school students in Cuentos used images and found objects to craft written and visual historical narratives. Their art projects used these objects to do justice to the contours of their favorite family member's life. The art-making process moved the students into the visual realms of Latino/a America and away from the written models I had given them. The translation of their families' biographies into art projects helped students go beyond the geographically limited, barrio-based historical essays in the Cuentos project.

The Cuentos students emphasized journeys, not barrios. Their projects cleaved to the journeys, choices, and obstacles that shaped their family member's life. Their narration of these transnational and translocal stories challenged my Latino barrio template. Their discussion of the emotional trajectory of their subjects' lives also caused some unease among some audiences in Tampa, graphically highlighting tensions around respectability and domesticity in Latino communities. Racial schooling in the Cuentos project often claimed kin with cultural citizenship, what Flores and Benmayor describe as the process in which "cultural phenomena—from practices that organize the daily life of individuals, families and the community, to linguistic and artistic expression—cross the political realm and contribute to the process of affirming and building an emerging Latino identity and political and social consciousness."[3] The racial schooling qua cultural citizenship came in two forms. First, some project sponsors expected student participants to represent what was implicitly respectable in a monolithic Latino culture. In the second form, I—as the Cuentos project director—expected students to recognize themselves in the written barrio narratives I shared with them. In both cases, stereotypes about cultural expression narrowed the ability of participants to lay claim to the variety of vibrant identities in which the students participated.

Tensions around respectability emerged when middle school students shared their sense of their domestic life with friendly publics across Tampa's public schools. The murmurs of "we do not need to hear that," which appeared when students discussed the multiple family arrangements that shaped their lives, showed how Cuentos students challenged idealizing gender norms established in the name of culture. When the Cuentos participants went beyond their immediate neighborhood to claim a larger geographical space for their biographies, they undercut the idea that a working-class Latino life started in one barrio experience. Moreover, the gender dynamics of many of these translocal family formations upset American stereotypes of geographically embedded nuclear families. Family arrangements were part of the Latino diversity in the Cuentos project.

Mobility and displacement underlay many of the Cuentos students' family stories; these themes were not in the Cuentos project curriculum. In response, students adopted and adapted historical genres from outside the classroom walls to more adequately represent the impact of history on their families' mobility. These genres—"aventuras sobre el mapa," "hidden lives," and the "via crucis"—used maps, images, and drawings to make each person's life connect to a world richer than their place in Hillsborough County. These genres demonstrate the creative challenge that Latinos faced when they brought an unrecognized life into the public sphere.

Contemporary Latinos, Racial Schooling, and the "Latin" Landscapes of Cuban Tampa

Latino racial schooling in Florida follows from the continuous reminder that Latinos are permanent recent arrivals, alien citizens in Mae Ngai's terminology. The economic growth of Hillsborough County has encouraged Latinos to settle in Tampa, but the geography of growth has complicated the ability of contemporary Latinos to see their reflection in Tampa's official Latin landscape. Still, the long-standing presence of Latino populations, the large numbers of Latinos, and the diversity of Latinos across Hillsborough County complicates this schooling of students simply as permanent foreigners.[4]

The diversity and number of Latinos in Hillsborough County is impressive. The 2000 census stated that twenty-two percent of the close to one million people who settled in Hillsborough County identified themselves as Hispanics or Latinos. Moreover, when asked to define their national origin, 56,680 identified themselves as other Latinos or Hispanics, 52,280 as Puerto Ricans, 35,321 as Mexicans, and 35,123 as Cubans.[5] Colombians, Dominicans, Hondurans, Ecuadorians, Nicaraguans, and Peruvians were the largest groups among the remaining forty thousand Latino residents.

This Latino diversity was evident in the student body. Although the vast majority of the Cuentos students were born in the United States, their narratives did not stay in the United States. There were eight Mexico-based biographies, four from Puerto Rico, and four from Texas. The remaining places covered were Connecticut, the Dominican Republic, Colombia, and Honduras, and Cuba and El Salvador were represented by two projects each. This school-aged diversity reflected the distribution of Latinos in Hillsborough County. The median age of the Latino population was thirty-one, but Puerto Ricans (twenty-eight) and Mexicans (twenty-three) had the lowest median age, and Cubans had the highest median age (thirty-eight). The median income for all these groups was roughly similar, with Dominican households earning the highest ($35,143) and Puerto Rican households the lowest ($31,008). The median household income for other Latino groups hovered around $33,000. This median household income is approximately $12,000 less than the general median income for Hillsborough County and $2,000 more than African American household incomes.[6] Latino households in Hillsborough County are both diverse and working-class. Since the establishment of Ybor City in 1885, economic growth has meant more Latinos and more Latino diversity in Hillsborough.

But the availability of particular jobs and housing to Latinos in Tampa has led to a pattern of checkerboard residential segregation. The largest concentrations of Latinos lay at the edges of Tampa. Puerto Rican, Central American, and South American households congregated at the western edge of historic West Tampa, keeping access to construction, industrial, and service sector employment, as well as work in the airport and the port of Tampa. Twenty miles away, in South Tampa, Puerto Rican, Dominican, and Tejano households maintained a connection to light industry, the tomato fields, and new residential subdivisions. In the northeast corner of Hillsborough County, Mexican, Puerto Rican, and Central American families settled in Plant City and took jobs in strawberry farms, canneries, and phosphate mines. Although Latino families in South Tampa and Plant City settled close to higher income neighborhoods in Hillsborough County, their children did not share in the educational benefits of this proximity. The Cuentos project took place in schools where the majority of students receive free lunches and more than half of the students are people of color.[7]

The schools in the Cuentos de mi Familia project emerge from the patchwork segregation wrought by patterns of suburban industrialization in agriculturally intensive areas. All these schools housed families with median incomes of less than thirty thousand dollars a year. The economic geography of Tampa places Latinos on the margins of urban life in Hillsborough County.

Each family's creative adjustments to limited labor market situations upset conventional American family ideals. The adults in the Cuentos project worked long hours in strawberry farms, tomato patches, phosphate mines, other people's houses, warehouses, short-haul trucking, laboratories, and light assembly factories. Students discussed their family's effort to live together over vast distances—and across highly policed borders. These long-distance situations stretched and warped household roles in ways that upset American family ideals. The translocal dimensions of Latino family life—leaving a child behind with siblings or grandparents in Honduras or Houston—disturb nuclear family ideals.[8] The ongoing child labor contribution to migrant households picking tomatoes in the fields of Indiana, Michigan, and Florida also challenges American family and labor law.[9] The threat of deportation also complicates any attempt to describe a regular undocumented family life.[10] Finally, the normative belief that most families own their houses, share the same citizenship, and that these houses are a refuge from a hostile world help render these structurally violent household situations nearly invisible.[11] When participants brought their domestic arrangements into public through their Cuentos, the variety of households among students unsettled the racial schooling implicit in a family values narrative.[12]

The Latin landscape in Tampa never included all groups participating in cigar manufacturing, and the current landscape reinforces these exclusions. In 1918, the people that the Circulo Cubano expelled on racial grounds established La Sociedad Marti-Maceo in 1918. Their ballroom became the marquee forum for black and Afro-Caribbean populations in Tampa. Afro-Cubans and Bahamians became heavily involved in civil rights mobilizations in Tampa and South Florida. Other Latinos capitalized on their service in machine politics and World War II. Some used their military connections to open GI Bill services, increase public employment for Latinos, and expand the political arena in West Tampa. The eclipse of cigars by cigarettes undercut shared black and Latino life in Tampa. In the 1960s, Latino West Tampa and Ybor City barely survived urban renewal, while federal highways paved over the historically black Central Avenue business district and forced Sociedad Marti-Maceo to tear down their Art Deco ballroom. Ybor City became the landscape that housed Latinidad in Tampa.[13] In the 1980s, the growth of tourism and retirement communities in Central Florida transformed Tampa into a key port for both of Orlando's growing industries. Midwestern retirees took I-75 to St. Petersburg, Sarasota, and Tampa, creating an ongoing construction boom in once-agricultural areas known for their strawberries, oranges, and phosphate mines. City boosters sought to capitalize on the movement of tourists, workers, and family members through Tampa. The Art Deco landscape created by "Latin" mutual aid societies in Ybor City became an alternative tourist attraction. Even though Ybor City became the national symbol for left-leaning Latino cigar-making communities, few Tampa Latins work in cigars. The economic landscape of Tampa places Cubans in the past and Latinos on the city's margins.

Lifting as We Climb: The ENLACE Project, Hillsborough County, and Cuentos de mi Familia

In the spring of 2003, I proposed the Cuentos de mi Familia project to the ENLACE project at the University of South Florida (USF). The project— Cuentos means a collaborative public history—asked each middle school student to complete three complicated tasks. First, complete a short research and interview-driven biography of a favorite family member. Then, combine images and photographs with parts of the biography to create a portable art project. After that, they were to present their project to all the families involved in the Cuentos project in a public space in their middle school. Finally, the director of the University of South Florida library would ask students and their families to consider donating their Cuentos art project and earlier drafts to the Special Collections division. The proposal sought to apply methods developed in neighborhood mapping projects run by the Smithsonian Latino Initiatives in Mount Pleasant, South Carolina, as well as the multi-ethnic archival projects sponsored by the Japanese American National Museum. ENLACE—the Latino outreach division at the University of South Florida—asked me to request participation from their seven partner middle schools across Greater Tampa.

I met with principals and ENLACE liaisons at all seven schools, and each agreed to participate. I requested funds from many Latino community groups. The Hispanic Professional Women's Association of Hillsborough County (HPWA), an organization with heavy involvement of Puerto Rican and Cuban American staff in ENLACE, was the only sponsor. They provided funds to cover the printing of educational materials, art materials, a camera, and a book for each student who participated in the project. ENLACE guaranteed transportation expenses and an administrative structure in each school. The USF Internal Review Board and the university–public school district liaison allowed the project to continue as long as there was no subsequent educational performance review for Cuentos students, which limited the policy implications of the Cuentos project.

Still, the schools recognized that Latino teens were in a good position to outline the future history of Latino Tampa. Each principal and teacher agreed to let selected students spend two hours a week during school hours with USF undergraduates enrolled in my Latino History course for twelve weeks. This was a sizable investment of time and experience by middle school students, USF undergraduates and faculty, ENLACE staff, and Hillsborough County School District employees. Surprisingly, the Cuentos project received substantial buy-in from seven schools across Hillsborough County. ENLACE—Hillsborough County gave the program the green light because there were stakeholders in local community organizations and were among middle school administrators who saw the value of such a project for Latino youth and their communities.

The ENLACE project itself dates back to national awareness of low Latino high-school graduation rates. In 1997, the W. K. Kellogg Foundation decided to intervene by providing one hundred thousand dollars in planning grants to thirteen university systems in areas with significant Latino populations.[14] In phase 2, the programs received close to a million dollars a year for five years. In Florida, the University of South Florida and Florida International University proposed county-wide systems to strengthen formal and informal connections among families and junior high schools, community colleges, and universities. Perhaps because of the emphasis on a linked fate, ENLACE-USF adapted Mary Church Terrell's motto for the National Association of Colored Women—"lifting as we climb"—as its official identity, and sought to transform at least two cultures: Latino families and the established university bureaucracy.

For the survival of Cuentos, I wanted the presentations to confirm the stakeholder's goals. The HPWA and ENLACE wanted Cuentos students to enter high school knowing that one of their family stories was already part of the permanent collection at the University of South Florida. As the project director and a professional advocate of Latino history, I wanted Florida-based university audiences to start recognizing the ways Puerto Rican, Mexican, Honduran, and other Latino youth were changing the (implicitly Cuban) Latino landscape of Tampa. I wanted Cuentos students to gain a sense of privilege regarding the elite public institution of higher education in Hillsborough County. Ultimately, these goals led to a disciplining uplift on the Cuentos de mi Familia project. Every student sought to make the accounts worthy of the Special Collections division. More important, all but one of the Cuentos students enrolled in high school, confirming that the project did not hinder their path to graduation.

Racial Schooling: Modeling Exemplary
Biographies in the Cuentos de mi Familia Project

The Cuentos project provided explicit models for students to follow as they transformed their household lives into recognizable public biographies. These writing models were chosen as counterpoints to the public Latino biographies available in Florida in 2003. The most prominent bio belonged to Republican candidate for the U.S. Senate, Melquiades Rafael (Mel) Martinez, who inundated Spanish and English media with his life story for his Senate campaign.[15] The story began with his experience being airlifted out of Cuba by the Pedro Pan project, and his subsequent life as a foster child in Central Florida picking up odd jobs and waiting for his parents' rescue from Cuba. The bio ended with his work as the mayor of Orlando and Secretary of Housing and Urban Development between 2000 and 2003, and glossed over his connections to Operation Rescue, the Cuban American National Foundation and real estate interests with Jeb Bush.[16] The campaign presented an "up by your bootstraps" format to make Mel's life stand in for free market politics and state-imposed "family values." This was the most circulated working-class biography in Hillsborough.

The World War II generation produced a number of biographies. The publication of Evelio Grillo's coming-of-age autobiography, *Black Cuban, Black American* in 2000, led to many appearances across Hillsborough County public schools. His book became required reading in magnet schools, a deep irony given the open exclusion he faced as a black man in Tampa.[17] Ferdie Pacheco, the fight doctor for Muhammad Ali, published frequently on the Ybor City roots of his career as a publicly minded doctor, philanthropist, and artist.[18] These stories emphasized Tampa's not quite so glorious past and their individual successes. The autobiographers presented themselves as successful strivers, as there were no children, no wives, no divorces, no disasters, and no explicit contradictions in their narratives. These were all ethnically and politically diverse "race leaders."[19]

These local biographies provided a difficult model for anyone writing on women or life trajectories that lay outside politics and teaching. They implied that people ought to be recognized in history projects only if they already lived a public life. I made sure students confronted Latino biographies that did not depend on public success to justify their importance. Piri Thomas's essay "Mami, aka Dona Lola" emphasized the emotional labor needed to maintain a family in difficult circumstances.[20] Pat Mora's essay on her Aunt Lobo—"good name for a dog, terrible name for a wonderful eccentric aunt"—used humor to describe the importance of kin outside the immediate family.[21] I used Mandalit del Barco's biographical anecdote "Hello Dollinks" because it focused on her mother, a small-town *Mexicana* who ended up principal of a San Francisco junior high school, and emphasized the challenges she faced in the workspace as well as her empathy with all kinds of immigrants.[22] Cuentos students also interacted with USF undergraduates—an ethnic mix of Latino and non-Latino (Filipino, Chippewa, Anglo-Scottish, Tampeño, Puerto Rican, Honduran, Nuyorican, and Colombian) students, ensuring a fuller spectrum of diverse family arrangements.

Breaking the Model Biography Format: Transforming Images in Cuentos de mi Familia

Students were probably aware that the scripts in the Cuentos project did not necessarily fit the parameters of their lives. After Cynthia de la Garza turned in all her consent forms, she asked me once again about the project. When she realized that she would be writing about her mother for two months, she cried out in surprise, "My mother! But I am much more interesting!" Cindy may have been correct, given that she was the top student in

Tomlin Middle School, had won scholarship funds to attend the public university of her choice in Florida, and had already decided that she was going to be a forensic scientist. Her pithy phrasing forced me—as project director—to confront the ways history, even family histories, have to be learned.

Cynthia—and all the Cuentos students—confronted deeply framing questions: Why were they part of a university-based *Latino* public history outreach project? What parts of their family member's story would they want to share with their fellow students? What models would they use to present their research in a Latino-themed public history project? What models would they reject? What did their audiences need to know when they read a Cuentos project? Cuentos students dealt these questions at a far earlier age than did established Latina/o Studies scholars.

The students responded to the four essays by picking a variety of protagonists—"favorite family members"—a spectrum that ranged from parents to aunts, uncles, grandparents, cousins, and older siblings.[23] They made the choices with models based in San Juan, New York, El Paso, Tucson, and San Francisco, but they came from a far wider mix of situations and places. In West Tampa, students came from Colombia, Connecticut, Cuba, Honduras, Puerto Rico, Peru, and Venezuela; and their stories involved light industry, construction, domestic work, small business, and light clerical work. In East Hillsborough and South Tampa, the students' families worked long-haul trucking, phosphate mining, tomatoes, strawberries, and domestic work. Most of the families in West Tampa had lived and worked in urban areas before their arrival. The families in South and West Hillsborough participated in rural and urban jobs during their settlement process, perhaps reflecting their rural origins as well as labor discrimination in the United States.

This variety of regional arrangements, migration stories, and family relationships did not fall into the plots provided by the model biographies. The students turned the blank spaces in the Cuentos project to their advantage. The manual provided only one visual text—a plain three-column, one-image bilingual handout biography of Eulalia Perez and Juan Seguin from the National Museum of American History.[24] The project provided a disposable camera, a large posterboard, art supplies, and the following guidelines: "Use the camera." There was minimal guidance for the use of posterboard and photographs, but Cuentos eighth graders used the posterboard as their basic platform. The two-dimensional posterboard meant that students could design something that could lie flat, stand alone, or hang against a wall. Unfortunately, the project manual did not go any further in this discussion. The posterboard's possibilities dominated the conversation regarding most

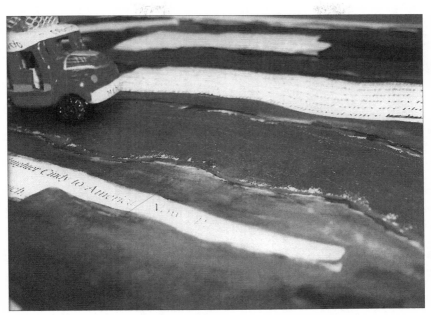

9.1. "Paulo Muñoz" (Transnational Chiva) by Karina Muñoz.

Cuentos projects. Cuentos students used the visual dimension to present biographies that fit their own sense of the world. The following section discusses the three main genres they used to present their stories: "aventuras sobre el mapa," "hidden lives," and the "via crucis."

Aventuras: Remapping Family Journeys

In the Cuentos weekly meetings, students used maps to indicate to one another where their families currently lived and had once resided. Students then used maps to indicate their family's journey to people outside their immediate Cuentos group. The maps provided a basis for archipelagos, triptychs, and layered objects that both shared and obscured various dimensions of family life.

A map project allowed Karina to place her father on the North American map. Karina Muñoz's father worked as a bricklayer and a clerk in the United States and as an accountant in Colombia. He stayed in the United States because he was able to send money home. Karina used a Chiva (a bus intended for the coffee region in Colombia as well as a classic folk souvenir)

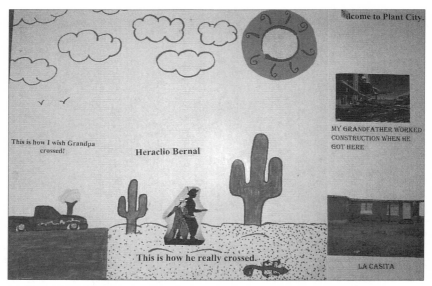

9.2. "Aventuras de Heraclio Bernal" (Lowrider Crossing) by Eduardo Bernal.

on an unpaved dirt road reaching across the Pacific Ocean and the Gulf of Mexico to show her father's crisscrossing journeys. Karina, who was born in Los Angeles and spent her childhood in Medellín, traced the contours of the paths that brought him through Bogotá, New York, Los Angeles, and Tampa.

Cuentos students also used border crossings to place their families across national landscapes. Eduardo Bernal used an iconic border landscape to restage his grandfather's journey across the desert and the chaparral into Texas. Heraclio was a young man who earned money by dancing at parties to set the mood, and by rearranging sod for other people's *ejido* plots in Arroyo, Nuevo Leon. He had an epically difficult desert crossing in the 1970s, during which some of his *compañeros* passed away. He worked difficult construction jobs in Houston, and eventually was able to save enough to own a small tomato farm in Plant City. Eduardo looked for ways of presenting both the achievements and the obstacles in Heraclio's life.

For Eduardo Bernal, his grandfather's journey across the desert is a tragic achievement. The misery and hardship Eduardo associated with this passage was something no one should bear, let alone his grandfather. Eduardo drew a lowrider pickup to demonstrate the way he wished his grandfather could have crossed: as a proud representative of the Plant City car club to which all three generations of his father's family belong.

This is a double commentary on the different ways people can move across "the border." This challenge to American narratives—that every person from Mexico should risk their lives to come to the United States—resonates with South Texas folklore.[25] The aggressive humor in Eduardo Bernal's project should remind audiences that the terror of border control still troubles teenagers far away from Nuevo Leon and the Texas borderlands. Eduardo uses the border as a counterpoint to highlight Heraclio Bernal's achievements—a house, a family, a car club, and a farm.

The two projects highlight the narrative possibilities in a three-dimensional format. Their landscapes link various imagined communities to physical landscapes excluded from American maps. The Chiva—a much-derided form of privatized public sociability—connects Paulo Muñoz's journey with other Colombians making their precarious way across rural and urban areas. Eduardo's juxtaposition of the car club pickup and the border interrupt two normative visions of Mexicano life. First, crossing the border in a custom pickup claims a Texas border space, and second, the international travel interrupts the neighborhood identity associated with car clubs. The stylish crossing that Eduardo wished for his grandfather troubles the idea that a border passages should have a grand and heroic hyper-visibility; Eduardo's depiction points out that border crossing should be an everyday routine not worthy of national attention.[26] The Cuentos landscape projects provide a counterpoint to the state-marketing strategies that translate the work of households into a colored dot on a county census map, convert individual biographies into Hispanic households, and translate places into national spaces.[27]

Faculty and students in the University of South Florida Department of Art participated in the second half of the project. In Pierce Middle School, Professor Rosalinda Borcila modeled ways of using found objects to communicate meaning, and some students followed her lead. Jemi Ponce focused on the way that color could transmit feelings. Her father happily cooperated with the project, taking the disposable camera to his work sites in Tampa. Jemi used the airy, sharp, and light blue sky in the photographs as the background to one posterboard. Here, she highlighted the journeys he took as a member of the merchant marine in Honduras, marking places like Athens, Paris, London, Sydney, and Hong Kong. She also included the traces of his second journey from Honduras across Mexico and Texas to Tampa on a photocopied map of the Gulf of Mexico. This posterboard carried a sunny and triumphant feeling.

Her other poster emphasized the parts of her father's life that were opaque to her. She used this space to emphasize her father's absent twin, his work as a candy seller while still a child, and his work in the military and at the air-

9.3. "My Dad" (Blue Sky) by Jemi Ponce.

port. She took photographs of older photographs to place him at a younger age in Honduras. These photographs have a darker, opaque, brown tone. This color provided the background for the aspects of his life that seem distant to her at this moment. She also used the brown background to connect her family's history to Honduras national history. She placed images of Honduran currency, the UNESCO world heritage site of Copan, and Mayan carvings on the lower and outside margins of the poster. These iconically Central American images anchor her father's life in Honduras. The diptych can be read separately and independently. For Jemi Ponce, her life in Honduras is still present in Tampa. The blue and brown posters are a reminder of her maturing in two separate places linked by her father's journeys.

Other students sought to depict the ways the past shadowed the present. Andrea Valeria Arcila found ways of portraying these ephemeral connections. Her father grew up in the northern border region between Colombia and Venezuela. In his experience, this region was part of both countries, but national borders denied the shared landscape. Andrea used a map to portray the connection between Venezuela and Colombia. But she was also interested in making sure her audience would always connect his biography to the landscape of his childhood. She photocopied her typewritten text onto a transparency. She then photocopied photographs from her father's past onto individual transparencies.

9.4. "Gerardo Arcila" (Memory Traces) by Andrea Valeria Arcila.

One image presents an altar boy separated by waves of text from the crucified Jesus. The text is present but difficult to read. This was one of Gerardo Arcila's iconic photographs from his childhood in Colombia. The other image is of her father and mother at the beginning of their relationship in Caracas. The yellow patch in the distance is the pale trace of the cover painted on the initial transparency. The text highlights the journeys across Venezuela and the United States her father took to keep his family together. Andrea wanted people to leaf through her book of transparencies, with images of her father's life in Colombia and Venezuela interposing and reframing the account of his life. For Andrea Arcila, the combination of transparencies provided a way to indicate the way she felt connected to her father throughout his travels.

Via Crucis: Difficult Passages in a Not-So-Ordinary Life

All students struggled to place the events in their protagonist's lives within a meaningful arc. The ongoing presence of the person, especially a mother, heightened the difficulty students faced in constructing the narrative. Cuentos students built a model that drew from the way stations in their protagonist's life. Students fell on this genre independently, using a via crucis model to tell a story through visual means. They drew images that highlighted dramatic moments in their family member's life. They placed the images on a flat vertical space. The montage offered no initial direction for the way the images should be read. The labeled and unlabeled drawings illustrated a central text—their biography of their protagonist—as if they appropriated the *via crucis* model from church to tell a written story through visual means. The relationship accrued significance when reading the Cuento authored by each artist. Like the Stations of the Cross depicted in church, the written text helps determine the interpretation of each way station. Students consistently drew on this genre across schools, independent of any direction from students or professors.

This form of visual narrative followed the depiction of the Stations of the Cross. The format offers members of a particular church the opportunity to reflect on the meaning of the passion and death of Jesus. These students found the relationship between image, text, and overall narrative in a via crucis to be the most satisfying way of communicating their families' Cuentos. The via crucis eschews the teleology of a classic "rags-to-riches," "foreigner-to-American" immigrant narrative. By focusing on the emotional weight of these points in their lives, these via crucis projects ask viewers and readers to meditate and ponder the emotional texture in each person's life. The individ-

9.5. "The Topping of the Cake" by Rocío Lopez Padilla

ual efforts behind the drawings help communicate the personal importance of the Cuentos to each student. Rocío Lopez Padilla chose five images that captured points of tension in her mother's life. The center panel has Angelica at the center of her family in Tampa, Florida. Rocío called her mother "the topping of the cake" because she keeps her siblings connected to one another. In her drawing, Rocío shows her mother resting in a chair, with her siblings overlaid on one another, again emphasizing the familial links wrought by her mother. The second central image is of a young woman peering through a window as she stands on a ladder. Rocío placed the woman off center, physically close to the margin. The white contours of the drawing emphasize a sense of separation from the world.

Both images reflect the feel of Rocío's writing. She chose to write the Cuento in spoken conversational English. Her first sentence begins, "I am doing history to get closer to my mother." Her biography emphasizes her mother's devotion to keeping herself in contact with family members across the United States: "My mom went through a lot of struggles in her life, so let's get back to her history. There are two great things about her. She did everything on her own and, she always had a positive attitude about everything."[28]

In a second drawing, the untouched background emphasizes the central figure. The line that separates the drawing from the panel lies at the center of the triptych, increasing the sense of separation—"she did everything on her own." The final image of the triptych still places her mom at the center of Rocío's family. Her airy images and light conversational tone mask a depth of trauma in her mother's life, such as her uncle's murder. Both drawings emblematize the connections and the loss. On the outlying panels, Rocío drew images meant to capture a mood. On the lower corner of the left triptych, she drew her mother enjoying her sense of early innocence in Austin, Texas. This drawing includes a younger girl playing in the city's famous parks and springs.

The last drawing—this one on the right panel of the triptych—captures the tone in Rocío's voice. In a small anecdote about Houston, Rocío describes how residents in her neighborhood helped her family out while her mother was working long hours. The drawings depict Rocío's descriptions of her siblings. The four children are unsupervised. Like the second picture, there are no distracting background effects. Unlike that picture, the wavy border around the drawing places the picture somewhere warm and distant. In her anecdote about Houston, Rocío and her siblings made their way on their own away from their house and arrive at a local bar. There, the patrons entertained and fed the children, making sure they got home by the time her mother came home from work. Rocío shows that this *cariño* is part of the web that linked her mother to her neighborhood.

Jaileen Torres used *cariño* to indicate the emotional labor and key way stations in her father's life. Her project, "Elvis Jr.'s Three Miracles," emphasizes transcendent moments in her father's life. In her essay, Jaileen emphasized her father's singing ability (which is where he got the nickname "Elvis"), his rebelliousness ("he used to sneak out at night to steal food"), and his career as a member of a music ensemble, Grupo Negro.

The first two miracles in his via crucis revolved around the births of Jaileen and her sister. The third was his miraculous survival from a horrifying freeway accident—"When he got up, a truck with a weird noise was coming my dad's way. My dad got on the horse and was ready to cross the rest of the street. Nevertheless, it was too late. The horse heard the noise and jumped up and then the truck just slammed into them." Elvis walked to his sister's house and collapsed, and then spent the next six months in a hospital. Jaileen's drawings thematize her father's role as a musical guide in her life in Tampa while he was still far away in Puerto Rico. The drawings mark Elvis Jr.'s way stations and leave the location unmarked, allowing viewers to place the images somewhere familiar.

Wildivina Rosario, in her essay, "My Mother and How We Came to Be," highlighted the disruptive presence of transnational mobility in the emotional life of her family. Hewing to her mother's conversation, Wildivina chose points that explained "how we came to be." Her via crucis highlights three stations in a Caribbean passage: "waiting," "getting our papers," and "together." Her conclusion hinted at the incomplete edge of the Cuentos. Wildivina concluded that "she taught me and my sister that no matter how life goes on, you are always going to have to go through changes, which practically meant that it didn't matter how hard you try to keep your normal life you are always going to change." The stories were ongoing, as most of the projects involved people who were still alive. Their domestic lives seem uncomfortably mutable. The students could not use the closure that seems to follow the model biographies provided by political campaigns, public schools, or even the Cuentos project itself, because the families in which they lived were still changing. The visual narratives—the Cuentos projects—could never arrive at an easy conclusion.

Conclusion

In the Cuentos I described, the students found ways to represent the actions that their "favorite family member" took at a point when their lives were changing. The unfinished lives of the authors and artists who put together the projects also undercut the linear national chronological nature of the other biographies. When students translated their essays into visual narratives, they complicated the normative disciplining that goes with the presentation of family stories. The Cuentos students made choices about their family members, and these choices also indicated the ways they placed themselves in the Americas. They adapted maps of small towns, countries, and even the globe to claim personal relationships to places beyond Hillsborough County. Their Cuentos emphasized obstacles overcome, difficult situations, and the challenges of unfamiliar jobs and neighborhoods. They pointed to the ongoing ways they built families in the United States and across other international borders. These ties—from Tampa to Texas, from Manhattan to Medellín—moved them across the boundaries of many barrios, neighborhoods, agricultural fields, *ejidos,* and small towns. The Cuentos participants made narrative choices that reflected their mobility and displacement. This variety of family arrangements, rural outlooks, and urban experiences exposed an unconsciously American national template I developed for the Cuentos projects. The Cuentos students transformed and challenged the

Latino-specific racial schooling that emphasized their place as minorities in the United States. Their narrative practices revealed their connections to a far wider world.

Like the majority of Americans, Cuentos students lived in rural and suburban areas. This settlement process underscores the large dimensions of Latino life in the United States that take place outside the barrios of Los Angeles, New York, Chicago, San Francisco, San Antonio, and Miami. The projects mapped out a variety of connections that placed the Cuentos students beyond the U.S.-based ethnic geographies. The Cuentos students' increasingly emphasized geographic mobility as the project wore on. The emerging historical narratives in the Cuentos de mi Familia project should force scholars to grapple again with the long history and diversity of working-class Latino experiences in places "beyond el barrio."[29]

The complexity of the stories presented a challenge to journalists who sought to bring Cuentos into the public eye. After reviewing the panoply of Cuentos narratives, the editors chose two narratives—a World War II veteran and a Cuban *balsera* fleeing the island on an improvised boat—that highlighted America's special position in the world. The coverage of the *balsera* story, one of two Cuban stories in the project, emphasized the Cuentos student's obligation to his mom, beyond her journey as a mechanic in Cuba and Africa. The second story focused on the only veteran—Manuel Dimas Castillo—whose journey dated back to World War II.[30] Castillo's more complicated and more representative Latino narrative—his boxing, the racist incidents that ended his career in Wyoming, his settlement in Plant City in the 1950s, and his thirty years in farm labor—was too complicated for the local newscast. The complexity of Latino lives in the Cuentos project challenges the unidirectional crossing within the immigrant scripts provided to Latinas and Latinos in contemporary American culture.

NOTES

1. Gary Mormino, *The Immigrant World of Ybor City: Italians and Their Latin Neighbors in Tampa, 1885–1985* (Gainesville: University Press of Florida, 1998). Nancy Hewitt, *Southern Discomfort: Women's Activism in Tampa, 1880–1920* (Urbana: University of Illinois Press, 2001). Susan Greenbaum, *More Than Black: Afro-Cubans in Tampa* (Gainesville: University Press of Florida, 2002). Cristina Garcia, *Havana USA* (Berkeley: University of California Press, 1997). Alejandro Portes, *City on the Edge: The Transformation of Miami* (Berkeley: University of California Press, 1993). Alejandro Portes, *Legacies: The Immigrant Second Generation* (Berkeley: University of California Press, 2001). Throughout this chapter, I use the term Latinidad to refer to historically specific and shifting characteristics attributed to people from Latin America and the Caribbean.

2. Susan Oboler, *Ethnic Labels, Latino Lives: Identity and the Politics of (Re)presentation in the United States* (Minneapolis: University of Minnesota, 1995).

3. William Flores and Rina Benmayor, "Constructing Cultural Citizenship," in *Latino Cultural Citizenship: Claiming Identity, Space, and Rights*, ed. William Flores and Rina Benmayor (Boston: Beacon Press, 1997), 6–7.

4. Mae Ngai, *Impossible Subjects: Illegal Aliens in the Making of Modern America* (Princeton: Princeton University Press, 2005), 7.

5. In Hillsborough County, other Hispanics and Puerto Ricans were the majority among Latino populations. In the 2000 Florida census, other Hispanics (1,003,643) outnumbered Cubans (833,120), Puerto Ricans (482,027), and Mexicans (363,925). http://factfinder.census.gov/.

6. This is different than in Miami-Dade County, where the median household income for Cuban Americans outstrips the average white household income.

7. http://www.floridacountiesmap.com/hillsborough_county.shtml, accessed October 28, 2008.

8. "The analytical category of queer upsets the strict gender roles, the firm divisions between public and private, and the implicit presumptions of self-sufficient economics in the respectable domestic household." Nayan Shah, *Contagious Divides: Epidemics and Race in San Francisco's Chinatown* (Berkeley: University of California Press, 2001), 13. Gina Pérez, *Near Northwest Side Story* (Berkeley: University of California Press, 2004). See also Pierrette Hondagneu-Sotelo, *Domestica: Cleaning and Caring in the Shadows of Affluence* (Berkeley: University of California Press, 2001). Pierrette Hondagneu-Sotelo, ed., *Gender and U.S. Immigration: Contemporary Trends* (Berkeley: University of California Press, 2003). Carol Stack, *All Our Kin: Survival Strategies in a Black Community* (New York: Basic Books, 1997). For a discussion of The Moynihan Report, see Douglas Massey and Robert Sampson, *The Moynihan Report Revisited: Lessons and Reflections After Four Decades* (New York: Sage Publications, 2009), 2–10.

9. See Jonathan Kozol, *There Are No Children Here* (New York: Basic Books, 1989).

10. For INS family discipline, see Ngai, *Impossible Subjects*, 202–225.

11. Stephanie Coontz, *The Way We Never Were: American Families and the Nostalgia Trap* (New York: Basic Books, 2000).

12. Pierrette Hondagneu-Sotelo, *Domestica: Cleaning and Caring in the Shadows of Affluence* (Berkeley: University of California Press, 2001).

13. Mormino, *Immigrant World*. Hewitt, *Southern Discomfort*. Greenbaum, *More Than Black*.

14. http://www.wkkf.org/default.aspx?tabid=75&CID=16&NID=61&LanguageID=0, accessed July 9, 2008.

15. http://martinez.senate.gov/public/index.cfm?FuseAction=AboutMartinez.Biography&CFID=45199290&CFTOKEN=82486311, accessed November 1, 2005.

16. William Yardley, "Both Parties Pin Hopes on Senate Race," *New York Times* (10/30/2004). Senator Martinez was one of fourteen thousand school children who were airlifted from Cuba in the mid-1960s and placed in Catholic foster families across the United States. Administered by the Catholic Church and endorsed by the State Department, the legacy of the program is mixed, though many of the children—like Senator Martinez and performance artist Ana Mendieta—went on to important public careers. Pedro Pan alum and political scientist María de los Angeles Torres has written the most

scholarly account in her monograph *The Lost Apple: Operation Pedro Pan, Cuban Children in the U.S., and the Promise of a Better Future* (Boston: Beacon Press, 2004). Unlike some of the other explorations, she also examines the long-term experience of these children in the United States.

17. Evelio Grillo, *Black Cuban, Black American: A Memoir* (Houston: Arte Publico Press, 2000).

18. Ferdie Pacheco, *Ybor City Chronicles: A Memoir* (Gainesville: University Press of Florida, 1994).

19. Hazel Carby, *Race Men: The Du Bois Lectures* (Cambridge: Harvard University Press, 2000).

20. Piri Thomas, "Mami, aka Dona Lola," in *Las Mamis: Favorite Latino Authors Remember Their Mothers*, ed. Joie Davidow (New York: Vintage, 2001), 67–77.

21. Pat Mora, "Tia Lobo," in *Latina: Women Write the Borderlands*, ed. Liliana Castillo-Speed (New York: Touchstone, 1995), 73–75.

22. Mandalit del Barco, "Hello Dollinks," in Davidow, *Las Mamis*, 35–42.

23. The Cuentos students featured eleven mothers, nine fathers, three grandfathers, two grandmothers, one stepfather, one aunt, one uncle, one sister, and one brother.

24. John McKiernan, "Eulalia Perez," and "Juan Seguin," NMAH handouts (Smithsonian, 1998).

25. José Limón, *Dancing with the Devil: Society and Cultural Poetics in South Texas* (Madison: University of Wisconsin Press, 1994). Américo Paredes, *Folklore and Culture on the Texas Mexico Border* (Austin: University of Texas Press, 1993).

26. Brenda Bright, "Heart Like a Car," *American Ethnologist* 25 (4): 583–609.

27. On the translation of experience into public policy documents, see Ralph Cintron, *Angel's Town: Chero Ways, Gang Life, and the Rhetorics of Everyday* (Boston: Beacon Press, 1998), 15–50.

28. http://www.cas.usf.edu/history/cdmf/Cuentos%20de%20mi%20Familia-Dowdell-Rocio-Lopez-Padilla.htm, accessed September 19, 2004.

29. Matt Garcia makes a similar theoretical claim for suburban Los Angeles County. Matt Garcia, *A World of Its Own: Race, Labor, and Citrus in Greater Los Angeles County* (Chapel Hill: University of North Carolina Press, 2001).

30. Lissette Campos, WFTS-TV morning show, accessed November 28, 2003.

————————————————————————————— 10 ——

The Mission in Nicaragua

San Francisco Poets Go to War

————————————————————— CARY CORDOVA ———

> This shared cement ground
> Surrounded by a sweet shop
> A fast food store and four bus stops
> Was renamed by
> WE THE PEOPLE
> From a radius of twenty miles or so
> "Plaza Sandino"
>
> —Nina Serrano

In the late 1970s, a community of poet-activists rechristened their usual gathering spot, the plaza above a subway station in the heart of the barrio, as "Plaza Sandino." Otherwise known as the BART station at Twenty-fourth and Mission streets in San Francisco's Mission District, their literary seizure of the land, in the name of Nicaraguan peasant hero Augusto Sandino (1893–1934), signaled the ways this public space in San Francisco had become a meaningful place to express solidarity with the leftist struggles in Nicaragua and elsewhere. The poet Roberto Vargas described the mood of the barrio as follows: "The Mission is now aware of itself as a body of many people, all tribes aware of themselves . . . There is a collective feeling of compassion for each other Nicas Blacks Chicanos Chilenos oppressed Indios. The sense of collective survival, histories full of Somozas Wounded Knees written on the walls: Muera Somoza Free Angela."[1] Seeing the fight to overthrow Anastasio Somoza's dictatorship in Nicaragua as intertwined with the fight to free Angela Davis was indicative of the poet-activists' efforts to build an internationalist civil rights movement in the barrio.

Nina Serrano's poem "I Saw It Myself on the Corner of Mission and Twenty-fourth Streets" perfectly illustrates the ways that protests at Plaza

Sandino collapsed transnational struggles into a single vision for change. She writes:

> We chanted / incanted
> circling circling
> circling circling
> "Pinochet Romero
> Y Somoza
> Son La Misma Cosa"
> And it was raining
>
> We chanted / incanted
> circling circling
> circling circling
> "se siente
> se siente
> Sandino esta presente"
> And it was raining
> Ending a three year drought.
>
> I saw it myself on the corner
> Of Mission and Twenty-Fourth streets[2]

According to the poem, "Pinochet, Romero, y Somoza Son La Misma Cosa" are the same thing. For Serrano, and for many others, the dictatorial heads of Chile, El Salvador, and Nicaragua (Augusto Pinochet, Carlos Humberto Romero, and Anastasio Somoza Debayle) had merged as a single oppressive entity. The brutality of these U.S.-sponsored, right-wing regimes propelled a global solidarity movement critical of U.S. politics and supportive of left-leaning guerrilla mobilizations.[3] Simultaneously, Serrano's poem celebrates the presence of Augusto Sandino ("Sandino esta presente" / Sandino is present), the heroic antithesis of these regimes, the soldier for the underdog, whose magical presence in the rain suggests an almost saintly ability to end a real and spiritual drought. In the poem, Sandino symbolizes hope for another way of life, not just in Nicaragua, but everywhere, and perhaps especially in the Mission.

At the time, the Mission District certainly might have benefited from some saintly guidance. In the late 1960s, the Mission average income was substantially below the city average, the unemployment rate was high, if not the highest in the city, and only 5 percent of graduates from the local high school continued on to college.[4] The socioeconomic circumstances of the Mission are exactly why it became a focal point for 1960s civil rights activists and artists, or "cultural workers," to demand social justice. Drawing on revolutionary struggles around the globe became a key means for cultural workers to advocate for revolutionary change at home. As Vargas writes, "My ideal is along the broad horizon of internationalism, the right to be free and to demand justice, although to reach this state of perfection it may be necessary to shed one's own and one's neighbor's blood."[5] The poet's sympathies for the working class propelled his interest in revolution, nonviolent or otherwise.

Poet-activist Alejandro Murguía describes how the neighborhood zeitgeist transformed his identity. In 1971, after reading Gabriel Garcia Marquez's *One Hundred Years of Solitude*, he states, "Suddenly we reinterpreted our existence, we were no longer exiled in the cold north, in the pale United States. We transposed our Latino roots from Central America, land of volcanoes and revolutions; from the Caribbean, land of palm trees and salsa music, and from Aztlán, land of lowriders and *vatos locos,* and fused these tropicalized visions to our barrio and made the concrete sidewalks, the asphalt streets, and the sterile buildings sway to a Latin beat."[6] By importing these tropicalized sensibilities, the dimensions of difference between Central America and the Mission District collapsed.

In many ways, Nicaragua came to represent a place where the problems of the Mission could be solved. Especially from 1972 to 1979, San Francisco cultural workers mobilized to support Nicaragua's Frente Sandinista de Liberación Nacional (FSLN) as part and parcel of local community organizing. Pro-Sandinista sentiment flourished in San Francisco, not simply out of sympathy for Nicaraguans, but because the situation abroad represented an inextricable extension of the problems defining life in San Francisco's Mission District. If the Sandinistas succeeded, Nicaragua promised to become a new and better Cuba, an amends for the loss of Chile in the 1973 coup, and a model for freedom and equality around the world, including within the United States. The activism of the Sandinistas articulated the Marxist ideals of San Francisco cultural workers and expressed their dissatisfaction with U.S. capitalism from a war front of their own, the Latino barrio of San Francisco. The parallels were ready-made, and the struggle was the same.

Like other chapters in this volume, especially the one by Ana Aparicio on Dominicans in New York, this essay situates "barrio politics" in a transnational context. Over the course of the 1970s, artists and activists used the ideals of revolution in Nicaragua to express the political needs of Latinos in San Francisco and in the Americas. In order to capture this history, one must go beyond seeing the barrio in solely domestic or local terms. At a time when, as poet Alejandro Murguía complained, "the typical Anglo American couldn't find Nicaragua or Colombia on a map, even if it bit them in the ass," cultural workers in the Mission established an intimate and often romanticized relationship with Nicaragua.[7] The imagined Nicaragua, circulated in San Francisco poetry, murals, and literature, propelled a leftist idealism for what could be. While many have heard of the Nuyorican poetry movement of the 1970s, few know that there was a similarly rich, transnational poetry movement evolving in San Francisco's Mission District.[8]

In order to document this largely unwritten history, I am turning to three poets: Nina Serrano, Roberto Vargas, and Alejandro Murguía. None of the three was ever "just" a poet. Rather, they drew inspiration from a wide array of Latin American revolutionary poets, including Ernesto Cardenal, Ruben Dario, Roque Dalton, and Pablo Neruda. All three participated in the Neighborhood Arts Program and became leading activists in the community. Together, they organized a long list of intersecting events—poetry readings, rallies, and demonstrations—all calling for revolution in Nicaragua. Two of the three, Murguía and Vargas, even went to Nicaragua to join as soldiers in the struggle.

Notably, only one of the three—Vargas—is Nicaraguan. Murguía identifies as Chicano, originally from Los Angeles, and Serrano is a Colombian American, originally from New York. In various ways, the cultural workers of San Francisco asserted their solidarity with the people of Nicaragua, regardless of whether they were of Nicaraguan origin. Their priority was to draw attention to a struggle that encompassed both Nicaragua and the Mission District in a much larger quest for revolutionary change.

San Francisco, la ciudad de los nicaragüenses[9]
—Ernesto Cardenal

One of the reasons San Francisco established such a strong solidarity movement with the Sandinistas in Nicaragua can be tied to its demographics. The city's large Nicaraguan American community had grown in tandem with trade routes between the United States and Nicaragua since the late 1800s, particularly owing to the coffee industry. In addition, a large influx of Nicaraguans came to the city just prior to, or in the wake of, the 1934 assassination of revolutionary leader Augusto Sandino. Most were supporters of Sandino, and with the ensuing rise to power of right-wing dictator Anastasio Somoza, they were unable to return to their home country for the next forty years. This was the case for poet Roberto Vargas, who has stated, "We came in the human wave fleeing the brutality of the Somoza regime that still rules the homeland."[10] These earlier communities were important in establishing strong neighborhood migration networks, comprising family, friends, and even friends of friends.

Though Central Americans had established a strong presence in San Francisco since the nineteenth century, the passage of the 1965 Immigration Act and increasing political turbulence prompted increased migrations over the course of the 1970s. The 1980 census shows that of the eighty-three thousand Latinos in San Francisco, 39 percent identified as of Mexican origin, 6 percent of Puerto Rican origin, 2 percent of Cuban origin, and 53 percent "of other Spanish origin."[11] The large percentage of, "other Spanish origin" is largely due to the city's sizable Central American populations, particularly from El Salvador and Nicaragua. Even so, the fact that no single nation dominated San Francisco's Latino population helped popularize a pan-Latino, or Raza, identity in local politics and subsequently encouraged activism across national borders.[12]

Close ties between San Francisco and Nicaragua solidified when a devastating earthquake tore Managua apart in 1972. The disaster took the lives of up to twenty thousand people and destroyed more than three-quarters of the city's housing and businesses.[13] San Francisco cultural workers sought to make a difference through fund-raising—for instance, Roberto Vargas started the Comite Civico Pro Liberación de Nicaragua to send aid. Once established, El Comite Civico organized rallies, poetry readings, lectures, and even produced radio and television shows.[14]

Significantly, the earthquake also revealed the scale of government corruption to the world, since most of the international efforts to send aid never reached beyond the coffers of the Somoza regime. The year 1972 proved a turning point, or as Thomas Walker notes, "the beginning of the end" for the Somoza regime.[15] By the mid-1970s, Walker adds, "Somoza stood out as one of the worst human rights violators in the Western hemisphere."[16]

Alternatively, the guerrilla Sandinista Front promised a radical social revolution. While the FSLN struggled with internal divisions, its ideology promised social justice for the masses. According to Carlos Fonseca, who later earned the title "Supreme Commander" of the Nicaraguan revolution, "The question is not only to bring about a change of the man in power, but to transform the system, to overthrow the exploiting classes and achieve the victory of the exploited."[17] In 1978, the FSLN published a twenty-five-point list of objectives that clearly established the revolutionary ambitions of the organization. Their intentions were to redistribute land, create an agrarian revolution, enhance labor conditions, control prices, enhance public transportation, provide utilities to rural areas, develop decent housing, provide free medical assistance and education to all in need politically incorporate indigenous communities, protect natural resources, eliminate torture and political assassinations, encourage free speech, and end discrimination against women.[18] The utopian ideals for social reform perfectly intersected with the ideals of community organizers in San Francisco.

The student protest movements of the late 1960s grew out of the Bay Area's history of radical and leftist politics. The richness of San Francisco's activism encompassed a wide array of intersecting issues, from the Native American takeover of Alcatraz, to the controversial trial of "Los Siete de la Raza," to the Third World Strikes at San Francisco State University, to the Black Panther breakfast programs. As such, support for the Sandinistas in Nicaragua was indicative of a more expansive cultural milieu.

San Francisco support for the Sandinistas swelled as migration from Nicaragua increased. Poet Ernesto Cardenal, who later became the revolution's Minister of Culture, describes how the cultures of San Francisco and Nicaragua merged in the Mission:

Como los puertorriqueños en Nueva York, los cubanos en Miami, y los mexicanos en Los Ángeles, eran los nicaragüenses en San Francisco. La calle Mission era la calle de los nicas; allí estaban los restaurantes y bares nicaragüenses, se vendía *La Prensa* de Managua, se bebía cerveza nicaragüense. Y allí había una oficina del Frente Sandinista: con la bandera rojinegra, retrato de Sandino, pósters revolucionarios; bajo la vigilancia y amenaza del FBI y de la CIA.[19]

(Like the Puerto Ricans in New York, the Cubans in Miami, and the Mexicans in Los Angeles, it was the Nicaraguans in San Francisco. Mission Street was the street of the Nicaraguans; there were Nicaraguan restaurants and bars, they sold Managua's newspaper *La Prensa*, they drank Nicaraguan beer. And there was even an office of the Sandinista Front: with the red and black flag, portrait of Sandino, revolutionary posters; under the threat and surveillance of the FBI and CIA.)

The politics of Nicaragua remapped the local landscape and the culture of the Mission in multiple ways. Not only did one find Nicaraguan food and drink in the Mission, but the neighborhood even served as a home for the FSLN. As poet Nina Serrano recalls, at the urging of her friend Roberto Vargas, "I went down to the Sandinista headquarters . . . right off Valencia Street . . . and met all the compañeros, who barely, almost all exiles, barely spoke English. . . . They wanted me to help them with organizing a group to speak to the American people about Nicaragua, and to stop U.S. intervention in Nicaragua. And as a result, I helped to form NIN—Nonintervention in Nicaragua." Serrano adds that her recruitment efforts largely consisted of organizing "the only people I knew, which were all the poets."[20] As Serrano's story makes clear, the physical presence of Sandinista organizations, including a Sandinista headquarters, had a radicalizing effect on the neighborhood.

One reporter later stated, "There is a quasi-joke among certain sectors here that half the Nicaraguan revolution was planned in back rooms around Mission Street."[21] In truth, it was hardly a joke. According to Ernesto Cardenal, "la célula sandinista de San Francisco era la más importante de los Estados Unidos."[22] (The Sandinista cell in San Francisco was the most important in the United States.) Obviously, organizing for the Sandinistas was safer in San Francisco than it was in Nicaragua. Former soldier Walter Ferreti states, "The FSLN could operate in the United States, could make demonstrations, and could publicly expose the cruelties of the Somoza dictatorship. We had an office and made propaganda against the regime."[23] Protections of free speech and free assembly facilitated San Francisco support for the Nicaraguan revolution. The Mission subsequently served as a second home to various high-profile revolutionaries, including Walter Ferreti, Casimiro Sotelo, Raul Venerio, Lygia Venerio, and Bérman Zúniga.[24]

Nonetheless, FBI infiltration and surveillance was also a reality. Ferreti adds, "Of course, the office was vandalized, the printing press was broken, and the files stolen. To this day we don't know if this was done by Somoza's agents or by the FBI. And of course, those of us who worked there were stopped in the streets or in our cars by the police. They would ask us where we were going and what we were doing. They would call us 'communists' and tell us to go back to Nicaragua."[25] Regardless of official U.S. or Nicaraguan interventions, San Francisco proved a key location to support a revolution.

Stoned on Liberation and Love at the Risk of Seeming Ridiculous
—Roberto Vargas

The sense of being part of the same struggle, "la misma cosa," profoundly shaped local Latina/o cultural production, from poetry, to filmmaking, to the visual arts. Cultural workers like Roberto Vargas, Nina Serrano, and Alejandro Murguía supported the revolution in Nicaragua as part of a larger internationalist vision of liberation. In 1975, writing in support of the Sandinistas in the neighborhood newspaper *El Tecolote*, Roberto Vargas declared, "Every Latino has the responsibility to work toward the liberation of our people. There is no neutral or middle ground, and we must join the struggle."[26] The fact that this perspective pervaded the neighborhood is evident in the newspapers, the poetry, and the culture at large. For example, choosing to shed any sign of objectivity, *El Tecolote* editorial staff declared agreement with Vargas: "In doing research for this article, two themes have come up consistently: U.S. intervention, whether direct or indirect, which clearly has been used to the detriment of the Nicaraguan people, and their courageous and continuous struggle for control over their own lives and country. As Latinos we are part of this same struggle. It is important to show our solidarity with the progressive struggles of all people and to support them in any way we can."[27] The ideology of transnational liberation shaped the neighborhood's cultural production, defined what it meant to be Latino, and contributed to the ways that action abroad and at home merged.

Roberto Vargas, born in Nicaragua but raised in San Francisco, was dedicated to bringing revolution to both places. According to Murguía, "Roberto took the concept of organizer and expanded it to mean everything: organizer of poetry readings, writing workshops, film and theater projects, community dances, and eventually even political marches and rallies for Nicaragua."[28] For Vargas, the struggle was clear. His 1971 book *Primeros Cantos* collected a group of socially conscious poems, highly critical of the capitalist system. Poems such as "Elegy Pa Esso," "They Blamed It on Reds," and "Elegy Pa Gringolandia" ridiculed American love for the dollar. In "Elegy Pa Gringolandia," Vargas fantasized about the death of capitalism:

> It seems . . . just the other day
> The Wall Street Journal (His Masters voice)
> Chanted extreme Unction rites
> To the tinkle of a no-sale cash register
> In the belly of the Stock-Exchange
> Amerikka Hemmoraged internally
> And died . . . Of an overdose of Hate
> (Did they blame it on reds?)
> (O say
> can you
> see . . .)

It seems . . . just the other day
A new world . . . began again
Chepito in Nicaraguan natural
Sticking life to drumskin
Splashing Tim-Timbale voodoo
On Santana's Mayan / pocho / Afro
Sinfonia (Jingo-Jingova)
And today the new children
Are STONED on Liberation
     And love. . . . (At the risk of
          seeming
       Ridiculous . . .)

For Vargas, the death of "Amerikka" birthed true liberation, a world returning to a mestizo culture of pounding drums and natural incantations of love. His dramatic reading of the poem, very much akin to the spoken word style of Beat and Nuyorican poets, is emphatically musical, playing with tempo and singing certain phrases ("O say / can you / see" and "Jingo-Jingova").[29]

The poem captures Vargas's idyllic hopes. "Amerikka" might practice egregious financial activities ("The tinkle of a no-sale cash register / In the belly of the Stock-Exchange"), but people have another choice: fight for liberation and love. He uses the line, "STONED on Liberation / And love . . . (At the risk of / Seeming / Ridiculous)" as a call to others to risk being passionate about the world. Like love, liberation induces a drug-like high, a sense of purpose, and a willingness to sacrifice one's self for the sake of something more profound. It is a philosophy that filtered through Vargas's poetry and into his everyday life.

In 1974, Vargas cofounded the *Gaceta Sandinista*, a San Francisco Spanish-language newspaper dedicated to covering the struggle in Nicaragua. The fact that San Francisco became the home of the only newspaper in the United States devoted to the Sandinista cause is illustrative of the Bay Area culture.[30] Officially a product of El Comite Civico Pro Liberación, the newspaper editorial staff reads like a list of Sandinista soldiers, including Casimiro Sotelo, Roberto Vargas, Raúl Venerio, Jr., and Walter Ferreti, who all served in San Francisco, while another set of "reporters" served in Los Angeles.[31] The newspaper provided information in a way that would have been impossible within Nicaragua without serious repercussions from the government. Much of the reportage focused on the conditions of political prisoners, the government's repressive violence and corruption, and the seemingly growing number of successful FSLN actions.

Gaceta Sandinista was just as much a product of San Francisco's independent publishing collectives as it was of FSLN organizing. Alejandro Murguía's experience illustrates the close ties that existed between *Gaceta Sandinista* and the various Third World publishing collectives that had mobilized throughout the city. After moving to San Francisco from Los Angeles in 1971, Murguía joined Editorial Pocho-Che, an organization first started in 1968 to serve the publishing needs of Latina/o writers and artists.[32] He also cofounded Third World Communications in 1972 and the Third World Poetry Series at San Francisco State in 1974.[33] As a writer, as an editor, and as an organizer, Murguía had a hand in bringing various projects to publication, including *Time to Greez! Incantations from the Third World* (1975) and a series of chapbooks that included the work of Jose Montoya, Roberto Vargas, Raul Salinas, and Nina Serrano.[34] As Murguía's repertoire expanded, he also became an editor for *Gaceta Sandinista* and the official Bay Area FSLN representative. Not coincidentally, Editorial Pocho-Che became part of the publishing arm for *Gaceta Sandinista*.[35] The rise of all these Third World publishing ventures is indicative of the internationalist spirit driving local support for the FSLN.

Relatively quickly, the revolution in Nicaragua became a pivotal part of Murguía's political and literary activism in the Mission. He first learned about Nicaragua through Vargas, who introduced him to the writings of Ernesto Cardenal in 1972.[36] It did not take much for Murguía to see Nicaragua as part of a larger struggle. As he writes in 1981, "Nicaragua was a classic confrontation: a puppet regime installed and supported by the United States, challenged by a National Liberation Front. Vietnam in the western hemisphere."[37] Angered by the disaster of U.S. policy in Vietnam, Murguía saw it as imperative to be engaged in the struggle in Nicaragua.

In his memoir, Murguía recalls his first demonstration for the FSLN in 1975: "We carried these beautiful black-and-red posters of Sandino silkscreened by La Raza Silk Screen Center, and we waved them at passing traffic and stood outside El Tico-Nica bar exchanging insults with Somoza sympathizers."[38]

The moment, captured in an *El Tecolote* photograph, shows a cheerful Murguía and Vargas leading a crowd of protesters down Mission Street with their signs of support for the Sandinistas. The image is also indicative of the way that events in Nicaragua were literally changing the face of the Mission, as artist Alfonso Maciel's posters became part of the Mission District land-

10.1 Roberto Vargas and Alejandro Murguía marching down Mission Street in support of the Sandinistas in 1976. Photograph by Alejandro Stuart. Image courtesy of *El Tecolote* Photograph Archive.

scape. And while Murguía's recollection indicates that Somoza sympathizers did exist in the Mission, the thrust of community organizing was decidedly in favor of the Sandinistas.

Remarkably, even the 1977 inauguration of the Mission Cultural Center, the result of a decade-long battle between cultural workers and city hall for neighborhood arts centers, was framed around the Sandinista cause. San Francisco's seemingly bottomless investments in high-art institutions like the symphony, opera house, and performing arts center spurred public demand for some sort of equivalent investment in low-income communities. After considerable protest, the city finally agreed to fund neighborhood arts programs and to invest in neighborhood cultural centers.[39] Murguía, as the first director of the Mission Cultural Center, and Vargas and Serrano in their roles as community organizers, contributed substantially to the new institution's political and artistic orientation.[40] Together, they were determined to create a place where residents could congregate, where art could be taught and shared, and where ideas could revolutionize the future of the barrio.

To mark the opening of the Mission Cultural Center, Vargas, Murguía, and Serrano wanted to create an event that would reflect the ideological future of the institution. They invited the Sandinista poet Ernesto Cardenal to speak at the opening. Cardenal not only served as the inaugural speaker, but, according to the Mission District's literary journal *Tin Tan*, he also "baptized a group of children, in a very moving ceremony in which he called on the spirits of greed, capitalism, egoism and Somoza, to keep out of these children."[41] Thus Ernesto Cardenal, the yet-to-be Minister of Culture of post-revolution Nicaragua, inaugurated the Mission Cultural Center in San Francisco. His presence symbolized the hope for social change that cultural workers sought to imprint on the community.

Taking Up Arms: Poets in the Revolution

By 1978, support for the Sandinista movement had become more widespread in the Bay Area, particularly as the Somoza regime seemed more likely to topple. In October 1978, the Mission Cultural Center sponsored a "Week of Solidarity with the People of Nicaragua." The events consisted of films, music, and poetry, featuring an impressive listing of poets, including Victor Hernandez Cruz, Diane di Prima, Jack Hirschman, Michael McClure, David Meltzer, Ricardo Mendoza, Janice Mirikitani, Ishmael Reed, and Alma Villanueva.[42] The diversity of the poets is reflective of the widespread support the Sandinistas had achieved in the Bay Area, and that was growing in the international arena. Of course, the ways that support should take form became an issue of debate, from different attitudes toward violent and nonviolent tactics to different approaches toward art.

In the Mission, as in Latin America, poets became not just figurative, but literal revolutionaries. Over the course of the 1970s, Murguía's and Vargas's activism reflected increasing personal risk, gradually shifting from publishing and protesting to taking over the Nicaraguan consulate. Fellow cultural worker Roxanne Dunbar-Ortiz recalls, "I happened to be working that day in the Treaty Council office in the Flood Building at Powell and Market, which was on the floor below the Nicaraguan consulate. When I heard the racket, I walked upstairs and saw the small band wearing black-and-red scarves over their faces. Even so, I recognized Roberto and Alejandro." Amazingly, they were not arrested because the authorities could not determine who had jurisdiction.[43]

As a Sandinista victory appeared increasingly imminent, Vargas and Murguía made the decision to join the fighting on the southern front. In fact, a team of sympathizers began training in the Bay Area hills in order to ready to serve as soldiers in Nicaragua. Murguía states, "During the period between October 1978 and June 1979, I devoted full time to organizing solidarity committees across the United States in support of the Nicaraguan people, as well as editing the journal, *Gaceta Sandinista*. In June of 1979, along with the compañeros 'Armando' and 'Danilo,' I left for Costa Rica to join in the Final Offensive." Murguía subsequently documented the fighting in two books, *The Southern Front* and *The Medicine of Memory*.[44]

While the decision to go to war undoubtedly expressed Murguía's and Vargas' passion for the politics, others found themselves more ambivalent about taking up arms. For example, Nina Serrano found herself caught between her activism and her pacifism. A Colombian American originally from New York, she moved to San Francisco in 1961 with hopes of joining the Beat counterculture. Her love of theatre and politics led her to become a writer for the San Francisco Mime Troupe. She also established her filmmaking career when she and her then husband, Saul Landau, produced *Que Hacer? What Is to Be Done?*, a film supportive of the Allende government in Chile, which they released at the same time as the 1973 coup. Still, she wrestled with turning to violence as a means to an end.

Serrano originally learned about the Nicaraguan struggle in 1969, while working on a play with the Salvadoran poet Roque Dalton in Cuba, and it was his dangerous life that caused Serrano to meditate on the role of violence in the pursuit of liberation. While she supported the struggle intellectually, her preference for nonviolence caused her enormous internal conflict. Serrano's poem "To Roque Dalton Before Leaving to Fight in El Salvador (Havana, 1969)" is indicative of her ambivalence, both loving this revolutionary figure, who was already larger than life in the minds of many, but also sensing that his life would end tragically. Her poem spins on the contradictory romance of revolution, as she finds herself caught between her values as an activist and as a humanist: "My love of man in conflict / with my love for this man." In the poem, Dalton jokes about his impending death, making light of something that is pinned on "revolutionary slogans." The ambivalence of the poem reflects how Serrano's appreciation for a people's revolution was tempered by her pacifism.

In 1979, Serrano and Lourdes Portillo grappled with the gendered roles of revolution in *Después del Terremoto*, a short film depicting the experiences of a woman who migrated from Nicaragua to the Mission "after the earthquake."[45] The film drew inspiration from its Mission District setting, using familiar places and local residents to act the parts (including a cameo by

Serrano). The two protagonists, Irene and Julio, are both Nicaraguan exiles, but their different politics create an irresolvable tension in their relationship. Early in the film, Irene learns that her former fiancé is in San Francisco after suffering three years of torture by the Somoza regime. The two try to reconnect, but their divergent experiences have undone the intimacy they once shared.

The film is a testament to the ways that cultural workers sought to radicalize the Mission, and the ways in which their efforts were also filtered by the everyday concerns of working people in the barrio. Julio, a passionate revolutionary, is more in tune with the politics of the filmmakers, but his rabid approach alienates the people he tries to reach. At a birthday party, Julio initiates a slide show to recruit assistance for the revolution, arguably much like the various slide shows organized by the Mission's Comite Civico. Julio talks over the images of poverty: "This shack is a school in our beautiful country—a country with thirty percent illiteracy. . . . This is a child dying of malnutrition. Yet, millions of dollars in U.S. aid are used by this corrupt dictator to buy arms and continue to keep our people under submission. This is an abuse of power. This is oppression." His audience is resistant. One woman responds, "For this stupidity the Immigration Department can deport us!" while another states, "We know all this, but we are not there, we are here." The responses echo popular sentiments in the neighborhood. The filmmakers, like Julio, are invested in transnational action, but they also empathize with the fears and concerns of new migrants and low-income residents.[46]

The filmmakers' treatment of Irene is complex, both appreciative of the dreams of a hard-working, underpaid woman, but also critical of someone who has turned away from the politics of her homeland. Irene is more interested in buying a television than in securing freedom in Nicaragua. Simultaneously, however, her experience as a working woman in the United States has generated a feminist consciousness. She has found more sexual freedom and independence in San Francisco than she ever knew in Nicaragua, as the filmmakers indicate in the first shot of her handling a book titled *Vida Sexual: Prematrimonial*. For her, the purchase of a television is emblematic of her freedom as a woman. Irene tells Julio, "I think that a woman must be independent, as I am becoming. To show you, I've just bought a TV." Both her friend and Julio tell her she is misguided in her purchase. Her friend says, "Nobody needs a color TV, especially you. You work six days a week, twelve hours a day! What are you going to do, put it in your pocket and watch it while you clean?" Irene responds, "You don't understand. I didn't have a TV."[47] The film is sympathetic toward Irene, but it also suggests the ways that new migrants are co-opted by the glamour of American capitalism. The film illustrates the ways that cultural workers pushed for radicalizing a community, and yet everyday life in the barrio often subsumed any interest in such large-scale issues.

Unexpectedly, Portillo and Serrano encountered criticism from their peers for making a fictional film. According to Portillo, "When I did that, it was a struggle against them [the Sandinista movement in the United States] and they disowned us in the process. . . . there was a break with them because they wanted us to do a documentary that they had been used to seeing— very factual, very political, very one-sided."[48] Portillo adds that some did not find the film radical enough. Criticized by those who might be most sympathetic, the film encountered even stronger disapproval in the industry, as it was unable to secure distribution in the United States, more than likely for the picture it painted of U.S. foreign policy.[49] The censorship is suggestive of the ways that political sympathies in San Francisco did not reflect the U.S. mainstream.

Después del Terremoto reflects a particular moment in the Mission, in the years after the earthquake and before the revolution, at a time when organizing for the Sandinistas was growing rapidly. Poets, activists, cultural workers, and soldiers came together in San Francisco and around the world to participate in the struggle. Nicaragua beckoned as a place that could overthrow a repressive government and form a utopian community. In 1979, the year that *Después del Terremoto* was released, the dreams of the FSLN and of San Francisco cultural workers came to fruition. After weeks of military advances, the FSLN took over the capital city of Managua on July 17, 1979. President Somoza fled to the United States, then Paraguay, while the Sandinista government declared the revolution's success. The dramatic change in leadership promulgated a pervasive hopefulness for the Left. Alejandro Murguía writes:

During May, June, and July of 1979, thousands and thousands of Nicaraguans, Latin Americans, Chicanos, Indigenous peoples, and North American progressives stormed out into the streets of cities in the United States, such as San Francisco, Los Angeles, Seattle, Tucson, New York, and Washington, D.C., in support of the final offensive that brought Nicaragua its long awaited liberation.[50]

The promise of Nicaragua spoke to the dreams of thousands of people in the United States.

After the Revolution

The victory of the Sandinistas was marked into the Mission District landscape. Casa Nicaragua, or Casa Sandino, as it was also known, was located at Twenty-fourth Street and Balmy Alley, a location that opened onto a growing collection of neighborhood murals. The building served as a gathering place, gallery, and information source for the Nicaraguan leftist community in San Francisco. The exterior of Casa Nicaragua illustrates how closely connected Bay Area cultural workers viewed the struggles in Chile and Nicaragua. A mural covered the building and featured "Chilean and Nicaraguan symbols beneath a handshake of support between the two countries."[51]

The linkage reflected the political concerns of the four mostly Chilean artists, known collectively as the Brigada Orlando Letelier, in honor of the Chilean diplomat assassinated in Washington DC in 1976. Letelier's two sons, Francisco and Jose, painted the mural with René Castro, another exiled Chilean artist, and Beyhan Cagri. The mural is similar to the "flat style" of murals that decorated Chile during the Salvador Allende government, which the Pinochet government subsequently sought to eradicate. The artists were completing the mural in the summer of 1979, just as the Sandinistas overthrew the Somoza government, so the mural also served as a celebration.[52]

After the revolution, rather than tapering off, the cultural exchange between San Francisco cultural workers and the Sandinistas continued to flourish. Murals, with their high visibility, proved a popular import into the new Nicaragua, particularly with the leadership of Nicaraguan Minister of Culture Ernesto Cardenal. As David Kunzle notes, "In the decade of Sandinista rule following the Triumph of the Nicaraguan revolution in 1979, close to three hundred murals were created in a tiny, poor country of three million or so inhabitants."[53] Among the Bay Area muralists to travel to Nicaragua were the Orlando Letelier Brigade, Miranda Bergman, Juana Alicia, and Susan Greene. Greene later remarked, "There is a part of me that would have liked to have stayed there, but we need all the people we can get for the struggle in the United States. ¡Sandino Vive!"[54]

The 1979 triumph of the Sandinistas prompted a shift in the direction of migration, as the new Nicaraguan government invited its U.S. supporters to participate in the revolution. Roberto Vargas and Casimiro Sotelo, both from the Mission, became Nicaraguan ambassadors. Nina Serrano's intimate connections with the country led her to translate Nicaraguan poetry and cofound Friends of Nicaraguan Culture. Both of Serrano's children left the Bay Area to live in Nicaragua for extended periods of time. As she states,

10.2 The building interchangeably referred to as Casa Nicaragua or Casa Sandino, with murals by the Brigade Orlando Letelier. Above, image from *El Tecolote*, March 1981. Image courtesy of *El Tecolote* Photograph Archive.

"For the next many years, many, many years, we produced international cultural exchanges, including music, art, theatre, and interchanges of travel—interchange between American artists and Nicaraguan artists."[55]

Of course, this story does not end in the way that the cultural workers hoped. The Sandinistas were unable to deliver the idealized, utopian vision that had attracted supporters. This, combined with President Ronald Reagan's and President George Bush's desire to unseat the Sandinistas, legally or otherwise, led to the fall of the Sandinista regime in the 1990 election. As Gary Prevost and Harry Vanden state, Reagan's Contra war "took 30,000 Nicaraguan lives, cost more than $12 billion in damages and bankrupted the Nicaraguan treasury."[56] The magnitude of U.S. military and diplomatic force ensured the election of a presidential candidate who would protect U.S. interests. For Serrano, "I was totally disheartened when they lost the election. It just was very, very painful."[57] Murguía still feels angry. He states, "After ten-plus years of a 'democratic-capitalist' government . . . Nicaragua is now the poorest country of Latin America, and in the Western Hemisphere is second only to Haiti in lowest per capita income. This is the great benefit of the Contra War sponsored by the United States."[58] For many, the hope of the

1970s was destroyed by the traumatic violence of U.S. intervention in Central America over the course of the 1980s.

Traditional assessments of the 1970s lead one to believe that the period was devoid of hope. Historian David Farber characterizes the 1970s as a period when "Americans too often felt that they faced nothing but bad choices." According to Farber, "Events lent themselves to a litany of despair: inflation up, employment down; oil prices out of control, American-made automobiles breaking down; factories closed, marriages over, homicide rates soaring; President Gerald Ford."[59] Indeed, economic stagflation, deindustrialization, and decreased public funding hit neighborhoods like the Mission District especially hard. Nevertheless, out of the barrio, a transnational social movement flourished with hope. The issues are not unrelated. The promise of Nicaragua in the 1970s embodied what cultural workers hoped to build in the Mission District and around the world. The culture of the Mission was instrumental in determining the role San Francisco would play in the Sandinista campaign. In the context of 1960s civil rights social movements, anti-Vietnam protests, and San Francisco liberalism, the Mission District became center stage for Latino arts organizing with a decidedly leftist bent.

U.S. support of the Contra War is well documented, but the story of popular American support for the Sandinista revolution is hardly recognized or taught. Acknowledging the history of this political activism and cultural production is not only imperative to understanding the political and aesthetic development of Latino arts in the Bay Area and beyond, but it is central to thinking about diaspora, transnational solidarity, and conflicted patriotism. Upon reflection, perhaps one of the most salient points to consider here is how the actions of these poet-warriors might be interpreted today. The act of fighting for enemy forces, or serving as an accessory for a community at odds with U.S. diplomatic policy, is not well tolerated today. But deciding to take part in these actions emerged from an internationalist vision of the world, a vision built on hope and driven by the desire to eradicate oppressive social and economic policies in and beyond the barrio.

NOTES

1. Roberto Vargas, *Nicaragua: Yo Te Canto Besos, Balas, y Sueños de Libertad* (San Francisco: Editorial Pocho Che, 1980), 22.

2. Nina Serrano, *Heart Songs: The Collected Poems of Nina Serrano (1969–1979)* (San Francisco: Editorial Pocho-Che, 1980), 102–103.

3. María Cristina Garcia, *Seeking Refuge: Central American Migration to Mexico, the United States, and Canada* (Berkeley: University of California Press, 2006), 3–8.

4. Marjorie Heins, *Strictly Ghetto Property: The Story of Los Siete de la Raza* (Berkeley: Ramparts Press, 1972), 25–27.

5. Vargas, *Nicaragua*, 21.

6. Alejandro Murguía, *The Medicine of Memory: A Mexica Clan in California* (Austin: University of Texas Press. 2002), 126–127.

7. Murguía, *Medicine of Memory*, 125.

8. Juan Felipe Herrera provides one of the few accounts of San Francisco's Raza literature in "Riffs on Mission District Raza Writers" in *Reclaiming San Francisco: History, Politics, Culture*, ed. James Brook, Chris Carlsson, and Nancy Peters (San Francisco: City Lights Books, 1998), 217–230.

9. Ernesto Cardenal referred to San Francisco as "the city of Nicaraguans" in *Las Ínsulas Extrañas: Memorias 2* (Madrid: Editorial Trotta, 2002), 475.

10. Vargas, *Nicaragua*, 16; Carlos Cordova, interview by author, San Francisco, March 5, 2003; Raquel Rivera Pinderhughes, with Carlos Cordova and Jorge Del Pinal, "Our Multicultural Heritage: A Guide to America's Principal Ethnic Groups," http://bss.sfsu.edu/raquelrp/pub/heritage_pub.html, accessed October 7, 2006; Brian J. Godfrey, *Neighborhoods in Transition: The Making of San Francisco's Ethnic and Nonconformist Communities* (Berkeley: University of California Press, 1988).

11. Godfrey, *Neighborhoods in Transition*, 111, 138; Wallace Turner, "Mission District Seeks New Identity," *New York Times*, August 3, 1981; George J. Sanchez, "Race, Nation, and Culture in Recent Immigration Studies," *Journal of American Ethnic History*, Summer 1999, 66–84.

12. Cary Cordova, "The Heart of the Mission: Latino Art and Identity in San Francisco" (Ph.D. Diss., University of Texas, Austin, 2005).

13. George Black, *Triumph of the People: The Sandinista Revolution in Nicaragua* (London: Zed Press, 1985), 59.

14. "Bay Area Support Group Aids FSLN Cause," *El Tecolote*, June 27, 1975, 8.

15. Thomas Walker, *Nicaragua: Living in the Shadow of the Eagle*, Fourth Edition (Cambridge, MA: Westview Press, 2003), 31.

16. Ibid., 33.

17. Carlos Fonseca, quoted in Black, *Triumph of The People*, 90.

18. Daniel Ortega Saavedra, Victor M. Tirado López, and Humberto Ortega Saavedra, "Why the FSLN Struggles in Unity with the People," *Latin American Perspectives*, Winter 1979, 108–113. According to the publication, "This document was published both in English and the original Spanish by *Gaceta Sandinista*, III (July–August 1978), in San Francisco."

19. Cardenal, *Las Ínsulas Extrañas*, 475. Translation by author.

20. Nina Serrano, interview with the author, April 16, 2003. Murguía also describes the creation of NIN in *Medicine of Memory*, 135.

21. Cynthia Gorney, "San Francisco: When the Golden Gate Leads Home," *Washington Post*, March 25, 1984.

22. Cardenal, *Las Ínsulas Extrañas*, 476.

23. Walter Ferrety [*sic*], "From Guerrilla Commander to Top Cop," in Philip Zwerling and Connie Martin, *Nicaragua: A New Kind of Revolution* (Westport, CT: Lawrence Hill, 1985), 5–6.

24. Francisco Flores, "Roberto Vargas: The Intersection of Personal Growth and Community Activism," *El Tecolote*, April 2001; Murguía describes the presence of some of these high-profile figures in *Medicine of Memory*, 130–146.

25. Ferrety, "From Guerrilla Commander to Top Cop," 5–6.

26. "Bay Area Support Group," *El Tecolote*, 8.

27. "Nicaragua: Its People, History, Politics, and Economy," *El Tecolote*, June 27, 1975, 5–7.

28. Murguía, *Medicine of Memory*, 122.

29. Audio recordings of Vargas and other poets are housed at the Freedom Archives in San Francisco.

30. Flores, "Roberto Vargas"; Michelle María Boleyn, "Two Writers in the Mission," *North Mission News*, March 1987, 15.

31. Editorial box, *Gaceta Sandinista*, San Francisco, December 1975.

32. Herrera, *Reclaiming San Francisco*, 217–230; Roderick Anthony Hernandez, "Pocho-Che and the Tropicalization of American Poetics" (Ph.D. Diss., Stanford University, 2000).

33. Alejandro Murguía, curriculum vitae, collection of the author; Murguía, *Medicine of Memory*, 118–125.

34. Janice Mirikitani et al., eds., *Time to Greez! Incantations from the Third* World (San Francisco: Third World Communications, 1975); Pocho Che Editorial publications included: Jose Montoya, *El Sol y los de Abajo, and Other RCAF Poems* (San Francisco: Ediciones Pocho Che, 1972); Vargas, *Nicaragua*; Serrano, *Heart Songs*; Raul Salinas, *Un Trip Through the Mind Jail, y Otras Excursions* (San Francisco: Editorial Pocho-Che, 1980).

35. Herrera, *Reclaiming San Francisco*, 217–230; Hernandez, "Pocho-Che and the Tropicalization of American Poetics."

36. Murguía, *Medicine of Memory*, 130.

37. Alejandro Murguía, "A Chicano Sandinista in Nicaragua," *Uno Magazine*, December 1, 1981.

38. Murguía, *Medicine of Memory*, 134. While Murguía describes this event as the first rally ever held for Nicaragua in the Mission District, the local paper covering the demonstration suggests significant activism preceded this event. See "Bay Area Support Group," *El Tecolote*, 8.

39. See Nora Gallagher, Ken McEldowney, Michael Singer, and Henry Weinsten, "Art for Harold's Sake: How Big Business Manipulates the Arts in San Francisco," *San Francisco Bay Guardian*, November 21, 1975; Ceci Brunazzi, "On the Performing Arts Center," *Arts Biweekly*, July 27, 1976, 3–4; and a series of oral history interviews collected by UC Berkeley's Regional Oral History Office, *The Arts and the Community Oral History Project: San Francisco Neighborhood Arts Program*, 1978.

40. Murguía, curriculum vitae; Gilberto Osorio, "Fight for a Mission Cultural Center," *El Tecolote,* July 1976, 8; Paul Kagawa, "Mission Shaff-ted," *Arts Biweekly,* February 15, 1977, 3–4; Scott Riklin, "Galería Museo: Mirror of the Mission," *Arts Biweekly*, November–December 1977, 3–4.

41. "Ernesto Cardenal in the Barrio," *Tin Tan*, vol. 2, no. 5, June 1, 1977, 13.

42. Events cited in poster for the event, collection of Gilberto Osorio.

43. Dunbar-Ortiz, *Blood on the Border: A Memoir of the Contra War* (Boston: South End Press), 2005, 42; Gilberto Osorio, interview with author, July 10, 2006.

44. Alejandro Murguía, *Southern Front* (Tempe, AZ: Bilingual Press / Editorial Bilingüe), 1990, 7; Flores, "Roberto Vargas"; Murguía, "Chicano Sandinista."

45. *Después del Terremoto / After the Earthquake*, dirs. Lourdes Portillo and Nina Serrano, 1979.

46. Ibid.

47. Ibid.

48. Rosa Linda Fregoso, *Lourdes Portillo: The Devil Never Sleeps, and Other Films* (Austin: University of Texas Press, 2001), 50–51.

49. Ibid.

50. Alejandro Murguía, "El Movimiento de Solidaridad en San Francisco, 1974–1979," *Barricada Internacional*, July 8, 1989, 39. Translation by author.

51. Tim Drescher, "The Brigada Orlando Letelier," *Community Murals*, Fall 1981, 5.

52. Ibid.

53. David Kunzle, *The Murals of Revolutionary Nicaragua* (Berkeley: University of California Press, 1995), 12.

54. Susan Greene, "Artists Brigade to Nicaragua," *Community Murals Magazine*, Fall 1984.

55. Serrano, interview with author, April 16, 2003.

56. Gary Prevost and Harry E. Vanden, *The Undermining of the Sandinista Revolution* (New York: St. Martin's Press, 1999), 2.

57. Ibid., 2–3; Serrano, interview with author, April 16, 2003.

58. Murguía, *Medicine of Memory*, 146.

59. David Farber, *Taken Hostage: The Iran Hostage Crisis and America's First Encounter with Radical Islam* (Princeton: Princeton University Press, 2005), 10.

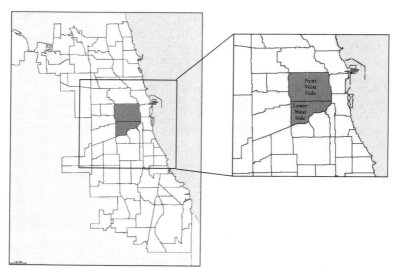

11.1 Near West Side and Lower West Side (Pilsen/18th Street), Chicago.

From the Near West Side to 18th Street

Un/Making Latino/a Barrios in Postwar Chicago

LILIA FERNÁNDEZ

In late 1971, a group of Mexican Americans gathered in Chicago's Pilsen/18th Street neighborhood to discuss the naming of a new Mexican community center opening in the area's east end.[1] The center would occupy the building of an old Catholic grammar school and adjoining church and rectory, which lay vacant for several years. St. Joseph's, or St. Joe's as it was known in the neighborhood, had long served a Slovakian immigrant population, but those residents and their second- and third-generation descendants had abandoned the neighborhood and the parish years before. The growing Mexican community in the area had obtained permission from the Archdiocese of Chicago to lease the facilities and operate a community center to serve local youth and families.

At their meeting, community members and leaders expressed passionate opinions about what the site should be named. Older professionals in the community, such as physician Dr. Jorge Prieto and Judge David Cerda, supported the name "Latin American Youth Center," a label that would clearly identify the community's purpose and ethnic heritage. Younger, more militant participants who had embraced the cultural nationalism of the Chicano Movement ardently called for a name in Spanish that would reflect the politics of a racialized national minority, not the traditional ethnic immigrant identity of the previous generation. According to one of the center's founders, Phil Ayala, "The more radical side [of the group] came up with [the name] 'El Centro de la Causa'" ("The Center for the Cause"). Tense debates over the center's name consumed the lengthy meeting. Ultimately, the group reached a compromise that would seemingly satisfy all involved: they adopted both names— the Spanish one to appease the younger radicals and the English version to satisfy state incorporation laws and more moderate middle-class sponsors.[2]

Despite the contrasting political views and generational differences, the establishment of the center marked an important moment for the Mexican people of Chicago's 18th Street neighborhood: they had asserted their presence and laid claim to the neighborhood. Mexican Americans quickly began efforts to establish other community-controlled centers and attract services for the growing population. The creation of institutions such as El Centro de la Causa, among other events, signaled the rooting of one of Chicago's quintessential Mexican barrios, the largest in the Midwest and one of the largest in the nation for over four decades.[3]

Latina/o barrios in contemporary urban America have become so naturalized as geographical entities that their origins, and specifically the structural conditions that historically led to their formation, have been forgotten. In the 1970s, Chicano historians documented the emergence of Mexican barrios in the Southwest as a result of the nineteenth-century American conquest of Mexico. They documented the structural racism, labor stratification, and residential segregation that created such communities. Historians of Puerto Rican migration have also documented the twentieth-century settlement of Puerto Ricans in ethnic enclaves in East Coast cities.[4] But in the late twentieth and early twenty-first centuries, such spatial formations have been reified and understood perhaps too simplistically as the logical and inevitable result of ethnic congregation.

Mexican Americans' settlement in Chicago's 18th Street community did not occur by accident. Their presence there is embedded in a history of racially based urban planning driven by market interests that dislocated them from the Near West Side neighborhood, known affectionately as "Taylor Street" (see figure 11.1). Mexican immigrants had a decades-long history in the Taylor Street area, but by the 1960s urban renewal, the construction of federal expressways, and the new University of Illinois Circle Campus had displaced much of the population. As a result, most families moved across the railroad tracks and settled in the historically eastern European Pilsen community (known officially by the Chicago Community Inventory as the Lower West Side). This chapter traces that movement and the efforts at community formation and activism in both neighborhoods. It illustrates the state's role (in this case, the municipal government of the city of Chicago) in making, then unmaking, then remaking the barrio.[5] In order to move "beyond el barrio," as the title of this anthology suggests, we must first closely examine its origins and determine how and why these spaces formed.

Settling on the Near West Side

Mexican immigrants began settling in Chicago and the Near West Side during World War I when workers were recruited to the city's railroads and steel mills. Comparable to the early East Los Angeles communities of Boyle Heights and Lincoln Heights, or the Puerto Rican *colonias* in New York City, the Near West Side was home to a heterogeneous working-class immigrant and second-generation population.[6] The area had been a port of entry for European immigrants for decades, and was one of the oldest neighborhoods in the city. In the mid to late nineteenth century, Irish and German immigrants made their homes there. By the turn of the next century, eastern and southern Europeans (Greeks, Italians, Russian and Hungarian Jews) began replacing the older stock. Densely crowded, dilapidated tenement buildings, which lacked plumbing or sewage systems, provided crude shelter for thousands of newcomers. In 1889, renowned social reformer Jane Addams chose the impoverished and overcrowded district to begin social settlement work and established the famous Hull House. The neighborhood's geographical location epitomized urban paradox—it stood immediately south and west of downtown but was one of the most neglected parts of the city.[7]

When European immigration decreased dramatically in 1924, greater numbers of Mexicans and southern African Americans began making their way to the Near West Side. The aged and neglected neighborhood was one of the least expensive places to live and one of the few areas besides the Black Belt that accepted racial minorities.[8] Although Mexicans had also moved to South Chicago, near the steel mills, and in the Back of Yards area, near the meatpacking houses, the Near West Side was their largest and most prominent settlement. It remained an extremely diverse community, symbolized best by the area's historic Maxwell Street open-air market, where a mélange of working-class people gathered to bargain, barter, sing, eat, preach the gospel, listen to music, and peddle their wares. Here, Mexicans walked among Italians, Greeks, Arabs, Gypsies, Jews, and Black Southerners. The area's diversity, however, belied the rigid physical segregation of African Americans who lived *within* Near West Side boundaries but generally did not live *among* Italians, Greeks, or other European immigrant neighbors. Ethnic whites often had slightly more tolerance for Mexicans and, thus, more frequently allowed them to live among "white" neighbors. In general, Mexicans enjoyed a more ambiguous racial position, at times considered just another immigrant group like Europeans, but at other times viewed as racially different like African Americans.[9]

Mexicans and a small number of other Latin American immigrants in the area had opened their own businesses as early as the 1920s, including restaurants, boarding houses, small grocery stores, and barber shops. They established mutual aid societies, athletic and fraternal clubs, and patriotic organizations. A handful of Spanish-language newspapers and periodicals were produced in the neighborhood during the 1920s and 1930s as well.[10]

In the 1930s, Chicago's Mexican population dropped to a third of its size as a result of the Great Depression and accompanying deportation and repatriation policies. The various social groups and service organizations that Mexicans managed to create in the neighborhood by the 1940s attest to the stable presence that some immigrants and their children were able to maintain despite economic instability. Area residents initiated various community organizations and groups designed to serve the largely immigrant, and largely impoverished, ethnic Mexican community. St. Francis of Assisi parish, which held its first Spanish-language mass in 1926, remained an institution in the community after the Depression. Mexican men who attended St. Francis established a fraternal organization, the Wildcats, in 1938. Their newsletter, the *St. Francis Crier*, regularly reported news about neighborhood residents, especially young men returning from military service during World War II. The church also sponsored youth clubs and offered recreational outings for second-generation teens. St. Francis's grammar school served many Mexican children as well.

Ethnic Mexicans officially numbered over 2,700 persons on the Near West Side in 1940, making up 9.5 percent of the foreign-born population and 2.0 percent of the neighborhood's total population. While this may seem small, Mexican settlement, like that of most other immigrants, was concentrated in a specific set of blocks, thus making them highly visible as a distinct racial group.[11] Relations with European Americans and African Americans were mixed: in some cases Mexicans had peaceful dealings with their Italian neighbors and others, but they also experienced racial tensions with Italians, Blacks, and Poles. By the mid-1940s the city's Mexican population began increasing again, numbering over twenty thousand. The neighborhood continued to serve as a port of entry for many incoming Mexican immigrants, *braceros*, Mexican American migrants, and a new group of Spanish-speaking labor migrants, Puerto Ricans.

Throughout the 1940s, Mexicans on the Near West Side developed various initiatives to address community needs and further plant roots in the neighborhood. In 1943, they formed the Mexican Civic Committee (MCC) under the sponsorship of the Chicago Area Project (CAP), a local juvenile delinquency prevention initiative. The MCC drew some of the city's few Mexican professionals to its board. The chair, Frank Paz, a Mexican immigrant from Michoacán, had an engineering degree from the University of Illinois at Urbana-Champaign and worked in the steel mills of the far South Side. The University of Chicago instructor Luis Leal, who would later become a renowned Chicano literary scholar, served as an officer as well before going off to serve in World War II.[12] In its goal to prevent juvenile delinquency, the MCC sponsored summer camps, classes, and other recreational programs for children. Overall, the MCC promoted education as the key to Mexican American upward mobility. It advocated a self-help philosophy, espousing notions of civic responsibility, community problem solving, and education as the means for social improvement.

The Status of the Mexican American in Chicago

In 1945 Mexican Americans called on the citywide Council of Social Agencies to better serve their social needs. The Council served as an umbrella organization for social service agencies throughout the metropolitan area, and had a Committee on Minority Groups that addressed minority concerns in matters of education and recreation.[13] That year at a Council-sponsored conference, Mexican American participants (including those from the MCC) protested their status as a "forgotten minority," a group that had gone overlooked by the social service agencies.[14] After much urging from Frank Paz and the MCC, the Committee on Minority Groups established a special Subcommittee on Mexican American Interests in February 1947. Paz became the subcommittee's first chair.[15]

The Subcommittee began planning and organizing for a city-wide conference for social service providers in the metropolitan area. On May 22, 1949, the Council of Social Agencies along with the Chicago Commission on Human Relations, social and welfare agencies, and leaders of the Mexican American community held a conference, "The Status of the Mexican American in Chicago." Paz provided opening remarks and set the tone for the meeting by examining the discrimination that Mexicans suffered in Chicago and how it had kept them from achieving the social mobility that European immigrants had enjoyed.[16] He began by astutely observing the "barrioization" of Mexicans in the city. "There is no neighborhood, that I know of, which has a publicly announced policy which says 'We do not rent to Mexicans,'" he remarked, "yet it happens—could it be accidentally?—that we find ourselves congregated in particular districts."[17] Paz pointedly observed the de facto residential segregation that Mexicans experienced. He addressed other issues such as employment discrimination and the failure of local social settlement houses, like Hull House, to include Mexican Americans in leadership positions.

In the end, conference attendees agreed on the need for "a city-wide, self-directed, non-profit organization for the purpose of serving as [the] representative voice for persons of Mexican American descent in Chicago." By June 1950, the organization was incorporated as the Mexican American Council (MAC), with Paz as the Council's first chair.[18] MAC noted, "The Mexican American is confronted with/manifold inter-related social problems. As a recent immigrant his [sic] income is low, his employment security uncertain, and his 'acceptance' by other ethnic groups in doubt. He faces numerous problems occasioned by his differences from his neighbors in language, culture, and educational opportunity. Judged by even the minimum of American standards of health and decency, he is in general 'ill-housed, ill-clothed, and ill-fed.'" The Mexican American Council, thus, sought "the better integration of the Mexican American into the life of his [sic] community in metropolitan Chicago."[19] Although Mexicans lived in three main settlements, their greatest concentration was on the Near West Side. The community and its leaders soon became the center of Mexican American sociopolitical advocacy. MAC faced the challenge, however, of serving ever-growing numbers of Mexican immigrants, Texas Mexicans (*Tejanos*), and Puerto Ricans. In March 1953, MAC estimated that over twenty-eight thousand Spanish-speaking people lived in the neighborhood.[20]

New migrants brought with them all the attendant problems of poor, recent arrivals, something that further compounded the already austere social conditions of Mexican American residents. Those who settled in the Near West Side area were drawn by the relatively low rents, proximity to jobs, and the presence of an already established Spanish-speaking community. As more Mexicans and Puerto Ricans arrived in the crowded, deteriorated community, they faced high unemployment rates, substandard housing, crowded schools, and high rates of poverty.[21] Many sought social services at Hull House, others turned to the Cordi-Marian Sisters, a Mexican order of nuns who provided daycare and programs for children and adults.[22] MAC provided assistance and referrals as well. Their health committee helped translate information for Spanish speakers. The housing committee assisted those who needed emergency shelter. The labor committee met with union representatives. The educational committee awarded scholarships to Mexican American high school graduates. Finally, the youth committee addressed the issue of juvenile delinquency.[23]

Barrio Interrupted

The Mexican Civic Committee and the Mexican American Council represented two significant initiatives of Mexican Americans on the Near West Side. The neighborhood also had an active interethnic community planning group, the Near West Side Planning Board (NWSPB), which in 1949 began plans for rehabilitating, improving, and conserving the district. The NWSPB regularly held open forums for community residents to provide input to future plans for the area and had widespread support. A meeting in March 1952 boasted the sponsorship of over eighty groups including neighborhood churches, public housing developments, schools, social service agencies, and civic groups. Mexican Americans were well represented by the Cordi-Marian Settlement, MAC, the MCC, the Mexican Methodist Church, the Manuel Pérez American Legion Post #1017, and St. Francis of Assisi parish.[24]

The NWSPB helped secure loans for local home owners to improve their properties as part of a larger community improvement effort. They also convinced the federal government to designate the area near Harrison and Halsted streets, the heart of the Mexican neighborhood, for urban renewal and proposed new affordable housing for area residents.[25] The urban renewal designation, however, inadvertently led to the neighborhood's demise. Initially, city hall supported the project and welcomed the improvement of the old and decayed district. Soon, however, the city betrayed the community's plans.[26] For several years, the Board of Trustees of the University of Illinois had been searching for a new campus in the Chicago area. Interested in the economic advantages of locating the school within city limits, the mayor insisted on finding a site within his jurisdiction. Debates raged for several years over the appropriate siting of the campus, with various communities and local leaders arguing in favor of and against various proposed locations. In late 1960, however, Mayor Richard J. Daley unilaterally offered the neighborhood's Harrison-Halsted site for the construction of the campus. The location had never been under consideration until that point (although a nearby railroad yard had been proposed). NWSPB members and local residents learned of the decision in local newspapers. Community women, mostly Italian American but some of them Mexican American, organized and challenged the city through pickets and lawsuits. They fought long and hard but ultimately lost the battle. In 1963, after the U.S. Supreme Court ruled against the neighborhood, the construction of the University of Illinois Circle Campus went forward.[27]

Entire blocks of neighbors were displaced as the university took the original redevelopment site plus even more acreage. Mexicans composed nearly 45 percent of families and 33 percent of single residents displaced by the university. Between 1960 and 1970, the area lost forty-seven thousand residents, nine thousand of whom were Mexican Americans.[28] The Mexican business district on Halsted Street, which provided Mexicans throughout the city, suburbs, and even further away with imported food products, *tortillerías*, *panaderías*, and other ethnic products, had to relocate. Neighborhood institutions such as social agencies and ethnic organizations dispersed or folded as well. Hull House, a long-standing, highly venerated institution, closed its doors after more than six decades of service to immigrants, and turned to city-wide rather than neighborhood-specific social programs for the poor.[29]

The displacement of Mexican Americans from the Taylor Street neighborhood has become part of a collective historical narrative for Mexican Americans throughout the Chicago area, but particularly for those who live in Pilsen/18th Street. Countless families tell stories of growing up in the neighborhood and eventually being forced to move as buildings were torn down for classroom facilities, athletic fields, parking lots, or housing for university students and faculty. María Ovalle, who grew up near Taylor Street, remembers as a child coming home from the fourth grade every day to see which buildings had been marked for demolition on her block: "I have a very, very clear recollection of this. . . . You would come home and if your [apartment building] was ready [to be torn down] it would have a circle with a cross on it. . . . And so, it would be really, really sad! You'd come home and the kids would [say], 'Oh, our house is going next,' and you'd have to move."[30] Families who had known one another for decades, or more recent arrivals who had just begun to establish roots in the neighborhood, were forced to find new housing elsewhere. As bulldozers razed area buildings, the majority of Taylor Street's Mexican families, and more than a few Puerto Ricans, reluctantly packed up and moved just south and west to the neighboring Lower West Side, more popularly known as Pilsen or 18th Street.

Re/Making the Barrio: From Taylor Street to 18th Street

The geographical movement of Mexicans from Taylor to 18th Street in the 1960s did not go uncontested. Eighteenth Street resembled much of the rest of Chicago, layered with generations of immigrants, highly segregated, and increasingly characterized by residential succession.[31] The neighborhood had historically been a port of entry for European immigrants, with Germans and Irish settling the area during the mid-eighteenth century. By the late 1800s and early 1900s, Czechoslovakian, Bohemian, Slovenian, Lithuanian, and Polish workers and their families moved in as they searched for housing close to their industrial workplaces.[32] Pilsen lay in the center of an industrial corridor, fringed by railroad tracks on the north, factories and warehouses on the east and south, and the south branch of the Chicago River. To the west, Pilsen flanked the neighboring Little Village (South Lawndale) community, which had a similar industrial and demographic composition. Pilsen was a decidedly working-class community.

The neighborhood was fairly impoverished and neglected. Housing stock was considerably older than in other parts of the city: less than 1 percent of Pilsen's housing had been constructed after 1940, while in outlying areas of Chicago as much as 30 percent of housing stock had been recently built. Multifamily apartment buildings outnumbered single-family homes.[33] European immigrants had economized space as much as possible. Many property lots contained two buildings, one in the front and one in the rear, each of which was divided into several small apartments to increase occupancy. Pilsen residents lived in very crowded conditions. For Spanish speakers, relocation from Taylor Street to 18th Street did not signal much of an improvement.

This contrasted sharply with the experience of European Americans. By the early 1960s, many of Pilsen's second- and third-generation ethnic whites had moved out to less crowded, better quality housing in neighborhoods to the south and west. Some of these families lived in neighboring Little Village (South Lawndale), with its slightly larger, less crowded homes, while the better heeled moved even further south and west to middle-class suburbs like Cicero and Berwyn. These stable, blue-collar bungalow communities lay further away from the city core. The simultaneous process of white flight and Mexican in-migration changed 18th Street and eventually the contiguous Little Village area as well. The construction of the University of Illinois Circle Campus had quickened the change in the racial composition of these neighborhoods.[34]

When Mexicans began arriving to 18th Street and Little Village, they encountered an already deteriorated community with an aging immigrant population that often expressed racial resentment toward these recent arrivals, regardless of whether they were U.S.-born transplants from Taylor Street or recent immigrants from Mexico.[35] Mexicans had historically held an ambiguous position within the city's racial order. Although they were immigrants, their cultural differences and darker skin color of some marked them as racially distinct, especially in relation to ethnic whites. Although many

European immigrants and their descendants had deep-seated ethnic and national antagonisms toward one another (i.e., Poles, Slavs, Czechs), they came together on the basis of their shared "whiteness" to battle the encroaching threat of darker people. By the 1970s, research conducted in Pilsen and Little Village revealed European immigrant anxieties about the changes in the community:

> [They] view the exodus [*sic*] of Mexicans, and to some extent the closeness of the blacks, as a threat to their very existence in every sense of the word. Informants often say that they do not object to Mexicans and blacks as such, but cannot hide a deep-seated anxiety concerning the changes they may bring in their own style of life and in the cultural and social atmosphere of the whole community.

Researchers explained that in the face of incoming Mexicans and African Americans, whose children attended their neighborhood public high school, "Czechs, Slovaks, Poles and Slovenians [were] sufficiently drawn together to overcome their historical pasts."[36]

The emergence of a "white" identity occurred in contrast to a nonwhite one. Second-generation Mexican Americans grew up with the experience of racial resentment from their neighbors and were explicitly told they were outsiders. Jesús García, for example, recalled as a youth hearing European Americans on the streets or in local businesses lament the fact that "these people" (the Mexican newcomers to Little Village) did not understand or respect the "traditions of the neighborhood," a phrase that masked underlying racial animosity.[37] Alicia Amador, a Mexican American woman, recalled explicit bigotry during her childhood:

> Racism was awful over there. People can not believe what we went through. I remember walking into a store with my brother and we were waiting [to be helped] and people were walking ahead of us [in line]. Finally, I told the proprietor, "We've been standing here. My brother wants to buy some candy." And he said, "We don't serve niggers here."[38]

On 18th Street, Mexicans and Mexican Americans had similar experiences. Carlos Valencia, who moved to Pilsen in 1958 when he was a teenager, remembered very tense relations in the predominantly Polish area. As one of the first Mexican families to cross the imaginary western racial boundary along Ashland Avenue, the Valencias encountered prejudice from their Polish neighbors. Valencia noted, "We were always fighting with the Polish guys. There was lots of tension."[39] Resident Cathy Alaniz told researchers in 1970 about an elderly Polish neighbor, Mrs. Zapolsky: "Whenever the [Mexican children] go down the stairs and pass her on the way, they hear her muttering, 'Mexicans!'" Zapolsky also referred to Alaniz's dark-skinned niece as "that black Mexican."[40]

Despite these conflicts, by the late sixties signs of a new ethnic community began to emerge on 18th Street. The 1970 census officially counted a population of more than twenty-four thousand Spanish-speaking people, composing 55 percent of the neighborhood's total population.[41] The community's poverty remained unchanged. Median family income measured less than $8,600, with sixteen percent of families living below the poverty line. Forty-nine percent of those employed in Pilsen worked in manufacturing. The community had one of the city's lowest levels of school completion: the median for adults over twenty-five was only 8.5 years of schooling. Residents were very young, with thirty-nine percent under eighteen years of age.[42] Such conditions prompted Mexican Americans to begin organizing and attracting more resources to their community.

As families began establishing new businesses, social networks, and community ties, many of the second generation began claiming 18th Street/Pilsen as a permanent Mexican community. Local youth and activists were shaped by the politics of the time: the civil rights, student, antiwar, women's, Chicano, and Puerto Rican movements that found expression both nationally and in Chicago. But the experience of displacement from the Near West Side, and the new position in which Mexicans found themselves within the area's ethno-racial landscape influenced them as well.

Some local activists worked in social service agencies, formed community-based organizations, and began building coalitions with other groups across the city. Others had more radical critiques of American society and envisioned revolutionary social changes that struck at the root of inequality. Those attracted by cultural nationalism gravitated to the burgeoning Chicano Movement. Like their counterparts in places like Los Angeles, those who identified as Chicanos in Chicago made demands for self-determination and community autonomy, protested against local power structures, and demanded greater social services. Chicanismo in Chicago, however, emerged in a context of traditional ethnic politics (including the Democratic Daley machine), racially shifting neighborhoods, and coalitions with other Latin American migrants, namely Puerto Ricans.[43] The particularities of Chicago's political history and ethno-racial landscape tempered some radical activism and promoted more moderate and "accommodationist" community politics among those who preferred to identify themselves as immigrants, akin to Europeans, rather than embrace a racial minority status.

The establishment of El Centro de la Causa, a community youth center, represented just one effort at claiming space for Mexicans in Pilsen, challenging social inequalities, and bringing social services to the community. In 1970, Father John Harrington, of the Providence of God parish in Pilsen's east end, informed two Mexican American workers at the Howell Settlement House, John Velásquez and Phil Ayala, about a vacant Catholic school and church building.[44] He suggested that it could possibly be reopened and used by the neighborhood. The school facilities included classrooms and a large gym that could be put to use by local youth as a recreational center and meeting place. Velásquez and Ayala successfully negotiated with the Archdiocese to lease the buildings and secured two paid staff positions as well. In November 1971, the building officially opened as "El Centro de la Causa, the Latin American Youth Center, Inc."[45]

El Centro initially focused on recreational and athletic programs aimed at gang-violence prevention primarily among young men. The director hired street workers to reach Mexican youth and draw them into the Center. Staff soon began applying for funding for other projects and quickly expanded their services to programs such as Servicios Sociales del Barrio (Neighborhood Social Services), Project Quetzalcoatl, the Chicano Mental Health Training Program (CMHTP), BASTA (literally, "Enough!" but an acronym also for Brotherhood Against Slavery to Addiction), and Dar A Luz (Giving Birth), a mother-infant health program. Women affiliated with the Center branched off in 1974 and formed a women's organization, Mujeres Latinas en Acción (Latina Women in Action), meant to specifically address the needs of women and girls. A fund-raising press release from the early 1970s explained El Centro's formation: "Over the years this community [the Mexican American population] has been ignored by federal, state, and city agencies that have been established to meet some of the needs of inner city residents. . . . There has been little interest on the part of city agencies to [expend] energy or monies to provide needed services for our community." The Center aimed "to provide an atmosphere which encourages adults to use their civil rights and responsibilities and which enables youth to realize their full potential."[46]

The CMHTP symbolized one of the Center's most successful, though short-lived, initiatives. The program sought to train local community residents as "bilingual bicultural paraprofessionals in the ever broadening field of mental health."[47] CMHTP received funding from the National Institute of Mental Health in July 1972. The program recruited Mexican American and Latina/o instructors and developed a Chicano-centric curriculum.[48] Over two dozen neighborhood residents enrolled in the courses. Students took classes at El Centro and completed internships in local mental health or social service agencies. Within four years, the program had successfully trained forty-eight residents, thirty-eight of whom received Associates Degrees, while fifteen continued on toward advanced degrees. The program placed a total of twenty students in mental health service positions, and fifteen in other human service jobs.[49]

Two years after opening, El Centro received a seventy-five-thousand-dollar grant for a demonstration project they called Servicios Sociales del Barrio. The program provided assistance to families and youth, largely in the form of casework, and included a research component that sought to identify needs and services that were not being met in the community. A group of men in the neighborhood also obtained funding to initiate a methadone clinic and drug rehabilitation program (BASTA). El Centro established a community library as well. The neighborhood had long been without a public library, and while many had petitioned the city to open one, El Centro's staff saw an opportunity to develop their own locally controlled space that would "supply the community with the information it needs to survive within a hostile environment, and to improve self-concepts by raising the level of consciousness about ourselves and our culture."[50] Project Quetzalcoatl provided encouragement and resources for local youth to attend college. This college recruitment program helped numerous young men and women apply and enroll in local colleges in the city and beyond.

El Centro represented a significant achievement for 18th Street's Mexican American community. In a short span of years, activists had succeeded in attracting substantial resources to serve the local population. Yet it was not the only center of activism in the community. Radical, leftist Latino groups took a more direct, confrontational approach to combat social inequality. A coalition of Mexican and Puerto Rican workers, calling themselves Asociación Pro Derechos Obreros (The Association for Workers' Rights, APO), organized in the late 1960s. In the early 1970s they staged bus boycotts and sit-ins to protest employment discrimination against Latinos by the Chicago Transit Authority. The Marxist-Leninist organization Centro de Acción Social Autónomo—Hermandad General de Trabajadores (Center for Autonomous Social Action–General Brotherhood of Workers, CASA-HGT) found a base among undocumented immigrants and their allies, and waged campaigns for their rights. Cultural nationalists (some of whom were affiliated with other organizations) reclaimed the local social settlement house, Howell House, which had long served European immigrants, and renamed it Casa Aztlán, reflecting a new, Chicano-centric orientation. Moderate and reformist activists led more traditional initiatives. In 1968, Mexican Americans successfully assumed leadership of the Pilsen Neighbors Community Council (PNCC), a Saul Alinsky–style Industrial Areas Foundation organization that focused on neighborhood beautification and operated a credit union and buying cooperative. A League of United Latin American Citizens (LULAC) chapter comprising attorneys, small businessmen, and skilled workers operated in the slightly more middle-class neighborhood of Little Village. LULAC provided scholarships for high school students and promoted greater educational attainment.

Women participated in these organizations but also took on specifically gendered concerns that affected them as women, mothers, and wives. After surveying neighborhood households and discovering the dire need for childcare, a group of seven mothers founded El Hogar del Niño (The Child's Home), a daycare center for local children. The female staff and participants at El Centro formed Mujeres Latinas en Acción to address domestic violence, runaway teenage girls, reproductive health, and employment training. Other mothers and residents fought for the construction of a neighborhood high school. Their boycotts and demonstrations ended in victory for local Mexican residents, who until then had to send their children a long distance to the only area high school. Residents named their new school Benito Juarez, after Mexico's first indigenous president. Still another group of activists established the Latino Youth Alternative High School for those labeled as "problem" students, including those who dropped out or were "pushed out" of the school system.

These community organizations, campaigns, and struggles emerged within a span of only a few years, from 1968 to 1975. Such efforts symbolized an adamant claim on the 18th Street community by Mexican American residents. The displacement of the Mexican community in the early 1960s from the Near West Side, their encounter with prejudice and discrimination, and their need to establish roots in a new neighborhood influenced the response of Mexican Americans to the social conditions of the barrio. Working within their specific environment and sociopolitical context, Mexican Americans shaped their conditions and sought to improve their lives as best they could.

Conclusion

The dismantling and remaking of the predominantly Mexican Near West Side barrio in postwar Chicago brings into relief the ways in which the state shapes and limits the possibilities of everyday life of Latinas/os in the United States. As much as working-class people have worked to create homes for themselves in urban communities, structural conditions and market imperatives ultimately determine the future of neighborhoods, the profitability and desirability of real estate markets, and the ethnic/racial composition of those communities. Eighteenth Street and the Near West Side, both of which have undergone tremendous demographic, physical, and economic changes, would hardly be recognizable in the twenty-first century to their inhabitants fifty, thirty, or even ten years ago. Just as Spanish-speaking immigrants and their children brought a new complexion to these neighborhoods decades ago, the national "re-urbanization" of middle- and upper-class whites is dramatically transforming inner-city neighborhoods again. The Near West Side and Pilsen, once discarded and forgotten districts, have seen a reversal of fortunes as developers have erected upscale housing, high-end shopping corridors, and fashionable art galleries and restaurants to attract young professionals. Condominiums, townhouses, and lofts have replaced empty lots, dilapidated frame houses, abandoned factories and warehouses, and the tenements of earlier generations. Students, professors, artists, and white-collar workers (perhaps descendants of those earlier residents?) have quietly displaced the most recent immigrants, who for decades made these neighborhoods their arrival point in the city. Just as in the sixties and seventies, activists are vocally claiming their community, but this time they are ardently defending it against the sweeping intrusion of gentrification that threatens to displace them once more. This newest phenomenon confirms yet again that market imperatives for the accumulation of capital, public discourses of racial animus, and the municipal and federal embodiment of the state continue to shape where and when Latinas/os have been able to put down roots, and where they will be able to make homes in the future.

The title of this anthology calls on us as scholars to move "beyond el barrio" in a theoretical sense. Yet we may also be moving away from el barrio quite literally, as national gentrification trends are reversing the white flight of half a century ago and foreshadowing the disappearance of the traditional inner city barrio of the twentieth century. Latino Studies scholars would be wise to explore more deeply the historical origins of this social formation before it vanishes completely and gets erased from our historical memories.

NOTES

1. I use the terms "Mexican" and "Mexican American" interchangeably (and sometimes jointly) throughout this chapter to denote both immigrants and U.S.-born or U.S.-raised people of Mexican descent.

2. Phil Ayala, interview with the author, 25 March 2004. El Centro eventually became a Catholic Charities agency and remained so until it closed its doors in 2006.

3. This includes the larger, contiguous areas of Pilsen and Little Village.

4. For historic accounts of Chicano barrios, see Albert Camarillo, *Chicanos in a Changing Society: From Mexican Pueblos to American Barrios in Santa Barbara and Southern California, 1848–1930* (Cambridge: Harvard University Press, 1979); Richard Griswold del Castillo, *The Los Angeles Barrio, 1850–1890: A Social History* (Berkeley: University of California Press, 1979); Lisbeth Haas, *Conquests and Historical Identities in California, 1769–1936* (Berkeley: University of California Press, 1995); and Ricardo Romo, *East Los Angeles: History of a Barrio* (Austin: University of Texas Press, 1983). For twentieth-century accounts, see George J. Sanchez, *Becoming Mexican American: Ethnicity, Culture, and Identity in Chicano Los Angeles, 1900–1945* (New York: Oxford University Press, 1993); and Matt Garcia, *A World of Its Own: Race, Labor, and Citrus in the Making of Greater Los Angeles, 1900–1970* (Chapel Hill: University of North Carolina Press, 2001). For accounts of Puerto Rican communities, see Carmen Teresa Whalen, *From Puerto Rico to Philadelphia: Puerto Rican Workers and Postwar Economies* (Philadelphia: Temple University Press, 2001); and Virginia Sánchez-Korrol, *From Colonia to Community: The History of Puerto Ricans in New York City* (Berkeley: University of California Press, 1994).

5. Due to limited space, I do not provide an exhaustive treatment of these dynamics. For a more in-depth analysis, in particular a treatment of Puerto Rican community displacement, see Lilia Fernández, *Brown in the Windy City: Mexicans and Puerto Ricans in Postwar Chicago* (manuscript under review).

6. See Sanchez, *Becoming Mexican American*; and Sánchez-Korrol, *From Colonia to Community*.

7. For a historical description of the Near West Side, see Thomas L. Philpott, *The Slum and the Ghetto: Neighborhood Deterioration and Middle-Class Reform, Chicago 1880–1930* (New York: Oxford University Press, 1978).

8. African Americans formed an enclave within the Jewish section of the neighborhood. Carolyn Eastwood, *Near West Side Stories: Struggles for Community in Chicago's Maxwell Street Neighborhood* (Chicago: Lake Claremont Press, 2002), 204.

9. Thomas Philpott argues that Mexicans were considered an immigrant group similar to European immigrants. Yet researcher Paul Taylor noted as early as 1932 that Mexicans had a shifting racial position in the local social order, at times ranked above African Americans, but at other times viewed as similar or even inferior to them. Gabriela Arredondo also argues that Mexicans experienced a great deal of racial discrimination from European immigrants and were racialized distinctly from them. See Philpott, *The Slum and the Ghetto*; Paul S. Taylor, *Mexican Labor in the United States*, Vol. II (New York: Arno Press, 1970, 1932); and Gabriela Arredondo, "Navigating Ethno-racial Currents: Mexicans in Chicago, 1919–1939," *Journal of Urban History* 30 (2004).

10. On Mexican immigrants in Chicago prior to World War II, see Gabriela F. Arredondo, *Mexican Chicago: Race, Ethnicity, and Nation: 1916–1939* (Urbana: University of

Illinois Press, 2008); and Louise Año Nuevo Kerr, "The Chicano Experience in Chicago: 1920–1970" (Ph.D. dissertation, University of Illinois, 1976).

11. Louis Wirth and Eleanor H. Bernert, eds., *Local Community Fact Book of Chicago* (Chicago: University of Chicago Press, 1949). See also Phil Ayala, interview with the author, 4 December 2003; and Adrian Canales, Mikale Haepp, Josue Olivas, and Amanda Rojas, "Movement and Settlement: A Lower West Side Story," based on an oral history interview with Jovita Duran, in *Telling Historias: Oral Histories from Chicago Based on the Curiosity of Youth and the Memories of Elders* (Chicago: n.p., 2002–2003).

12. Nelson A. Rockefeller to Ernest Burgess, February 10, 1943, box 89, Chicago Area Project Collection (hereafter CAP), Chicago Historical Society; "Report on the Conference on the Mexican Americans in Chicago," n.d., box 147, Welfare Council of Metropolitan Chicago Records (hereafter WC), Chicago Historical Society; Jesse A. Jacobs, "Notes on Conversation with Clifford Shaw re: Future of the Mexican Civic Committee," 17 February 1944, box 373, WC; and Clifford Shaw to Mexican Civic Committee, n.d., box 89, CAP.

13. The Committee on Minority Groups addressed issues affecting Chicago's Black population, as well as other "minority" issues such as Japanese American resettlement. Horace Cayton, one of the authors of the famous *Black Metropolis: A Study of Negro Life in a Northern City* (1945), chaired the Committee. See box 145, WC.

14. See "Minutes of the Meeting of the Committee on Minority Groups, Wednesday, October 23, 1946," box 145; and "A Brief History of the Committee on Minority Group Relations, Division of Education and Recreation, Welfare Council of Metropolitan Chicago," October 1950, box 145, WC.

15. "Minutes of the Meeting of the Committee on Minority Groups," 26 February 1947, box 145; "Minutes of Meeting of the Executive Committee of Division on Education and Recreation," 20 February 1947, box 147; and "Minutes of the Meeting on Mexican American Interests," 7 May 1947, box 147, WC.

16. Eileen McMahon, for example, chronicles the remarkable upward mobility and assimilation that Irish immigrants experienced in Chicago as they successfully integrated into civil service jobs, municipal politics, and lower-middle-class neighborhoods usually within two generations. See *What Parish Are You From? A Chicago Irish Community and Race Relations* (Lexington: University of Kentucky Press, 1995).

17. "Report on the Conference on the Mexican Americans in Chicago"; and Frank Paz, "Status of the Mexican American in Chicago," speech given at conference, box 147, WC.

18. The Subcommittee on Mexican American Interests had accomplished its goals and thus disbanded. See "A Brief History of the Committee on Minority Group Relations, Division of Education and Recreation, Welfare Council of Metropolitan Chicago," October 1950, box 145, WC; and untitled document, Mexican American Council, April 1953, box 88, CAP.

19. Untitled document, Mexican American Council, April 1953, box 88, CAP.

20. Louise Hutchinson, "Quiet 'Revolt' Making City Happier Place for Mexicans," *Chicago Tribune* (March 29, 1953).

21. See, for example, Tom Littlewood, "Mexicans Are Chicago's Least Understood Group," *Chicago Sun-Times* (October 19, 1953).

22. Phil Ayala, interview with the author, 4 December 2003; and Duran oral history.

23. See Hutchinson, "Quiet Revolt."

24. Near West Side Planning Board, flyer, March 1952, box 88, CAP.

25. Near West Side Planning Board pamphlet, n.d.; James C. Downs to Clayton C. Meyers, 21 July 1955; "Proceedings of the Fifth Anniversary Meeting of the Near West Side Planning Board," 27 October 1953; all in box 92, CAP.

26. See Near West Side Community Council, *Near West Side Chronicle* (October 1958): 7, in Near West Side Community Committee Records (NWSCC), Special Collections, University of Illinois at Chicago.

27. For more details, see Eastwood, *Near West Side Stories*; George Rosen, *Decision-Making Chicago-Style: The Genesis of a University of Illinois Campus* (Urbana: University of Illinois Press, 1980); and Fred W. Beuttle, Melvin G. Holli, and Robert V. Remini, *The University of Illinois at Chicago: A Pictorial History* (Charleston, SC: Arcadia Publishing, 2000).

28. Eastwood, *Near West Side Stories*, 269; and Evelyn Kitagawa and Karl E. Taeuber, eds., *Local Community Fact Book: Chicago's Metropolitan Area, 1960* (Chicago: Chicago Community Inventory, 1963), 71.

29. Unfortunately, a historic mural, the first ever painted by a Mexican in Chicago, Adrian Lozano, was torn down during the demolition of Hull House; see David A. Badillo, "Incorporating Reform and Religion: Mexican Immigrants, Hull-House, and the Church," in *Pots of Promise: Mexicans and Pottery at Hull-House, 1920–40*, edited by Cheryl R. Ganz and Margaret Strobel, 31–54 (Urbana: University of Illinois Press, 2004), 50–51. The story of Taylor Street's Mexican community resembles that of Chavez Ravine, a Los Angeles Mexican American community that was also displaced by the construction of a major institution, Dodger Stadium. See Eric Avila, *Popular Culture in the Age of White Flight: Fear and Fantasy in Suburban Los Angeles* (Berkeley: University of California Press, 2006), chapter 5.

30. María Ovalle, interview with the author, 6 June 2004. The term "house" did not necessarily mean a single-family home, but rather any family residence. Most buildings in the area, in fact, were multifamily apartments.

31. For a discussion of race and housing (and specifically, the issue of public housing, which in Chicago has come to represent the confluence of race and housing), see chapter 5 of Gregory D. Squires, Larry Bennett, Kathleen McCourt, and Philip Nyden, *Chicago: Race, Class, and the Response to Urban Decline* (Philadelphia: Temple University Press, 1987). For a classic study of race, housing, and the creation of low-income African American public housing in Chicago, see Arnold R. Hirsch, *Making the Second Ghetto: Race and Housing in Chicago, 1940–1960* (Cambridge: Cambridge University Press, 1983).

32. In 1940, Pilsen was populated entirely by European immigrants and their descendants. Seventy-one percent of residents were "native white," and twenty-nine percent "foreign-born white." This foreign-born population consisted of Poles (31 percent), Czechs (23 percent), Yugoslavians (13 percent), Lithuanians (12 percent), Italians (8 percent), and other smaller ethnic groups; Wirth and Bernert, *Local Community Fact Book of Chicago*.

33. In 1960, 23 percent of housing units were owner-occupied. Kitagawa and Taeuber, *Local Community Fact Book*, 76–77. See also Mary Bakszysz and Kay Guzder, "Description of the 18th and 26th Street Communities," n.d. (ca. 1970), and "Pilsen," n.d., in *El Centro de la Causa* private archives (hereafter ECC); and Chicago Association of Commerce and Industry, *Community Area Data Book for the City of Chicago: 1975 Census Data by 75 Community Areas* (Chicago: Chicago Association of Commerce and Industry, ca. 1976), vi.

34. A white pastor at the Millard Congregational Church in Little Village, Pastor Anderson, explained to researchers in 1969 that he was leaving the neighborhood because the congregation could not support him anymore. There were only 130 members remaining in his church, and 50 percent of them had moved out of the area to Cicero or Berwyn but still came back to the neighborhood on Sundays for church. Bohemian families, Anderson claimed, moved out after their children graduated from eighth grade because they did not want to send their children to Farragut High School, where they would mix with Black students. See Sister María del Rey and Mary Bakszysz, "Operation of the Millard Congregational Church," 9 September 1969, ECC.

Such racial change was occurring throughout the South Side of Chicago in the 1960s as African Americans pressed beyond the borders of the hyper-segregated Black Belt, and whites responded by abandoning their communities. See McMahon, *What Parish Are You From?*

35. Alicia Amador, interview with the author, 26 March 2004; also Mrs. and Mrs. Brevenick interview with Elisabeth Houston, 21 July 1969; Sister María Del Rey and Mary Bakszysz, "Operation of Millard Congregational Church," 9 September 1969; Cathy Alaniz, interview with Emile Schepers, 15 September 1970; all in ECC.

36. Anonymous, "The Middle European Community of South Lawndale," 6, 7, ECC. See also Bakszysz and Guzder, "Operation of Millard Congregational Church." The ethnic differences among European immigrants were embodied in the "national" parishes that the Catholic Archdiocese established for each national group. Poles, Italians, Germans, and Irish initially worshipped separately in their own churches. By the 1960s, however, as a result of racial succession and changing dynamics, those ethnic barriers gradually dissolved and "white ethnics" found more in common with one another. McMahon, *What Parish Are You From?*, 38, 101, and chapter 2.

Numerous scholars have documented this dynamic of "investing" in whiteness in the mid-twentieth century. See, for example, George Lipsitz, *The Possessive Investment in Whiteness: How White People Profit from Identity Politics* (Philadelphia: Temple University Press, 1998); and Thomas J. Sugrue, *The Origins of the Urban Crisis: Race and Inequality in Postwar Detroit* (Princeton: Princeton University Press, 1996). Arnold Hirsch traces how European American "ethnics" became white through their opposition to Blackness in *Making the Second Ghetto*, chapter 6. Thomas Guglielmo notes that although Italians were always racialized as white, they consciously claimed their whiteness beginning in the 1940s to distinguish themselves from African Americans in Chicago; see his *White on Arrival: Italians, Race, Color, and Power in Chicago, 1890–1945* (Oxford: Oxford University Press, 2003).

37. Jesus Garcia, interview with the author, 22 June 2004.

38. Amador interview.

39. Carlos Valencia, personal communication with the author, 20 June 2004. Poles had a history of racial enmity toward Mexicans dating back to the 1920s. See Arredondo, *Mexican Chicago*, chapter 2; and Taylor, *Mexican Labor*.

40. Emile Schepers interview with Cathy Alaniz, 15 September 1970, ECC. Arredondo documents the historic ethno-racial enmity that Poles had for Mexicans in *Mexican Chicago*.

41. Researchers and community leaders assumed a *significant* undercount, especially of the undocumented.

42. Chicago Fact Book Consortium, *Local Community Fact Book Chicago Metropolitan Area: Based on the 1970 and 1980 Censuses* (Chicago: Chicago Review Press, 1984), 364, 453.

43. By "traditional ethnic politics," I refer to the practice of ethnic political bosses who often controlled neighborhoods or particular communities through patronage jobs, nepotism, and political machines. Richard J. Daley, who reigned as city mayor from 1955 to 1976, epitomized such politics.

44. St. Joseph's was a victim of the white flight that left many Catholic churches abandoned during the 1960s and 1970s.

45. Reverend John M. Harrington, "A Ministry of Social Justice: A Parochial Model in a Mexican American Community" (Doctor of Ministry dissertation, St. Mary of the Lake Seminary, 1981), 10. See also John Harrington, personal communication with the author, 10 December 2004; and Archdiocese of Chicago, *A History of the Institutions of the Archdiocese of Chicago*, Vol. II (Chicago: Archdiocese of Chicago, 1981), 857.

46. "El Centro de la Causa/Latin American Youth Center, Inc.," press release, n.d., ECC; and Archdiocese of Chicago, *History of the Institutions*, 859.

47. Chicano Mental Health Training Program, funding application to the Department of Health, Education, and Welfare, 30 September 1972, ECC.

48. "Chicano Mental Health Training Program," n.d.; syllabi, Chicano Mental Health Training Program; "The Chicano Mental Health Training Program—Abstract" (August 1973), 1; all in ECC; also Ayala interview, 25 March 2004.

49. Phil Ayala to Dr. Bertrand Brown, Director of Department of Health, Education, and Welfare, National Institutes of Mental Health, 12 May 1976, ECC; and Ayala interview, 25 March 2004.

50. El Centro Board of Directors, "Meeting Minutes," 22 March 1973, ECC. See also Servicios Sociales case files, ECC; and Humberto Martinez, "BASTA: A Chicano Addict Rehabilitation Program," n.d., ECC. Documents reveal that Euro-Americans had negative opinions overall toward El Centro and especially towards the BASTA program. "Research Results of Community Survey," n.d., ECC. "El Centro de la Causa Library" n.d., ECC.

12

Transglocal Barrio Politics

Dominican American Organizing in
New York City

ANA APARICIO

Over the past two decades, Dominican American activists working
in the northern Manhattan neighborhood of Washington Heights have initiated projects that have reshaped that neighborhood and the local political
landscape. In this process, they have established and utilized numerous networks that include and extend beyond local and transnational Dominican
circles; these networks include African Americans, Puerto Ricans, Cubans,
and progressive whites. While they use these networks, they have also
helped to transform them. This chapter will focus on the ways and reasons
Dominican American activists work through these multiple networks, and
on the implications this work has for the way we theorize contemporary
"barrio politics."[1]

This chapter takes as its central question the debate over the significance
of the "local" in a globalized world, particularly when examining immigrant
politics in the United States. When discussing New York–based Dominican
American organizing, I am often asked about the extent to which local concerns compete with transnational practices in the realm of politics. Are new
generations of Dominican American activists tied exclusively to the neighborhood of Washington Heights or to Dominicans? Can we not begin to
look at the ways that people are identifying with various populations and
localities? That is, could we not theorize on how people are simultaneously
becoming transnational, global, and local—or "transglocal"—in a globalized world? These questions are raised particularly in relation to the work
that emphasizes the central place of the local in recent trends in Dominican
American politics (Aparicio 2006; Ricourt 2002). One could ask, "Haven't we
moved beyond the strict boundaries of place-specific, provincial notions of
community?" In fact, yes, people do move between or across borders—physically, socially, economically, and culturally. The growing body of literature on

transnationalism highlights these trends. In analyses of Dominican transnationalism, neighborhoods like Washington Heights, New York, and Jamaica Plain, Boston, are often described as the quintessential contemporary transnational communities, with Dominican social and political groups regularly working across various boundaries (Duany 1994; Levitt 2001). Precursors to this kind of dynamic political life can be found in the work of organizations like the Young Lords Party. In the 1960s and 1970s, this organization worked across cities in the United States and with activists in Puerto Rico. They also worked across ethno-racial group definitions; that is, from their inception they had close ideological and social ties to activists in groups like the Black Panther Party. An exploration of the history of organizations like the Young Lords further explicates the transglocal as a concept that necessarily considers the local, the global, and the transnational. This notion of the transglocal incorporates lessons from these varied analyses to offer a more nuanced and multifaceted reading of Latino/a politics, forcing us to reconsider the very nature and complexity of local barrio politics.

Recent texts on U.S.-based Dominican politics (Levitt 2001; Ricourt 2002; Aparicio 2006) point out that the transnational sphere is one space in which Dominicans living in places like New York City and Boston practice and alter politics. Peggy Levitt's work, building on the earlier literature on transnationalism (e.g., Basch et al. 1994), delves into the complex nature of this transnational work among contemporary transmigrants such as Dominicans living in Boston and in Lawrence, Massachusetts. Foundations like the Inter-America Foundation have also taken note of the growing role of transnational networks among Dominican organizations; in recent years, they discovered that many of the organizations they funded in the Dominican Republic developed projects and products that eventually found their way to organizations in the United States. In 2004, the Foundation held meetings with scholars and community organizers who worked with Dominican populations in Miami, New York, and Boston to ascertain how they could begin to work with this understanding of the way Dominican organizers—in the Dominican Republic and in the United States—occupied local *and* transnational spaces. It is clear to whoever takes an even cursory glance at political life in Washington Heights (or in the Dominican Republic) that networks span geopolitical borders. Transnational practices are important, and today's technology and economic forces make such practices more urgent. But this does not suggest that geopolitical borders no longer exist, or more important, that immigrants move across these borders with facile acrobatics. State power continues to exert tremendous force. And place matters much.

In order to understand people's lives and their political projects, we must understand the local context in which their lives and work are embedded; the role of the state and state policies are part and parcel of this context. Further, I propose that even when acknowledging and analyzing the way people work across prescribed borders (of geography, group identity, class, etc.), that we not forget that for most people, particularly racially marginalized populations, the local is of paramount importance. The local is where people carry out their daily lives and struggles. When thinking about the work to which Dominican American activists commit themselves, local concerns— allocation of resources, political representation, government accountability, service provision, gentrification—matter to them because they see local residents confronting these issues daily. What I am proposing is that we not think of it as a zero-sum game, where either the local or the transnational reigns supreme in matters political.

A reading of Dominican American politics—particularly that which is grounded in the northern Manhattan neighborhood of Washington Heights—necessitates a complex reading of all the layers that make up this ever-expanding project. Dominican American activism can only be understood by bringing together all the varied threads that span time and geography. An analysis of Dominican American politics requires that we figure out methods to understand the multiple ways in which activists work through the transnational, local, global, and diasporic. In essence, I am suggesting that when thinking of the local "barrio politics" of Washington Heights, we consider three very important factors. First, through their work local activists draw on multiple histories. Second, for decades now, Dominican American activists have been working across group boundaries. And finally, these organizers regularly reach out beyond the neighborhood, and sometimes beyond the nation, to construct new dynamics that bear fruit in local politics. This analysis of the transnational nature of some Dominican life and organizing, while not unfamiliar to many who think carefully about transnationalism, is not one that is often put forth by policy makers or pundits—or even by some academics, for that matter, who often still reify "el barrio" or the local as the only way of organizing or engaging in political activity.

Histories in Washington Heights

The first matrix that one must understand when thinking of Dominican American politics in Washington Heights is one that is engulfed by history. This is not about a history that is resurrected solely for the purpose of contextualizing facts, which then allow us to understand how people arrived at a particular situation. The significance of history in the telling of this particular "barrio story" moves beyond contextual utility; activists often call on history to make certain claims, to demand rights, to challenge structural inequalities, and to build their political networks. For the purpose of this chapter, there are only three histories to which I draw the reader's attention: political and activists' histories from the Dominican Republic, a history of Dominican immigration and settlement in Washington Heights, and the histories of Dominican American organizers' connections to other activists of color in New York.

Dominican Republic

The mass exodus of Dominicans to New York occurred after the assassination of dictator Rafael Leonidas Trujillo in 1962. During this same year, the United States established a U.S. Consulate's office in the Dominican Republic for the explicit purpose of issuing scores of passports[2] and visas in order to eliminate potential unrest and militancy in the country. In 1965, when the United States ordered and carried out a military invasion of Santo Domingo, massive unrest flourished in the capital city. The U.S. Immigration Reform Laws of 1965 also created the conditions under which emigration would occur. Many Dominicans who arrived at this time did so for economic reasons. Others arrived as de facto political exiles, remaining in close contact with political organizing efforts based in the Dominican Republic. In efforts to continue to play a role in island political life, they created political organizations in New York City. As one local organizer recalled:

> The progressive movement within the Dominican movement in the United States . . . all those who made up the foundation of this movement were comrades who survived the persecutions in the Dominican Republic. . . . They had an organization [in New York City]: Asociación Dominicana. They had another called Enriquillo. . . . I can't forget to mention Alfredo White. Alfredo White established the first Dominican community center here in Washington Heights, but the majority of the leaders of those organizations here were, the majority, they were ex-combatants of the Guerra de Abril [the April War] from the side of the Constitutionalists and the majority of them . . . they arrived here [in the United States] once [Joaquín] Balaguer came into power. In other words, the majority arrived

here between 1966 and 1968. At that time they established a Dominican Committee for Human Rights, a Dominican Committee of the Dominican-Haitian Committee of Friendship. . . . There was a very active movement. Again, their ideology was to organize the people not just to play dominoes but to organize the people so that the people would mobilize. (translation mine)[3]

Two organizers—Marcos Villegos and Emiliano Luis Montenegro—who helped to establish some of the most prominent organizations in Washington Heights were part of this militant Dominican émigré population. In the Dominican Republic, both Villegos and Montenegro formed part of the leadership of the radical Marxist militant organization Linea Roja in the late 1970s and 1980s. Both fled the Dominican Republic due to poverty and political persecution. Both men, like most political refugees of the time, arrived in the United States as young adults in their late twenties. And they arrived with a leftist, community-based orientation to civic participation, grounded in anti-imperialist Marxist ideology. Many were also involved in political efforts that extended to various Latin American countries, namely Cuba, Nicaragua, and later El Salvador. This suggests that a more complex reading of political motivation, discourse, and strategies is in order. It was their anti-imperialist ideology that propelled many of these activists to work with those struggling for justice. They worked across Latin America and the Caribbean because of U.S. imperialist politics and practices in the region. When discussing their solidarity with organizations like the FMLN in El Salvador, one group of Dominican organizers drew parallels with their own nation's history with U.S. empire (primarily U.S. invasion and puppet dictatorships). This political capital helped to shape Dominican community organizing. Many from the current ranks of local leadership arrived at this time (and entered the New York City public education system), or are children of those who emigrated during these years. During these early years of mass migration, many Dominicans—including political activists–assumed that their stay in New York was temporary. They believed that after saving money or after political turmoil on the island country abated, they would return to their homes in the Dominican Republic. As such, many sought employment and enrolled their children in New York schools but continued to receive news about politics in the Dominican Republic, and mobilized accordingly.

Some political exiles led chapters of leftist political parties from the Dominican Republic. Organizers from Linea Roja met in New York, forming a chapter of the radical group in their new home. They elected leaders and representatives to meet with comrades in the Dominican Republic. This group remained active until the mid-1980s. The purpose of the political clubs was to keep those living in New York abreast of affairs in the island country and rally support—political and economic—for projects in which their island compatriots were involved. These clubs also kept people in close contact with one another while adjusting to life in New York, providing a mechanism of social support for newly arrived immigrants.

Political unrest continued after the 1965 U.S. invasion, and in 1978, when the newly elected Partido Revolucionario Dominicano (PRD) took control of the Dominican government, many activists—in the Dominican Republic and the United States—protested the PRD's signing of an economic development agreement with the IMF. Many key political figures continued to direct their lens toward the Dominican Republic. Although an interest in "homeland politics" remains an important aspect of many organizations, one cannot overlook the reasons for the specific political agendas and orientations of the early political clubs in Washington Heights' Dominican community. As one organizer indicated, "These [clubs] were our refuge. We had a role in helping to democratize the island. We were here, but our hopes for revolutionary change in the Dominican Republic could not die. It just couldn't." The political situation in the Dominican Republic propelled Dominicans to organize these clubs. The 1960s and 1970s were particularly difficult times for leftist movements in the Dominican Republic. As one political exile explained:

The period between 1972 to 1978 was difficult. . . . During that time the principal student leaders were assassinated, and more than four thousand people were in prison, and approximately seventy or eighty people were disappeared. . . . Today young people don't think that to criticize and to use the right to think for oneself [is a big thing]. . . . [They believe] that it's something natural and it should be that way. I'm happy that they think this way. But in my time, thinking had a very high price. Even the way that you dressed [could be dangerous]. For example, if you put on black pants and a green shirt, simply because someone gave it to you and you didn't have anything else, you would be arrested and you would get beaten up and they tortured you so that you would say that you led, that you knew people from [the movement] 14 de junio. If you put on black pants and red socks they would do the same to you so that you would say that you knew about the MPD. And when there were fights between military groups and they killed [one of their own], well, be ready that a group of young people would be imprisoned and serve a sentence. A comrade here at work in the school served seven years in prison, seven years, the mention of which brings him to tears. That was a long time ago but that was seven years of his life [he lost] for nothing. They grabbed him, they found him at home, and they took the supposed evidence. They gave him a weapon, which they said they found in his house. It was with that weapon that they had killed a Sergeant in San Francisco de Macorís, and he paid for that, something he did not do. (translation mine)

Stories and events like these reached Dominicans living in Washington Heights. They were part of the raison d'etre of political clubs. Their politics were rooted in an anti-imperialist ideology whose goal was radical social/structural change.[4] Crucial to an understanding of this era of Dominican transnationalism is an analysis of the political climate in the Dominican Republic at the time this organizing was most fervent. It is also important to assess the political ideologies of the activists involved in transnational politics; as noted earlier, many were also involved in solidarity movements in multiple countries throughout Latin America, regardless of their own country of origin.

Political and social clubs still operate in Washington Heights, often attracting the newly arrived. In the spring of 2000, when Dominican presidential campaigning was in full swing, New York–based offices of political parties organized caravans, fund-raisers, and speaking engagements throughout Washington Heights. There is no question that island, or "homeland," politics have a space in the neighborhood, but Dominicans have also developed organizations to empower, to provide services, and to obtain resources for those living in New York City.

Many of the political exiles arrived in New York with the desire to continue to effect change in the Dominican Republic. Their goal was to create a truly democratic nation and to see the masses return to this island nation. They created various political and social clubs in Washington Heights, which brought many activists together and worked to support the projects of compatriots who remained in the Dominican Republic. In the 1980s, however, activists began to reconsider the idea that the masses would one day return home. What follows is an exploration of the reasons for such a shift in perspective. The projects they subsequently undertook give us a better understanding of the ways they developed local politics by maneuvering through networks that extended beyond the co-ethnic and local.

Taking Root in the Local

The shift from organizing almost exclusively for "homeland" politics to organizing to empower Dominicans locally spanned the better part of the 1980s. This decade proved to be a turning point for Dominican American community building in New York (Georges 1984; Ricourt 2002; Torres-Saillant 1998). Its development rested on the convergence of a series of factors. First, upon wrestling with the *aquí-allá* (here-there) debate, a large contingent of Dominican community organizers let go of "home" and began orienting their work toward New York–based issues. The reasons for this shift include: an understanding that the radical structural change they envisioned for the Dominican Republic was not close at hand; in the twenty-plus years of residence in New York City, Dominicans had begun to establish firm roots; and Dominican populations and neighborhoods had grown considerably, as had their concerns. And so they began to establish locally focused organizations. Second, many young organizers began to graduate from New York City public schools and the City University of New York. This new, second generation of activists took the networks and political experiences garnered in these institutions into their organizing in Washington Heights. Third, Dominican American activists established local organizing and connected to other people of color in New York, primarily Puerto Rican and Black organizers and elected officials. And finally, established leadership and external institutions began to offer resources to organizations in the Dominican American community of Washington Heights; this included the Dinkins mayoral administration of the late 1980s and early 1990s. These factors helped channel Dominican organizing in a new direction and developed into a critical era of activism for the Dominican American community.

Even two decades after the first wave of Dominican emigrants, many organizers still believed that their stay in New York was temporary. But as revolutionary prospects diminished on the island, local residents and activists debated the permanence of the Dominican community in the United States and began to alter their organizing efforts. Was the Dominican immigrant population going to return to the island country or did activists need to plan for another scenario? In local organizations and in everyday settings, residents and activists debated prospects for this community, and projections hinged on the realization that this population was not a group of transient sojourners that would return en masse to the Dominican Republic. Local activists—from the first generation of radical émigrés and the second generation raised in New York—began to come to terms with the fact that the Dominican population in New York was setting roots in the United States, and that it was their duty to secure a degree of civic participation and empowerment for this population. One of my interlocutors explained that guiding their efforts in these early days was a political ideology that included questions of inclusion, exclusion, and racialization in the United States:

> During that time it was en vogue to discuss Stalin's book, *The National Question*. We discussed if Dominicans living here were part of the multinational nation or if we were a minority exploited in the United States. That caused a division in the group. There was one group that said we Dominicans are here, we're staying, *y pa'l carajo con la República Dominicana* [to hell with the Dominican Republic]. The other sector, to which [Emiliano Luis] belonged, said there's a group that will stay but there's also a group that will go back. We have to be responsible for both groups. The first group was more firm, and they left *Linea Roja*. . . . They founded *ACDP* . . . the focus would be organizing the community, the tenants. That was going to be the focus.

But intent alone did not catapult Dominicans into major organizations. Initially, Dominican organizers attempted to gain entry into preexisting organizations in the neighborhood. Although there were many community-based organizations providing services to residents of Washington Heights, Dominican activists ultimately felt that existing organizations did not adequately address or meet the needs of the newly arrived Dominican population. As one local activist explained, the organizations established by others in the early 1980s did not include Dominicans in their boardrooms or in their program development.[5]

By the 1980s, some of the more prominent community activists had curtailed their organizing around politics in the Dominican Republic—the "transnational" political emphasis—and agreed that they needed to organize and address some of the issues they all confronted as New Yorkers. One Alianza Dominicana leader explained:

> We made a conscious decision that we were going to focus here, because in the mid-eighties there was a very strong awareness and somewhat of a debate in the community, so were we here permanently or temporarily as a group, because if we were here temporarily then obviously the agenda had to be different, we had to prepare to leave. And many of us knew that we were here permanently. That meant we had to create institutions that could support our permanent presence.

These organizers analyzed the nature of existing community organizations in Washington Heights and concluded that although there were many social and political clubs, none represented—nor attempted to represent—the Dominican presence and none attempted to address their New York–based concerns such as housing, employment, and health care. Local activists began to meet to discuss how they might contribute to the development and empowerment of the Dominican population residing in New York City. Those centrally involved included the leftist organizers from the Dominican Republic. When developing these new locally geared projects, they not only utilized the networks and political experiences garnered from a history in politics in the Dominican Republic, but they also infused these local initiatives with the same kind of political ideology that led them to work for democracy and justice in the Dominican Republic, Cuba, and so forth. That is, the history from the Dominican Republic was transported to and worked to enliven efforts geared toward the local in Washington Heights.

The new generation of U.S.-educated activists joined with fellow activists who had been involved with organizing for "home" politics in discussing the future of the Dominican population residing in New York. In fact, younger Dominican activists were the first to recognize the need to structure their own programs that would address the needs of the Dominican community. The issues raised during this time—the near-exclusion from established institutions—led many activists to focus on building routes in the United States. The issues that activists addressed included the nature of "belonging" and entitlement in the United States. One of the founders of Alianza Dominicana, and the current director of a community development program, explained:

> Something was emerging at the time. . . . There was an obvious community presence . . . in [Washington] Heights, needs coming up, young people coming out of college looking to make their mark on the day. . . . The first manifestation was some people ran for [the local community] school board and won. . . . They had a presence for the first time. So the community had begun to show its face. . . . I was painfully aware of something called the Washington Heights–Inwood Task Force that was formed in the late seventies by [Mayor Ed] Koch. Everyone but Dominicans [was included], there was one Latino there, but he was a landlord. There was also a task force and a lot of committees. Early on in that work, or as a result of that work, there were three things done in this community, which is the part that is really a milestone . . . in the development of this community. Three agencies were formed in 1978, 1979: Northern Manhattan Improvement Corporation, the Washington Heights–

Inwood Development Corporation, and the Washington Heights–Inwood Coalition. . . . They were formed to address really discrete stuff [such as housing and social services]. [Dominican activists were worried] that these were things set up with interlocking boards and that these agencies were gatekeepers . . . It was amazing the same people were on the boards . . . so we [Dominicans] ended up organizing [our own organizations].

When Dominicans attempted to secure space for their fledgling organizations, they experienced a degree of hostility from the local white leadership. One founder explained the way the local community board of the late 1980s—composed of the old white leadership of the neighborhood—attempted to stall the progress of Alianza Dominicana as they requested office space:

[In order to get the space] the Housing Authority had asked, because that was community space, . . . they asked for some show of support. We had to go before the community board and ask them for, would you give us a letter of support, or a resolution of support or what have you? . . . [The] Housing Authority said what they wanted was more or less a formality and it was a very small space . . . a chunk of it someone had already committed it to the Heisman Foundation and they were going to do childcare and this little space was going to be [Alianza Dominicana]. From where these people [i.e., the Heisman Foundation] came is a mystery. It turns out they were never able to do stuff there. . . . They didn't do it. They didn't even know how to run a childcare center. And [Alianza Dominicana] couldn't get that space because it had already been committed. Anyway, when we go that night to the community board meeting, to get support . . . as we were making our case in the public session . . . in comes this person who . . . created massive confusion by asking for this same space.

I asked him why this person, someone he recognized as non-Dominican, wanted this space:

They wanted it, they heard we wanted it. . . . I ended up on community board floor making some quick alliances with the non-Dominicans and managed to get the support . . . it was quite a scene. . . . It was a good indication that people just did not want this to happen. Not letting it happen. So we navigated that struggle and got some space . . . But it was a given we were gonna get it [from the Housing Authority] but it shows you a lot about the process [and] what happens with racism.

In a proactive manner, local leaders of the Dominican community began to map out political routes in New York City.

In the early 1980s, a twenty-year-old Dominican man, Miguel Amaro, approached the leaders of the old guard of Dominican activists—those who were part of the leftist organization Linea Roja—with plans to organize an annual Dominican parade. One activist who was present recalled, "He said I want to talk to you in secrecy but I have a plan to organize here and I want you to be the guiding force." The old guard agreed to meet, explaining, "We did it because he was a young leftist militant." One activist present during one of the initial meetings stated that when this young man left the room, everyone present thought he was misdirecting his efforts:

> We really believed he was crazy. [We believed] the Dominican community wasn't about that. The Dominican community was into organizing itself to go back. But Miguel [Amaro] was able to understand the feelings of the community before us, the famous leftist leaders. He understood where the community was going and saw that one thing that brought a sense of pride and a sense of patriotism was organizing a parade. And he did it.

In 1981, Amaro founded the Dominican Day Parade, then known as el Festival Dominicano, with its first realization as a march down Audubon Avenue that August. Hundreds of people arrived to celebrate Dominican pride in the streets of Washington Heights. The effort to build a force in the United States, however, would also need the support and political savvy of the old guard of first-generation activists. The turning point for those old guard activists, who believed they would return to the Dominican Republic, was the 1984 Dominican elections. As one activist explained:

> The turning point for the mentality of the community was in 1984. [It occurred after] the disaster of the government of the PRD. Because with the government of 1978 we didn't have much hope . . . because the most conservative of the PRD rose to power. But in 1982 the number of people that came from the militant Left [in the Dominican Republic] . . . there were dozens of *compañeros* and *compañeras* that went back because Salvador Jorge Blanco represented the intellectual side of the party. With him there were people with berets with stars on the front demonstrating their respect for Ernesto Ché Guevara and what he symbolized. And so all these young intellectuals from 1982 rise to power [in 1984] and this was the government, probably the most corrupt that has been seen in the history of

the Dominican Republic. . . . The external debt shot up, the [Dominican] peso lost so much value, and approximately eleven or twelve ministers in the government divided amongst themselves what [former president and Trujillo cabinet member Joaquín] Balaguer typically divided between five hundred generals or wealthy families in the country. So during the government of Salvador Jorge Blanco, ten or eleven people were able to gather thousands of millions of pesos. Some of the young poor people that we used to see and organize with in the university were among those in the government . . . traveling to buy Arabian horses and with a Dominican plane at their disposal. . . . Those were our *compañeros*. . . . The hope we Dominicans had that there would be a positive change in the country and that we would return, well that diminished.

At this point, many activists began to understand the permanence of the Dominican community in the United States. This ideology was advanced by the rising second generation coming of age in the Dominican community, a part of the history that is a cornerstone of contemporary Dominican American politics (Aparicio 2006).

Working Across Barrios

The desire to establish a local presence and power was strong among Dominican American organizers in Washington Heights in the 1980s, as was the political repertoire garnered from years of struggle in the Dominican Republic. As crucial as these elements were for Dominican American activism in Washington Heights, there were other key factors in the political history of this contemporary New York barrio. They include networks—both horizontal and vertical, grassroots as well as electoral—with leadership from other New York groups, namely African Americans and Puerto Ricans. Dominican Americans created these networks and working relationships with established leadership and with grassroots activists; this has been one of the crucial layers of Dominican American politics that has often gone overlooked. One of the key alliances in the electoral sphere was with David Dinkins.

In 1989, after serving as Manhattan Borough President for four years, David Dinkins launched a campaign for the New York City mayoral seat. In his successful campaign against Mayor Ed Koch for the Democratic primaries and against Republican candidate Rudolph Giuliani, Dinkins sought the support of the city's Black, Latino, and white populations. Among those who answered his call were the director and a founding board member of Alianza Dominicana, and Guillermo Linares, a local organizer who just a couple of years later became the first Dominican elected to office in the United States. Dinkins ran a successful campaign, becoming the city's first black Mayor (Day 1990; Sanjek 1998). Dinkins garnered the endorsement of Blacks, Latinos, and whites. Perhaps more than any New York political figure before him, David Dinkins was able to create an inter-ethnic, inter-racial network in mainstream city politics. As Barbara Day (1990, 174) states, "Dinkins's victory was earned by an alliance of organized labor, African-Americans, Latinos, prochoice women, lesbians, and gays."

Dinkins's success was also a success for local Dominican organizing. Dinkins selected one of the cofounders of Alianza Dominicana to lead his transition team. Guillermo Linares also served on that team. In his reading of the city as a "mosaic" of peoples, Dinkins sought to create an administration that included people of color in a way very different from that of his predecessor, Ed Koch. Dinkins appointed a number of Dominicans to different high-level offices, including head of the Office of Hispanic Affairs, Assistant Commissioner for the city's Department of Employment, and Deputy Commissioner. The three Dominicans in these high-ranking positions had formed part of the group that founded Alianza Dominicana. Their connections to the Dominican community of Washington Heights remained important as they served under Dinkins. For example, in 1991 Dinkins established the Beacon Initiative. Conceived as a community-based organization partnership with local schools, this initiative created programs and provided services to communities throughout the city. In the first year, eight organizations were selected to lead Beacon programs. Each lead organization received half a million dollars from the city, and Alianza Dominicana was among them. The founding director stated, "In the Dinkins administration those of us that were on the inside worked very much to strengthen what was on the outside." The growth of Alianza Dominicana and other programs throughout the city could not have occurred had Dominicans not established a working partnership with David Dinkins and other Black politicians and local organizers.

Another important series of networks developed in a less formal way, primarily among youth activists. Young Dominicans raised and educated in New York, who were at the forefront of much of the new activism, extended the reach of already established community-based organizations. They served as cultural and financial brokers, connecting Dominican associations to established Puerto Rican leaders, many of whom they met in the City University of New York, the city's public university system, in the late 1980s and 1990s. It was at this very moment that the Dominican community began to appear as a local political force. Although a number of Dominican individuals were, by this time, in positions of leadership in city government, local Dominican activists felt that the general population of Dominicans was still disproportionately disenfranchised.

The second generation, along with those of the first generation who were now focusing more on New York issues, began to make connections to other Latino and Black activists in New York schools in their attempts to gain access to power and resources and challenge racialized class and power structures. Mariana Bidó, one of the activists involved in Linea Roja and the early years of Asociación Comunal de Dominicanos Progresistas (ACDP) became involved with La Liga Por la Lucha Revolucionaria, or the Revolutionary League, in which Amiri Baraka was one of the principal figures. The League was involved in a movement to liberate political prisoners in the United States. Ties to Puerto Rican and Black organizers and organizations—such as Bidó's ties to El Puente, a Puerto Rican organization and school in Brooklyn, and, earlier, to Amiri Baraka—were important. In fact, Puerto Ricans signed the incorporation papers of the ACDP because first-generation Dominican leaders of the organization could not sign the nonprofit paperwork themselves because they were not yet U.S. citizens. Obtaining 501(c)(3) status was crucial given that this organization, along with many others, believed it was necessary to secure funding from external agencies.

At the same time this was occurring, a series of young organizers—ranging in age but all younger than thirty—frustrated with the poor education and police brutality to which young Dominicans were subject in New York, established local, grassroots, activist organizations in Washington Heights. This population established the two organizations at the center of my own fieldwork. It is important to note that these individuals were first generation, second generation, and the so-called 1.5 generation.[6]

During the 1980s and early 1990s Dominicans of both generations came together to establish some of the most well-known and influential community organizations in Washington Heights. These organizations have, from the time of their incorporation as nonprofits, focused on confronting local issues in New York. Although it may appear that organizing focused primarily on the Dominican "co-ethnic" community, the organizers were clear that they must reach out to other organizers of color in order to build stronger institutions, political capital in the city, and, for some, a stronger grassroots movement for social justice. Similar processes of racialization, deindustrialization, and government disinvestment in public education that other people of color face also shaped Dominicans' lives and prospects.

Although many might not recognize the role that inter-ethnic/racial collaborations played in developing Dominican power, all local residents witness the fruits of that labor. Today, Dominican American organizers are trying to use all the skills and networks established during the 1980s and 1990s to secure a place on the national political scene. In 2002, Guillermo Linares ran for New York State Senate. The Dominican American National Roundtable has secured offices in Washington DC. The director of one of the organizations involved explained these national efforts:

> We have a yearning and a need to be in Dominican communities throughout the United States that don't have the level of support that are required. So we're looking a lot now toward organizing nationally, organizing us as a community. We may surge now as the third largest Latino community in the nation, I think we will actually after the census. So that means we have to really begin to organize from a national perspective.

Dominican American organizers learned from and worked with other organizers of color to develop a Dominican entry into local politics. Working with other activists of color—particularly Puerto Ricans and African Americans—was an essential element of early Dominican political developments in New York City. As a result, Dominican American youth and educational organizations grew in number, scope, and funding in the 1980s and 1990s.

By the 1990s, many organizers and academics began to speak of the "Dominican American" and what needed to be done to gain some real power in the United States. Unlike earlier waves of white immigrant groups, Dominicans' status and prospects would continue to be delineated by racial codes and racialization processes operating in concert with contemporary socioeconomic shifts in the United States (Hernandez 2002; Torres-Saillant 1998).

Dominican American activists, especially those who have spent the majority of their political lives battling U.S. racism and imperialism, understand that in building bridges with numerous community they are, in effect, creating a larger movement. They reach out beyond the local but keep an eye focused on the ways their work and collaborations affect the local. For example, Dominican American organizers have worked with other immigrant groups in the United States demanding amnesty, with Haitians fighting for justice in the Dominican Republic, and with those working with solidarity efforts with Cuba. These young Dominican American organizers have altered the work and meanings around the Black diaspora in ways that extend beyond the local New York scene as well, shifting the definitions of Blackness in relation to Haitians. Dominicans have questioned and attempted to change the racialization of Haitians by organizing to change the lived experiences of racial discourse, of state-sanctioned racism hiding behind the guise of nation and citizenship.

Much of their collaborative work has taken place around issues of state violence. In the 1990s, youth leaders of major Dominican organizations worked with Puerto Rican activist Richie Perez and others to combat police brutality on the streets of New York City. These same organizers went on to establish a multi-ethnic anti-imperialist, anti-racist organization called Azabache (Aparicio 2007). In all these projects, Dominican American youth activists see themselves as part of a larger collective confronting similar concerns. Their "community," therefore, is one that begins to extend beyond the local, beyond the transnational (as popularly conceived), and into the diasporic transglocal.

Conclusion

So what does this all mean for the way some activists are reconceptualizing Dominicanidad, race, diaspora, and power? What does this all suggest about the way we understand and theorize "barrio politics"? The various threads that I have suggested make Dominican American politics in Washington Heights strong are numerous, multilayered, and forever intertwined. In order to grapple with the local, we must analyze the multiple ways activists reach across histories and geographies to garner local power. We cannot look at a geographic site, or local barrio, as an island suspended in time. An understanding of local and transnational patterns requires that we document and contextualize the ways in which historical roots in a place, under certain political conditions, continue to matter in structuring new social and political patterns. Additionally, when examining the barrio, we need to look at spaces and groups that exist beyond this one locale. In the case of Dominican Americans in Washington Heights, New York, this means that we need to further document the continuing significance of history, transnationalism, and diasporic organizing in local activism. These factors are part of the context and the content of Dominican American organizing in Washington Heights—they are part of what make up this transglocal barrio at this time.

NOTES

1. Portions of this chapter were originally published in Aparicio 2006.

2. Prior to this moment in political history, only a select few from the elite sectors of Dominican society under Trujillo were granted passports from the Dominican government.

3. Some interviews were conducted in Spanish and I provide translations where noted.

4. The role that New York has played in the diasporic political projects of Caribbean populations stretches back to the nineteenth century. Political exiles from Cuba and Puerto Rico developed their work and political projects from New York throughout the nineteenth and twentieth centuries (Aparicio 2005; Oboler and Gonzalez 2005).

5. This seemed to follow a trend in the city's ethnic and racial political divisions, a product of a long history of politics in New York and Mayor Ed Koch's overtures to solidifying divisions along racial lines (Mollenkopf 1992).

6. The "first generation" consists of those who, as adults, emigrated from their home country to another. The "second generation" is commonly understood to mean those who were born to immigrant parents in the new country of residence. The "1.5 generation" also refers to children of immigrants; however, they are different from the second generation because the "1.5ers" were born in their parents' country of origin and emigrated as children.

REFERENCES

Aparicio, Ana. 2005. "Latinos in New York," entry in Oboler and Gonzalez, eds., *Oxford Encyclopedia of Latinos and Latinas in the United States.*
———. 2006. *Dominican Americans and the Politics of Empowerment.* Gainesville: University Press of Florida.
———. 2007. "Contesting Race and Power Through the Diaspora: Second-Generation Dominican Youth in the New Gotham." *City and Society* 19(2): 179–201.
Basch, Linda, Nina Glick Schiller, and Cristina Szanton Blanc. 1994. *Nations Unbound: Transnational Projects, Postcolonial Predicaments, and Deterritorialized Nation-States.* London: Gordon and Breach Publishers.
Day, Barbara. 1990. "New York: David Dinkins Opens the Door." In *Fire in the Hearth: The Radical Politics of Place in America.* Mike Davis, Steven Hiatt, Marie Kennedy, Susan Ruddick, and Michael Sprinker, eds. New York: Verso.
Duany, Jorge. 1994. *Quisqueya on the Hudson: The Transnational Identity of Dominicans in Washington Heights.* Dominican Research Monograph Series. New York: CUNY Dominican Studies Institute.
Georges, Eugenia. 1984. "Dominican Diaspora: Putting Down Roots?" *Hispanic Monitor* (May 1984): 6.
Hernández, Ramona. 2002. *The Mobility of Workers Under Advanced Capitalism: Dominican Migration to the United States.* New York: Columbia University Press.
Levitt, Peggy. 2001. *The Transnational Villagers.* Berkeley: University of California Press.
Mollenkopf, John. 1992. *A Phoenix in the Ashes: The Rise and Fall of the Koch Administration.* Princeton: Princeton University Press.

Oboler, Suzanne, and Deena J. Gonzalez, eds. 2005. *The Oxford Encyclopedia of Latinos and Latinas in the United States*. New York: Oxford University Press.

Ricourt, Milagros. 2002. *Dominicans in New York City: Power from the Margins*. New York: Routledge.

Sanjek, Roger. 1998. *The Future of Us All: Race and Neighborhood Politics in New York City*. Ithaca: Cornell University Press.

Torres-Saillant, Silvio. 1997. "Diaspora and National Identity: Dominican Migration in the Postmodern Society." *Migration World Magazine* 25(3): 18–22.

———. 1998. "Visions of Dominicanness in the United States." In *Borderless Borders: U.S. Latinos, Latin Americans, and the Paradox of Interdependence*. Frank Bonilla, Edwin Melendez, Rebecca Morales, and María de los Angeles Torres, eds. Philadelphia: Temple University Press.

About the Contributors

ANA APARICIO is Assistant Professor in the Department of Anthropology and in the Latino Studies Program at Northwestern University. She is the author of *Dominican Americans and the Politics of Empowerment*, which received the 2006 Association for Latina and Latino Anthropologists Book Award Honorable Mention. She is also the coeditor of *Immigrants, Welfare Reform, and the Poverty of Policy*.

ADRIAN BURGOS, JR., is Associate Professor of History at the University of Illinois, Urbana-Champaign, and the author of *Playing America's Game: Baseball, Latinos, and the Color Line*. His academic articles have appeared in *Journal of Sport and Social Issues, Journal of Negro History*, and *CENTRO: Journal of the Center of Puerto Rican Studies*. He is currently working on *Harlem's Numbers King: A Life Story of Alejandro Pompez*.

DOLORES INÉS CASILLAS is Assistant Professor of Media Studies in the Department of Chicana and Chicano Studies at the University of California, Santa Barbara. Her current manuscript, based on her award-winning dissertation, examines the political relationship between U.S. Spanish-language radio and Latino listeners throughout the twentieth century.

MARÍA ELENA CEPEDA is Associate Professor of Latina/o Studies at Williams College, and author of *Musical ImagiNation: U.S.-Colombian Identity and the Latin Music Boom*. She has published in the journals *Popular Music and Society, Latino Studies, Identities, Women and Performance*, and *Discourse*, among others, and is editorial assistant and translator of *Musical Migrations: Transnationalism and Cultural Hybridity in Latin/o America*, edited by Frances Aparicio and Cándida Jáquez.

CARY CORDOVA is Assistant Professor in the Department of American Studies at the University of Texas, Austin. She has published in *Latino Studies* and *Voices of Art*, and is in the process of completing her manuscript,

"The Heart of the Mission: Latino Art and Identity in San Francisco." She also has served as a public historian and oral historian for various institutions, including the Texas Parks and Wildlife Department and the Archives of American Art, Smithsonian Institution.

LILIA FERNÁNDEZ is Assistant Professor at The Ohio State University in the Department of History, with affiliations in Latina/o Studies, Women's Studies, and Comparative Studies. Her most recent essay, "Of Migrants and Immigrants: Mexican and Puerto Rican Labor Migration in Comparative Perspective, 1942–1964," appears in the *Journal of American Ethnic History* (Spring 2010). Her manuscript, "Brown in the Windy City: Mexicans and Puerto Ricans in Postwar Chicago, 1945–1975," is currently under review.

FRANK A. GURIDY is Associate Professor of History and African and African Diaspora Studies at the University of Texas, Austin. He has published essays in the *Radical History Review, Caribbean Studies, Social Text*, and, most recently, *Cuban Studies*. His book, *Forging Diaspora: Afro-Cubans and African Americans in a World of Empire and Jim Crow*, examines the institutional relationships and cultural interactions between Cubans and U.S. Americans of African descent from the U.S. intervention of 1898 until the eve of the outbreak of the Cuban Revolution.

LOURDES GUTIÉRREZ NÁJERA is Assistant Professor in Latin American, Latino, and Caribbean Studies and Anthropology at Dartmouth College. She is currently revising a manuscript for publication on Zapotec transnational migration, and has contributed essays to *Urban Anthropology, Latino America: A State-by-State Encyclopedia*, and *Health Education Quarterly*. She also serves as the coordinator for the Gender and (Im)migration Workshops at the Rockefeller Center at Dartmouth College and serves on the Executive Board of the Society for the Anthropology of Work.

JOHN MCKIERNAN-GONZALEZ is Assistant Professor in the Department of History at the University of Texas, Austin. He has worked on a variety of exhibits and public programs with the Smithsonian Institution, and recently finished the digital radio recovery project, Onda Latina. His work focuses on the ways Latinos have historically negotiated the intersection of public health, public space, and citizenship. He is completing his manuscript, "Fevered Measures: Connecting Public Health and Race at the Texas-Mexico Border, 1848–1942."

PABLO MITCHELL is Associate Professor of History and Comparative American Studies at Oberlin College. He is the author of *Coyote Nation: Sexuality, Race, and Conquest in Modernizing New Mexico, 1880–1920*, which was awarded the 2007 Ray Allen Billington Prize by the Organization of American Historians. His next book project is "West of Sex: Colonialism and the Making of Mexican America, 1900–1930." In 2008, he was named one of ten 2008 Emerging Scholars by the magazine *Diverse: Issues in Higher Education*.

DEBORAH PAREDEZ is a poet, Associate Professor of Theatre, and Associate Director of the Center for Mexican American Studies at the University of Texas, Austin. She is the author of *Selenidad: Selena, Latinos, and the Performance of Memory* and the poetry volume *This Side of Skin*. She is a founding member of CantoMundo, a national organization dedicated to fostering and supporting Latina/o poetry. Her current research focuses on performances by Black and Latina/o divas.

GINA M. PÉREZ is Associate Professor and Director of the Comparative American Studies Program at Oberlin College. Her book, *The Near Northwest Side Story: Migration, Displacement, and Puerto Rican Families*, was awarded the Delmos Jones and Jagna Scharff Memorial Prize for the Critical Study of North America, by the Society for the Anthropology of North America. She is currently working on a new manuscript, "Creating Better Citizens: Latina/o Youth, JROTC, and the American Dream," based on ethnographic research with Latina/o youth in Northeast Ohio.

HALEY MICHAELS POLLACK is a PhD candidate in the History Department at the University of Wisconsin, Madison. She was awarded the Ida and Isaac Lipton Award in 2009 for her work on Jewish masculinity and the Galveston immigration movement. Her dissertation will look at sites of memory and violence in the San Francisco Bay Area.

HORACIO N. ROQUE RAMÍREZ teaches at UC Santa Barbara. His research and writing have appeared in the *Journal of the History of Sexuality*, *The Organization of American Historians Magazine of History*, and *CENTRO: Journal of the Center for Puerto Rican Studies*. He is coediting an anthology on *Queer Oral Histories* and guest editing an issue of the *Journal of American Ethnic History* on "Homoerotic, Lesbian, and Gay Ethnic and Immigrant Histories." His forthcoming book is *Memories of Desire: An Oral History from Queer Latino San Francisco, 1960s–1990s*.

Index

Levitt, Peggy, 49, 254
Lewis, Oscar, 4–5
LGBTQ communities, 107, 181
La Liga Por la Lucha Revolucionaria, 267
Linares, Guillermo, 266, 268
Lindsay, John, 86
Linea Roja, 257, 261, 264, 267
Lipman, Pauline, 174, 183n15
Lipsitz, George, 7, 251n36
Little League World Series (LLWS), 81–82, 87–89
LLWS. *See* Little League World Series
LMJ. *See* Lorain Morning Journal
"The Local and the Global" (Hall), 30
Lopez, George (comedian), 46
López, George (actor), 131
López, Josefina, 131, 134, 148n23
Lopez Padilla, Rocío, 189; "The Topping of the Cake," *205*, 205–6
Lorain, Ohio: African Americans in, 149, 151, 155–56, 160; Americanization Board of, 154; Cubans in, 151–52; Latinas/os in, 149–67, 177, 179–81; Mexicans in, 149–53, 157–60, 164; Native Americans in, 155, 161–63, 165; Puerto Ricans in, 13, 149–67
Lorain Morning Journal (*LMJ*), 13, 154–57, 160–64
Los Angeles: Koreans in, 63–64; Mexicans in, 3–4; Zapotecs in, 63–80
Lowriders, 200, *200*, 213
Lozano, Adrian, 250n29
LULAC. *See* League of United Latin American Citizens
Lutz, Catherine, 177

MAC. *See* Mexican American Council
Machismo, 3
Maciel, Alfonso, 220
Macombs Dam Park, 87, 95–97
Maderazo, Woodard, 41
Madrea, Felipe, 115, *116*
Magnet schools, 174
Majority minority role, of Latinas/os, 169
Maldonado, Jesse Anthony, 115, *116*
Maldonado, Severando, 152

"Mami, aka Dona Lola" (Thomas), 197
Mantle, Mickey, 85
Marcano, Arturo, 93
Marginalization: of immigrants, 51–52, 58, 64–65; by race, 255; of Yalaltecos, 69, 74, 76–77
Marielitos, 189
Marine Corp, 178–79, 182n2
Mariscal, Jorge, 174
Marketing, multicultural, 170–71, 182n1
Marquand, Clotilde, 155
Marquand, Henry, 155
Marshall, Penny, 85
Martin, Jean, 162–63
Martin, Ramon, 151
Martinez, Leonides, 165
Martinez, Melquiades Rafael (Mel), 196, 209n16
Martínez, Pedro, 90
Massey, Douglas S., 27
Maxwell Street market, 235
MCC. *See* Mexican Civic Committee
McClure, Michael, 222
McKiernan-González, John, 14
McMahon, Eileen, 249
Medal of Honor, 171
The Medicine of Memory (Murguía), 223, 230n38
Mejia, Pedro, 159, 167n25
Melting pot, 176
Meltzer, David, 222
Memory, 3, 12; AIDS and, 103–28
Mendieta, Ana, 209n16
Mendoza, Ricardo, 222
Mestizos, 69
Methadone clinics, 245
Mexican American Council (MAC), 238–39
Mexican Civic Committee (MCC), 236–37, 239
"Mexican Community in Lorain, Ohio" (Jacinto), 150
Mexican Damsel's Club, 157
Mexican Methodist Church, 239
Mexican Mutual Club, 157
Mexican regional music, 45, 55, 58

Mexicans: in Chicago, 15, 233–52; dominance of, 59n2; in Lorain, Ohio, 149–53, 157–60, 164; in Los Angeles, 3–4; racial issues and, 150; in San Francisco, 44–45, 47–48, 215
"Mexicans in New York City" (Edson), 150
"Mexicans in Pittsburgh" (Edson), 150
"Mexicans in Saginaw" (Edson), 150
"Mexicans in Sioux City, Iowa" (Edson), 150
Mexican Young Man's Club, 157
Miami, Cubans in, 60n5
Microcredit associations, 65, 72–74, 76, 78n8
Migration: Bracero program and, 175; of Yalaltecos, 66–69
Militarization: of gender roles, 168, 181; of Latinas/os, 168–86
Military service, and citizenship, 170
Military values, 168–86
Milk, Harvey, 127n27
Minuteman Project, 169, 175, 183n10
Mirikitani, Janice, 222
"Mis Dos Patrias" (My Two Countries), 45
Mission Cultural Center, 221–22
Mission district, of San Francisco, 211–31
Mitchell, Pablo, 13, 149–67
Mixe language, 67, 77n5
Mobility, 191, 237
"El Mojado Acaudalado" (The Wealthy Wetback), 45
Molina, Natalia, 5
Monolingualism, 38
Montenegro, Emiliano Luis, 257, 261
Montgomery, Martin, 53
Montoya, Jose, 220
Mora, Pat, 190, 197
Moreno, Arthur, 112
Moreno, Candido, 155
Morley, David, *Home Territories*, 44, 46
Mothers, absent, 12, 129–48
Mujeres Latinas en Acción (Latina Women in Action), 244, 246
Multicultural marketing, 170–71, 182n1
Muñoz, Karina, "Paulo Muñoz," *199*, 199–201

Muñoz, Paulo, *199*, 199–201
Murguía, Alejandro, 213–14, 220–23, *221*, 225, 227; *The Medicine of Memory*, 223, 230n38; *The Southern Front*, 223; *Time to Greez! Incantations from the Third World*, 220
"Musical imagi/nation," 29–30, 39
Mutual aid societies, 194, 236
"My Dad" (Ponce, J.), 201–2, *202*
"My Mother and How We Came to Be" (Rosario), 207

Naficy, Hamid, 50
Nash, Ilana, 129, 146n1
National Association of Colored Women, 196
National belonging, 30–35
National Capital Immigrant Coalition, 31
National Council of La Raza, 182n4
National Institute of Mental Health, 245
Nationalism, 3
National Museum of American History, 198
The National Question (Stalin), 261
National Tube Company, 151
Native Americans, 38; in Lorain, Ohio, 155, 161–63, 165
Nativist backlash, 169
Navarro, Emilio, 86
Near West Side Planning Board (NWSPB), 239
Neighborhood Arts Program, 15, 214
Nelson, Elmer, 163
Neoliberal movement, 182
Neruda, Pablo, 214
New York (city): Dominicans in, 15–16, 253–71; Puerto Ricans in, 3, 81–99, 234–35, 253, 260; queerness in, 266; transnationalism in, 253–71
New York Yankees, 11, 85, 94
Ngai, Mae, 192, 209n4
Nicaragua: revolution in, 211–31; U.S. intervention in, 217–18, 225, 227–28
Nicaraguans, in San Francisco, 14, 211–31
Nickel Plate Railroad, 159
NIN. *See* Nonintervention for Nicaragua

Yalaltecos: belonging and, 70–71; marginalization of, 69, 74, 76–77; migration of, 66–69

Yankee Stadium, 84–87, 95–97

Yo soy Betty, la Fea (television program), 12, 138

"Yo Soy el Army" slogan, 170–71, 182n1

Young Lords Party, 254

Zapotec language, 63, 67, 73, 77n1

Zapotecs, in Los Angeles, 63–80

Zero tolerance policies, 177

Zúniga, Bérman, 217

Made in the USA
Columbia, SC
11 March 2021